ENCYCLOPEDIA
FROM
A TO Z

AN ILLUSTRATED ENCYCLOPEDIA
FOR YOUNG READERS

TORMONT

HOW TO USE THE ENCYCLOPEDIA

Using this encyclopedia is very simple. Just look for the topic that interests you in the **index** at the back of the book, then go to the listed page.

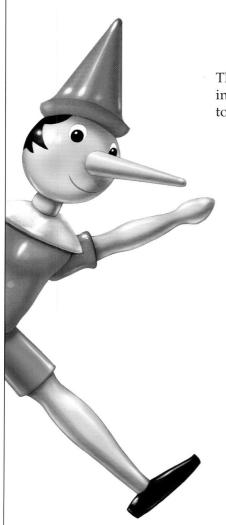

The **first block** introduces the topic.

The **caption** explains the illustration.

The **second block** provides more information.

The **third block** completes the explanation.

BEES

Bee is the common name for the 20,000 species of insects belonging to the Apoidea family in the Hymenoptera order. Some bees are ¹⁄₁₀ of an inch (2 mm) long, and others are a little over 1 inch (3 cm) long. Bees live in a rigid caste system. The swarm has thousands of worker bees but just one queen bee, which is about twice the size of the other bees. Worker bees are sterile female bees, and only the queen bee can reproduce. She is inseminated in flight by *drones*, which are male bees.

Beekeeper – The bee-keeper wears a special suit and protects his face and hands when he collects honey. He smokes out the bee-hive to stun the bees, then he raises the roof on the apiary and removes the frames covered with honey. The honey is then extracted through centrifugation.

The bee carries pollen from one flower to another.

Honeycombs (below) are hexagonal, a shape that limits the amount of material wasted. Combs are made of wax secreted by the bee's wax-secreting glands.

Hives hang on branches or are built in holes. Beekeepers keep bees in houses called apiaries, where the bees build honeycombs.

Honey comes in different colors and flavors:
1. Eucalyptus honey
2. Linden honey
3. Acacia honey
4. Orange flower honey
5. Chestnut honey

Bees – Thousands of bees work in the hive: some produce wax to build combs, which are six-sided cells where the eggs and honey are deposited. Other bees are in charge of cleaning the hive; they also keep it cool by beating their wings. Bees that make honey are called *honeybees*.

The swarm – When the hive is too crowded, the queen abandons the hive, bringing with her almost half of the worker bees. The swarm of bees clusters on a branch until it chooses a new place to build the hive.

Colored signals
Bees see colors that are invisible to humans. These colors on flowers are nectar guides, a kind of landing strip for bees so they can reach the sweet nectar.

Colors humans can see.

Colors bees can see.

51

1. Honeycombs.
2. The queen bee leaves the queen cell.
3. The bee sucks nectar from the flowers.
4. Nanny bees feed the larvae.

The **main illustration** presents the topic.

Mating – When the queen bee is one week old, she takes her first mating flight. Hundreds of male bees called *drones* try to mate with her, but only a few are successful. After the mating period, the males are chased away. The inseminated queen bee lays up to 2,000 eggs per day. She will lay more than 2 million eggs during her lifetime (4 or 5 years).

Secondary illustrations show interesting details.

A bee only stings if it is provoked. Its stinger is attached to a poison sac.

Life in the hive – Worker bees live for about one month. During the first days they clean the combs and feed the larvae. Around the tenth day they start building combs and taking reconnaissance flights. Then they guard the hive and keep enemies away. Finally, they gather nectar and collect pollen.

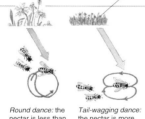

Coded dance
Worker bees perform special dances, using the sun as a reference, to inform other worker bees where and how far away the nectar is. The inclination and speed of the dance indicate the direction.

Round dance: the nectar is less than 330 ft (100 m) away.

Tail-wagging dance: the nectar is more than 330 ft (100 m) away.

Larvae – After three days, the eggs deposited by the queen bee turn into larvae. They are fed royal jelly by nanny bees, then honey and pollen. The larvae turn into pupas, then become adult bees.

A bee's head looks like that of a space alien: it has eyes that can see in any direction, long antennas, and a strange trunk-like mouth.

The encyclopedia is divided into three sections:

FROM A TO Z
From AFRICA to ZEBRAS, 196 topics in alphabetical order.

VISUAL DICTIONARY ✓
from ASSEMBLY LINE to THE WORLD IN STATISTICS, 21 illustrated topics full of details and special views.

DICTIONARIES
Dinosaurs, Famous Tales and Authors, Health and Medicine, Mythology.

FARM ANIMALS, FIELDS AND MEADOWS, FLOWERS, INSECTS

52

The **box** highlights a special concept.

Cross reference
The hand points to other topics to see in the encyclopedia for related information. Illustrations from the **Visual Dictionary** are marked with a ✓.

TABLE OF CONTENTS

From A to Z

AFRICA

Africa is the world's third largest continent. Its population is unevenly distributed: the Mediterranean area and eastern Africa have large cities and are more densely populated than the deserts, forests, and savannas. The nomadic way of life is still very much alive in Africa, in tribes like the Tuaregs.

Noble Tuaregs in their characteristic dark blue clothes.

Tuareg tents are made with animal skins or carpets.

Tuaregs – This tribe of the Sahara Desert makes its living through trade, crafts, and raising camels and horses. The Tuaregs live in feudal-type communities divided into four social classes.

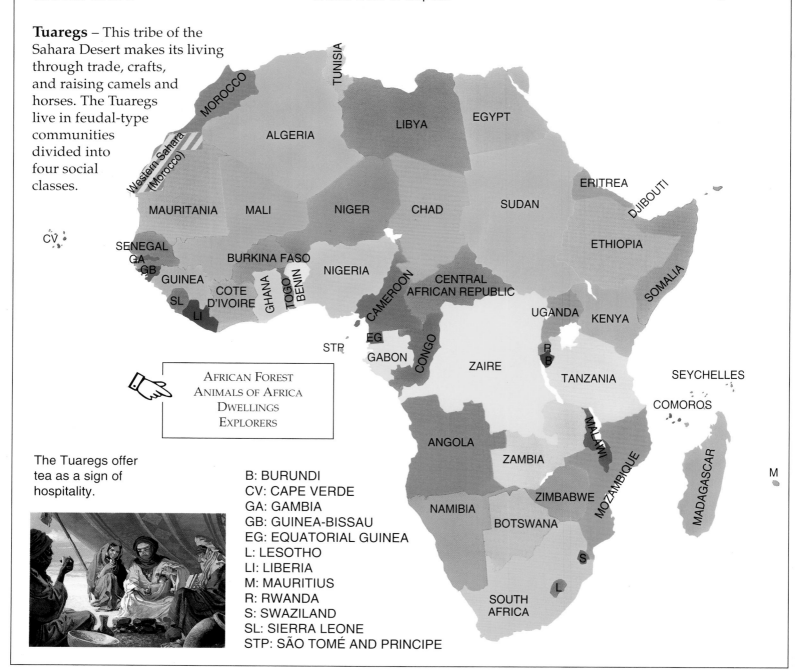

AFRICAN FOREST
ANIMALS OF AFRICA
DWELLINGS
EXPLORERS

The Tuaregs offer tea as a sign of hospitality.

B: BURUNDI
CV: CAPE VERDE
GA: GAMBIA
GB: GUINEA-BISSAU
EG: EQUATORIAL GUINEA
L: LESOTHO
LI: LIBERIA
M: MAURITIUS
R: RWANDA
S: SWAZILAND
SL: SIERRA LEONE
STP: SÃO TOMÉ AND PRINCIPE

MOROCCO
TUNISIA
Western Sahara (Morocco)
ALGERIA
LIBYA
EGYPT
MAURITANIA
MALI
NIGER
CHAD
SUDAN
ERITREA
DJIBOUTI
ETHIOPIA
CV
SENEGAL
GA
GB
GUINEA
BURKINA FASO
NIGERIA
CENTRAL AFRICAN REPUBLIC
SOMALIA
SL
COTE D'IVOIRE
GHANA
TOGO
BENIN
CAMEROON
UGANDA
KENYA
LI
STP
EG
GABON
CONGO
ZAIRE
R
B
TANZANIA
SEYCHELLES
COMOROS
MALAWI
ANGOLA
ZAMBIA
MOZAMBIQUE
MADAGASCAR
M
ZIMBABWE
NAMIBIA
BOTSWANA
S
L
SOUTH AFRICA

African Countries

COUNTRY	CAPITAL	AREA	POPULATION	LANGUAGE	CURRENCY
Sudan	Khartoum	967,570 sq mi (2,505,813 sq km)	30,120,000	Arabic, English, native languages	Sudanese pound
Algeria	Algiers	919,665 sq mi (2,381,751 sq km)	28,540,000	Arabic, French	Algerian dinar
Zaire	Kinshasa	905,430 sq mi (2,344,885 sq km)	44,100,000	French, Lingala, others	zaire
Libya	Tripoli	679,588 sq mi (1,759,998 sq km)	5,250,000	Arabic, Italian, English	Libyan dinar
Chad	N'djamena	495,790 sq mi (1,284,000 sq km)	5,586,500	French, Arabic, Sara, others	CFA franc
Angola	Luanda	481,388 sq mi (1,246,700 sq km)	11,000,000	Bantu, Portuguese	kwanza
Mali	Bamako	478,856 sq mi (1,240,142 sq km)	9,400,000	Bambara, French	CFA franc
Niger	Niamey	478,800 sq mi (1,240,000 sq km)	9,280,000	Hausa, Djerma, French	CFA franc
Ethiopia	Addis Ababa	435,217 sq mi (1,127,127 sq km)	56,000,000	Amharic	birr
South Africa	Capetown and Pretoria	471,476 sq mi (1,221,030 sq km)	45,095,450	Afrikaans, Zulu, English, Xhosa	rand
Mauritania	Nouakchott	397,984 sq mi (1,030,700 sq km)	2,300,000	Arabic, Wolof, French	ouguyia
Egypt	Cairo	386,690 sq mi (1,001,450 sq km)	62,360,000	Arabic	Egyptian pound
Tanzania	Dar es Salaam	364,907 sq mi (945,037 sq km)	28,700,000	Swahili, English	Tanzanian shilling
Nigeria	Abuja	356,727 sq mi (923,853 sq km)	101,200,000	Hausa, Yoruba, Ibo, English	naira
Namibia	Windhoek	318,718 sq mi (825,418 sq km)	1,651,550	English, Afrikaans, native languages	Namibian dollar
Mozambique	Maputo	309,518 sq mi (801,590 sq km)	18,115,250	Portuguese, native languages	metical
Zambia	Lusaka	290,608 sq mi (752,618 sq km)	9,446,000	English, native languages	kwacha

	COUNTRY	CAPITAL	AREA	POPULATION	LANGUAGE	CURRENCY
	Somalia	Mogadishu	246,217 sq mi (637,655 sq km)	7,347,000	Somali, Arabic, Italian, English	Somali shilling
	Central African Republic	Bangui	240,550 sq mi (622,980 sq km)	3,200,000	French, Sangho	CFA franc
	Botswana	Gaborone	231,817 sq mi (600,360 sq km)	1,392,400	English, Setswana	pula
	Madagascar	Antananarivo	226,677 sq mi (587,050 sq km)	13,862,300	Malagasy, French	Malagasy franc
	Kenya	Nairobi	224,977 sq mi (582,646 sq km)	28,800,000	Swahili, English	Kenya shilling
	Cameroon	Yaoundé	183,582 sq mi (475,442 sq km)	13,500,000	Fang, Bamileke, Duala, French	CFA franc
	Morocco	Rabat	172,426 sq mi (446,550 sq km)	29,200,000	Arabic, Berber, French	dirham
	Zimbabwe	Harare	150,814 sq mi (390,580 sq km)	11,140,000	English, Bantu	Zimbabwean dollar
	Congo	Brazzaville	132,056 sq mi (342,000 sq km)	2,500,000	French, Lingala, Kikongo	CFA franc
	Côte d'Ivoire (Ivory Coast)	Yamoussoukro	124,502 sq mi (322,462 sq km)	14,295,000	French, Akan, Kru, Malinke	CFA franc Voltaic, Malinke
	Burkina Faso	Ouagadougou	105,870 sq mi (274,200 sq km)	10,420,000	Dioula, French, others	CFA franc
	Gabon	Libreville	103,354 sq mi (267,667 sq km)	1,155,000	French, Fang, others	CFA franc
	Guinea	Conakry	94,932 sq mi (245,857 sq km)	6,550,000	Fulani, Malinke, Soussou, French	Guinean franc
	Uganda	Kampala	91,142 sq mi (236,040 sq km)	19,573,000	English, Swahili, Luganda	Uganda shilling
	Ghana	Accra	92,100 sq mi (238,537 sq km)	17,700,000	English, Akan, Mossi, Ewe, Ga-Adangme	cedi
	Senegal	Dakar	75,754 sq mi (196,190 sq km)	9,007,000	Wolof, Pulaar, French, others	CFA franc
	Tunisia	Tunis	63,175 sq mi (163,610 sq km)	8,900,000	Arabic, French	Tunisian dinar
	Eritrea	Asmara	46,845 sq mi (121,320 sq km)	3,580,000	Afar-Bilen, Kunama	Ethiopian birr

COUNTRY	CAPITAL	AREA	POPULATION	LANGUAGE	CURRENCY
Malawi	Lilongwe	45,747 sq mi (118,484 sq km)	9,800,000	English, Chichewa	kwacha
Benin	Cotonou, Porto Novo	43,483 sq mi (112,622 sq km)	5,500,000	French, Fon, Yoruba, Somba	CFA franc
Liberia	Monrovia	43,000 sq mi (111,370 sq km)	3,000,000	English and native languages	Liberian dollar
Sierra Leone	Freetown	27,700 sq mi (71,740 sq km)	4,750,000	English, Mende, Krio, others	leone
Togo	Lomé	21,925 sq mi (56,785 sq km)	4,400,000	French, Gur and Kwa languages	CFA franc
Guinea – Bissau	Bissau	13,948 sq mi (36,125 sq km)	1,125,000	Portuguese, Crioulo	Guinea-Bissau peso
Lesotho	Maseru	11,720 sq. mi (30, 355 sq km)	1,993,000	English, Sesotho	loti
Equatorial Guinea	Malabo	10,830 sq mi (28,051 sq km)	420,000	Spanish, pidgin English, Fang, others	CFA franc
Burundi	Bujumbura	10,747 sq mi (27,834 sq km)	6,262,400	French, Kirundi	Burundi franc
Rwanda	Kigali	10,169 sq mi (26,338 sq km)	8,600,000	French, Kinya Rwanda	Rwanda franc
Djibouti	Djibouti	8,495 sq mi (22,000 sq km)	421,320	Arabic, French	Djibouti franc
Swaziland	Mbabane	6,704 sq mi (17,363 sq km)	967,000	Siswati, English	lilangeni
Gambia	Banjul	4,363 sq mi (11,300 sq km)	990,000	English, Mandinka, Wolof	dalasi
Cape Verde	Praia	1,557 sq mi (4,033 sq km)	436,000	Portuguese, Crioulo	Cape Verdean escudo
Mauritius	Port Louis	718 sq mi (1,860 sq km)	1,127,800	English, French-Creole	Mauritian rupee
Comoros	Moroni	838 sq mi (2,170 sq km)	550,000	French, Arabic	CFA franc
São Tomé and Príncipe	São Tomé	370 sq mi (958 sq km)	140,000	Portuguese	dobra
Seychelles	Victoria	175 sq mi (453 sq km)	72,700	French-Creole, English	Seychelles rupee

AFRICAN FOREST

A thick, lush rainforest grows in the heart of Africa around the Congo River and the region of the great lakes. The intertwined tree branches almost totally block out the sunlight and the climate is extremely humid. There are sandalwood, mahogany, ebony, palm, banana trees and mangroves, and the ground is covered with ferns and orchids. All kinds of wild animals live in this green forest, including leopards, crocodiles, scaly anteaters and poisonous snakes.

monkey

The hornbill has a yellow beak with a helmet-like protuberance and a long tail with ten feathers.

African forest:
1. Leopard
2. Duiker
3. Serval
4. Okapi
5. Guenon
6. Hornbill
7. Scaly anteater
8. Baboon
9. River hog
10. Gorilla
11. Python

AFRICA
ANIMALS OF AFRICA
APES AND MONKEYS
BIRDS
CROCODILES
SNAKES

Strange mammals
Duikers are small, shy nocturnal antelopes with two horns. Okapi, with brown striped legs, are very rare giraffes. River hogs, which look like wild boars, have large ears, red fur and a white mane.

ALCOTT, LOUISA MAY

LITTLE WOMEN

"Margaret, the eldest of the four, was sixteen … with large eyes, plenty of soft, brown hair, a sweet mouth, and white hands, of which she was rather vain. Fifteen-year-old Jo was very tall, thin, and brown, and reminded one of a colt, for she never seemed to know what to do with her long limbs, which were very much in her way. She had sharp, gray eyes, which appeared to see everything. Her long, thick hair was her one beauty, but it was usually bundled into a net, to be out of her way. Beth was a rosy, smooth-haired, bright-eyed girl … with a shy manner, a timid voice, and a peaceful expression which was seldom disturbed. Amy, though the youngest, was a most important person – in her own opinion at least. A regular snow maiden, with blue eyes, and yellow hair curling on her shoulders, pale and slender, and always carrying herself like a young lady mindful of her manners."

Louisa May Alcott (1832–1888) was an American author who became very famous with her novel *Little Women*. She also wrote *Good Wives*, *Little Men* and *Jo's Boys*.

"Being still too young to go often to the theater, and not rich enough to afford any great outlay for private performances, the girls put their wits to work … Very clever were some of their productions … No gentlemen were admitted, so Jo played male parts to her heart's content …"

"For two or three hours the sun lay warmly in the high window, showing Jo seated on the old sofa, writing busily. Quite absorbed in her work, Jo scribbled away till the last page was filled, when she signed her name with a flourish and threw down her pen … She put on her hat and jacket as noiselessly as possible, and going to the back entry window, got out upon the roof of a low porch, swung herself down to the grassy bank, and took a roundabout way to the road."

AUTHORS AND POETS
CHILDREN'S LITERATURE

ALEXANDER THE GREAT

Alexander was the son of Philip II, the King of Macedonia. Before he turned thirty, he had conquered most of the lands then known to mankind. That is why he was called *Magno*, which means Great. When Alexander became king in 336 B.C., Macedonia was a small kingdom. Alexander left Macedonia to conquer the Persian empire of Darius III. He founded the city of Alexandria in Egypt and was proclaimed pharaoh. He then headed eastwards, conquered Mesopotamia and occupied Susa, Persepolis, Ecbatana, and Babylon. Alexander even arrived as far as the Indus Valley.

a bust of Alexander

356 B.C.: Born to Philip II and Olympiade.
338 B.C.: Fights at Chaeronea.
336 B.C.: Takes the throne after his father's death.
335 B.C.: Subdues rebellions, destroys the city of Thebes.
334 B.C.: Defeats Darius III.
333 B.C.: Conquers the Persians in Issus.
331 B.C.: Defeats Darius and occupies Babylon and Susa.
327 B.C.: Reaches the Indus Valley.
326 B.C.: Blocks the army of King Porus.
323 B.C.: Dies of fever at 33 years of age.

According to prophecy, whoever undid the Gordian knot would rule all of Asia. Alexander severed it with his sword.

The Phalanx – Macedonian infantry fought in a *phalanx* formation: the soldiers in the first row aimed their spears at the enemy and their fellow soldiers held their long spears on a diagonal.

EGYPTIANS, GREEKS, INDIA
MEDITERRANEAN CIVILIZATIONS, PERSIA
☞

Hellenistic Age
Alexander's armies covered close to 12,400 mi (20,000 km). The Greek language and civilization reached remote populations and mingled with Oriental culture. And so the Hellenistic Age was born.

16

AMERICA

The American continent is formed by two distinct continental land masses — North America and South America. These two land masses are connected by a narrow strip of land which, together with the Antilles Islands, forms Central America.

Central America – This region is made up of all the countries south of Mexico to Panama, as well as the adjacent Antilles Islands. *Dominica, Saint Lucia, Antigua and Barbuda, Barbados, Saint Vincent and the Grenadines, Grenada*, and *Saint Kitts and Nevis* are all found in Central America. The *Panama Canal*, completed in 1914, links the Atlantic and Pacific Oceans.

The Navajo Indian tribe has preserved many of its ancient cultural traditions such as sand painting (below).

CANADA

UNITED STATES OF AMERICA

MEXICO

BAHAMAS

CUBA

H

DR

JAMAICA

B

GUATEMALA

HONDURAS

ES

NICARAGUA

COSTA RICA

PANAMA

B: BELIZE
ES: EL SALVADOR
H: HAITI
DR: DOMINICAN REPUBLIC

South America – Together with Central America, this region is also known as *Latin America* because most of its colonizers were Spanish or Portuguese. Today, many different ethnic groups live in South America. Most people live in the large cities along the coast. Zones with a more hostile climate – such as the Amazon, Patagonia, and the Tierra del Fuego at the very southern tip of the continent – are less populated.

Weaving on Lake Titicaca.

TRINIDAD AND TOBAGO

VENEZUELA

GUYANA

SURINAME

French Guiana

COLOMBIA

ECUADOR

PERU

BRAZIL

BOLIVIA

PARAGUAY

CHILE

ARGENTINA

URUGUAY

ANIMALS OF NORTH AMERICA,
ANIMALS OF SOUTH AMERICA,
EXPLORERS,
NATIVE AMERICANS,
WASHINGTON, WILD WEST

The Andes form the world's longest mountain chain: 4,700 mi (7,600 km) long!

Lake Titicaca, between Bolivia and Peru, lies at 12,500 ft (3,810 m) above sea level. The local population uses canoes made of woven reeds to sail on the lake.

The Andes
This is the world's longest mountain chain. La Paz in Bolivia, at an altitude ranging from about 10,650 to 13,250 ft (3,250 to 4,100 m), is the world's highest capital city. Even the railway that crosses the Andes reaches a record-breaking altitude of 15,843 ft (4,829 m)!

COUNTRIES OF NORTH AND CENTRAL AMERICA

COUNTRY	CAPITAL	AREA	POPULATION	LANGUAGE	CURRENCY
Canada	Ottawa	3,852,088 sq mi (9,976,140 sq km)	29,600,000	English, French	Canadian dollar
United States	Washington, D.C.	3,619,047 sq mi (9,372,610 sq km)	263,815,000	English	US dollar
Mexico	Mexico City	761,660 sq mi (1,972,547 sq km)	93,900,000	Spanish, Amerindian languages	Mexican peso
Nicaragua	Managua	50,000 sq mi (129,494 sq km)	4,206,000	Spanish	córdoba
Honduras	Tegucigalpa	43,281 sq mi (112,090 sq km)	5,500,000	Spanish	lempira
Cuba	Havana	42,806 sq mi (110,860 sq km)	10,937,630	Spanish	Cuban peso
Guatemala	Guatemala City	42,045 sq mi (108,889 sq km)	11,000,000	Spanish	quetzal
Panama	Panama City	30,195 sq mi (78,200 sq km)	2,600,000	Spanish, English	balboa
Costa Rica	San José	19,730 sq mi (51,100 sq km)	3,420,000	Spanish	Costa Rican colón
Dominican Republic	Santo Domingo	18,816 sq mi (48,730 sq km)	7,510,000	Spanish	Dominican peso
Haiti	Port-au-Prince	10,714 sq mi (27,750 sq km)	6,540,000	French, Creole	gourde
Belize	Belmopan	8,867 sq mi (22,965 sq km)	214,000	English	Belizan dollar
El Salvador	San Salvador	8,124 sq mi (21,040 sq km)	5,900,000	Spanish	Salvadoran colón
Bahamas	Nassau	5,380 sq mi (13,939 sq km)	256,600	English	Bahamian dollar
Jamaica	Kingston	4,243 sq mi (10,990 sq km)	2,550,000	English	Jamaican dollar
Dominica	Roseau	290 sq mi (751 sq km)	82,600	English, French patois	East Caribbean dollar
Saint Lucia	Castries	239 sq mi (620 sq km)	156,000	English	East Caribbean dollar

COUNTRY	CAPITAL	AREA	POPULATION	LANGUAGE	CURRENCY
Antigua and Barbuda	Saint John's	171 sq mi (442 sq km)	65,000	English	East Caribbean dollar
Barbados	Bridgetown	166 sq mi (431 sq km)	256,400	English	Barbados dollar
Saint Vincent and the Grenadines	Kingstown	131 sq mi (340 sq km)	117,340	English, French patois	East Caribbean dollar
Grenada	Saint George's	131 sq mi (340 sq km)	94,500	English	East Caribbean dollar
Saint Kitts and Nevis	Basseterre	104 sq mi (269 sq km)	40,000	English	East Caribbean dollar

RECORDS IN AMERICA

● **The largest bay:** Hudson Bay, which covers an area of 475,800 sq mi (1,232,300 sq km) and has 7,623 mi (12,268 km) of coast.

● **The largest gulf:** The Gulf of Mexico covers an area of about 615,000 sq mi (1,592,800 sq km).

● **The longest river:** The Amazon River is about 4,000 mi (6,448 km) long. Since it has so many different branches, it is difficult to determine its exact length.

● **The highest lake:** Lake Titicaca, in the Andes between Bolivia and Peru, is at 12,500 ft (3,810 m) above sea level.

● **The tallest waterfall:** Angel Falls in Venezuela, with a 3,212 ft (997 m) vertical drop.

SOUTH AMERICAN COUNTRIES

	COUNTRY	CAPITAL	AREA	POPULATION	LANGUAGE	CURRENCY
	Brazil	Brasilia	3,286,723 sq mi (8,511,957 sq km)	160,737,400	Portuguese	novo cruizeiro
	Argentina	Buenos Aires	1,068,380 sq mi (2,766,890 sq km)	34,300,000	Spanish	Argentine peso
	Peru	Lima	496,260 sq mi (1,285,216 sq km)	24,000,000	Spanish, Quechua, Aymara	nuevo sol
	Colombia	Bogotá	439,767 sq mi (1,138,910 sq km)	36,200,250	Spanish	Colombian peso
	Bolivia	Sucre and La Paz	424,195 sq mi (1,098,581 sq km)	7,900,000	Spanish, Quechua, Aymara	boliviano
	Venezuela	Caracas	352,170 sq mi (912,050 sq km)	21,000,000	Spanish	bolivar
	Chile	Santiago	292,280 sq mi (756,950 sq km)	14,200,000	Spanish	Chilean peso
	Paraguay	Asunción	157,047 sq mi (406,752 sq km)	5,358,000	Spanish, Guaraní	guaraní
	Ecuador	Quito	109,490 sq mi (283,560 sq km)	10,890,000	Spanish, Quechua	sucre
	Guyana	Georgetown	83,000 sq mi (214,969 sq km)	725,000	English, Amerindian dialects	Guyana dollar
	Uruguay	Montevideo	68,040 sq mi (176,224 sq km)	3,220,000	Spanish	Uruguayan peso
	Suriname	Paramaribo	63,043 sq mi (163,270 sq km)	430,000	Dutch, Sranantonga	Suriname guilder
	Trinidad and Tobago	Port of Spain	1,980 sq mi (5,128 sq km)	1,270,000	English	Trinidad and Tobago dollar

* **French Guiana** is an overseas department of France.

AMPHIBIANS

Amphibians are animals that live in water during their larval stage but as adults can also live on land. As they grow, their respiratory apparatus changes. When they are young they live under water and have gills like fish, but when they become adults they develop lungs so they can breathe air. Almost all amphibians lay their eggs in water, and these eggs turn into larvae.

Orders – Amphibians are divided into three orders: anura (frogs and toads), urodela (salamanders and newts), and apoda or gymnophiona (limbless amphibians). Amphibians do not live in the sea, desert areas, or polar regions.

Crested newt – This amphibian lives among the reeds lining the banks of a pond or marsh. The males of this species turn a brighter color during the mating season.

Colors – Many amphibians are quite colorful and some have glands in their skin that secrete poisonous toxins.

Frog eggs (about 4,000 each hatch) are covered with gelatin. Tadpoles have a tail and gills but no legs. As they grow into frogs, their front legs appear first.

ANIMALS (STRANGE)
CAMOUFLAGE
EVOLUTION
HIBERNATION

Frog (left) – Frogs have long back legs, webbed feet and smooth skin. Many have odd names: *bull-frog, hairy frog, sheep frog, leopard frog,* and *goliath frog.* But all frogs have sticky pads on their front feet for a better grip. Their large bulging eyes press against the inside of their mouths to help them chew.

Toad (left) – The toad has a squat body covered with warts. Even though it is ugly and slimy, it is very useful to farmers because it eats insects that harm crops. It quickly flicks out its long, sticky tongue to capture insects. Unlike the frog, the toad lives on land and only returns to the water to lay its eggs.

The salamander is an expert climber. It lives mainly on trees, and when it climbs down to the ground it hides in humid holes. Like other amphibians, the salamander absorbs water through its skin, and even breathes through its skin in what is called cutaneous respiration.

ANIMALS OF AFRICA

Dromedary (below)
Thanks to the fat in its single hump, the dromedary can go without food for extended periods. It can also survive for up to eight days without water.

The savanna in East Africa is a huge prairie. The area's thick grass is yellow during dry spells and turns green after the rains. Trees are sparce, but the giant baobab grows here as well as the acacia. It is the region's wildlife that captures the imagination: herbivores such as rhinoceros, giraffes, gazelles, zebras and antelopes share the savanna along with predators: lions, leopards and cheetahs. Hyenas, jackals, and vultures are carnivores that eat the carcasses of dead animals. In the deserts to the north live dromedaries, snakes and scorpions.

The chimpanzee (above) lives in clans in equatorial Africa.

Giant pangolin – (above)
This nocturnal animal rolls into a ball when attacked. Its strong armor is covered with bony plates.

AFRICA,
AFRICAN FOREST,
APES AND
MONKEYS,
CAMOUFLAGE,
ELEPHANTS,
ENDANGERED
SPECIES, GIRAFFE,
RHINOCEROS,
WILDCATS, ZEBRAS

The savanna at the foot of Mount Kilimanjaro:
1. lesser kudu
2. Grant's gazelle
3. impala
4. korrigum
5. ostrich
6. guinea fowl
7. egret
8. zebra

ANIMALS OF AUSTRALIA

The Australian plains are full of spiny bushes and shrubs. Ferns, palm trees, and mangroves grow luxuriantly in the forests on the northern coast. Since it has been isolated from other continents for millions of years, Australia is home to many strange animals such as the kangaroo and spiny anteater, which are not found anywhere else in the world. Some animals, such as the platypus and the varanus, have maintained their prehistoric traits. Many colorful birds, such as the lyrebird and bird of paradise, are also found in Australia.

Spiny anteater or echidna – The young hatch, one at a time, from eggs the mother places in its abdominal pouch.

Kangaroo – Females have just one baby at a time. The baby is kept in the mother's abdominal pouch; this pouch has four teats, only two of which provide milk.

The platypus (above) is an unusual mammal that lays eggs. It has a flat duck bill and palmed feet that help it swim.

Koala – This nocturnal marsupial lives in eucalyptus trees in the forest. It is an excellent climber and eats only eucalyptus leaves. The koala is a very gentle animal and opens its eyes wide in surprise when disturbed. It is about 24 in (60 cm) long and its newborn babies are about an inch (2 cm) long.

ANIMALS (STRANGE), BIRDS WITH BRIGHT COLORS, MAMMALS, OCEANIA

Animals of the Australian bush:
1. and 2. Flying opossum
3. Emu
4. Cuscus
5. Tasmanian wolf (now extinct)
6. Wallaby
7. Parrot
8. Koala
9. Kangaroo
10. Varanus
11. Spiny anteater
12. Platypus
13. Cassowary

ANIMALS OF EUROPE

Fawn (below)
A fawn is a baby deer. It has reddish fur in the summer that turns dark gray in winter.

Europe has many different environments and climates. The Arctic regions are inhabited by polar bears, arctic hares, wolves, wolverines, and reindeer. Brown bears and lynx live in the taiga, made up of coniferous forests. The Mediterranean areas are inhabited by chamois, ibexes, stags, and deer that live in the mountains. Seals, sea lions, and birds such as loons and seagulls live in the coastal areas of northern Europe.

Marten – This animal, also found in Asia and America, is an excellent climber that lives in forests and parks. It eats mice, berries, fruit and nuts.

Fox – This fine hunter sneaks into towns in search of food.

The female fox (left) has 3 to 8 pups at a time.

In the forest – Marmots, which live in colonies, dig tunnels with many entrances and use piercing whistles to communicate with each other. Other furry animals found here include the nocturnal dormouse, the badger and the marten.

The European forest:
1. Roe deer
2. Brown bear
3. Blackbird
4. Stag
5. Fallow deer
6. European badger
7. Squirrel
8. Hare
9. Boar
10. Polecat

BEARS
EUROPE
HEDGEHOG
SQUIRRELS

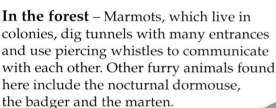

ANIMALS OF NORTH AMERICA

North America has many different habitats. Coyotes, prong-horned antelopes, and bison live in the vast prairies. Prairie dogs hide in their burrows underground and always leave one animal standing guard to launch shrill whistles when a coyote is near. Opossums, skunks, and bears live in the forests of North America while lynx and rattlesnakes live in the southern deserts.

Virginia opossum
This marsupial has a pointy snout, hairless ears, five digits per paw, and sharp teeth. It plays dead if it senses danger. A female can give birth to up to 25 babies in five minutes, although only about 6 will survive. After 4 or 5 weeks in their mother's pouch, the babies will move on to her back.

The striped skunk (above) secretes a smelly liquid to ward off its enemies.

The North American prairie:
1. Bison
2. Prong-horned antelopes
3. Coyote
4. Prairie dogs
5. Owl
6. Grouse
7. Horned lark
8. Ground squirrel
9. Rattlesnake

The red lynx (above) has excellent eyesight.

AMERICA, ANIMALS OF SOUTH AMERICA, BEARS, BOVINES, RACCOONS, RAPTORS, SNAKES

ANIMALS OF SOUTH AMERICA

White-lipped peccary

South America is full of contrasts, from dry prairies to snowcapped mountains to tropical forests. The vast prairies, called the *pampas*, are home to small armadillos, nandus, deer, and rodents such as maras and vizcachas that dig burrows underground. Giant anteaters, parrots, sloths, giant armadillos, peccaries, pumas, and jaguars live in the tropical forests.

👉 AMERICA,
ANIMALS OF NORTH AMERICA,
ANIMALS (STRANGE),
BIRDS WITH BRIGHT COLORS,
RODENTS, WILDCATS

The South American prairie:

1. Giant anteater
2. Patagonian mara or hare
3. Nandu
4. Pampas deer
5. Giant armadillo
6. Crested screamer or chaja
7. Long-legged maned wolf
8. Giant paca
9. Six-banded armadillo
10. Viscacha
11. Jaguarundi
12. Wild rabbit
13. Golden agouti
14. Capybara

Guanaco (below) – This Andean animal, related to the llama, lives in herds at 12,800 ft (4,000 m). In the fall, the female descends to the valley to give birth.

Puma – The puma lives in the forests, mountains and pampas. At night it hunts small mammals and birds.

Nandu – The nandu, which weighs about 55 lb (25 kg) and is about 5½ ft (1.7 m) tall, is smaller than the African ostrich. It has soft feathers and no tail; its three-toed feet have no rear spurs.

ANIMALS OF THE POLAR REGIONS

The Arctic is not a continent: it is the land and sea surrounding the North Pole inside the Arctic Circle. Antarctica at the South Pole, however, is the coldest continent on Earth. It is larger than Europe but it is uninhabited outside of scientific research stations. It is extremely cold in these regions, but forms of life have adapted to these difficult weather conditions.

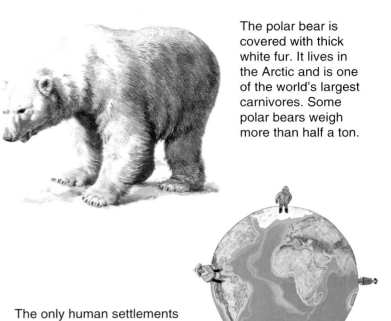

The polar bear is covered with thick white fur. It lives in the Arctic and is one of the world's largest carnivores. Some polar bears weigh more than half a ton.

The only human settlements at the South Pole are scientific research stations.

Arctic populations
The Inuit (above) live in Greenland, Canada, and Alaska, with related populations in Eastern Siberia. They hunt and fish and build igloos for shelter during their expeditions. The Lapps live in Northern Europe.

The walrus has a thick layer of fat beneath its skin. It uses its tusks to pull itself out of the water.

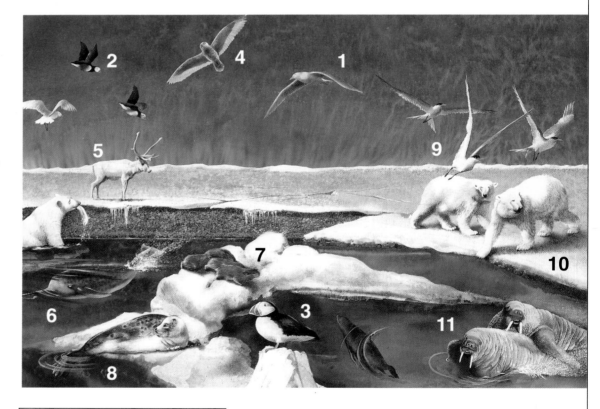

At the North Pole:	6. Narwhal
1. Northern fulmar	7. Lemming
	8. Common seal
2. and **3.** Puffin	9. Stern
4. Snowy owl	10. Polar bear
5. Arctic reindeer	11. Walrus

Reindeer – This ruminating mammal is over three ft (1 m) tall and about six and a half ft (2 m) long. It weighs 330 lb (150 kg) and has light gray fur and large antlers. Reindeer live in the tundra and in the taiga of Eurasia and eat moss, lichens, and herbs. They are raised for their hides, meat, and milk.

Animals at the South Pole – Blue whales swim among icebergs in the cold Antarctic Sea. These whales, which can reach 65 ft (20 m) in length and weigh up to 100 tons, eat plankton and small fish. Many countries have banned the hunting of these whales. Albatrosses soar through the skies of the South Pole, where twenty different species of penguins – including the Gentoo penguin, crested penguin, King penguin, and Emperor penguin – frolic in the sea. Elephant seals live on the shores: the males of this species have an unusual trunk-like snout.

Of all the land above the sea, about 10% is located in the polar regions where it is covered with ice.

Penguins are amusing animals that love to play on the ice.

The male Emperor penguin incubates the only egg laid by the female. He keeps it warm by balancing it on top of his feet and covering it with a thick roll of skin and feathers.

Penguins – These birds cannot fly because their wings have been transformed into fins. They are covered with thick feathers and have webbed feet and a tail that acts like a rudder. A thick layer of fat beneath their skin protects them from the cold. Penguins are excellent swimmers and can dive to a depth of about 65 ft (20 m) in search of food.

ANTARCTICA
BEARS
TUNDRA

At the South Pole:
1. Albatross
2. Leopard seal
3. Blue whale
4. Elephant seal
5. Gentoo penguin
6. King penguin
7. Crested penguin
8. Seal

ANIMALS – SOME STRANGE EXAMPLES

Nature is full of surprises! Some animals have very odd traits: some look like their prehistoric ancestors and others have learned to protect themselves by changing color.

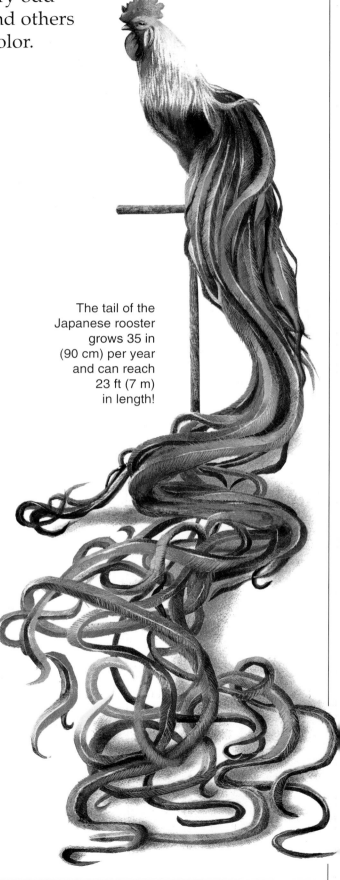

The tail of the Japanese rooster grows 35 in (90 cm) per year and can reach 23 ft (7 m) in length!

Platypus – This animal, which lives in Australia, is a combination of a bird and a mammal. Even though it has a duckbill and lays eggs, it suckles its young. The platypus is awkward on land but is a great swimmer thanks to its webbed feet and flat tail.

Flying dragon – This reptile has wings that are bright orange on top and blue with black speckles underneath. It glides easily from one tree to another and is perfectly camouflaged among the leaves. It lives in the Philippines and Indonesia.

Armadillo – This animal's name means "small armored creature" in Spanish. The armadillo lives in North, South, and Central America. Its body is covered with jointed armor plates that form bony rings and look like tractor tracks. Armadillos eat insects and dig tunnels with their strong paws.

Slender loris – This mammal lives in the forests of southern India and Sri Lanka. It hangs all day from the trees and hides its head between its paws. It has very large, glowing eyes. Thanks to its natural 'headlights,' the slender loris is most active at night. After a six-month gestation period, the female gives birth to twins.

Slender loris

Rhinoceros hornbill – This bird, found in the tropical rainforests of Asia, Africa and Oceania, has a bright red growth on its bill. During the hatching period, the male finds a hollow tree for the female. Once she is inside, he seals the hole with mud, leaving his companion inside to hatch the eggs.

Poison dart frog – This frog lives in the forests of Central and South America. It has a powerful poison that protects it from enemies. Some Native Americans use this poison for their arrowheads because it instantly paralyzes all kinds of animals.

The black and orange striped poison dart frog.

AFRICAN FOREST,
AMPHIBIANS,
ANIMALS OF AUSTRALIA,
ANIMALS OF SOUTH
AMERICA,
CAMOUFLAGE,
FISH

Echidna – This animal (below), also known as the *spiny anteater*, lives in New Guinea. It has a long curved snout, a dark brown coat with whitish quills, and three or four claws on each paw.

Four-eyed fish
This fish lives along the tropical coasts of America at the shallow mouth of a river. It keeps its bizarre bulging eyes half out of the water. Due to refraction, the part of the eye beneath the water level looks detached from the half above, so it seems like this fish has four eyes!

ANTARCTICA

Antarctica, the sixth continent, extends around the South Pole. It covers a total area of 5,447,385 sq mi (14,107,637 sq km). Antarctica, which is formed by land and huge blocks of floating ice called icebergs, is the coldest continent on Earth. The sun shines day and night for six months, then not at all for the other six months. Roald Amundsen from Norway was the first explorer to reach the South Pole in 1911.

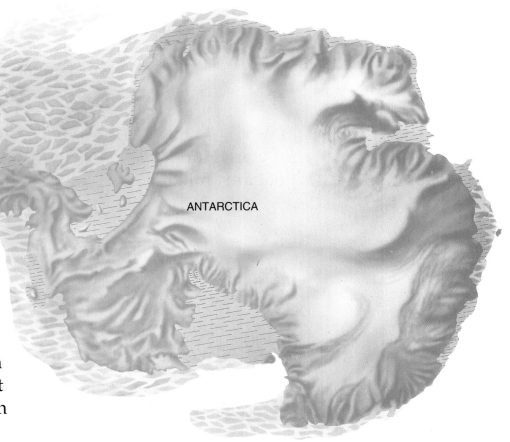

ANTARCTICA

Penguins live in colonies only in and around Antarctica. They are excellent divers and can reach a depth of 65 ft (20 m).

☞

ANIMALS OF THE
POLAR REGIONS,
EXPLORERS

No inhabitants – No traces of native populations have ever been found on this continent. Even today, Antarctica has no inhabitants other than scientists at research stations belonging to different countries. Antarctica is also a very inhospitable place for animals. Only the coasts are populated — by sea lions, penguins, seagulls, and albatross, which are all animals that catch fish in the sea. Whales and killer whales live in the icy ocean.

The albatross, like other birds that live in these frozen lands, hatches just one egg and protects it from the cold by keeping it under its wings.

ANTS

There are about ten thousand species of ants. Life is frenetic in the ant hill and each ant has a precise job to do within the colony. The queen is the only fertile female and lays up to one million eggs during her lifetime. The older ants gather food, then pass the food to the younger worker ants so they can feed the larva. Worker ants are sterile females with many different tasks: they make tiny bricks out of chewed dirt and use them to build the rooms in the ant hill and dig tunnels. Some species of worker ants also raise aphids, tiny insects that are "milked" to obtain a nutritious nectar.

Thanks to special glands, ants leave scent trails so that they can find their way around.

The queen ant lays more than 20,000 eggs per day in the royal chamber.

Dangerous – Ants can carry things much heavier than themselves. South American army ants, which are constantly on the move, will devour any animal in their path.

Supplies – Ants store seeds, crumbs, pieces of fruit and leaves, and capture small animals. Ants even grow mushrooms: they plant them on rotting leaves and then water them.

FIELDS AND MEADOWS
INSECTS

Ant hill:
1. Workers transporting food
2. "Milking" aphids
3. Workers cutting leaves
4. A captured bee
5. Ants with bellies full of nectar
6. Food storage
7. Young queens

APES AND MONKEYS

Pygmy marmoset
The smallest of all monkeys, it weighs around 4½ oz (125 g) and lives in the rainforests of the Upper Amazon. It has large bulging eyes, a round head, and very fine, soft fur.

Orangutans, gibbons, gorillas and chimpanzees are anthropoid (human-like) apes with a large brain and no tail. Macaques, baboons, colobus, and marmosets belong to another smaller group. All apes and monkeys have large eyes, small ears and a flat nose. Their forelimbs have hands that are able to grasp and deftly maneuver objects.

Only the New World monkeys have prehensile tails, which means that they can curl their tails around the branch of a tree to keep their balance.

Crab-eating macaque
(right) – These macaques from Southeast Asia have long tails and whiskery brown faces. They fish for crabs and other shellfish. Scientists used the crab-eating macaque to develop the polio vaccine.

In the 1960s small Rhesus monkeys were sent into space and returned unharmed.

Celebes macaque from Indonesia

Apes and monkeys eat insects, fruit, leaves and birds' eggs, but bananas are their favorite treat.

Chimpanzee
These anthropoid apes have arms longer than their legs. Chimps walk on all fours but keep their backbone straight. The female (right) has a gestation period of 9 months and gives birth to a baby that weighs about 5 lb (2 kg).

AFRICAN FOREST
ANIMALS OF AFRICA
ASIAN JUNGLE
ENDANGERED SPECIES
MAMMALS

ARABS

Nomadic and semi-nomadic Arab tribes have lived in the Arabian peninsula since 1000 B.C. These tribes, which were often at war with one another, were united by Mohammed (570–632 A.D.), who was a shepherd and guide of merchant caravans. Mohammed wrote the *Koran* in which he proclaimed himself God's prophet and urged the people to accept *Allah* as their one and only God. He fled from Mecca to Medina in 622. This date, called *Hegira* in Arabic, marks the first day of the Muslim era. When Mohammed died, his successors, the *caliphs*, kept spiritual and secular power over the desert tribes in the name of Allah.

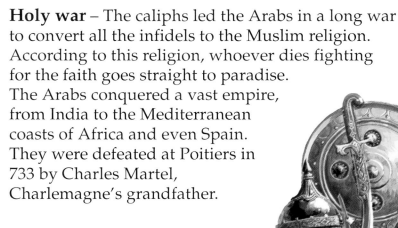

Culture – The Arabs were key in the development of medicine, mathematics, astronomy, and map-making. Below, the remains of the *Bibi Khanum madrasha* (a mosque housing a school) built in 1399, in Samarkand, Uzbekistan.

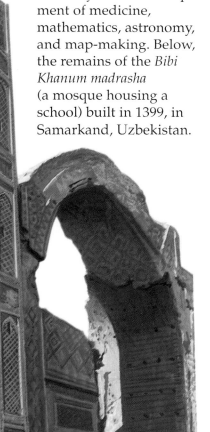

Holy war – The caliphs led the Arabs in a long war to convert all the infidels to the Muslim religion. According to this religion, whoever dies fighting for the faith goes straight to paradise. The Arabs conquered a vast empire, from India to the Mediterranean coasts of Africa and even Spain. They were defeated at Poitiers in 733 by Charles Martel, Charlemagne's grandfather.

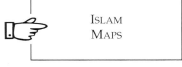

☞ ISLAM
MAPS

ARCHITECTURE

Architecture is the art and science of designing and constructing buildings and other structures. Architects are inspired by aesthetic standards and seek well-balanced proportions. However, they must also apply structural and functional techniques.

The Sphinx at Giza in Egypt is 240 ft (73 m) long and 66 ft (20 m) tall. It has a lion's body and its head represents Pharaoh Khafre.

The Parthenon, the temple dedicated to Athena, the patron goddess of Athens.

Classical architecture – The Parthenon is a marble temple that was built between 447 and 438 B.C. on the hills of the Acropolis in Athens. It was designed in the Doric style with 8 columns at the front and back and 17 columns on both sides.

Roman architecture – The Romans skillfully combined artistic inspiration and functionality in the construction of palaces, amphitheaters, aqueducts, and bridges.

The Roman Forum
1. Temple dedicated to a god
2. City wall
3. Equestrian statue
4. Two-horse chariot
5. Senator
6. Gladiator
7. Litter carried by slaves

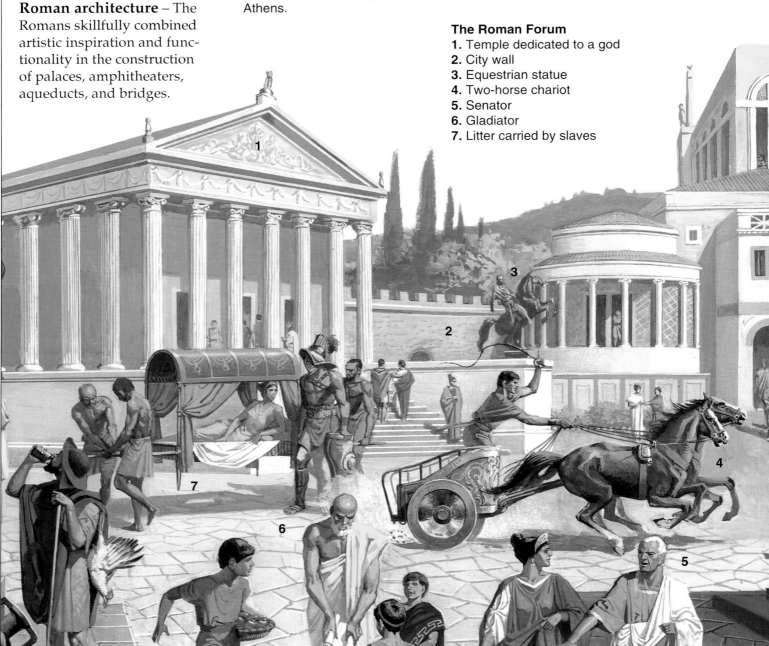

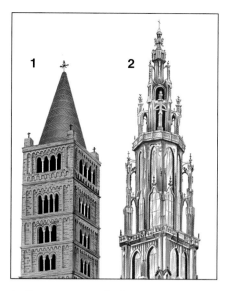

1. Romanesque bell tower
2. Gothic bell tower

Romanesque and Gothic styles

The Romanesque style was developed between the 11th and 12th centuries. Simplicity and austerity are the trademarks of this architectural style. The Gothic style developed at the end of the 12th century and spread throughout Europe up until the 16th century. Its characteristic spires and round arches seem to defy the laws of gravity and make buildings look even taller.

Modern architecture

At the beginning of the 20th century, architecture was greatly influenced by technology. New materials such as iron, steel, glass, and reinforced concrete were used for construction. Architecture adopted simple and functional styles to get the most out of limited available space.

Between 1887 and 1889, French architect G.A. Eiffel built the 984 ft (300 m) tall Eiffel Tower, entirely made of iron, for the Paris Exposition.

BUDDHISM, EGYPTIANS, GLASS, GOTHIC CATHEDRAL ✓, GREEKS, HINDUISM, ISLAM, NEW YORK CITY ✓, RENAISSANCE ✓, ROMANESQUE CHURCH ✓, ROMANS, SKYSCRAPERS ✓

Today, towering skyscrapers are built in the centers of large cities to take advantage of the limited available space. Above, the Empire State Building in New York, 1,250 ft (381 m) tall, built in 1931 by architects Shreve, Lamb, and Harmon.

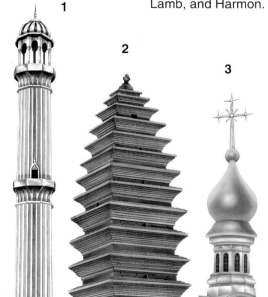

1. A minaret of the Jamma Masjid mosque in Delhi.
2. A Chinese pagoda in Tianning.
3. The Monastery of the Caverns in Kiev.

Religion and architecture

Christian cathedrals, Buddhist pagodas, Islamic mosques, and Tibetan monasteries: each religion has its own architectural style that distinguishes its places of worship, where the faithful meet to pray, and monasteries, where monks and priests live.

ARTISTS

Early forms of art existed during prehistoric days: many grottoes and caves have been found with ancient paintings that depict hunting scenes. The mosaics and frescoes of ancient Crete, Greece, Rome and Central America portray daily life and religious rites. The art of painting flourished in the 1400s and has continued down through the centuries with European artists such as Leonardo da Vinci, Michelangelo, Titian, Tintoretto, Goya, Monet, Cézanne, van Gogh, Picasso, Klimt, Mirò and Dalì.

Above: The Altamira Caves in Spain contain magnificent Stone Age paintings.

Egyptian art – Numerous frescoes let us reconstruct the daily life of Egyptians (left: fishing on the Nile). Even writing was an art: *hieroglyphics* were composed of *ideograms*, which are symbols that represent ideas.

Titian (Tiziano Vecellio) (ca. 1490–1576) Titian arrived in Venice at a very young age and was a student of Giorgione, a great master of the Venetian school of painting. Titian's later works revealed the influence of Michelangelo. Titian embodied the triumph of expressive realism and created a style that influenced masters such as Tintoretto and the Dutch painters Rembrandt and Rubens.

According to an anecdote, when Emperor Charles V knelt down and picked up a brush that his favorite artist Titian had dropped, the emperor exclaimed, "Titian deserves to be served, even by a king!"

Michelangelo (1475–1564) – Michelangelo was an artist of the Italian Renaissance. His love of form, expressed in his sculptures, is also evident in his paintings, where the human figure plays a dominant role. Michelangelo's greatest masterpiece is the ceiling of the Sistine Chapel, a masterpiece that took him four years to finish.

Michelangelo was also a great sculptor. His marble masterpieces include *David* and the *Pietà*.

Pablo Picasso (1881–1973) This Spanish artist and sculptor moved to Paris in 1904. The city inspired his blue period, followed by a more cheerful rose period. He and fellow painter Braque created Cubism, characterized by geometric forms. A giant of 20th century art, Picasso is especially famous for *Les Demoiselles d'Avignon* (1906–1907) and *Guernica* (1937).

Vincent van Gogh
(1853–1890) – Van Gogh was a Dutch painter whose early works were influenced by Impressionism, a movement that emerged in France in the second half of the 19th century. His works expressed the desperation and anguish of a tormented soul. His psychological pain can be seen in the dramatic use of color and violent brush strokes. Van Gogh killed himself in 1890.

HUMAN ANCESTORS
LEONARDO
RENAISSANCE ✓

ASIA

Asia is the largest and most populous continent on Earth. Asia and Europe, which are physically separated by the Ural mountain chain, form one single territory called Eurasia. As the land is so vast, it has many different physical characteristics.

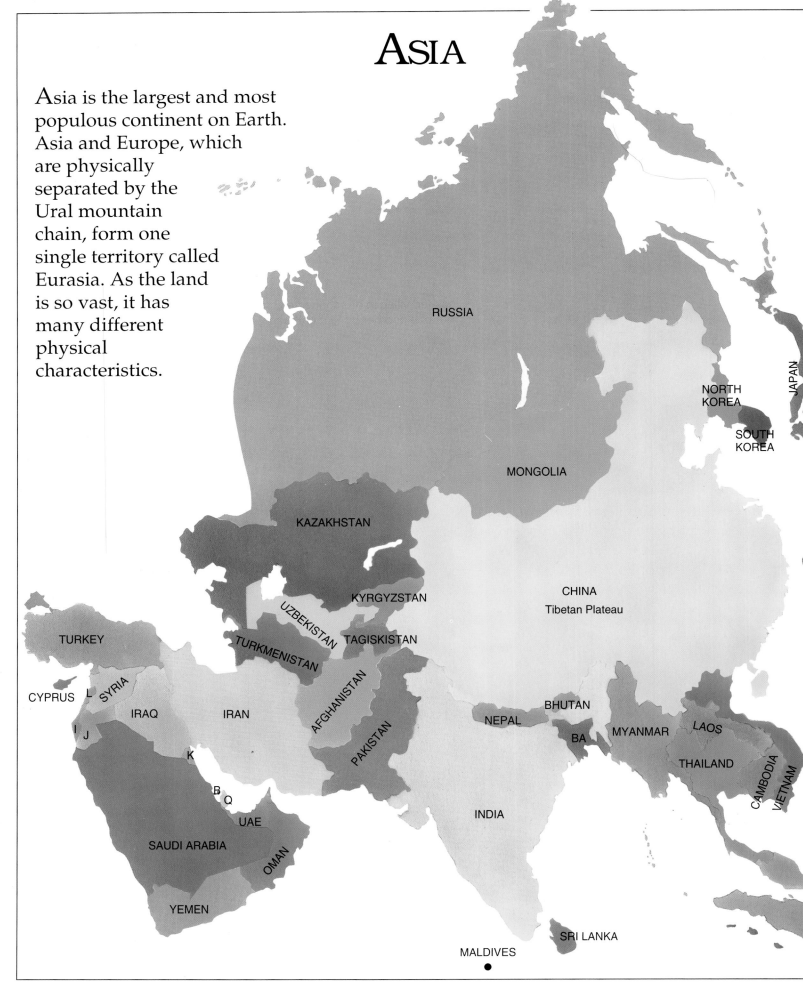

RUSSIA

JAPAN

NORTH KOREA

SOUTH KOREA

MONGOLIA

KAZAKHSTAN

CHINA
Tibetan Plateau

KYRGYZSTAN

UZBEKISTAN

TAGISKISTAN

TURKEY

TURKMENISTAN

CYPRUS

L

SYRIA

IRAQ

IRAN

AFGHANISTAN

BHUTAN

NEPAL

BA

MYANMAR

LAOS

I

J

K

PAKISTAN

THAILAND

CAMBODIA

VIETNAM

B

Q

UAE

SAUDI ARABIA

OMAN

INDIA

YEMEN

SRI LANKA

MALDIVES

Many different populations – The huge Asian territory is inhabited by many different people. *Mongols* mostly live in China and central-eastern Asia. *Arabs, Armenians, Caucasians, Persians,* and *Singalese* live in the western and southern areas. Over the centuries, these and other peoples have intermingled.

Above: A costume celebration. Tibetan traditions are greatly influenced by Tibet's geographical position in the mountains and by the Chinese and Indian cultures.

Isolated villages are connected with one another by foot paths and small bridges (left) that cross deep valleys.

For Tibetans, hospitality is sacred.

Tibet – This is an autonomous region in China. Its territory is almost entirely occupied by the world's largest plateau that bears its name. Very tall mountain chains rise above this plateau and are interrupted by deep, narrow valleys. Sitting on these mountains are the large monasteries of Buddhist monks that used to rule over this land, under the leadership of the Dalai Lama. The Tibetan population, concentrated in the southern valleys, lives mainly from raising yaks and sheep.

The yak is a typical animal of the region. It is a sturdy bovine with long, woolly fur. The yak is often used as a means of transport along the steep trails that cross the mountains.

'AN

PHILIPPINES

BR

INDONESIA

B: BAHRAIN
BA: BANGLADESH
BR: BRUNEI DARUSSALAM
UAE: UNITED ARAB EMIRATES
J: JORDAN
I: ISRAEL
K: KUWAIT
L: LEBANON
Q: QATAR
S: SINGAPORE

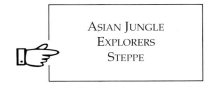

ASIAN JUNGLE
EXPLORERS
STEPPE

ASIAN COUNTRIES

	COUNTRY	CAPITAL	AREA	POPULATION	LANGUAGE	CURRENCY
	China	Beijing	3,705,676 sq mi (9,596,960 sq km)	1,203,100,000	Cantonese, Mandarin	yuan
	India	New Delhi	1,269,437 sq mi (3,287,590 sq km)	936,600,000	Hindi, English, others	Indian rupee
	Saudi Arabia	Riyadh	757,040 sq mi (1,960,582 sq km)	18,700,000	Arabic, English	riyal
	Indonesia	Jakarta	735,324 sq mi (1,904,344 sq km)	203,580,000	Bahasa, Javanese, Austronesian languages	Indonesian rupiah
	Iran	Teheran	636,342 sq mi (1,648,000 sq km)	64,300,000	Farsi	rial
	Mongolia	Ulan-Bator	604,294 sq mi (1,565,000 sq km)	2,493,600	Mongolian	tughrik
	Pakistan	Islamabad	310,424 sq mi (803,936 sq km)	131,542,000	Urdu, English	Pakistan rupee
	Turkey	Ankara	301,405 sq mi (780,580 sq km)	63,405,500	Turkish	Turkish lira
	Myanmar (Burma)	Yangon (Rangoon)	261,989 sq mi (678,500 sq km)	45,104,000	Burmese, Karen, Shan	kyat
	Afghanistan	Kabul	250,000 sq mi (647,500 sq km)	21,250,000	Dari, Pashto	afghani
	Yemen	Sana'a	203,865 sq mi (527,970 sq km)	14,730,000	Arabic	rial (North Yemen) dinar (South Yemen)
	Thailand	Bangkok	198,470 sq mi (514,000 sq km)	60,200,000	Thai (Siamese)	baht
	Iraq	Baghdad	168,766 sq mi (437,072 sq km)	20,600,000	Arabic, Kurdish	Iraqi dinar
	Japan	Tokyo	145,885 sq mi (377,815 sq km)	125,500,000	Japanese	yen
	Malaysia	Kuala Lumpur	127,326 sq mi (329,750 sq km)	19,724,000	Malay, English, Chinese	ringgit
	Vietnam	Hanoi	127,255 sq mi (329,566 sq km)	75,400,000	Vietnamese	dong
	Philippines	Manila	115,840 sq mi (300,000 sq km)	73,266,000	Philippino, English	Philippine peso

COUNTRY	CAPITAL	AREA	POPULATION	LANGUAGE	CURRENCY
Laos	Vientiane	91,429 sq mi (236,800 sq km)	4,837,000	Lao, French	kip
Oman	Muscat	82,030 sq mi (212,458 sq km)	2,125,000	Arabic, English	Omani rial
Syria	Damascus	71,498 sq mi (185,180 sq km)	15,452,000	Arabic	Syrian pound
Cambodia	Phnom Penh	69,903 sq mi (181,035 sq km)	10,600,000	Khmer, French	riel
Nepal	Kathmandu	54,367 sq mi (140,800 sq km)	22,000,000	Nepali, Newari	Nepalese rupee
Bangladesh	Dhaka	55,598 sq mi (143,998 sq km)	128,095,000	Bangala, English	taka
North Korea	Pyongyang	46,544 sq mi (120,540 sq km)	23,500,000	Korean	won
South Korea	Seoul	38,031 sq mi (98,480 sq km)	45,554,000	Korean	won
Jordan	Amman	34,448 sq mi (89,213 sq km)	4,100,000	Arabic	Jordan dinar
United Arab Emirates	Abu Dhabi	29,184 sq mi (75,581 sq km)	2,925,600	Arabic	dirham
Sri Lanka	Colombo	25,332 sq mi (65,610 sq km)	18,343,000	Sinhala, Tamil	Sri Lankan rupee
Bhutan	Thimphu Punakha	18,000 sq mi (46,620 sq km)	1,800,000	Dzongkha	ngultrum
Taiwan	Taipei	13,895 sq mi (35,988 sq km)	21,500,000	Mandarin	New Taiwan dollar
Israel	Jerusalem	8,020 sq mi (20,772 sq km)	5,500,000	Hebrew	shekel
Kuwait	Kuwait City	6,880 sq mi (17,820 sq km)	1,800,000	Arabic, English	Kuwaiti dinar
Qatar	Doha	4,247 sq mi (11,000 sq km)	534,000	Arabic	Qatari riyal
Lebanon	Beirut	4,015 sq mi (10,400 sq km)	3,700,000	Arabic, French	Lebanese pound
Cyprus	Nicosia	3,572 sq mi (9,251 sq km)	736,600	Greek, Turkish	Cyprus pound

COUNTRY	CAPITAL	AREA	POPULATION	LANGUAGE	CURRENCY
Brunei Darussalam	Bandar Seri Begawan	2,226 sq mi (5,765 sq km)	292,000	Malay, English, Chinese	Brunei dollar
Bahrain	Al-Manamah	240 sq mi (620 sq km)	576,000	Arabic, English	Bahrain dinar
Singapore	Singapore	244 sq mi (632 sq km)	2,900,000	English, Chinese, Malay, Tamil	Singapore dollar
Maldives	Malé	115 sq mi (298 sq km)	261,300	Dhivehi	Maldivian rufyaa

RECORDS IN ASIA

● **The largest continent:** Asia, about 17,183,000 sq mi (44,500,000 sq km).

● **The deepest ocean trench:** the Mariana Trench, in the Pacific Ocean, 35,840 ft (10,924 m).

● **The largest archipelago:** Indonesia, with 13,000 islands.

● **The deepest lake:** Lake Baikal, in central Siberia, 5,315 ft (1,620 m).

● **The largest lake:** Caspian Sea, 143,244 sq mi (370,973 sq km).

● **The widest delta:** the delta of the Ganges River, about 28,960 sq mi (75,000 sq km).

● **The tallest mountain:** Mount Everest in the Himalayan Mountain Chain, 29,028 ft (8,848 m).

● **The largest plateau:** the Tibetan Plateau, about 77,220 sq mi (200,000 sq km).

● **The deepest valley:** Kali Gandaki, in the Nepalese Himalayas, 14,435 ft (4,400 m).

● **The highest mountain pass:** the Karakoram Pass, 18,290 ft (5,575 m).

● **The highest capital city:** Lhasa (Tibet – China), 11,910 ft (3,630 m).

ASIAN JUNGLE

Monsoon winds sweep over Southeast Asia: in the winter the winds blow out to sea and are cold and dry. In the summer they bring rain inland from the sea. The high temperatures and rain favor the growth of the jungle. The trails are covered with *lianas*, or hanging vines, and lined with coconut trees, rosewood trees, and flowered bushes. Crocodiles and birds with long legs such as the ibis and the marabou live in the swamps. Many types of monkeys swing from one liana to another without ever touching the ground. Cobras and pythons slither along the ground while tigers and leopards lie in wait for their prey.

APES AND MONKEYS, ASIA, BIRDS, CROCODILES, SNAKES, TIGERS, WILDCATS

The proboscis monkey lives on the island of Borneo. The male makes its large nose swell to attract a female.

Tiger – The tiger lives in Asian forests from Siberia to India. This agile feline bites its prey on the back of the neck or throat to kill it. Everyone remembers *Shere Khan*, the terrible tiger in Rudyard Kipling's novel, *The Jungle Book*.

1. Python
2. Squacco heron
3. Ibis
4. Crocodile
5. Mallard
6. Jacana
7. Mandarin duck
8. Archer fish
9. Catfish
10. Fire-bellied toad
11. Moorhen

ASTRONOMY

Stars are classified according to color.

Astronomy is the science of the stars and dates back to the time of the ancient Babylonians and Egyptians. People then were so fascinated by the starry sky that they thought the Sun and the Moon were gods. At that time, the stars could only be observed with the naked eye. The first telescope was invented by Galileo in the 17th century.

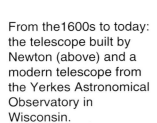

From the 1600s to today: the telescope built by Newton (above) and a modern telescope from the Yerkes Astronomical Observatory in Wisconsin.

Stars and galaxies
Stars differ in size, temperature, and luminosity, and their colors range from white to blue and dark red. Stars are grouped together in *galaxies*: Each galaxy contains billions of stars.

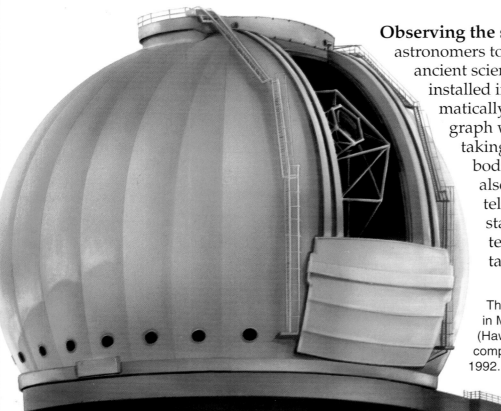

Observing the sky – The equipment used by astronomers today is quite different from what ancient scientists used. Today, telescopes installed in modern observatories can automatically follow a chosen star and photograph wide areas of the sky in sequence, taking a zoom shot of all the celestial bodies it finds. Artificial satellites are also important for they have special telescopes that transmit images of stars. Together these advances in technology have led us to important discoveries about the universe.

The telescope in Mauna Kea (Hawaii), completed in 1992.

CONSTELLATIONS ✓, EARTH, MOON, OPTICS, SPACE TRAVEL, SUN

AUTHORS AND POETS

Through their prose and poetry, authors and poets describe their own personal outlook on life and express sentiments, fantasies, emotions, and ideas. Literature encompasses many different styles and topics.

Homer (ca. 8th century B.C.) was a blind poet who supposedly wrote *The Iliad* (which tells the story of the Trojan War) and *The Odyssey* (about Ulysses' journey from Troy to Ithaca).

Dante Alighieri (1265–1321) was a Florentine poet who wrote the *Divine Comedy*. This book tells of his imaginary voyage (below) to Hell, Purgatory, and Paradise, guided first by the poet Virgil, then by his beloved Beatrice, and finally by Saint Bernard.

ALCOTT
CHILDREN'S LITERATURE
ELIZABETH I
FAIRY TALES AND FABLES
GREEKS
MELVILLE
MYTHS AND LEGENDS
STEVENSON
SWIFT

Charles Dickens (1812–1870), an English author, wrote *Oliver Twist*, *David Copperfield* and *Pickwick Papers*, where he described many humorous characters (above). Dickens denounced the injustices of his day, but his stories always have a happy ending.

The French author Honoré de Balzac (1799–1850) published more than 90 books that together make up *La Comédie Humaine* (The Human Comedy), which describes society during his day.

William Shakespeare (1564–1616) was a great English poet and playwright of the Elizabethan Age. His famous works include *Romeo and Juliet*, *Henry IV*, *The Taming of the Shrew*, *A Midsummer Night's Dream*, *Hamlet*, *Othello*, *King Lear*, *Macbeth*, and *The Tempest*.

BARBARIANS

The Roman Empire fell between 395 and 476 A.D. Foreign invaders, called barbarians, came from eastern Europe and central Asia: they were Franks, Visigoths, Ostrogoths, Lombards, Burgundians, Vandals and Huns. Attila, also known as the Scourge of God, was the leader of the Huns. He attacked the Eastern and Western empires repeatedly and won much territory. However, he failed at Constantinople (443) and in Gaul (451). He pillaged northern Italy but never reached Rome. He died in his sleep in 453 and was buried with his treasure. He was succeeded by his sons, who divided the empire among them.

Huns torched the cities they conquered, which is why it was said, "Grass never grows where Attila has passed."

Vikings – These people settled in the western areas of Scandinavian (Norway today) in the 6th century. They were fine sailors and built light, fast warships called *drakkars*, as well as heavier and sturdier merchant ships called *knorrs*.

How barbarians dressed

Barbarian warriors were nomads who dressed in colorful tunics or sleeveless jackets, goatskin pants and a square or rectangular cape held together with metal clasps. They often wore furs to protect themselves from the cold.

The Vikings attacked many ships along the coasts of Europe.

Celts – Between 725 and 480 A.D. the Celts became an important force in central and western Europe. They lived in clans governed by warrior nobles. The priests, called *druids*, were very influential and performed sacrifices, handled legal matters, and advised the king. *Bards*, who were poets and musicians, sang the praises of the leaders' exploits.

Greeks and Romans called all people who lived beyond their borders *barbarians*, from the sound *bar-bar*, an imitation of the "babble" of an unknown language.

Celtic artisans forged magnificent metal weapons and jewelery that displayed druid symbols.

Clothing – The women wore long robes under a tunic. Cloaks and furs protected them from the cold. Metal buckles, pins and clasps with geometric designs decorated the women's garments.

Teutons – Indo-European populations settled in Germany around the 3rd century B.C. and were called Teutons, meaning "men who raise a war cry." They were a fierce semi-nomadic people (below) who hunted but also occasionally farmed and raised animals. Their homes were straw huts with a dome roof, which were easy to rebuild.

Teutonic, or German, women were important members of the clan and followed their husbands in times of peace and war.

ERIC THE RED
FASHION
INDIA
ROMANS
VIKING VILLAGE ✓

BEARS

brown bear

There are many bear species in Europe, Asia, and North and South America. The Malayan bear, the smallest, is just 4 ft (1.2 m) tall. The polar bear, however, reaches almost 10 ft (3 m) in height and weighs as much as 1,500 lb (700 kg). The giant panda can weigh up to 250 lb (115 kg). It feeds almost exclusively on bamboo. It has poor eyesight but an extremely keen sense of smell.

Grizzly – A type of brown bear, the grizzly reaches about 8 ft (2.5 m) in length. It lives in the forests of the Rocky Mountains in the U.S. and Canada.

Spectacled bear (right): This carnivore lives in the Andes and is the only type of bear in South America.

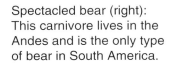

Himalayan black bear (right) – This bear has black fur and a pale V-shaped marking on its chest. It has good hearing and is an agile climber. The Himalayan black bear is vegetarian.

Behavior of the brown bear
If a bear is surprised or bothered, it stands up on its hind legs, waves its huge paws and growls. It spends the winter in a protected den. The mother bear (right) carefully supervises her cubs. If danger arises, she pushes them up into the trees, then climbs down to fight.

Children love teddy bears. The real thing isn't so cuddly!

ANIMALS OF EUROPE, ANIMALS OF NORTH AMERICA, ANIMALS OF THE POLAR REGIONS, ENDANGERED SPECIES, HIBERNATION, MAMMALS

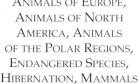

BEES

Bee is the common name for the 20,000 species of insects belonging to the Apoidea family in the Hymenoptera order. Some bees are 1/10 of an inch (2 mm) long, and others are a little over 1 inch (3 cm) long. Bees live in a rigid caste system. The swarm has thousands of worker bees but just one queen bee, which is about twice the size of the other bees. Worker bees are sterile female bees, and only the queen bee can reproduce. She is inseminated in flight by *drones*, which are male bees.

Beekeeper – The beekeeper wears a special suit and protects his face and hands when he collects honey. He smokes out the beehive to stun the bees, then he raises the roof on the apiary and removes the frames covered with honey. The honey is then extracted through centrifugation.

The bee carries pollen from one flower to another.

Hives hang on branches or are built in holes. Beekeepers keep bees in houses called apiaries, where the bees build honeycombs.

Honeycombs (below) are hexagonal, a shape that limits the amount of material wasted. Combs are made of wax secreted by the bee's wax-secreting glands.

Honey comes in different colors and flavors:
1. Eucalyptus honey
2. Linden honey
3. Acacia honey
4. Orange flower honey
5. Chestnut honey

Bees – Thousands of bees work in the hive: some produce wax to build combs, which are six-sided cells where the eggs and honey are deposited. Other bees are in charge of cleaning the hive; they also keep it cool by beating their wings. Bees that make honey are called *honeybees*.

The swarm – When the hive is too crowded, the queen abandons the hive, bringing with her almost half of the worker bees. The swarm of bees clusters on a branch until it chooses a new place to build the hive.

Colored signals
Bees see colors that are invisible to humans. These colors on flowers are nectar guides, a kind of landing strip for bees so they can reach the sweet nectar.

Colors humans can see.

Colors bees can see.

1. Honeycombs.
2. The queen bee leaves the queen cell.
3. The bee sucks nectar from the flowers.
4. Nanny bees feed the larvae.

Mating – When the queen bee is one week old, she takes her first mating flight. Hundreds of male bees called *drones* try to mate with her, but only a few are successful. After the mating period, the males are chased away. The inseminated queen bee lays up to 2,000 eggs per day. She will lay more than 2 million eggs during her life-time (4 or 5 years).

A bee only stings if it is provoked. Its stinger is attached to a poison sac.

Life in the hive – Worker bees live for about one month. During the first days they clean the combs and feed the larvae. Around the tenth day they start building combs and taking reconnaissance flights. Then they guard the hive and keep enemies away. Finally, they gather nectar and collect pollen.

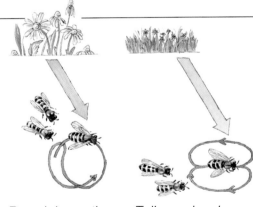

Coded dance
Worker bees perform special dances, using the sun as a reference, to inform other worker bees where and how far away the nectar is. The inclination and speed of the dance indicate the direction.

Round dance: the nectar is less than 330 ft (100 m) away.

Tail-wagging dance: the nectar is more than 330 ft (100 m) away.

Larvae – After three days, the eggs deposited by the queen bee turn into larvae. They are fed royal jelly by nanny bees, then honey and pollen. The larvae turn into pupas, then become adult bees.

A bee's head looks like that of a space alien: it has eyes that can see in any direction, long antennas, and a strange trunk-like mouth.

FARM ANIMALS, FIELDS AND MEADOWS, FLOWERS, INSECTS

BIRDS

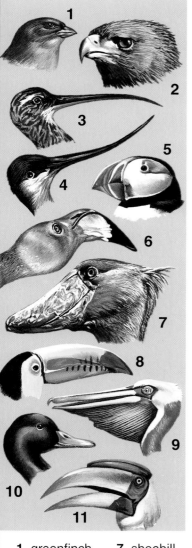

Birds are vertebrates that evolved from reptiles millions of years ago when their forelimbs turned into wings with feathers used for flight. They have light, hollow bones, very powerful wing muscles and a beak without teeth.

1. greenfinch
2. golden eagle
3. curlew
4. avocet
5. puffin
6. flamingo
7. shoebill
8. toucan
9. pelican
10. mallard
11. rhinoceros hornbill

Beaks – The horny beak, composed of bone and keratin, is stiff at the tip but soft at the base. The shape of a bird's beak varies with the species, depending on the kind of food it eats.

chiff-chaff

hawfinch

blackbird

thrush

Feathers are often brightly colored. In many bird species the male has more colorful feathers in order to attract the female during the mating season.

redstart

Feathers
Since feathers trap heat and do not absorb humidity, they are perfect insulators. Birds periodically shed their feathers, a process called *molting*.

Non-migratory or migratory

Birds that live all year round in the same place are *non-migratory*. Birds that migrate according to the season are called *birds of passage*. They leave their habitat in the fall in search of a warmer climate and more food, and return in spring.

chaffinch

orange canary

starling

nightingale

rufous-bellied niltava

yellow canary

Japanese nightingale

greenfinch

goldfinch

Nest – Some birds are born helpless and must stay in the nest several weeks being fed. Other species, such as ducks and gulls, are well-developed at birth and leave the nest within a day of hatching. They quickly learn to fly and feed themselves.

robin

AFRICAN FOREST,
ASIAN JUNGLE,
BIRDS WITH BRIGHT
COLORS, DINOSAURS,
MARSHLAND,
MIGRATION, PELICANS,
PETS, RAPTORS,
TUNDRA

BIRDS WITH BRIGHT COLORS

Some birds, like parrots, sport very colorful feathers, and others, like the toucan from tropical America, even have colorful beaks. In some species only the males are colorful, a characteristic they use to attract females during the mating season. The male peacock has a brilliant tail, for example, but the female is very drab.

Kingfisher: This bird waits until it spots a fish, then dives into the water and spears its prey with its long beak.

Cordon bleu – This bird lives in the forests of Malaysia and in central and eastern Africa. It is as large as a sparrow but has a long, colorful tail. The male has a bright red spot beneath its eyes. The cordon bleu flies in small, noisy flocks and uses its beak to skillfully weave its nest.

Peacock – Native to India, this bird reaches 6 ft (2 m) in length, including the tail. Only the male (above) has colorful feathers. In Roman mythology the peacock was considered the sacred bird of Juno.

cordon bleu

Gouldian grassfinch

Gouldian grassfinch – The birds in the Australian grassfinch family sport feathers in brilliant jewel-like colors. The most colorful is the Gouldian grassfinch. Because these finches are prized for their beauty, they are popular with pet owners, who also find them easy to feed. Unfortunately, the Gouldian population is steadily declining.

Paradise tanager (left) – These birds of passage are distinguished by seven brilliant colors. They live in the rainforests of South America, where their shrill whistle-like call can be heard.

Crowned pigeon (above) Very common in New Guinea, this pigeon is the largest in the world. It can grow to the size of a turkey.

Macaw (above right) One of the world's largest parrots, the macaw's tail can reach 3 ft (1 m) in length. It lives in Central America and in the Amazon.

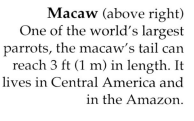

Topaz hummingbird (left) – These tiny birds live only in North and South America. Their wings beat so quickly (22 to 78 beats per second) that they are able to hover over a flower while foraging for food.

Magpie Several types of blue magpies live in Southeast Asia. One of the most beautiful is the Chinese magpie (above), which can be found from the Himalayas to Sumatra and Borneo.

Bird of paradise (right) Most of the species live in New Guinea. Many types of birds of paradise are monogamous, that is, they mate for life, and the male and female take care of the young.

ANIMALS OF AUSTRALIA, ANIMALS OF SOUTH AMERICA, BIRDS

BLOOD CIRCULATION

Blood is pumped by the heart through a dense network of *arteries*, *veins*, and *small capillaries* to reach all parts of the body. Blood consists essentially of a yellowish liquid called *plasma* which contains *white blood cells*, *red blood cells*, and *platelets*.

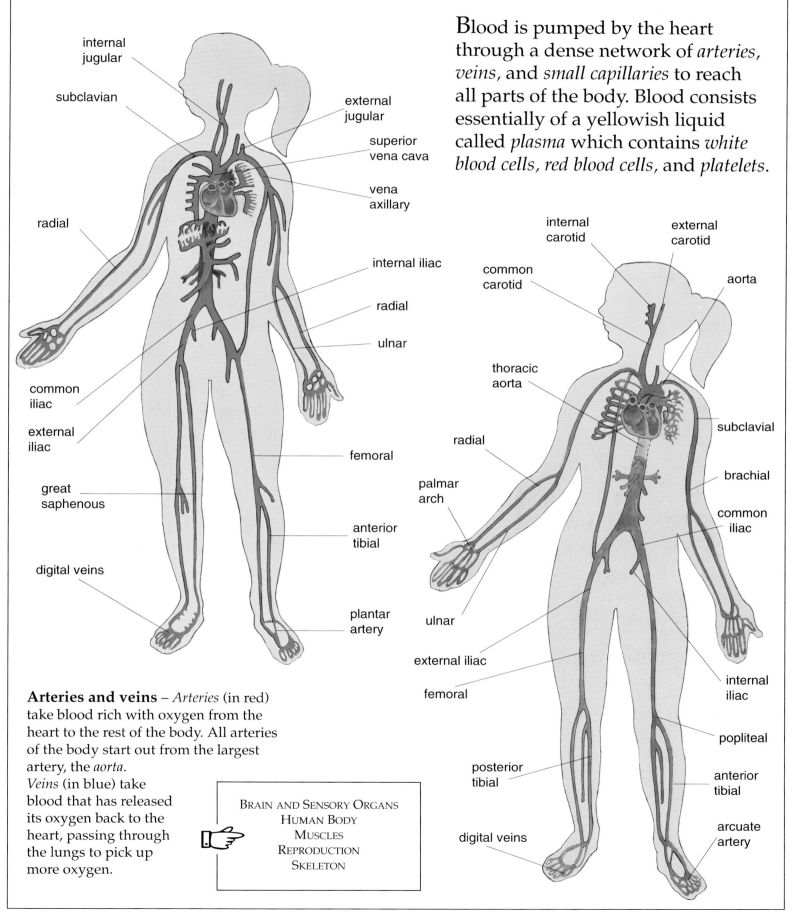

internal jugular

subclavian

external jugular

superior vena cava

vena axillary

radial

internal iliac

radial

ulnar

common iliac

external iliac

femoral

great saphenous

anterior tibial

digital veins

plantar artery

internal carotid

external carotid

common carotid

aorta

thoracic aorta

subclavial

radial

brachial

palmar arch

common iliac

ulnar

external iliac

femoral

internal iliac

popliteal

posterior tibial

anterior tibial

digital veins

arcuate artery

Arteries and veins – *Arteries* (in red) take blood rich with oxygen from the heart to the rest of the body. All arteries of the body start out from the largest artery, the *aorta*.
Veins (in blue) take blood that has released its oxygen back to the heart, passing through the lungs to pick up more oxygen.

BRAIN AND SENSORY ORGANS
HUMAN BODY
MUSCLES
REPRODUCTION
SKELETON

BOLIVAR, SIMON

Simon Bolivar studied in Europe, then returned to Venezuela, inspired by ideals of liberty and democracy. He decided to dedicate his life to help the Spanish colonies in South America gain their independence. In 1810 Simon Bolivar took part in an insurrection against the Spanish in Caracas. He and his volunteer army liberated Venezuela in 1813. He took full control of the country in 1814, but was later forced to flee. Simon Bolivar returned to create a confederation of South American states in 1816. He freed New Granada and was proclaimed President of the Republic of Gran Colombia in 1819.

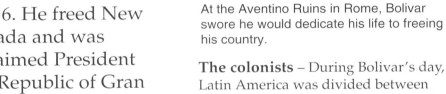

Simon Bolivar (1783–1830) was called *The Liberator*.

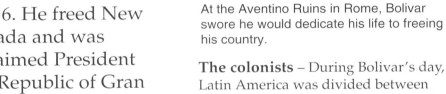

At the Aventino Ruins in Rome, Bolivar swore he would dedicate his life to freeing his country.

The colonists – During Bolivar's day, Latin America was divided between colonies ruled by Spain and Portugal. The colonists who lived there increasingly felt the need to become independent so they could manage the resources of their countries on their own, without having to answer to the mother country.

Bolivar led his fellow countrymen in the insurrection against Spain.

The end of a dream – Peru and Ecuador were annexed to Gran Colombia in 1822. The northern section of Peru became the Bolivar Republic in 1825 and later Bolivia, in honor of Simon. Some countries in the confederation tried on several occasions to become autonomous.

Simon Bolivar finally left politics after the Panama Congress (1826), when he realized that his dream of creating a great confederation had fallen apart.

CHRISTOPHER COLUMBUS,
PRE-COLUMBIAN
CIVILIZATIONS

BOOKS

Johannes Gutenberg's invention of the printing press dates back to the 15th century. This system allowed printers to mass produce books, which lowered their cost and made them accessible to everyone. Today, books are printed with machinery that can produce thousands of pages per hour.

The first book printed by Gutenberg (1455) was a Bible in Latin.

Rolled sheets – In ancient days books were made with sheets of parchment paper rolled around two wooden pegs. In fact, the word *volume* comes from a Latin word that means rolled up sheets. Only later was it possible to make books by binding the pages together.

COMPUTERS
GUTENBERG
MONASTERIES

Scribes – In the Middle Ages books were *manuscripts*, that is, they were written down and copied by hand by monks. They transcribed the texts of ancient Greek and Latin authors in their original language. The first books in *vulgar tongue*, meaning in the language spoken by the people, appeared after the printing press was invented.

Books in the Middle Ages were decorated or *illuminated* with colored drawings called *miniatures*.

Author's idea

Manuscript

Printing press

Layout on the computer

A book — printed and bound

How books are made today

The book is the *author's* creation. He or she sends a *manuscript* (usually written on computer) to a *publisher*. If accepted, the book is then *edited*. The *illustrator* creates illustrations to go with the text. The *graphic designer* designs the book cover and prepares the text and the layout for the color illustrations; today this is often done on computer. The *typesetter* prepares the text for printing. The *photolithographer* prepares the films for printing. The *printer* prints the book on large sheets that are folded, cut, and bound together with the cover.

BOVINES

Bovines belong to the *Bos* genus that includes Asian and African buffaloes, cows, and bison. They have split hooves that seem to form two toes. All domestic species *(Bos taurus)* come from the auroch, which originated in India during the Tertiary Period and became extinct in Poland in 1627. Bovines were first tamed by primitive peoples about 5,000 years ago. Today there are about 12 billion domestic bovines all over the world.

A calf drinks about 2.5 gallons (10 liters) of milk per day.

a Jersey cow with calf

William F. Cody, better known as Buffalo Bill.

Buffalo – This is another name for the American bison. The buffalo was the most important resource of Native American tribes whose customs, lifestyle, and art revealed this close tie. *May your soul quickly fly to your ancestors, the four spirits, and to the buffaloes from whence you came!* These were the words the medicine man would chant over dying people. There were 60 million bison in North America in 1700. But starting in 1865, they were gradually all but exterminated to make way for the construction of the Union Pacific Railroad, the first railroad in America. By 1889, there were only 835 buffaloes left. They were sent to live on protected wildlife reserves where there numbers began to increase again. Today there are 50,000 buffaloes in North America.

American buffalo

Chartley bull

European bison

yak

Yak – This animal lives in Tibet. It has thick black hair and horns that can reach 35 in (90 cm). It weighs between 1,300 and 1,500 lb (600-700 kg).

Different species – Cows are raised for work, milk, or beef. The best milking breeds are Brown Alpine, Frisian, Guernsey, and Jersey cows. The best beef breeds are Piedmont, Simmenthal, Chianin, Shorthorn, Aberdeen-Angus, Hereford, Charolais, and Limousin cattle.

Oxen have thick horns.

They use their tail as a fly-swatter.

Work oxen used to pull carts but in most places they have been replaced by farm machinery.

Indian buffalo – The Indian buffalo originated in India and Borneo and was later raised in Africa, Europe, Australia, and South America. It has long, curved horns and sturdy legs. It lives near water and is frequently used in rice cultivation.

Indian buffalo

brown Alpine cow

Frisian cow

Ruminants – Bovine stomachs are divided into four different chambers. Once the grass has been swallowed, it goes to the rumen where it is partially digested. Then it moves into the reticulum where it is rolled into balls. These balls are regurgitated and then ruminated or chewed. The cud then passes into the omasum, and then finally into the abomasum, where it is fully digested.

The bovine stomach is divided into four parts:
1. Rumen   **3.** Omasum
2. Reticulum   **4.** Abomasum

Language – Bovines communicate by moving their heads. If they are feeling aggressive, they paw at the ground with their hooves, then they lower their horns and attack.

anoa

zebu

Rift Valley ox

ANIMALS OF NORTH AMERICA, FARM ANIMALS, MAMMALS

61

THE BRAIN AND SENSORY ORGANS

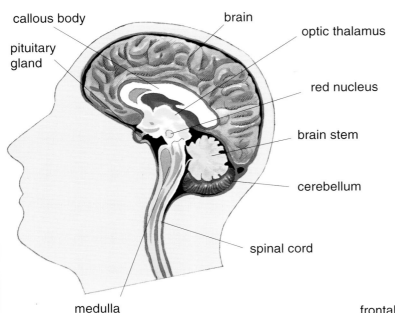

callous body
brain
optic thalamus
pituitary gland
red nucleus
brain stem
cerebellum
spinal cord
medulla

The brain controls all parts of the body through a network of nerves. The *central nervous system* is formed by the *brain* (cerebrum, cerebellum and medulla) and the *spinal cord*. The *peripheral nervous system* is made up of nerves. The organs of the five major senses (sight, hearing, smell, taste, and touch) send impulses to the brain through the peripheral nervous system.

Sight – This sense lets the eye see everything around us. Reflections of light pass through the *cornea* and *lens* to reach the *retina*, where they hit the *photoreceptors* linked to the brain through the *optic nerve*. The eye is like a camera: the images are projected much smaller and upside-down onto the retina.

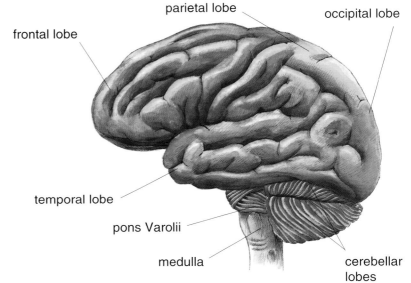

parietal lobe
occipital lobe
frontal lobe
temporal lobe
pons Varolii
medulla
cerebellar lobes

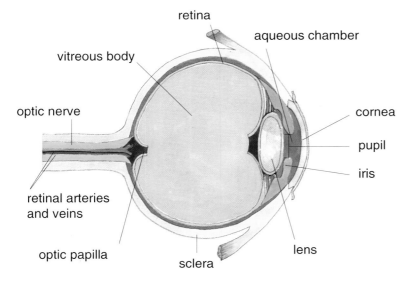

retina
aqueous chamber
vitreous body
optic nerve
cornea
pupil
iris
retinal arteries and veins
optic papilla
sclera
lens

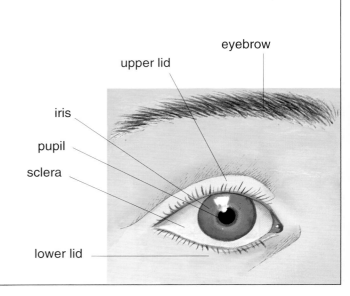

eyebrow
upper lid
iris
pupil
sclera
lower lid

62

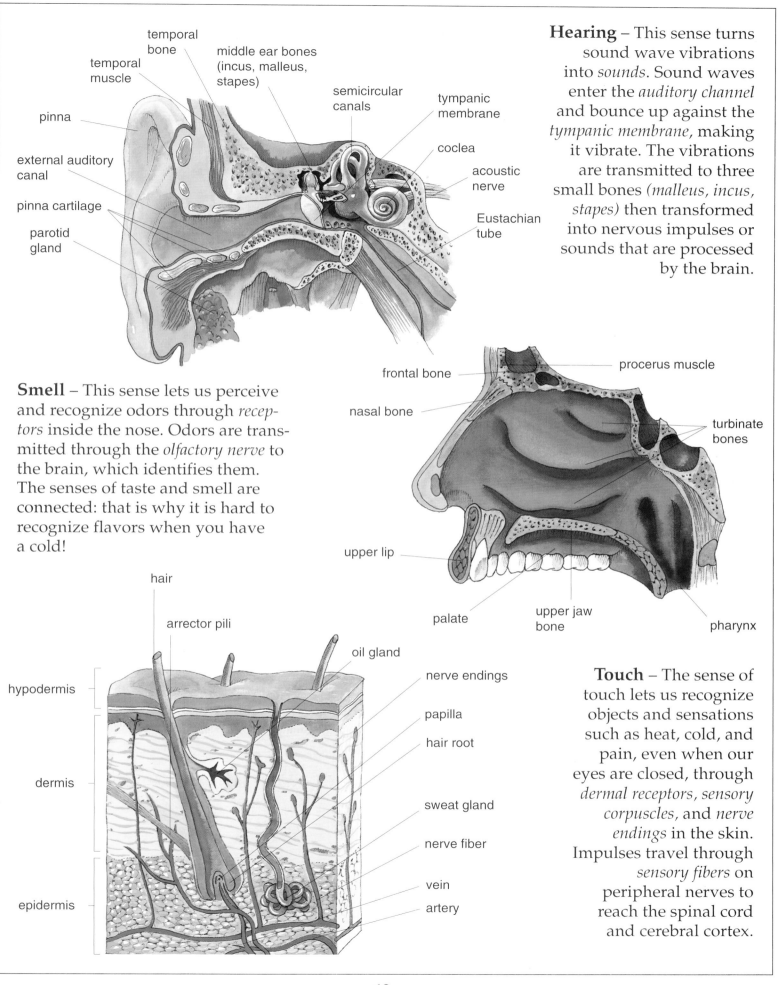

temporal muscle

temporal bone

middle ear bones (incus, malleus, stapes)

pinna

semicircular canals

tympanic membrane

coclea

external auditory canal

acoustic nerve

pinna cartilage

Eustachian tube

parotid gland

Hearing – This sense turns sound wave vibrations into *sounds*. Sound waves enter the *auditory channel* and bounce up against the *tympanic membrane*, making it vibrate. The vibrations are transmitted to three small bones (*malleus, incus, stapes*) then transformed into nervous impulses or sounds that are processed by the brain.

Smell – This sense lets us perceive and recognize odors through *receptors* inside the nose. Odors are transmitted through the *olfactory nerve* to the brain, which identifies them. The senses of taste and smell are connected: that is why it is hard to recognize flavors when you have a cold!

frontal bone

procerus muscle

nasal bone

turbinate bones

upper lip

palate

upper jaw bone

pharynx

hair

arrector pili

oil gland

nerve endings

papilla

hair root

sweat gland

nerve fiber

vein

artery

hypodermis

dermis

epidermis

Touch – The sense of touch lets us recognize objects and sensations such as heat, cold, and pain, even when our eyes are closed, through *dermal receptors, sensory corpuscles,* and *nerve endings* in the skin. Impulses travel through *sensory fibers* on peripheral nerves to reach the spinal cord and cerebral cortex.

Taste – This sense lets us distinguish flavors. *Taste buds* on the tongue send nerve impulses to the brain. Certain parts of the tongue are better at recognizing some flavors than others. The tip of the tongue recognizes sweet and salty flavors easier, the back recognizes bitter tastes and the sides, acid tastes. In general, sweet and salty flavors are the easiest to recognize.

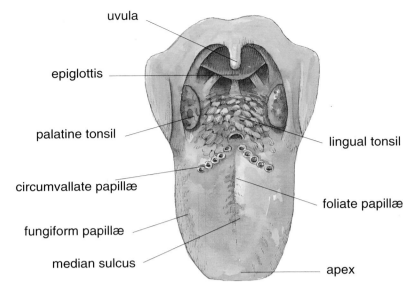

uvula
epiglottis
palatine tonsil
circumvallate papillæ
fungiform papillæ
median sulcus
lingual tonsil
foliate papillæ
apex

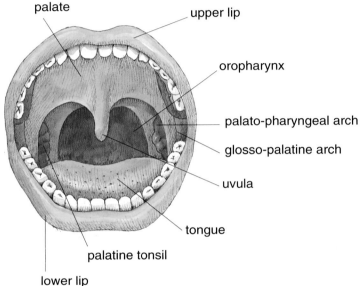

palate
upper lip
oropharynx
palato-pharyngeal arch
glosso-palatine arch
uvula
tongue
palatine tonsil
lower lip

Tongue – The tongue, which is covered in mucous, is very flexible because it has 17 different muscles. There are about one thousand taste buds on the surface of the tongue that recognize flavors.

BLOOD CIRCULATION,
HUMAN BODY,
MUSCLES,
REPRODUCTION,
SKELETON

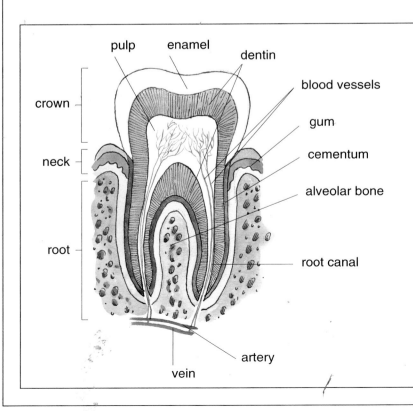

pulp   enamel
dentin
blood vessels
gum
cementum
alveolar bone
root canal
crown
neck
root
artery
vein

Teeth – Teeth are covered with a material called *dentine* that is harder and denser than bone. Dentine is covered with strong white *enamel*. The *crown* is the visible part of the tooth that is used for chewing; the *pulp* inside contains blood vessels and nerves. The root secures the tooth to the bone. Deciduous teeth (also called baby teeth) are the first ones to appear. After six years of age, 32 permanent teeth start to grow *(8 incisors, 4 canines, 8 premolars, 12 molars)*. Canines are pointed molars, premolars are large and flat, and incisors are sharp and narrow. If teeth are not brushed regularly, food particles may remain stuck between them and can cause *dental plaque* and *cavities*.

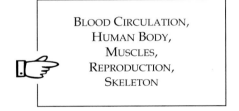

BUDDHISM

About 600 million people all over the world follow the teachings of Buddhism, a religious-philosophical doctrine that preaches serenity, tolerance, and universal love. Buddhism was founded by Prince Siddhartha Gautama (565 B.C. – 486 B.C.), who gave up wealth and riches when he was 30 and dedicated his life to the search for the *Four Noble Truths*. When enlightenment came to him, he realized he had to give up earthly desires and live in peace to be truly happy. This is why his disciples called him *Buddha*, which means the Enlightened One.

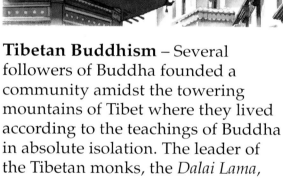

Below: the *wheel of life*, which represents the eternal cycle of birth and rebirth.

Above and below: statues of Buddha in meditation.

Tibetan Buddhism – Several followers of Buddha founded a community amidst the towering mountains of Tibet where they lived according to the teachings of Buddha in absolute isolation. The leader of the Tibetan monks, the *Dalai Lama*, also governed the country before China invaded Tibet in 1959.

Places of worship
The oldest Buddhist temples are called *stupas*. The large central dome houses the relic chamber, which is covered with a box-like structure topped with a round disc on a pole.

 ARCHITECTURE, CHRISTIANITY, HINDUISM, INDIA ISLAM, JUDAISM

When Siddhartha took refuge in the forest, a tree bent its branches to shelter him so that no one would disturb his meditation.

Nirvana – To achieve complete happiness (*nirvana*), a Buddhist must free him/herself from the material world by following the rules of the *Noble Eightfold Path*.

BUTTERFLIES

Butterflies go through four different stages in their life cycle: 1) egg, 2) larva or caterpillar, 3) chrysalis or pupa, and 4) adult. The change from one stage to another is called a metamorphosis. The caterpillar hatches from the egg and starts eating leaves and other plants. It wraps silk threads around its body, forming a chrysalis inside a cocoon. When the adult finally emerges from the cocoon, it opens its wings, which are covered with tiny colored scales.

mountain beauty

The caterpillar produces silk threads for the cocoon.

Day and night
Brightly colored butterflies are seen during the day while moths, which come out at night, have pale or drab colors and fold their wings along the sides of their body when at rest.

owl butterfly

Butterflies have an elongated tube on their mouth used for sucking liquids and drinking nectar.

Above:
1. Madagascar moon moth
2. dead-leaf butterfly
3. morpho
4. daetrhia
5. parasa reginula
6. Rajah Brooke's birdwing

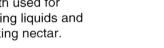

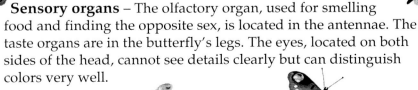

Sensory organs – The olfactory organ, used for smelling food and finding the opposite sex, is located in the antennae. The taste organs are in the butterfly's legs. The eyes, located on both sides of the head, cannot see details clearly but can distinguish colors very well.

swallow-tail

red admiral

brimstone

cinnabar

Jersey tiger moth

6-spot burnet

peacock

purple emperor

small Apollo

bronze underwing

anglewing

fritillary

FIELDS AND MEADOWS
INSECTS
MIGRATION

CAMOUFLAGE

Even humans camouflage themselves by wearing clothes that blend in with the surrounding vegetation. Soldiers wear military camouflage, for instance.

Several animals can *camouflage* themselves, which means they can blend in with their surroundings. A fish may look exactly like a stone, a butterfly can resemble a flower, and an insect can look just like a leaf. This strategy helps predators surprise their prey and animals hide from their predators.

From top to bottom: leopard, zebra, giraffe, cheetah.

Seasonal camouflage

Many animals' fur changes color in different seasons. In the summer (1) the marten has dark brown fur so it blends in with the countryside. In winter (2) its fur becomes pale so it can blend in with the snow.

Japanese marten

Fish – Rays and soles are difficult to see because they live on the sea floor and their mottled coloring blends in with the sand.

In the African savanna
Some animals have spotted or striped fur that helps them hide in the savanna brush.

Chameleon (above) – This amphibian changes color (green, yellow, brown) almost instantly to blend in with its surroundings. Special cells in its skin open and close in the process. These changes help it hide from its predators.

The scorpion fish (below) sits motionless on the bottom of the sea and blends in with the rocks.

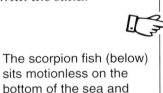

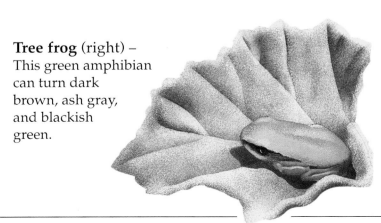

Tree frog (right) – This green amphibian can turn dark brown, ash gray, and blackish green.

AMPHIBIANS, ANIMALS OF AFRICA, ANIMALS (STRANGE), FISH, GIRAFFE, REPTILES, SEASONS, TIGERS, TUNDRA, WILDCATS, ZEBRAS

CASTLES

During the Middle Ages, the castle was a fortified building governed by a lord who lived there with his family. After the Crusades, new defensive building techniques were developed. Castles, which were more fortified than ever, were surrounded by double and triple walls with narrow slits used by soldiers to shoot at the enemy without being seen. In the 13th century, the castle became the administrative center of society. It was made up of three parts: the *wall* (with towers and a moat), a *dungeon* (a protected area where weapons and treasures were stored), and the lord's residence. Between the 15th and 16th centuries, the castle became an aristocratic mansion: the castles in the Loire Valley of France are a good example.

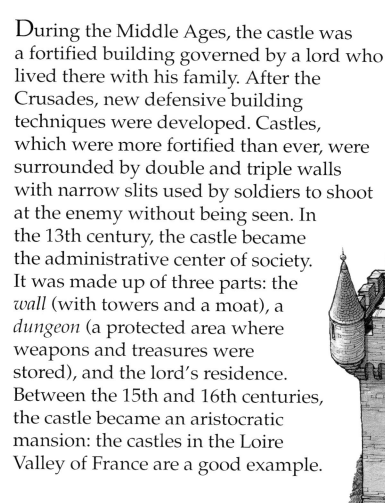

Fairy Tales – Castles are the setting for many fairy tales: *Sleeping Beauty, Snow White and the Seven Dwarfs, Cinderella, Puss in Boots, Bluebeard,* and *The Princess and the Pea*.

Jousting tournaments were often held in castles to entertain guests.

DWELLINGS, FAIRY
TALES AND FABLES,
KNIGHTS,
MIDDLE AGES

CATHERINE THE GREAT

Catherine, whose real name was Sophia Augusta Frederica, was the daughter of a German prince. She married Grand Duke Peter, the heir to the Russian throne, in 1745. Sophia was an intelligent and cultured woman. She learned Russian, converted to the Russian Orthodox religion, and was re-baptized Catherine. Six months after her husband became czar under the name of Peter III, she took over the throne with the help of the Imperial Guards. Catherine continued the expansionist politics of Peter the Great. She declared war on Poland and conquered White Russia, Volhynia, Podolia, Lithuania, and Courland. In the first Russo-Turkish war of 1768–1774, Russia acquired territory in the Crimea. After the second war (1787–1792), the border of Russia was extended all the way to the Dnestr River delta.

1729: Born in Stettin.
1745: Marries Peter III.
1762: Becomes empress.
1773–1775: Peasant uprising.
1774: Russia gains territory in the Crimea.
1792: Catherine's dominion extends to the Dnestr River.
1796: Dies in Saint Petersburg.

Catherine promoted many reforms and founded schools so that girls could also receive an education. Only members of the nobility, however, had access.

WOMEN OF HISTORY

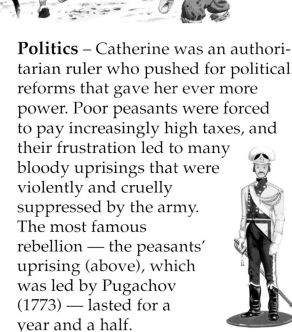

Under Catherine's reign, the Russian borders stretched from Poland to the Pacific and to China in the south.

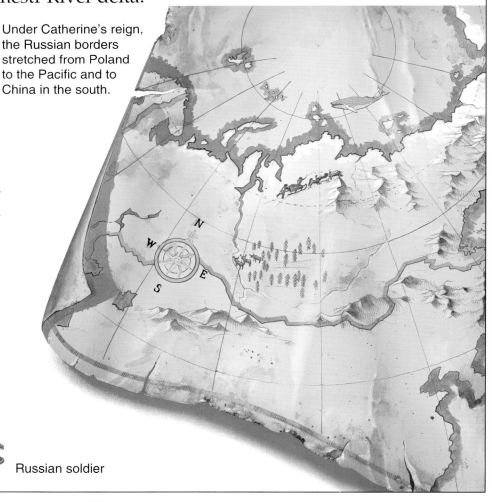

Politics – Catherine was an authoritarian ruler who pushed for political reforms that gave her ever more power. Poor peasants were forced to pay increasingly high taxes, and their frustration led to many bloody uprisings that were violently and cruelly suppressed by the army. The most famous rebellion — the peasants' uprising (above), which was led by Pugachov (1773) — lasted for a year and a half.

Russian soldier

CATS

Like the lion and the tiger, the domestic cat belongs to the feline family. Very quick and agile, cats have preserved their hunting instinct, even though they are now pets. In fact, all five senses of the cat are very well-developed, and cats use more than 16 different sounds to communicate. The cat probably descends from the wild African cat which appeared about one million years ago and was tamed by the Egyptians around 2000 B.C. to rid storehouses of mice. Many breeds have evolved since then. Today, there are nearly five hundred million cats around the world.

Cornish rex

Siamese

bicolor Persian

British tabby shorthair

blue Persian

The cat has retractable claws that are usually tucked away, but when a cat attacks, its claws spring out from its strong paws.

Domestic cat
The cat is a very independent animal but can also be very affectionate. It purrs when it is happy and uses its rough tongue to keep its fur smooth, shiny and clean.

tortoiseshell

sphinx

Breeds – There are more than 100 official breeds of cats. Some are purebreds, while others are mixed-breeds, obtained through cross-breeding.

The cat's eyes in the dark and in the light.

Magical eyes – Depending on the breed, a cat's eyes can be slanted, round, or almond-shaped. The pupils become narrow slits when there is a great deal of light, and they dilate (grow larger) in the dark. This is why cats can see very well at night.

The ancient Egyptians considered cats to be sacred animals. When they died, cats were mummified and preserved in cat-shaped sarcophaguses (below).

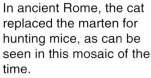

In ancient Rome, the cat replaced the marten for hunting mice, as can be seen in this mosaic of the time.

In fairy tales – Cats are frequently the heroes of fairy tales and cartoons: the clever *Puss in Boots*, the adorable *Aristocats*, *Sylvester* the cat, and *Tom* from *Tom and Jerry*.

This ancient Egyptian illustration (left) shows a cat wearing a leash. Even Leonardo da Vinci was impressed by the agility of cats (above right). A cat drawn by Picasso (right).

Kittens – A cat has from 2 to 5 kittens after a gestation period of 9 weeks. Kittens are born with their eyes and ears closed, so they use their sense of smell to locate their mother and find her teat. Kittens are weaned after about two months when they start eating solid food.

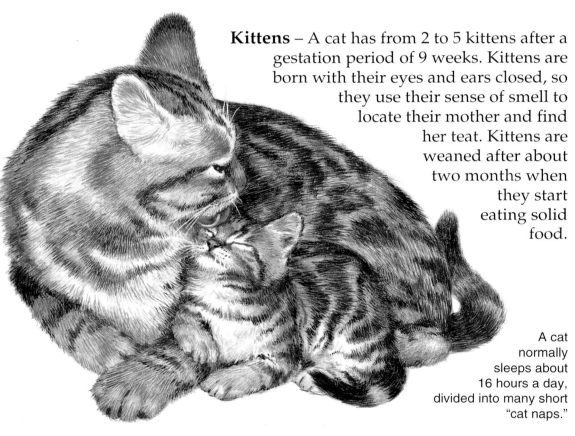

A cat normally sleeps about 16 hours a day, divided into many short "cat naps."

When a cat falls, it regains its balance by using its tail as a rudder. It rotates its head and body so it lands on all four feet.

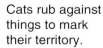

Cats rub against things to mark their territory.

Burmese

Playtime – Kittens love to play and wrestle with each other. They will chase after anything that moves or rolls: string, balls of yarn, plastic balls, etc. These games are very useful because they learn to hunt and protect themselves. They also develop the strength, intelligence, courage, and agility they will need as adults.

MAMMALS
PETS
WILDCATS

CAVES

A cave is a natural hollow formed by water rushing through rocks. The Flint Ridge and Mammoth cave systems in Kentucky are the world's longest set of connecting caves — 329 mi (530 km) long. The deepest cave in the world is the Jean Bernard Abyss in France — 5,036 ft (1,535 m) deep.

Bat – This able predator uses its claws to catch frogs and mice twice its size.

Stalactites and stalagmites – Drops of water rich in calcium carbonate form cone-shaped deposits inside caves. *Stalactites* hang from the ceiling and *stalagmites* project upwards from the cave floor.

1. Pygmy bat
2. Long-eared bat
3. Blind beetle
4. Bathysciola beetle
5. Speomolopo
6. Blind rhadinid beetle
7. Subtroglofilo
8. Brown centipede
9. Cave shrimp
10. Millipede
11. Olm
12. Eyeless amphipod

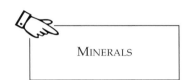

The olm, 12 in (30 cm) long, is a blind, cave-dwelling salamander. It has four legs and swims with its strong tail.

MINERALS

CEREALS

Flour and many other food products for humans and animals come from grains, which are rich in starch and protein. Wheat, rice, corn, barley, oat, rye, sorghum and millet are all grains. Bread made from wheat flour or other grains is an important food staple in the West, while rice is the most important food for many people in the Far East.

sliced bread

rye bread

whole-wheat bread

country-style bread

French breadstick

crusty bun

pita bread

soft bun

How bread is made – The baker takes flour and adds water, salt, and yeast, then kneeds or mixes everything together. The dough is covered and left to rest overnight in a warm place. In the morning, the baker cuts the dough up and shapes the pieces into buns, sticks, or loaves, which are put in the oven for about a half hour until the crust turns golden brown.

NUTRITION
PLANTS (USEFUL)

Millers used to grind the wheat in mills.

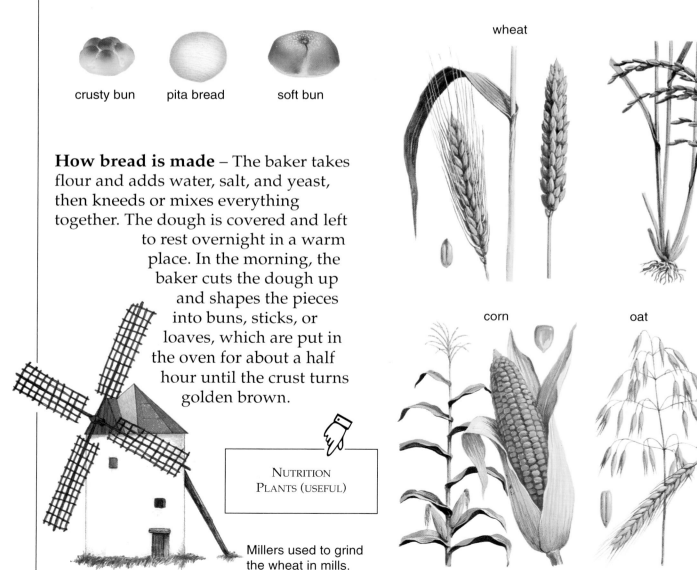

wheat

rice

corn

oat

barley

CHARLEMAGNE

Charlemagne (742–814) was also known as Charles the Great due to his courageous deeds. The son of Pepin the Short, king of the Franks, Charlemagne was a remarkable military leader. He defeated the Avars, Danes, Slavs, Saxons, and Bavarians before being crowned Holy Roman Emperor by the pope on Christmas night in 800 A.D. Political unity was thus re-established in the West and sanctioned by the Roman Catholic Church.

Charlemagne in a medieval tapestry.

Below: *Charlemagne and the Frankish army in Paris*, a fresco by J. Schnorr von Carolsfeld (1826).

Charlemagne wanted a plain throne (above) like that of legendary King Solomon which was described in the Bible.

The Holy Roman Empire – The empire stretched from the Pyrenees to the Danube River and from the North Sea to central Italy. Charlemagne divided the land into *counties* and *marquisates*, which were ruled by *counts* and *marquis* who pledged their allegiance. *Missi Domenici* were officials who maintained contacts between the regions of the empire. Even though he could hardly read or write, Charlemagne loved knowledge, so schools for young people were founded throughout the empire. The *Palatine School* at the Aquitaine court was the most famous.

Pope Leon III crowned Charlemagne in Rome on Christmas night in the year 800.

MIDDLE AGES ☞

CHARLES V

Charles V (1500–1558) reigned over a huge territory that stretched from Europe to America. He fought for years with Francis I of France for dominance of Europe. He was crowned emperor of the Holy Roman Empire by Pope Clement VII in 1530. Despite the many wars fought during his reign, Charles could not stop the spread of Protestantism. He abdicated in 1556, dividing his possessions between his brother, Ferdinand, and his son, Phillip II.

"The sun never sets on my kingdom!" Charles V used to boast, and he was absolutely right: when the sun set in Europe, it rose in the Spanish colonies of America.

Territories and conquests – Charles V inherited a huge empire from his mother, Joan the Mad of Spain, and his father, Phillip of Hapsburg. Under the reign of Charles V the Holy Roman Empire returned to its ancient splendor and grandeur.

EXPLORERS, GOTHIC CATHEDRALS ✓

Charles V's armies conquered vast territories in South America and brought valuable treasures back home.

CHILDREN'S LITERATURE

Robert Louis
Stevenson

Walter Scott

Louisa May
Alcott

Many books that are now considered children's classics were originally written for adults. This is true of *Treasure Island*, by Robert Louis Stevenson, and *Gulliver's Travels*, by Jonathan Swift. *Ivanhoe*, a historical novel by Walter Scott, describes England in the days of Richard the Lion-Hearted. Louisa May Alcott wrote *Little Women*, very popular among young readers.

The *novel* is a form of literature that describes real or imaginary situations: the *plot* is based on a series of adventures experienced by various *characters*.

Adventure books – The American author Jack London (1876–1916) wrote adventure books for adult readers that are still very popular with children today. His books describe the relationship between people and untamed nature. His novels speak of courage, friendship, and loyalty. London's most important books include *White Fang* and *The Call of the Wild*, and short stories such as *Burning Daylight*, *Martin Eden*, and *The Sea Wolf*.

The map shows where the gold rush took place: this is the setting for London's book *The Call of the Wild*.

CHINESE

The Chinese civilization started developing around 2000 B.C. in the Yellow River valley. Shi-Huangdi united China for the first time under the Ch'in Dynasty in 221 B.C. Construction on the *Great Wall of China* began during this period to defend the Northern borders. After a long siege in 1215, Genghis Khan conquered Beijing. The Ch'ing Dynasty, the last dynasty in China, fell in 1911 and the country was proclaimed a republic. A civil war and hostilities with Japan broke out and ended in 1949 with the victory of the Communists under Chairman Mao Tse-Tung.

Above: Chinese potters. Blue and white porcelain vases from the Ming Dynasty (14th century) are particularly valuable.

Marco Polo – (1254–1324) When this Venetian merchant and explorer was 17 years old, he accompanied his father Niccolò and his uncle Matteo on an overland journey from Venice to Beijing. They were sent to deliver a message from Pope Gregory X to the Kublai Khan, the Chinese emperor (below). Marco Polo narrated his adventures in a book entitled *Il Milione*.

Chinese farmers working in the fields.

The Chinese philosopher Confucius lived in the 5th century B.C. His doctrine was based on ethics, harmony, and moderation.

Inventions
The Chinese invented the compass. They were the first to make paper from tree bark and they also devised a printing system. The Chinese also invented gunpowder, which they used for fireworks.

GREAT WALL OF CHINA ✓, GUTENBERG, JAPANESE, KHAN, WEAPONS

CHOCOLATE

Theobroma cacao, the cocoa plant, originally comes from tropical America. The Aztecs, who lived in Mexico more than 500 years ago, were the first to use the beans of this plant to prepare hot chocolate. When Cortez conquered Mexico in 1521, he sent a shipload of cocoa beans to Europe. Hot chocolate became extremely popular in the 18th century. At the beginning of the 19th century, the Swiss Cailler produced the first chocolate bars and the Dutch Van Houten invented a process to make cocoa powder.

The Aztecs served hot chocolate in a solid gold chalice to their emperor Montezuma (above).

The first cafés, public places where people could drink chocolate and coffee, were opened in Europe in the 18th century.

The cocoa plant – Each fruit (left) contains about 40 beans. The characteristic chocolate aroma is released from the beans when they are left to ferment for one week in crates covered with banana leaves.

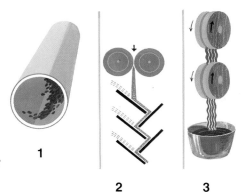

Production process
After the cocoa beans have fermented and dried in the sun, they are cleaned and toasted (1). Then the bean is separated from the shell (2), ground (3), and a paste is prepared.

1

2   3

Cocoa paste is made from crushed beans and is blended for hours with sugar and milk. The mixture is then poured into chocolate molds.

In the 18th century hot chocolate was a very fashionable drink at the French court, in Italy, and with German and Dutch royalty.

PLANTS (USEFUL),
PRE-COLUMBIAN
CIVILIZATIONS,
RECIPES

CHRISTIANITY

The Bible comprises the *Old Testament* and the *New Testament*. The New Testament, specific to Christianity, comprises the four *Gospels* that narrate the life of Jesus Christ, who was born in Bethlehem in Palestine and died on the cross. Through his sacrifice, humanity is said to be delivered from sin. After his death, his twelve apostles, led by *Peter*, preached the new religion that over the centuries has spread throughout the world.

Early Christians

Many Roman emperors such as Nero and Diocletian ruthlessly persecuted the Christians, who were forced to hide underground in the *catacombs* to celebrate their religious rites. Freedom of religion was only granted in 313 through the *Constantine Edict*.

Christians in the catacombs

The lamb (above) is an old Christian symbol: it represents the innocent victim that was sacrificed.

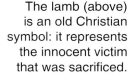

BUDDHISM,
GOTHIC CATHEDRAL ✓,
HINDUISM, ISLAM,
JUDAISM, MONASTERIES,
ROMANESQUE CHURCH ✓,
ROMANS

Gospel – This word means *good news*. The four Gospels were written in the 1st century A.D. by the evangelists *Matthew (1)*, *Mark (2)*, *Luke (3)* and *John (4)*. According to tradition, Jesus was born on December 25, Christmas day. The Gregorian calendar starts the year Jesus was born.

At Christmas *a crèche* is prepared to celebrate Jesus' birth: the first one was made by Saint Francis of Assisi in 1223. The tradition of decorating pine trees (right) dates back more than one thousand years and supposedly originated in Germany.

CHRISTOPHER COLUMBUS

Christopher Columbus (1451–1506) received permission from Isabel of Castille, the queen of Spain, to form a fleet of three caravels to search for a western passage to the Indies. He left the port of Palos in August 3, 1492, and landed on an island in the Bahamas, which he named San Salvador. He proceeded on his journey and sailed to Cuba and Haiti. Columbus was convinced he had reached the Indies: he made three other voyages before he died and never realized that he had discovered a whole new continent.

Columbus sailed from the port of Palos with three caravels: the *Niña*, the *Pinta*, and the *Santa Maria*.

Christopher Columbus was supposedly born in Genoa, Italy, in 1451.

America – The new continent was called America in honor of Amerigo Vespucci, the Italian explorer who sailed in 1501 on a new voyage to South America.

New products such as cocoa, potatoes, corn, tobacco, tomatoes and pineapples were brought to Europe from the Americas. Explorers imported animals such as parrots that Europeans had never seen before.

BOLIVAR, EXPLORERS,
NATIVE AMERICANS,
PRE-COLUMBIAN
CIVILIZATIONS

CHURCHILL, SIR WINSTON

Sir Winston Churchill was Britain's greatest modern statesman. For more than thirty years he served his country as a member of Parliament, a Minister, Chancellor of the Exchequer, and first lord of the admiralty. Churchill became Prime Minister of a coalition government in 1940. During World War II he became a symbol of Britain's will to resist the German onslaught, and he never doubted England would win the war.

Winston Churchill (1874–1965) making the famous "V", the sign for *victory*.

Nobel Prize – Churchill was the author of several historical works, including a collection of essays entitled *World War II* for which he won the Nobel Prize for Literature in 1953.

Cold War – After the war, Churchill became the leader of the opposition in Parliament. During a speech in a city named Fulton in the United States, he presented his theories on the need to stop Soviet expansion. This contributed to the beginning of the *Cold War*, a long period of great tension and hostility between the Soviet Union and America. Churchill became Prime Minister again from 1951 to 1955.

Left: a scene from the Battle of England (1940), where the RAF (Royal Air Force) fought the German Luftwaffe.

WEAPONS
WORLD WARS

CINEMA

The first motion pictures date back to the end of the 19th century when brothers Louis and Auguste Lumière presented their first film on December 28, 1895 in Paris. They invented a machine called the *cinématographe* that was used for filming and projecting moving pictures.

French brothers Louis and Auguste Lumière are considered the pioneers of motion pictures.

1. *The Magic lamp* (ca. 1600)
2. Thomas Edison's *Kinetoscope* (1889)
3. Horner's *Daedaleum* (mid-19th century)

These machines were invented to project moving pictures.

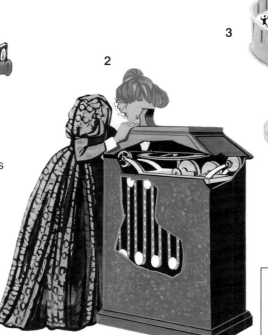

Sound and color – In the beginning, movies (called *silent pictures*) were in black and white and had no sound. A pianist in the theater played background music that accompanied the action on the screen. The first movie with sound, *The Jazz Singer*, was made in 1927 and starred Al Jolson, a famous actor of Broadway musicals. The first deluxe color film was *The Enchanted Forest*, a Walt Disney animated cartoon made in 1932.

☞ COMPUTERS, INFORMATION SCIENCE, PHOTOGRAPHY, SCIENTISTS AND INVENTORS, WALT DISNEY

Movie camera with hand crank.

Special effects – Today computers are used in films to create special effects. For example, by superimposing an imaginary scene over a real image, you can show dinosaurs interacting with real actors. You can also create three-dimensional images with the computer.

COMPUTERS

The computer is like an electronic brain. It processes data, which is the information supplied, by following a series of specific instructions — a *program*. The computer has a memory made up of microchips that let it store data. Computers are used for many purposes, including scientific research, industrial technology, space travel, and telecommunications.

screen

hard drive

keyboard

mouse

Input devices

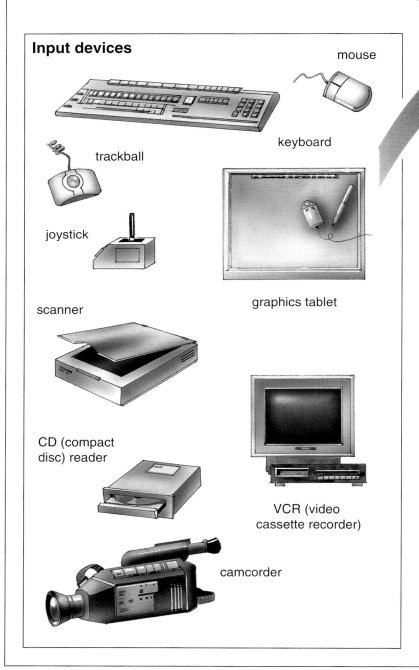

mouse

keyboard

trackball

joystick

graphics tablet

scanner

CD (compact disc) reader

VCR (video cassette recorder)

camcorder

Data storage devices

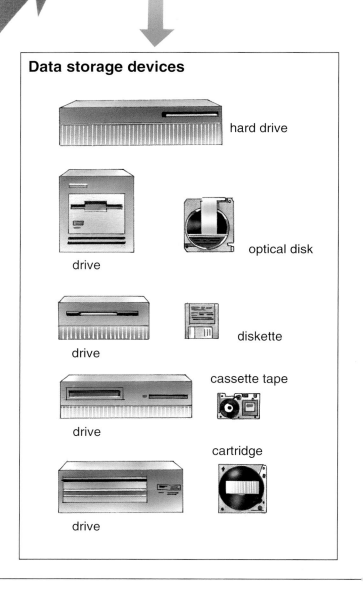

hard drive

drive

optical disk

drive

diskette

drive

cassette tape

cartridge

drive

Communication devices

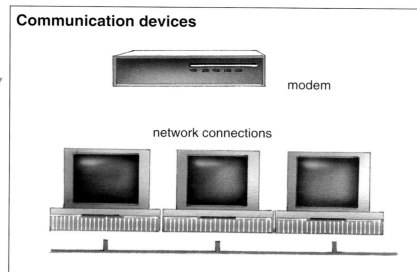

modem

network connections

Internet – This communications network links millions of computers worldwide. On the Internet, interactive communication takes place in real time. If you want to go on-line or access the Internet, you need a personal computer, modem, telephone line, and communications software.

Output devices

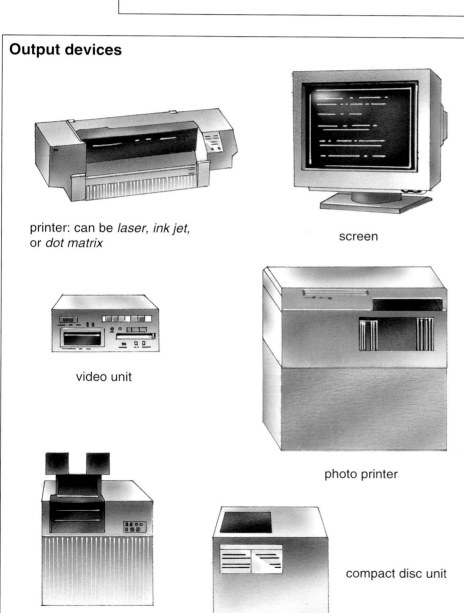

printer: can be *laser*, *ink jet*, or *dot matrix*

screen

video unit

photo printer

microfilm recorder

compact disc unit

Hardware and software
Hardware refers to the parts inside the computer. *Software* is the name given to programs the computer uses to perform different tasks. There is software for *videogames*, *calculations*, *word processing*, and *computer graphics*.

The history of the computer
Blaise Pascal built a mechanical calculating machine in 1642. Charles Babbage from England designed the first mechanical computer in 1834 that could be programmed with perforated cards. This invention, however, was too complicated to be built at the time. The first entirely electronic computer, the ENIAC — Electronic Numerical Integrator and Computer — was built in 1946 by American engineers J. Presper Eckert Jr. and John Mauchly.

BOOKS,
INFORMATION SCIENCE,
NEW WORDS,
SCIENTISTS AND
INVENTORS

CROCODILES

During the era of the dinosaurs one hundred million years ago, the crocodile's ancestors lived in swamps. These reptiles, which can reach 23 ft (7 m) in length and live for more than 100 years, belong to three families: the *alligator*, whose teeth are all hidden when it closes its mouth; the *crocodile*, whose fourth tooth is visible when the mouth is closed; and the *gavial*, characterized by a long narrow snout. Crocodiles are very agile in the water, but when they are out of the water they drag themselves along the ground with their short stumpy legs. These cold-blooded animals bask in the sun to store heat.

Crocodiles can swallow huge prey without chewing.

Gavial of the Ganges
This reptile has a long, narrow snout and sharp teeth. Its upper jaw has 54 teeth, and the lower jaw has 48.

There are two species of alligators: one from Mississippi and the other from China, which is in danger of extinction.

Eggs
The female crocodile lays her eggs and covers them with soil. She guards them from predators until they hatch, after about three months. Baby crocodiles make croaking sounds like frogs.

Crocodile – The crocodile has 19 teeth on its upper jaw. It stays in the water at night and lives on land during the day. It has a body temperature of around 77°F (25°C). The most famous types of crocodiles are the *Orinoco crocodile* and the *Nile crocodile*.

Peewit – This small bird sits on the crocodile's back and pecks away at the parasites. It even enters the crocodile's mouth to get at food particles between its teeth.

AFRICAN FOREST,
ASIAN JUNGLE,
DINOSAURS,
MARSHLAND, REPTILES

DANCE

In Crete (ca. 1000 B.C.), young Mycean dancers performed dangerous yet spectacular rituals with bulls called *taurocatapsie*.

Since the dawn of humanity, the art of dance has expressed human emotions and feelings. It has been a form of prayer, a ritual, and a form of entertainment. *Ethnic* and *folk dances* reflect the traditions and cultures of people from all over the world. But sometimes, we dance just for the fun of it!

Ballet – Even though its origins date back to the 9th century, ballet did not become a chore-ographed form of entertainment until the 14th century. In the 16th century, the *ballet de coeur* (with dances and songs) was performed at the French court, and the *comédie ballet* and *opéra ballet* were developed in the 17th century. The Royal Dance Academy was opened in 1661. A new style, the *Romantic ballet*, was introduced with *La Sylphide*, a ballet created by Filippo Taglioni for his daughter Maria in 1832. *Modern ballet* was developed thereafter and introduced by the Ballets Russes in 1911. Since then, a great many styles have come together in what is collectively known as *modern dance*; the dancer and choreographer Martha Graham has been one of its greatest influences.

Dancers with a tambourine (1) and castanets (2).

MUSIC AND MUSICIANS

Swan Lake (below) is one of Tchaikovsky's most famous ballets.

Ballet shoes with reinforced toes.

Classical ballet movements always start with one of the five basic positions.

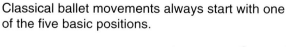

DINOSAURS

Dinosaurs, a kind of reptile whose name means *terrible lizard*, first appeared 225 million years ago. They quickly multiplied and dominated the Earth for a very long time. Thanks to fossil finds, we can piece together the skeleton, but we cannot determine the color because the skin has not been preserved. Dinosaurs were probably colorful animals like our lizards and reptiles. The coral snake, for example, has white, red, and black stripes, and the chameleon turns many different colors. Dinosaurs became extinct 65 million years ago.

The diplodocus was one of the largest animals on land: it reached almost 100 ft (30 m) in length.

It is impossible to know exactly what color dinosaurs were.

The Komodo dragon is a prehistoric species that still exists today. It is 10 ft (3 m) long and lives in Oceania.

1. Diplodocus
2. Stegosaurus
3. Pteranodon
4. Brachiosaurus
5. Ankylosaurus
6. Tyrannosaurus rex

pteranodon

Eggs – The shell was hard yet porous so air could penetrate it. Since the shell was made of a bonelike substance that the baby absorbed as it developed, it became thinner as the baby dinosaur grew, then finally broke.

Eras – Four geologic eras of the Earth — *Cenozoic, Mesozoic, Paleozoic,* and *Precambrian* — are in turn divided into periods that include different epochs. Large dinosaurs appeared on Earth during the *Jurassic Period,* in the Mesozoic Era.

In museums
Paleontology is the study of fossils, of their origin and evolution. Paleontologists compare prehistoric skeletons with the skeletons of other dinosaurs that have already been identified. Afterwards, the bones are placed upon a metal structure that holds them together. If a bone is missing, it is replaced with a plaster or plastic copy.

Tyrannosaurus rex means *king lizard.* It lived 70 million years ago.

Tyrannosaurus rex
The Tyrannosaurus rex was the largest carnivorous dinosaur, measuring about 50 ft (15 m) long. It stood upright and had powerful rear legs, while its forelimbs were small and only had two fingers.

Still among us

It is believed that birds are descendants of the dinosaurs. Birds' feet, like those of the dinosaurs, are covered in scales. Notice how the profile of a chicken resembles that of a dinosaur. In fact, featherless chicks just out of their shell look like strange lizards!

Pteranodon

This flying reptile had wings like a bat, with flaps of skin that attached them to the side of its body. It soared over the sea to catch fish.

Immersed in water

The brachiosaurus, like other dinosaurs, became so huge and heavy as it evolved that it could hardly move. Some scientists believe that it started to live in water so it wouldn't have to support its own weight — almost 50 tons! Its neck was long like a giraffe's.

The brachiosaurus weighed as much as ten elephants!

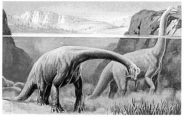

The stegosaurus, with pointy plates, was up to 30 ft (9 m) long.

The dimetrodon, a crested reptile, lived during the Carboniferous period near the end of the Paleozoic era.

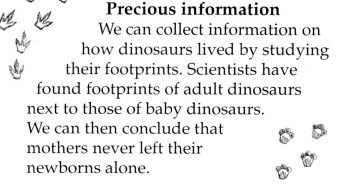

Precious information

We can collect information on how dinosaurs lived by studying their footprints. Scientists have found footprints of adult dinosaurs next to those of baby dinosaurs. We can then conclude that mothers never left their newborns alone.

Above: a battle between a duck-billed dinosaur or trachodont and a Tyrannosaurus rex.

Morganucodontid, a small rodent that lived about 150 million years ago.

BIRDS, CROCODILES, EVOLUTION, FOSSILS, REPTILES, STEPPE

Why did dinosaurs disappear? – There are many theories, but none has yet been proven. Perhaps early mammals ate their eggs. Dinosaurs may have became too large and slow and gradually died of starvation. There might have been a rapid change in the Earth's temperature or a meteor shower that created a cloud of dust and shut out the sun. Earthquakes and volcanic eruptions may also have had this effect.

The evolution of the horse: 1. Eohippus **2.** Orohippus **3.** Mesohippus
4. Parahippus **5.** Pliohippus, most similar to today's horse
6. Przewalski's horse, the only prehistoric horse still existing today.

Dogs

The dog is a descendant of the common wolf and was the first animal to be tamed by humans more than 10,000 years ago. It has very keen senses of hearing and smell. Dogs live between 8 and 15 years (1 year in a dog's life corresponds to about 7 years in a human's life). Smaller dogs usually live longer than large ones. Some dogs guard and protect their owner's property and most can be trained to obey. A dog loves praise and is often so loyal he will sacrifice his life for his owner.

German shepherd
The German shepherd has a well-developed sense of smell and is very intelligent. It has thick brown and black fur. Used in the past as a shepherd's dog, today the German shepherd is used for defense, as a guide dog for the blind, in Alpine rescue missions, and as a police dog.

German shepherd

A dog must always have a bowl of fresh water within reach, especially when it is hot out.

The Siberian husky, which is related to the wolf, is the best companion to have in Arctic regions and is used to pull a sled.

Siberian husky

Watch dogs – All dogs can be trained to obey, but training requires time, patience, and a knowledge of canine psychology. Not all large breeds are good watch dogs, and only a few have the instinct to protect like the *German shepherd*, *Doberman pinscher*, *boxer*, *schnauzer*, and *rottweiler*.

A dog that lives outdoors needs a waterproof dog house as shelter.

Doberman pinscher

Breeds – A breed is created when certain traits are transmitted from one generation to the next. Pure bred dogs have a *pedigree* (a family tree) that proves their origins. Dogs born from two different breeds of dogs are called *mongrels* or *mutts*.

Saint Bernard – These dogs are used to rescue people lost in the snow during an avalanche.

Bulldog
This dog with a flat face, short legs, and short hair was originally raised in England to fight bulls.

Great Dane – The male reaches a height of about 32 in (80 cm) and can weigh 132 lb (60 kg). It is a fine guard dog but not too aggressive.

Record – The largest breeds are the *Old English mastiff* and the *Saint Bernard*. The smallest are the *Chihuahua* and the *Yorkshire terrier*.

Great Dane

dachshund

Yorkshire terrier

Small dogs
Although it is a small dog, the *Yorkshire terrier* is aggressive. The *dachshund* is courageous and good at hunting.

chihuahua   Saint Bernard

At home – *Basset hounds, poodles, Pekinese, Chihuahuas, cocker spaniels,* and *Yorkshire terriers* are affectionate breeds. Several dogs which are favorite pets today were once used for other purposes: the poodle was used as a pointer and the cocker spaniel used to hunt woodcocks, a kind of bird.

bobtail

Hunting dogs – These dogs have a keen sense of smell and love to hunt. Breeds such as the *pointer*, the *English setter*, the *Irish setter*, and the *Gordon setter* stand motionless, pointing out the prey, until the hunter arrives. The *German spaniel* and *golden retriever* take the prey back to their master. *Foxhounds* are used during fox hunts on horseback.

greyhound

Greyhound – This slender canine with an arched back is the fastest dog in the world. It can run about 40 mph (65 km/h) and is used as a hunting dog because it also has excellent eyesight.

Mammals
Pets

Irish setter

93

DWELLINGS

Thanks to the discovery of caves with graffiti and rock paintings, we now know that prehistoric men and women lived in caves to protect themselves from fierce animals and the cold. Each civilization has created its own architectural style according to particular lifestyles and climate. Therefore, Nordic homes usually have a sharply pitched roof to prevent snow from accumulating. Homes in warm countries, however, often have no inclined roof at all, but a terrace where rain water is collected and stored.

Prehistoric dwellings
Caves were the first places where prehistoric men and women lived. Pile dwellings (right) were built in swampy zones to protect their inhabitants from the water.

A tent village built by nomads in the Sahara Desert of Africa.

Dome-shaped huts in eastern Africa.

Medieval castle – The castle, originally a fortified village, became the residence of the feudal lord and the hub of political and economic life. The fortified castle was built in strategic places and was protected by walls and moats. In times of war, people from the surrounding countryside sought refuge in castles.

Igloo – Built by the Inuit for temporary shelter from the Arctic cold, an igloo is made of a whale bone frame covered with blocks of ice that form a dome. People enter through a low, narrow entrance.

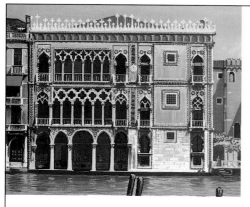

Ca d'Oro – This Venetian Gothic building with Moorish influences (left) was built in Venice on the Grand Canal from 1421–1440 by architects M. Raverti and G. Bon.

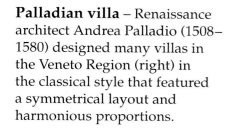

Pagodas – Japanese cities look very modern, but many homes have preserved elements of the ancient style such as the pagoda roof with blue tiles and sliding walls covered with rice paper.

Palladian villa – Renaissance architect Andrea Palladio (1508–1580) designed many villas in the Veneto Region (right) in the classical style that featured a symmetrical layout and harmonious proportions.

Eighteenth-century English architecture (left) was inspired by the classical style using columns and a triangular-shaped pediment.

Homes in the Middle East are painted white to reflect sunlight and to keep the temperature cooler inside.

AFRICA, CASTLES,
HUMAN ANCESTORS,
INUIT VILLAGE ✓,
JAPANESE,
VIKING VILLAGE ✓

American architect Frank Lloyd Wright (1869–1959) designed the famous *Falling Water* home for the Kauffman family at Bear Run, Pennsylvania.

Northern European homes – In the 16th century the facades of Northern European homes had brick and stone decorations, built-in windows, and sloped or step-like roofs. Row houses (right) sat on busy roads and housed offices and shops.

EARTH

How was the Earth born? No one is sure, but scientists speculate that billions of years ago an incandescent cloud of gas and dust gave rise to particles that condensed and solidified. These particles grew bigger and bigger as they rotated in the surrounding matter. The central nucleus of this cloud became the Sun and the smaller nuclei formed the planets of our solar system.

Movements of the Earth – The Earth's crust is formed by tectonic plates in constant, though barely noticable, movement. The present appearance of the Earth is the result of millions and millions of years of activity. Our planet will continue to change. The illustrations below show the movements of the plates over time. Notice how the continents have shifted.

Originally, the Earth's surface was a sea of lava.

How it formed – About 4.5 billion years ago the incandescent mass called *magma* started to solidify. About 3,500 million years ago the Earth started to cool gradually and shrank in size. The solidified layer crinkled, thus forming mountains.

The layers of the Earth
If we could cut into the Earth (see figure to the left), we would see three layers: a hard, cold outer layer called the *crust*, a middle layer (the *mantle*) made of liquid incandescent material and a solid, boiling *core* made of iron sulfide and iron.

Submerged land and seas – When the Earth's crust was cooling and mountains were forming, rocks released great amounts of steam that accumulated in the sky and formed huge clouds. At a certain point torrential rains began to fall, a process that lasted thousands of years. Water filled all the depressions on the Earth's crust and formed rivers, ponds and oceans. The layer of clouds became thinner and the Sun started to shine and warm the Earth.

The Suez Canal (Egypt)

Lake Niriz (Iran)

During space walks, astronauts wear special suits that re-create the Earth's atmosphere.

Observing Earth from space
The first photographs taken from space ships showed the Earth as a ball floating in space, with two-thirds of the surface covered by water and one-third by land.

Atmosphere – The Earth is covered with a gaseous layer called the atmosphere, which is rich in oxygen. If humans want to travel into space, where there is no atmosphere, they must wear special suits that provide oxygen and also compensate for the different *atmospheric pressure* (the weight of the air above us).

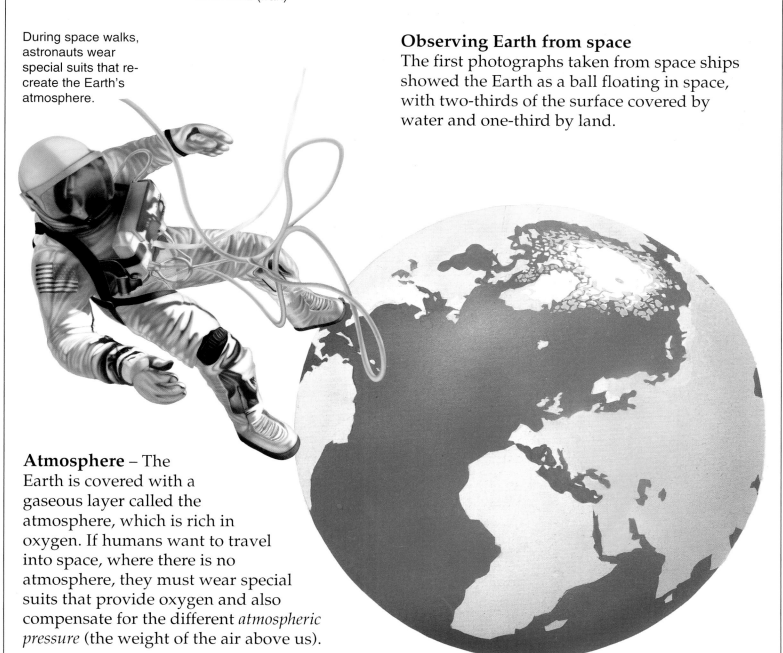

Photographing the Earth – Today artificial satellites take detailed pictures of the surface of the Earth, its atmosphere and other planets, and send the data back to Earth. The information gathered increases our knowledge and helps predict the weather, earthquakes, tides and other phenomena.

The Soviet Union launched *Sputnik I*, the world's first artificial satellite, on October 4, 1957. It remained in orbit until January 4, 1958. Since then, satellites have become more and more sophisticated.

ASTRONOMY, MAPS, MINERALS, MOON, MOUNTAINS, SEA, SEASONS, SOLAR SYSTEM, SPACE TRAVEL, SUN, TIME ZONES, VOLCANOES

The only man-made monument that can be seen from space is the Great Wall of China.

The illustration (right) shows what farmland looks like from an airplane.

ECOLOGY

The term *ecology* was introduced in 1868 by a German scholar named Haeckel. Today this science is very important due to worsening environmental problems such as pollution and the excessive exploitation of natural resources.

Acid rain – Rain that becomes acidic due to pollution in the atmosphere. Acid rain has caused the death of forests and lakes around the world.

Biodegradable – A substance that can be broken down and dissolved by living organisms (such as bacteria or fungi). Many chemical products such as plastic are not biodegradable and therefore pollute the environment.

Biosphere – The parts of the Earth where living beings are found; it includes the *atmosphere*, *lithosphere*, and *hydrosphere*.

CFCs (Chlorofluorocarbons) – Artificial substances that destroy the ozone layer and contribute to the greenhouse effect. CFCs are found in some spray cans and are used in refrigerators and air conditioners.

Chernobyl – In this town in the Ukraine, the explosion of a nuclear reactor at a power plant in 1986 released radioactive substances into the atmosphere, causing severe environmental contamination.

Demographic growth – An increase of the world population, which is now more than 5 billion people. Since the Earth has limited resources, many scientists propose reducing the birth rate to achieve zero growth.

Ecology – A branch of biology that studies the relationships between living organisms and the environment.

Energy – The means to do work. There are many types of energy: some, like oil, are polluting, while others such as solar energy or wind energy are natural and do not harm the environment.

Environment – The physical and biological system in which plant and animal life develops.

Environmental degradation – Worsening environmental conditions on Earth.

Environmentalist – A person who studies and actively works to protect the environment.

Eutrophication – Imbalance caused by an excessive amount of plant nutrients (such as nitrogen and phosphorus) in lakes and rivers. These nutrients cause an overgrowth of algae, which kills animal life by depriving it of oxygen. This problem is linked to the use of detergents and fertilizers.

Extinction – The disappearance of a form of life (plant or animal). An example of an extinct species are dinosaurs, which disappeared 65 million years ago.

Garbage sorting – Glass, paper, aluminum, batteries, and food scraps are divided and placed into separate containers so they can be recycled or disposed of in the most environmentally-friendly way available.

Greenhouse effect – A gradual increase of the Earth's temperature caused by environmental problems and imbalances.

Green Party – A group of environmental activists who care deeply about the environment and work to protect it through political means.

Greenpeace – An international environmental activist organization founded in 1970.

Nature – Animals and plants in their pristine state, untouched by humans or artificial substances.

Nuclear – Relating to atomic energy.

Organic agriculture – A natural farming method that does not use chemical fertilizers or pesticides.

Overconsumption – The excessive use of products that leads to the depletion of natural resources.

Ozone – A gas that acts as a protective layer in the upper atmosphere, shielding the Earth from the sun's ultraviolet rays. The destruction of the ozone layer is due to industrial pollution and the use of CFCs.

Pesticide – A chemical substance used to destroy parasites (insects and other pests) that harm crops.

Pollution – The contamination of the environment through emissions of chemical or synthetic substances.

Recycling – Turning garbage into reusable materials.

Vegetarian – A person who does not eat meat, poultry, or fish. Some vegetarians, eat products that come from animals such as milk, eggs, honey, and cheese. Others, called vegans, do not eat or use any animal products at all.

WWF – An acronym for *World Wildlife Fund*, an international environmental association founded in 1961.

Toucans live in the tropical forests of South and Central America. Like many other animals, they are threatened by the deterioration of their natural habitat.

Eutrophication – Many substances used by humans, such as detergents and chemical fertilizers, end up in our rivers, lakes, and oceans. These substances cause eutrophication, which is an excessive growth of algae and plants. As a result, the oxygen in the water decreases and many animal species die.

Gaia – According to ancient Greek mythology, Gaia was the goddess of the Earth, mother of all life. Today this word refers to a philosophy that sees the planet as a living creature that functions as a single organism. We must learn to respect the balance of nature and of natural resources and realize that these resources are limited. Below, a symbolic image representing Mother Nature.

Ecosystem – This refers to all the relationships that exist between living organisms and their environment. There is a special balance in nature whereby every living creature (both plants and animals) interacts with its environment. There is a constant exchange of energy and matter within each ecosystem. Therefore each component is an indispensable piece of the puzzle needed for the survival of the ecological community.

ENDANGERED SPECIES
ENERGY
TREES AND LEAVES

Water pollution harms marine life. Above, a seagull trying to eat a tar-covered fish.

EGYPTIANS

sarcophagus
with mummy

The earliest human settlements developed in the fertile valleys of the Nile River in the 4th millennium B.C. Egyptian society was organized in a hierarchy: the *pharaoh*, or Egyptian king, had absolute power and reigned over priests, government officials, warriors, craftsmen, peasants, and slaves. The Egyptians were very advanced in the fields of mathematics, geometry, astronomy, medicine, and surgery. Alexander the Great invaded Egypt in 332 B.C. and founded the city of Alexandria, which became the greatest cultural center of the Hellenistic Age.

Below: The gold mask of the pharaoh *Tutankhamen* (18th dynasty). His tomb was found intact in 1922 by archeologists H. Carter and G. Carnarvon.

The pharaoh was considered the son of the sun god. The gold scepter and whip, studded with precious gems (left), were symbols of his power.

Pyramids – These constructions were monumental tombs built for the pharaohs of Egypt (3rd–17th dynasty). The *burial chamber* housed the pharaoh's mummy. Each pyramid took decades to build and employed a large part of the population. The most famous pyramids are the Khufu, Khafre, and Menkaura pyramids at Giza.

Pharaohs – Thutmos III, Amenhotep II and III, and Ramses I and II (18th–20th dynasty) defended Egypt's borders from Hittite invaders. Akenaton IV tried to introduce monotheism (the cult of Aton). Nefertiti, his wife, was famous for her beauty. Her bust can be seen in the Egyptian Museum of Berlin. The last pharaoh was Nectanebo II.

Workers used wooden logs and strong ropes to drag blocks of stone weighing as much as 2 tons up to the top of the pyramids.

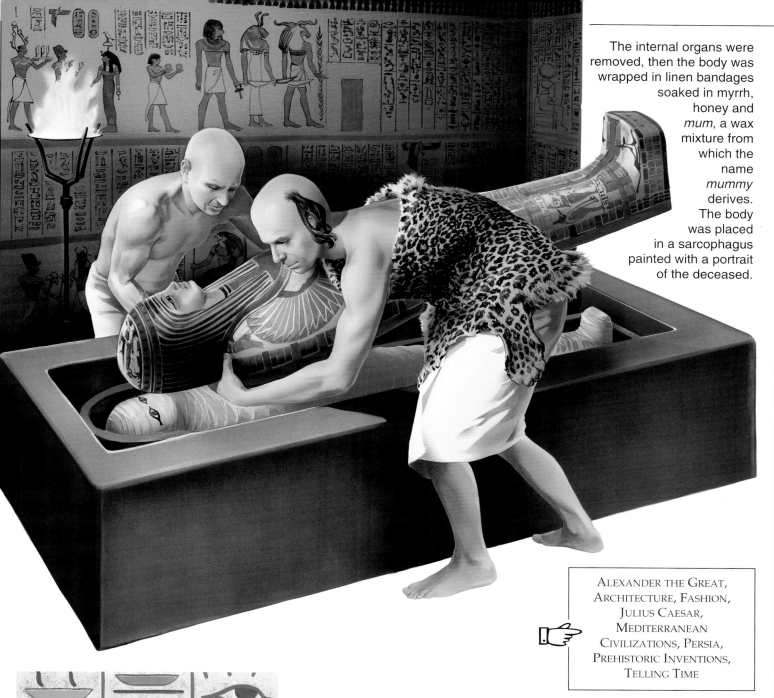

The internal organs were removed, then the body was wrapped in linen bandages soaked in myrrh, honey and *mum*, a wax mixture from which the name *mummy* derives. The body was placed in a sarcophagus painted with a portrait of the deceased.

ALEXANDER THE GREAT, ARCHITECTURE, FASHION, JULIUS CAESAR, MEDITERRANEAN CIVILIZATIONS, PERSIA, PREHISTORIC INVENTIONS, TELLING TIME

Gods and goddesses – *Anubis* was the god of mummification, *Osiris* was the god of the dead and *Isis* was his wife. *Horus* was the god of the living, and *Ra* was the sun god. *Hator* celebrated joy and love, and *Aton* was the creator of the universe.

Hieroglyphics – This type of writing is not considered a real alphabet because it is made up of *ideograms* (symbols that represent concepts). In 1822, J.F. Champollion became the first to understand this written language when he managed to decipher the hieroglyphics on the *Rosetta Stone*.

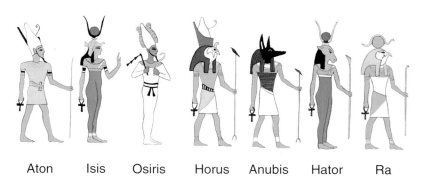

Aton   Isis   Osiris   Horus   Anubis   Hator   Ra

ELECTRICITY

Since ancient times, people have realized that certain objects attract when rubbed. Scientific investigation of electricity truly began in the 18th and 19th centuries.

The voltaic pile (left) was one of the first devices able to produce a regular current of electricity. It consisted of alternating disks of copper and zinc soaked in an acid. Batteries still work according to the principles of Volta, but different materials are used.

Alessandro Volta (1745–1827) gave his name to a unit of measurement *(volt)*.

One of the first electric lamps.

Lightning rod – During a thunderstorm in 1752, Benjamin Franklin flew a kite with a metal wire tied to a key near the ground. Sparks flew from the key, and Franklin was nearly electrocuted! But he had discovered how to build a lightning rod! In another experiment he placed metal wires on the roof of a building, down the walls to the ground. When the wires were hit by lightning, electricity was conducted to the ground.

Practical applications – In 1821 British chemist and physicist Michael Faraday proved that electricity could be used as a source of energy, and ten years later built the first electric generator. In 1860 Joseph Swan invented the first electric light bulb, but it stayed lit only for a very brief time. Twenty years later he and Thomas Edison produced the first practical light bulb. This invention created the need for great quantities of energy, so Edison built the first electric power plant in 1882.

ENERGY, HOUSEHOLD APPLIANCES, SCIENTISTS AND INVENTORS

Italian physicist Antonio Pacinotti (1841–1912) invented the first reversible electromagnetic machine — the dynamo.

ELEPHANTS

The elephant is the largest land mammal, with a lifespan of about 60 years. It uses its trunk for eating, breathing and for taking a shower! The elephant's two ivory tusks, which never stop growing, are actually incisors. Its molars wear down with time and help identify the animal's age.

African elephant (above) – The African elephant is larger than the Asian elephant and has bigger ears. Long valued by hunters for its ivory tusks, the African elephant is now protected by law, and most of them live in nature reserves.

Asian or Indian elephant (opposite) This elephant has small triangular ears. Unlike the African elephant, it can be easily trained and is used as a beast of burden.

Mammoth
This ancestor of the elephant became extinct at the end of the Pleistocene era. Smaller than the elephant, the mammoth had long hair, small ears and curved tusks about 10 ft (3 m) long.

Baby elephants
They are born after a gestation period of 22 months and weigh about 220 lb (100 kg) at birth. Baby elephants can already stand about 15 to 30 minutes after they are born. They are nourished by their mother's milk for the first four years.

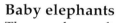
A mother elephant helps its young by pulling its trunk.

Left: An African elephant in its natural habitat.

Strange but true
Elephants make shrill trumpeting cries if they are frightened or disturbed, and wave their ears to demonstrate aggressive behavior. They usually sleep standing up.

ANIMALS OF AFRICA
MAMMALS

ELIZABETH I

Born in 1533, Elizabeth was only three years old when her mother, Anne Boleyn, was condemned to death and beheaded by her husband, Henry VIII, king of England. Elizabeth's sister, Mary I (known as Mary Tudor), was queen from 1553–1558; during this time she tried to restore the Catholic religion and imprisoned her Protestant sister Elizabeth in the Tower of London. Despite murder attempts, Elizabeth became queen of England at the death of her sister Mary in 1558 and wisely ruled over her country.

Left: *The Ermine Portrait* (1585) attributed to W. Segar.

1533: Elizabeth is born to Henry VIII and Anne Boleyn.
1536: Anne Boleyn is accused of treason.
1554: Elizabeth is imprisoned in the Tower of London.
1558: Elizabeth takes the throne.
1559: She reaffirms the power of the Anglican Church with the Act of Supremacy.
1587: Elizabeth condemns Mary Queen of Scots to death.
1588: Her navy battles the Spanish Armada.
1603: Elizabeth dies.

Besides music and literature, theater also flourished: the plays of William Shakespeare (1564–1616) were performed during the Elizabethan Age.

Mary Stuart – Mary Queen of Scots (1542–1587) abdicated the throne in favor of her son James in 1567. The Catholics, backed by the King Philip II of Spain, involved her in a conspiracy plot against Elizabeth I. Elizabeth found out and condemned Mary Queen of Scots to death.

Elizabeth I appointed Sir Francis Drake (above) to attack the Spanish colonies in America.

AUTHORS AND POETS
FASHION
PIRATES
WOMEN OF HISTORY

King Philip II of Spain sent his navy of 129 ships, the Armada, to conquer England. The fleet was defeated by the English, and many of the Spanish survivors lost their lives in ocean storms.

ENDANGERED SPECIES

Each day a plant species becomes extinct somewhere in the world, an event that causes a chain reaction: it leads to the extinction of the animal species that depended on it. Habitats and species are interconnected in a delicate balance that humans have upset with hunting, deforestation and pollution.

The lynx is a wildcat with a spotted coat and tufted ears. The Eurasian and European lynx are becoming extremely rare. There are still species in the northern regions of North America. Many wildcats are protected species, such as the leopard and cheetah.

Only a few thousand orangutans (below) still survive in Indonesia and Malaysia. Other apes risking extinction are the mountain gorillas in the African tropical forest.

Tiger – The largest cat, the tiger lives in the forests of southern Asia and Siberia. Since the bones and other parts of the tiger are prized in traditional Chinese medicine, the animal has been systematically hunted for centuries. Three tiger sub-species have become extinct (the Bali tiger, Javan tiger and Caspian tiger), and today there are only 7,000 tigers left in the world.

Falconer goat – Location: Himalayan region. Population: rapidly declining. Cause of extinction: hunted for its horns.
African elephant – Location: central Africa. Population: 650,000. Cause of extinction: hunted for its ivory tusks.
Florida panther – Location: southern Florida. Population: less than 50. Cause of extinction: deforestation.
Saiga – Location: steppes of Kazakhstan and Mongolia. Population: about 500,000. Cause of extinction: hunted for its horn.
Komodo dragon – Location: islands of Indonesia. Population: 700–1,000. Cause of extinction: pollution of its habitat.

The giant panda with cub. The panda is the symbol of the World Wildlife Fund.

Many birds of prey such as the condor are endangered species. Even the bald eagle (above), the national bird of the United States, risked extinction. Since it has been declared a protected species, however, it has successfully reproduced and grown in number.

Pandas – These animals, the rarest bears in the world, live in Tibet and Nepal at altitudes of up to 9,600 ft (3,000 m). There are two species of panda: the giant panda (with black and white fur) and the red panda. Pandas eat bamboo almost exclusively.

Sea turtles – These reptiles also risk extinction. Tortoises often mistake plastic bags for jellyfish and suffocate when they swallow the bags.

Sea turtle eggs hatch in the sand. As soon as they are born, the baby turtles head for the sea, but most are eaten by birds and crabs—only the luckiest ones survive.

Protecting nature – More than 100 countries have signed CITES, the Convention on International Trade in Endangered Species. Not only animals but also plants, such as orchids and cactus, are protected by this agreement. Other associations that protect the environment are WWF (World Wildlife Fund), Greenpeace and Europe Conservation. Several organizations have been formed to protect marine life, especially whales.

African species – Many animals in Africa such as the chimpanzee and African elephant (hunted for its ivory tusks) are endangered. Rhinoceros (hunted for their horns) are also endangered: there are less than 22,000 rhinos left.

Australia, Africa and North and South America have natural parks and large reserves where animals live protected.

Left: A giraffe, an African animal that is not an endangered species.

Dodo (below) – This flightless turkey-sized bird with a strong beak and short legs was already rare when it was first discovered in the Mauritius Islands in 1507. The dodo became extinct in 1860 after being hunted by Portuguese sailors.

ANIMALS IN AFRICA,
APES AND MONKEYS,
ECOLOGY, GIRAFFE,
OCEANIA, RAPTORS,
REPTILES, TIGERS,
WILDCATS

ENERGY

Steam, coal, hydroelectricity, oil and nuclear power are the most commonly used sources of energy. Renewable and non-polluting sources, such as solar and wind power, are being investigated more thoroughly.

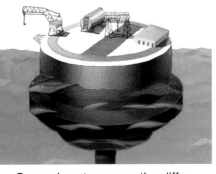

Several systems use the difference in the temperature between the water at the bottom of the sea and the temperature on the surface to produce electrical energy.

Wind turbines
Generators can be built where the wind is strong and constant. Large propellers that turn in the wind are connected to equipment that stores the energy produced.

Electric power plants
These plants use heat (from coal and oil), hydroelectric power or nuclear energy to produce electricity.

High-tension lines carry electricity produced in electric power plants.

Solar energy – Solar panels, which use sunlight to produce electricity, are called photovoltaic panels because they use particles of light called photons. Solar panels are also used on space satellites (below). Thermal panels, on the other hand, use the heat from the sun to produce energy.

ECOLOGY, ELECTRICITY, SCIENTISTS AND INVENTORS, SUN, TRANSPORTATION

ENGINES

There are many types of engines, including steam-powered, electric, diesel, internal-combustion, and jet engines. Most engines today convert fossil fuels like coal or oil into the mechanical energy required to drive a machine. Even though they function according to different principles, engines all have the same purpose: to do the hard work that used to be performed by humans and animals.

A cross section of a Jaguar E-type sports car, with a six-cylinder engine that reaches a speed of about 160 mph (250 km/h).

Right: A *four-stroke* gasoline engine, in which each piston completes a four-stroke cycle. The pistons slide into the cylinders where air mixes with tiny drops of gasoline. The pistons then move up and compress the mixture. An electric spark produced by the spark plug ignites this flammable mixture and the explosion slides the pistons down again. Finally, the pistons move up and the spent fuel leaves the cylinder.

Diesel engines, which are often used in trucks and trains, use diesel fuel instead of gasoline. Instead of spark plugs, they have *injectors* that spray the diesel fuel into the cylinders. The air inside the cylinders is compressed and overheated. As a result, the fuel explodes on its own, without the need for a spark.

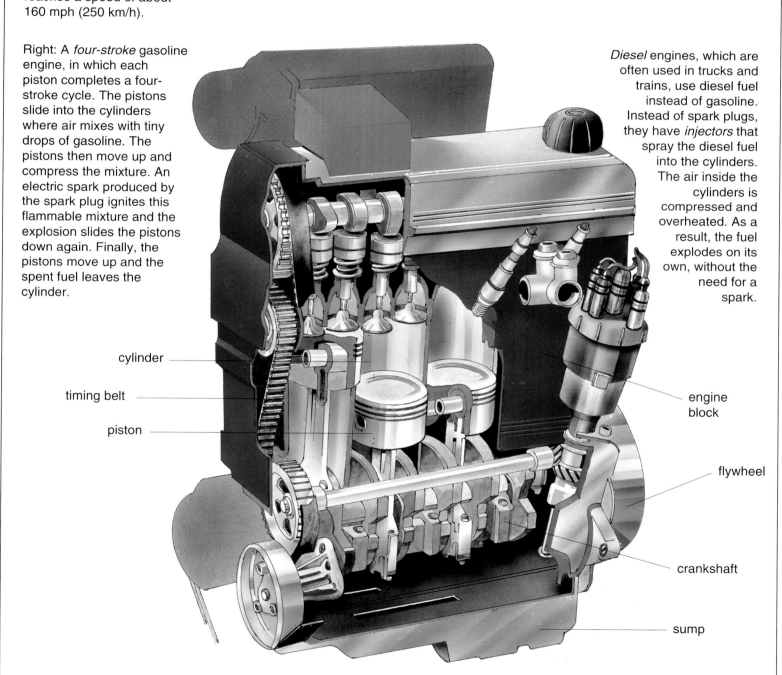

cylinder

timing belt

piston

engine block

flywheel

crankshaft

sump

Steam – James Watt invented the steam engine in 1765 and in so doing paved the way for the Industrial Revolution. Still today the *watt* is used as a unit to measure power. Steam engines were used to drive industrial machines, locomotives, and trolley cars like this one used in London during the last century (left).

Electric engines – Right, an electric-powered submarine designed by Goubers (1889). The electric current used to power the engine may be DC (direct current) or AC (alternating current).

This toy locomotive is powered by alcohol.

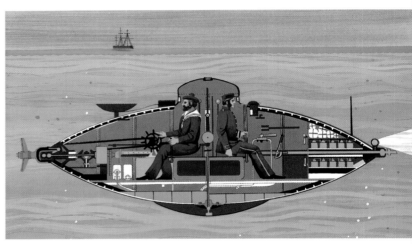

A cross-section of the Concorde.

Jet engine – The first jet engine was patented in 1930 by F. Whittle. Almost all modern aircraft use a *jet turbine engine*. Air enters the inlet diffuser and the air compressor, a fan with rapidly rotating blades, pushes it into the combustion chamber where it is heated by the fuel. The gases produced by igniting the fuel are expelled through the jet nozzle, which thrusts the aircraft forward. The expelled gases drive a turbine that in turn powers the air compressor; thus the cycle continues.

In the future – Gasoline and diesel engines pollute the air because they produce exhaust fumes. Some car manufacturers are studying cars with electric engines that are quiet and do not pollute. However, existing electric car batteries do not last long enough to provide sufficient autonomy.

ASSEMBLY LINE ✓
STEAM
☞ TRANSPORTATION

ERIC THE RED

Eric (ca. 940–1007), a Viking navigator, was called Eric the Red because of the color of his hair. He settled in Iceland and in the year 985 organized an expedition where he discovered Greenland. He returned the following year with 25 ships and 5,000 Viking colonists. Colonization of Greenland continued with his son, Leif Ericsson, who is thought by some historians to be the first man to reach the coasts of North America, an area he named Vinland.

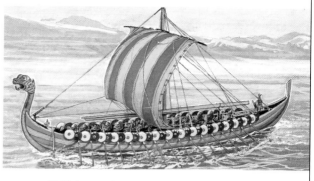

Viking ship – Besides being a rapid means of transport for cargo and men, the ship was also a symbol of wealth and prestige. When important leaders died, they were often cremated on a funeral pyre placed on top of their ship, which was then buried or burnt and left to sink off shore.

People in Viking villages raised animals and fished. When the colonists arrived in Greenland, they brought with them animals and many raw materials (like wood) that were scarce in Greenland.

The prow of Viking ships was often carved with a dragon.

Navigation – Viking ships were very advanced for their time, but because of their low sides, many of them sunk. In memory of dead sailors who never returned from their voyage, stone monuments were built, carved with *runes*, letters of the Scandinavian alphabet that were supposed to possess magical powers.

BARBARIANS
EXPLORERS
SAILING SHIPS ✓
TRANSPORTATION
VIKING VILLAGE ✓

EUROPE

Europe is a densely populated continent with more than 700 million people. The majority of the early inhabitants were white. With immigration over the past few decades, the face of Europe has changed; people of all races and colors live in Europe today. Some ethnic groups, such as the Lapps, have maintained their ancient traditions.

The tundra is the home of Lapp settlements. The traditional tents are built with a frame of tree branches covered with reindeer skins.

The Lapps keep their traditions alive and decorate their reindeer with the same bright colors used in their traditional native dress.

EEC – In 1957, the European Economic Community was founded to promote the balanced growth of countries and to create a free trade market for raw materials, labor and capital. On November 1, 1993, the EEC became the European Union (EU). Member countries are Austria, Belgium, Denmark, Finland, France, Germany, the United Kingdom, Greece, Ireland, Italy, Luxembourg, the Netherlands, Portugal, Spain and Sweden.

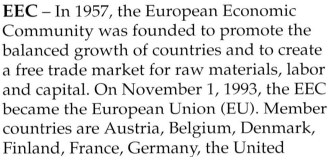

ICELAND

IRELAND

UNITED KINGDOM

PORTUGAL

SPAIN

Lapland – This northern region in the Arctic Circle is inhabited mainly by Lapps, once a nomadic people that used sleds and skis to travel. Today most Lapps live in settlements where they fish and raise reindeer. The subarctic climate in Lapland is very cold all year round. The ground stays frozen and it snows occasionally. The vegetation consists of conifers, lichens, moss and small shrubs.

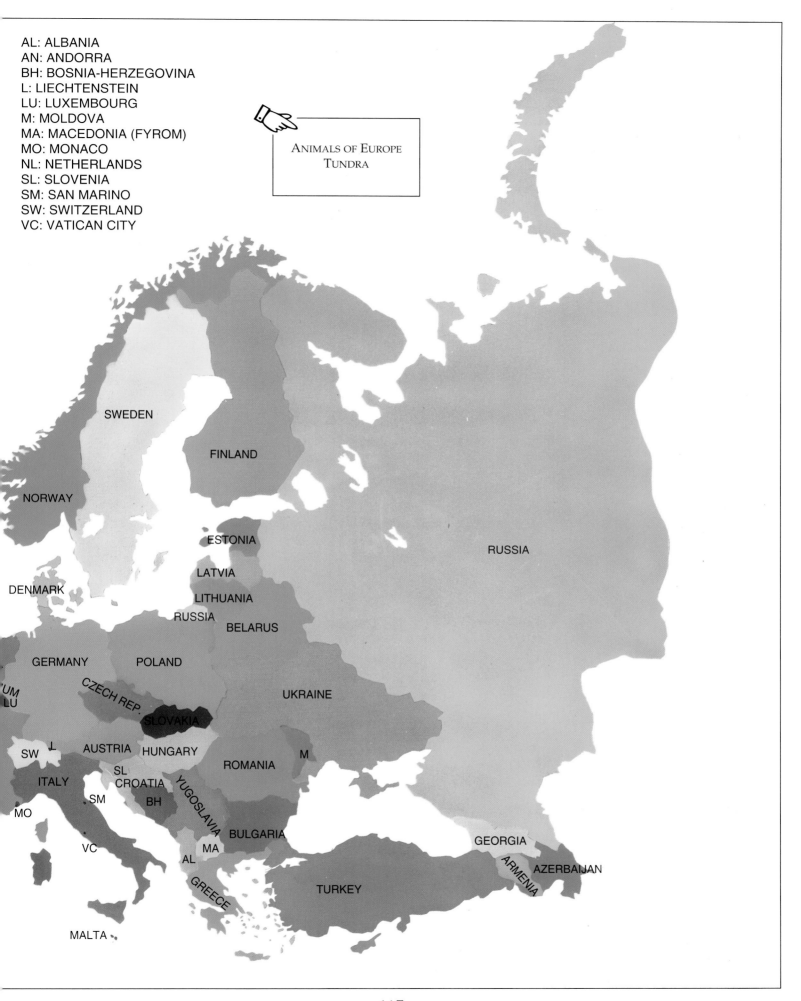

AL: ALBANIA
AN: ANDORRA
BH: BOSNIA-HERZEGOVINA
L: LIECHTENSTEIN
LU: LUXEMBOURG
M: MOLDOVA
MA: MACEDONIA (FYROM)
MO: MONACO
NL: NETHERLANDS
SL: SLOVENIA
SM: SAN MARINO
SW: SWITZERLAND
VC: VATICAN CITY

ANIMALS OF EUROPE
TUNDRA

SWEDEN

FINLAND

NORWAY

ESTONIA

LATVIA

DENMARK

LITHUANIA

RUSSIA

RUSSIA

BELARUS

GERMANY

POLAND

UM
LU

CZECH REP.

UKRAINE

SLOVAKIA

SW

AUSTRIA

HUNGARY

M

ITALY

SL

ROMANIA

CROATIA

YUGOSLAVIA

SM

BH

MO

BULGARIA

VC

MA

GEORGIA

AL

ARMENIA

AZERBAIJAN

GREECE

TURKEY

MALTA

COUNTRIES IN EUROPE

	COUNTRY	CAPITAL	AREA	POPULATION	LANGUAGE(S)	CURRENCY
	France	Paris	211,225 sq mi (547,030 sq km)	57,840,000	French	French franc
	Spain	Madrid	194,828 sq mi (504,567 sq km)	39,300,000	Spanish	peseta
	Sweden	Stockholm	173,743 sq mi (449,960 sq km)	8,778,000	Swedish	krona
	Germany	Berlin	137,815 sq mi (356,910 sq km)	81,088,000	German	Deutsche mark
	Finland	Helsinki	130,137 sq mi (337,030 sq km)	5,029,000	Finnish, Swedish	markka
	Norway	Oslo	125,190 sq mi (324,220 sq km)	4,315,000	Norwegian	krone
	Poland	Warsaw	120,735 sq mi (312,680 sq km)	38,792,000	Polish	zloty
	Italy	Rome	116,314 sq mi (301,230 sq km)	58,262,000	Italian	Italian lira
	United Kingdom	London	94,532 sq mi (244,820 sq km)	58,295,000	English	British pound sterling
	Romania	Bucharest	91,705 sq mi (237,500 sq km)	23,181,000	Romanian	leu
	Greece	Athens	50,946 sq mi (131,940 sq km)	10,647,000	Greek	drachma
	Bulgaria	Sofia	42,825 sq mi (110,910 sq km)	8,775,000	Bulgarian	leva
	Iceland	Reykjavik	39,770 sq mi (103,000 sq km)	265,000	Icelandic	krona
	Yugoslavia (Serbia and Montenegro)	Belgrade	39,520 sq mi (102,350 sq km)	11,102,000	Serbo-Croatian	Yugoslav new dinar
	Hungary	Budapest	35,920 sq mi (93,030 sq km)	10,319,000	Hungarian	forint
	Portugal	Lisbon	35,555 sq mi (92,080 sq km)	10,562,000	Portuguese	escudo
	Austria	Vienna	32,173 sq mi (83,823 sq km)	7,987,000	German	schilling

	COUNTRY	CAPITAL	AREA	POPULATION	LANGUAGE(S)	CURRENCY
	Czech Republic	Prague	30,438 sq mi (78,703 sq km)	10,408,000	Czech	koruna
	Ireland	Dublin	27,127 sq mi (70,280 sq km)	3,550,000	Irish, English	Irish pound
	Lithuania	Vilnius	25,203 sq mi (65,200 sq km)	3,876,000	Lithuanian, Russian	litas
	Latvia	Riga	24,891 sq mi (64,100 sq km)	2,749,000	Lettish, Russian	lat
	Croatia	Zagreb	21,821 sq mi (56,513 sq km)	4,666,000	Serbo-Croatian	Croatian dinar
	Bosnia-Herzegovina	Sarajevo	19,733 sq mi (51,233 sq km)	3,202,000	Serbo-Croatian	dinar
	Slovakia	Bratislava	18,926 sq mi (48,845 sq km)	5,432,000	Slovak	koruna
	Estonia	Tallinn	17,406 sq mi (45,080 sq km)	1,625,000	Estonian, Russian	kroon
	Denmark	Copenhagen	16,632 sq mi (43,075 sq km)	5,188,000	Danish	krone
	Netherlands	Amsterdam	16,027 sq mi (37,330 sq km)	15,543,000	Dutch, Frisian	guilder
	Switzerland	Bern	15,937 sq mi (41,275 sq km)	7,085,000	German, Raeto-Romansch, French, Italian	Swiss franc
	Belgium	Brussels	11,781 sq mi (30,513 sq km)	10,063,000	French, Dutch (Flemish)	Belgian franc
	Albania	Tirane	11,096 sq mi (28,737 sq km)	3,415,000	Albanian, Greek	lek
	Macedonia	Skopje	9,924 sq mi (25,333 sq km)	2,160,000	Macedonian, Albanian	denar
	Slovenia	Ljubljana	7,818 sq mi (20,248 sq km)	2,050,000	Slovenian	Slovenian tolar
	Luxembourg	Luxembourg	998 sq mi (2,586 sq km)	405,000	Luxembourgisch, German, French	Luxembourg franc
	Andorra	Andorra-la-Vella	181 sq mi (450 sq km)	65,000	Catalan, Spanish	French franc, peseta
	Malta	Valletta	122 sq mi (320 sq km)	369,000	Maltese, English	Maltese lira

	COUNTRY	CAPITAL	AREA	POPULATION	LANGUAGE(S)	CURRENCY
	Liechtenstein	Vaduz	62 sq mi (161 sq km)	30,000	German	Swiss franc
	San Marino	San Marino	23.9 sq mi (62 sq km)	24,300	Italian	Italian lira
	Monaco	Monaco	0.75 sq mi (1.94 sq km)	31,000	French	French franc
	Vatican City		0.17 sq mi (0.44 sq km)	830	Italian	Italian lira

EUROPEAN RECORDS

• **The longest mountain chain:** the Carpathian Mountains, 808 mi (1,300 km).

• **The longest river:** the Volga River, 2,194 mi (3,531 km).

• **The largest lake:** Lake Ladoga in Russia, 7,104 sq mi (18,400 sq km).

• **The tallest waterfall:** the Gavarnie Waterfall in the French Pyrenees, 1,384 ft (422 m).

• **The largest island:** Great Britain, 88,764 sq mi (229,885 sq km).

• **The largest peninsula:** Scandinavia, 308,890 sq mi (800,000 sq km).

• **The most important port:** Rotterdam Port in the Netherlands.

• **The highest capital:** Andorra-la-Vella, 3,510 ft (1,070 m).

• **The longest train tunnel:** the Chunnel, 31.5 mi (50.5 km)

• **The most populated capital:** Moscow, with 9,100,000 inhabitants.

CONFEDERATION OF INDEPENDENT STATES

	COUNTRY	CAPITAL	AREA	POPULATION	LANGUAGE(S)	CURRENCY
	Russia	Moscow	6,593,250 sq mi (17,075,200 sq. km)	149,910,000	Russian	ruble
	Kazakhstan	Alma-Ata	1,048,827 sq mi (2,716,253 sq km)	17,376,000	Kazakh	tenge
	Ukraine	Kiev	233,107 sq mi (603,700 sq km)	51,847,000	Ukrainian	karbovanets
	Turkmenistan	Ashkhabad	188,470 sq mi (488,100 sq km)	4,075,000	Turkmen, Russian	manat
	Uzbekistan	Tashkent	172,755 sq mi (447,400 sq km)	23,000,000	Uzbek, Russian	som
	Belarus	Minsk	80,160 sq mi (207,600 sq km)	10,437,000	Byelorussian, Russian	Belarusian ruble
	Kyrgyzstan	Bishkek	76,614 sq mi (198,417 sq km)	4,770,000	Khirgiz	som
	Tajikistan	Dushanbe	55,261 sq mi (143,116 sq km)	6,155,000	Tajik, Russian	Tajik ruble
	Azerbaijan	Baku	33,438 sq mi (86,600 sq km)	7,790,000	Azerbaijani, Russian	manat
	Georgia	Tbilisi	26,890 sq mi (69,641 sq km)	5,725,900	Georgian	coupon
	Moldova	Kishinev or Chisiniau	13,007 sq mi (33,687 sq km)	4,473,000	Moldavian	leu
	Armenia	Yerevan	11,505 sq mi (29,800 sq km)	3,557,000	Armenian	dram

The CIS (Confederation of Independent States) was formed in 1991 after the republics in the former Soviet Union proclaimed their independence. The first countries that joined this new confederation were Russia, Ukraine, Belarus, Kazakhstan, Turkmenistan, Uzbekistan, Moldova, Armenia, Kyrgyzstan, Tajikistan, and Azerbaijan. Georgia joined in 1993. Three Baltic countries — Lithuania, Estonia and Latvia — did not join and declared their complete independence.

EVOLUTION

Life first appeared in the great sea that covered most of the Earth about 3 billion years ago. The first living creatures were one-cell organisms. After a few million years of evolution, fish appeared, then amphibians. About 325 million years ago the first reptiles appeared and 100 million years later, the dinosaurs arrived. The first warm-blooded mammals appeared soon after, but only after the dinosaurs disappeared.

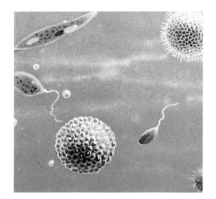

The first microscopic living creatures formed colonies (above). More complex multi-cell organisms (right) came later.

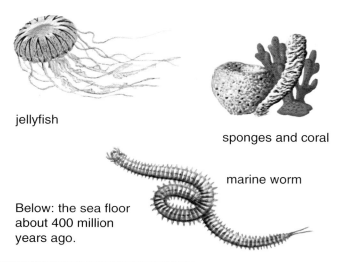

jellyfish

sponges and coral

marine worm

Below: the sea floor about 400 million years ago.

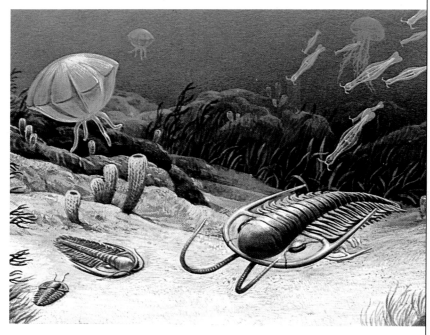

primitive coral (above)

arrow worms

starfish (below)

Reconstruction of a primeval forest.

The moschops, a primitive reptile.

The seas dried up – Many fish were able to breathe out of water for short periods of time (above). These fish probably evolved into the first amphibians, which then branched into many different species. Several amphibians started producing eggs with hard shells and no longer needed to live in water: the early reptiles descended from these amphibians.

Pteranodons were not birds, but reptiles.

AMPHIBIANS
DINOSAUR
REPTILES
SEA

121

EXPLORERS

Since ancient times, explorers have been driven by the spirit of adventure and the desire to discover new and bountiful lands. The Phoenicians and then the Greeks explored the Mediterranean; the Romans colonized Britain; and during the Middle Ages, the Arabs explored the Sahara while the Vikings established settlements in Greenland.

In Greek mythology, Odysseus explored unknown lands on his return voyage from Troy to Ithaca.

Marco Polo (ca.1254–1324), a Venetian merchant, explored Asia and even traveled to China. He narrated his adventures in a book that inspired many European explorers.

Great explorers
1. Eric the Red, a Viking warrior and explorer (ca. 940–1007).
2. Christopher Columbus set sail with three ships to discover a new route to India.
3. Portuguese navigator Vasco da Gama (1469–1524) reached the Indian port of Calicut.
4. James Cook made three voyages to the Pacific.
5. The famous meeting of explorers Stanley and Livingstone at Lake Tanganyika in East Africa.
6. Roald Amundsen from Norway was the first to reach the South Pole.

Christopher Columbus (1451–1506), an Italian explorer from Genoa, landed on the American coasts on October 12, 1492, yet he never realized he had discovered a new continent.

One of the three caravels (small light sailing ships) Columbus used to cross the Atlantic and reach the New World.

A new era – The great age of sailing and explorations began during the 15th and 16th centuries thanks to improved sails and nautical inventions such as the compass and the single rudder. The Spanish and Portuguese traders sought a sea route to the Indies (the land of precious cargo and spices) in order to avoid the long and dangerous voyage by land.

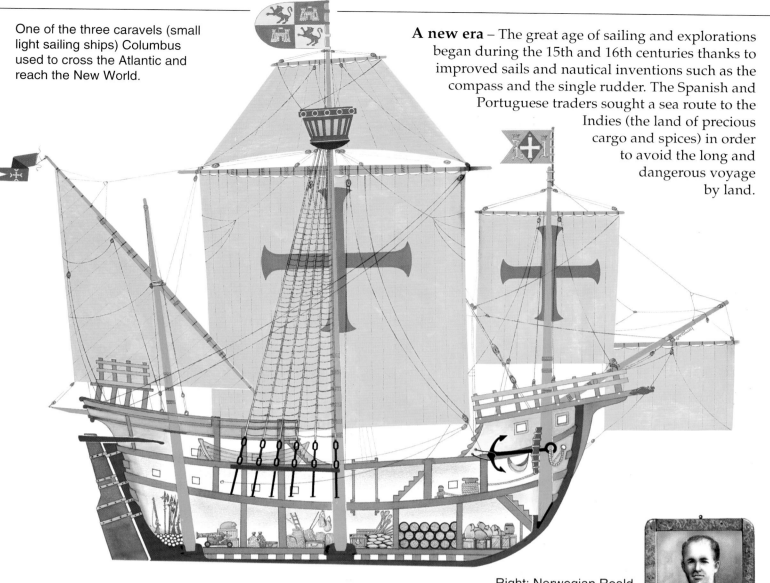

Ferdinand Magellan (1480–1521), the Portuguese navigator.

Magellan – He was the first to circumnavigate the globe. Magellan set sail from Spain, traveled along the South American coast to Patagonia and gave his name to the strait separating South America from Tierra del Fuego. He then crossed the Pacific Ocean and reached the Philippines, where he was killed. The only remaining ship crossed the Indian Ocean, sailed around Africa and returned to Spain in 1522.

Right: Norwegian Roald Amundsen (1872–1928) reached the South Pole in 1911. He flew over the North Pole in 1926 aboard the dirigible *Norge*.

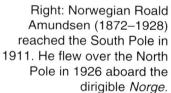

Left: Robert Scott (1868–1912), the British explorer, reached the South Pole but Roald Amundsen preceded him by five weeks.

David Livingstone (1813–1873), from Scotland, was given up for lost during his search for the Nile River. He was discovered by the journalist and explorer Henry M. Stanley near Lake Tanganyika.

Right: English captain James Cook (1728–1779) made three long voyages in the Pacific Ocean. He first explored the South Seas and Tahiti, then traveled to New Zealand and the Hawaiian Islands.

AFRICA, AMERICA, ANTARCTICA, ASIA, CHARLES V, CHRISTOPHER COLUMBUS, ERIC THE RED, MAPS, PRE-COLUMBIAN CIVILIZATIONS, SAILING SHIPS ✓

FAIRY TALES AND FABLES

A fairy tale is a fanciful story about humans and fantastic creatures such as fairies, witches, ogres, elves, and gnomes. A fable is a short story, often with a moral, where animals portray human vices and virtues. The most famous fables were written by the Greek poet Aesop (6th century B.C.), the Roman writer Phaedrus (ca. 20 B.C.–50 A.D.), and the French writer Jean de La Fontaine (1621–1695).

The Fox and the Grapes, a fable by Aesop.

Puss in Boots (fairy tale by C. Perrault)
"Once upon a time there was a cat that was so clever he turned his master, a poor miller, into a wealthy man..."

Cinderella (fairy tale by C. Perrault)
"'Cinderella,' said the Fairy Godmother, 'I'll turn that pumpkin into a carriage and these mice into fine white horses. You may go to the Prince's Ball, but the spell will break at the stroke of midnight!' With a touch of her magic wand, the Fairy Godmother turned Cinderella's miserable rags into an exquisite gown..."

Little Red Riding Hood (fairy tale by C. Perrault)

"The little girl jumped in fright when a deep voice asked, 'Where are you going, pretty little girl, all alone in the woods?' 'Grandma is sick, so I'm going to her house at the end of the woods to bring her some cookies.' replied Little Red Riding Hood. The wolf licked his whiskers, said good-bye to Little Red Riding Hood, then rushed off to Grandma's house to get there first...'"

The Three Little Pigs

"Once upon a time there was a Big Bad Wolf who wanted to eat three little pigs... The wisest and cleverest pig built a solid brick house the wolf could not enter...'"

AUTHORS AND POETS
CASTLES
CHILDREN'S LITERATURE
WALT DISNEY

Snow White (fairy tale by the Brothers Grimm)

"As soon as Snow White bit into the apple, she fell to the ground. The witch cackled as she walked away, 'Now I'll be the fairest one of all...'"

The Adventures of Pinocchio (by C. Collodi)

"Pinocchio was returning home to his father, Gepetto, to bring him the gold coins. On his way home he met up with a half-blind Cat and a lame Fox who said, 'Trust us, Pinocchio! We know a magic field where you can plant your golden coins and collect many, many more…'"

Farm Animals

Each farm animal has its home: bees have a hive, sheep have a pen, cows have a barn, chickens have a chicken coop, horses have a stable and pigs have a pigsty. Farms are sometimes called ranches in the United States and *fazendas* in Brazil. And they can specialize in raising different animals: *Gauchos*, or cowboys, in Argentina raise cattle, ostriches are raised in South Africa, and sheep are raised in New Zealand. In fact, there are twenty times more sheep than people in New Zealand!

Sheep – Its fleece becomes thicker in winter and is sheared in spring. Expert sheep shearers can cut off the fleece of a sheep in 60 seconds! The fleece is then washed and degreased, then carded, spun, dyed, and woven.

The goat (above) eats everything, even prickly bushes.

Ruminants – Cows are ruminants. They swallow grass without chewing it. The grass travels down to the first of the four parts of the stomach, then it moves into the second where it is rolled into little balls. It is regurgitated and finally chewed before it passes into the third and fourth parts of the stomach where it is digested.

Once cows were used as beasts of burden. Today they are raised to produce milk, meat, and leather.

Milk – A cow produces more than 1000 gallons (4,000 liters) of milk each year and a calf drinks between 2.5 and 3 gallons (10 – 12 liters) each day. As soon as the milk is drawn, it is pasteurized to kill all the germs by quickly bringing it to the boiling point for a few seconds. Cream is obtained from the skimming process, and butter from beating the cream. Yogurt is made by adding enzymes to milk, and cheese is pro- duced by coagulating milk with whey. All of these products and others made from milk are called dairy products.

bull

Males and females – A bull is a male bovine that is raised to breed with the cow. An ox is a male bovine that cannot breed because it has been castrated (its sexual organs have been surgically removed). An ox is gentler but much stronger than a bull.

Eggs – A hen lays about 250 eggs the first year, then fewer and fewer every year. The eggs we eat have not been fertilized. Eggs, which are protected by a calcium shell, contain a yellow yolk that floats in the egg white. To produce a chick, the hen must first mate with a rooster. Chicks are hatched after a 20-day incubation period.

hen and chicks

The turkey is raised for its tender meat.

The goose (right) – The goose, a web-footed bird whose orange beak has a serrated edge, is a descendant of the wild gray goose raised by the Egyptians, Greeks, Romans, and Chinese. It eats grass or a mash made from seeds. It also swallows small stones to help grind the food in its stomach. Goose down is used as stuffing for pillows and covers because it provides excellent insulation from the cold.

Chickens – When the sun sets, chickens fall asleep in the chicken coop, huddling next to each other to keep warm. They wake at dawn when the rooster crows, then scratch the ground looking for seeds and worms. Chickens roll in the sand or dust to clean their feathers.

The donkey and the mule – The donkey, which is smaller than the horse, has a large head and ears and small hooves. The mule is the hybrid offspring of a male donkey and a female horse. The mule himself can never breed.

donkey

1. English saddle
2. The large, comfortable American saddle suited for long rides.

1

The horse – There are about 70 million horses in the world, but the number of breeds has dwindled over the years. Today, horses are used much less in farming and their work is mainly done by farm machines.

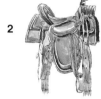

2

cart horse

There are about 200 breeds of horses today, like the elegant Arab horse, the fast purebred, and the strong Dutch cart horse.

On the farm – Rabbits live in a rabbit-hutch. They are herbivores that eat twice a day and can weigh 22 lb (10 kg) and grow to about 16 in (40 cm) in length. Domestic rabbits have less well-developed senses of smell, sight, and hearing than wild rabbits, but their reproductive capacity is greater. The female rabbit can have up to six bunnies several times a year.

BEES
BOVINES
HORSES
MAMMALS

The female rabbit gives birth to her bunnies in a corner of the rabbit-hutch that has been lined with soft tufts of her fur.

The rabbit – Its eyes are placed in such a way that it can look ahead and to the side. Its rear paws are longer than the front ones.

The Jewish and Islamic religions do not allow their followers to eat pork, which is considered impure.

The pig – The pig belongs to the swine family. It has a bristly heavy body, short legs, and strong hooves. It also has a curly tail like a corkscrew. The pig is omnivorous, which means it eats everything: flour, beets, and potatoes, but also roots, acorns, snails, and leftovers from dinner. Pigs drink up to 2.5 gallons (10 liters) of water per day. A *boar* is a male pig and a *sow* is a female pig.

Baby pigs are called sucklings. Twelve are born at a time.

A very useful animal
Humans use all parts of the pig. Pig meat, or pork, is used to make salami, ham, bacon, baloney, and sausages. Its bristles are used to make paint brushes and hair brushes. Its tanned hide becomes leather and its intestine is used as casing for salami and sausages.

FASHION

Clothing — like music, art, and architecture — defines a specific historical period. Starting in the Renaissance period, clothes began to express the personality of the person wearing them, as well as his or her social class. Clothes also had to satisfy people's desire for novelty, and so *fashion* was born. The pictures below show how clothes have changed over the centuries and how one style often blends with another. Thanks to today's means of communication, fashions change rapidly.

1. primitive humans
2. Egyptians
3. Greeks
4. Romans
5. early Middle Ages

6. late Middle Ages
7. medieval Germans
8. Elizabethan period
9. 17th century Dutch
10. 17th century French

The Golden Age – During the reign of Elizabeth I (above), England became a great power and experienced a time of great splendor. The clothing in that period was sumptuous and decorated with pearls and jewels.

1. hooped underskirt, or crinoline (16th century)
2. stiff lace collar, or ruff (17th century)
3. lace fan (18th century)
4. straw hat with flowers and ribbons
   (end of 19th century)
5. corset (end of 19th century)
6. embroidered handbags (end of 19th century)
7. parasol with lace and ribbons

11. 18th century English
12. 18th century French
13. 18th century German
14. Late 18th century French
15. 19th century French

16. 19th century English
17. 19th century English and
    German
18. from 1930 to 1950
19. from 1950 to 1990

BARBARIANS, EGYPTIANS,
ELIZABETH I, GREEKS,
HUMAN ANCESTORS,
JAPANESE, MIDDLE AGES,
ROMANS

FIELDS AND MEADOWS

Beneath the grass and flowers is an invisible world of animals and insects that live underground. Moles and mole crickets dig deep tunnels, while locusts and worms burrow near the surface. These animals break up the hard soil and fertilize it as well.

Mole – This animal is almost blind, but it hunts larvae and worms with its very keen sense of smell. It digs tunnels with its strong front paws.

Meadow flowers (from left to right): clover, four-leaf clover, dandelion, dandelion seed, daisy.

Animals in the meadow (right)	3. worm
1. snail	4. mole
2. ladybugs	5. mole cricket
	6. ant eggs

Pollination (above) – Butterflies (1), ladybugs (2), bees (3), and wasps (4) carry pollen from the stamens of one flower to the pistil of another flower.

ANTS, BEES, BUTTERFLIES, FLOWERS, INSECTS

FISH

Today more than 20,000 fish species have been identified. They are all cold-blooded vertebrates, with either a bony skeleton or a cartilaginous one. Their skin is covered with scales. To move, fish use their fins—abdominal and pectoral—or just a single fin—caudal, anal or dorsal.

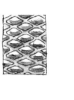

Types of scales (from left to right): ganoid, as in the garfish; ctenoid, as in the perch; placoid, as in the shark; cycloid, as in the salmon.

A prehistoric fish called the *cladoselache*.

Gills – These respiratory organs, located on both sides of the head, contain many blood vessels. Oxygen in the water enters the mouth and passes through the gills, where it is absorbed by the blood.

Scales – These small, overlapping bony plates cover the skin. Each scale is imbedded in a pocket-like cavity. The scale is protected by a skin-like membrane.

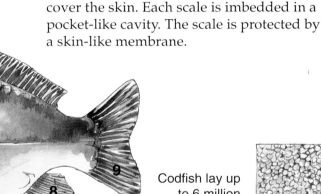

Codfish lay up to 6 million eggs at a time.

Anatomy of a carp:
Body parts: **1.** head; **2.** back; **3.** dorsal fin; **4.** pectoral area; **5.** pectoral fin; **6.** ventral fin; **7.** lateral line; **8.** anal fin; **9.** caudal (tail) fin.

Skeleton: **1.** skull; **2.** spinal column; **3.** ribs; **4.** fin rays; **5.** pectoral fin rays; **6.** hypural bone.

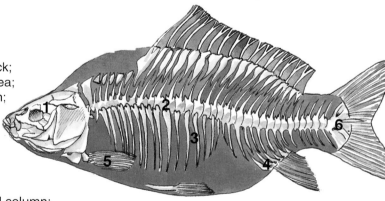

In the spring – Many fish migrate in springtime, seeking the best place to spawn. Females lay their eggs, which they leave unguarded, on the bottom of the lake, river or sea. Some species, such as the dogfish, hammer-head fish and shark, do not lay eggs but give birth to their young.

Internal organs: **1.** gills; **2.** heart; **3.** swim bladder; **4.** esophagus; **5.** liver; **6.** intestine; **7.** stomach; **8.** kidneys; **9.** urinary bladder; **10.** anus.

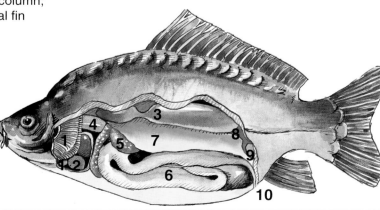

The swim bladder deflates when the fish swims near the bottom of the sea. It inflates when the fish reaches the surface of the water.

Eels – The European species migrate from fresh water to the Sargasso Sea to spawn. An eel cannot reproduce until 10 to 15 years of age.

Salmon – Salmon return to where they were born to lay eggs. A salmon can weigh up to 33 lb (15 kg) and measure nearly 4 ft (1.2 m) long.

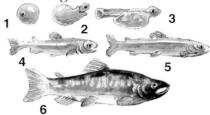

Salmon development:
1. fertilized egg; **2.** an egg hatching; **3.** pre-larval stage; **4.** the young, called a *parr*; **5.** smolt; **6.** adult male.

Piranha – This bony fish, which can measure up to 2 ft (60 cm) long, lives in South American rivers. Because of its aggressive nature, it is also called tiger fish. When an animal enters piranha-infested waters, these ferocious fish attack it and strip the flesh right down to the bone. Piranhas also attack humans.

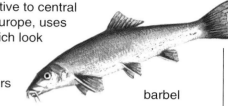

piranha

The barbel, native to central and western Europe, uses its barbels, which look like whiskers, to explore the bottoms of rivers and streams.

barbel

Trout – Salmon, trout and chars belong to the same family, and many people confuse them. Lake trout and brook trout are actually char. Only "true" trout have black speckles. The rainbow trout is a highly prized game fish found in many parts of the world.

Sturgeon – This freshwater fish swims upstream in spring to lay its eggs. The species found throughout Europe reaches almost 13 ft (4 m) in length. Some females contain as much as 220 lb (100 kg) of eggs, which are prized as a source of caviar.

All trout have black spots.

1. whitefish
2. dace
3. trout
4. sturgeon
5. pike
6. perch
7. mussel

carp

ANIMALS (STRANGE), CAMOUFLAGE, MIGRATION, OCEAN DEPTHS, PETS, SEA, SEA FLOOR, SHARKS

FLOWERS

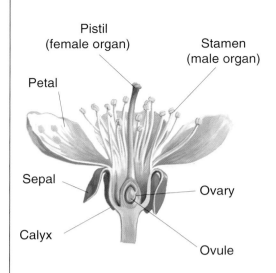

Pistil (female organ)

Stamen (male organ)

Petal

Sepal

Calyx

Ovary

Ovule

Plants had no flowers when dinosaurs roamed the Earth more than 70 million years ago. In fact, flowers only appeared after many insect species had developed. Bees, butterflies, flies and mosquitoes, which fly from one flower to another, allow plants to reproduce. Other animals such as hummingbirds and bats also feed on the nectar of flowers and transport the pollen.

How flowers reproduce

Flowers are the reproductive organs of plants. The pollen inside the stamen of a flower is carried by insects or the wind to the pistil of another flower, where it fertilizes the ovule. A fruit then develops whose seeds will grow into a new plant.

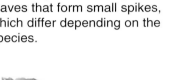

Meadow grass has long, narrow leaves that form small spikes, which differ depending on the species.

Clover

The most widespread species is red clover, which has three leaves and a purplish red flower. A four-leaf clover is rare and is thought to bring good luck.

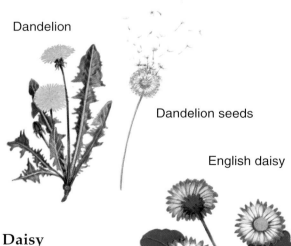

Dandelion

Dandelion seeds

English daisy

Daisy

Many types of daisies grow wild in fields or are grown in gardens. They are herbaceous plants that belong to the composite family.

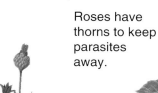

Colors, fragrances, and shapes

There are many varieties of flowers. Some have round petals, while others have oval or pointed ones. Flowers come in all the colors of the rainbow, and their fragrance is often strong so they can attract insects.

Anemones come in a wide variety of colors.

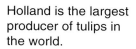

Holland is the largest producer of tulips in the world.

Wild violets grow in the woods in spring.

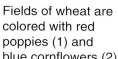

Roses have thorns to keep parasites away.

1

2

Fields of wheat are colored with red poppies (1) and blue cornflowers (2).

BEES, FIELDS, GARDENING, HERBAL MEDICINE, INSECTS, SEEDS, TREES AND LEAVES

Beautiful and useful

The geranium is often used to decorate balconies in the summer. There are many types of geraniums: some are climbing species, while others have single or double flowers. They come in shades of white, red, or pink and some have a strong scent. The essence of geraniums is used to make mosquito repellent.

Water lilies are aquatic plants.

The daffodil has a strong fragrance. The most popular varieties are the *poet's daffodil* with white flowers and a yellow heart and the *yellow daffodil*.

135

FOSSILS

The ocean floor during the prehistoric age, where fish with armor plates and powerful jaws used to live.

When many prehistoric fish, insects and plants died, their bodies remained trapped in sediment (left by water, wind or other erosive elements). The soft parts would decompose, but the hard parts became mineralized or petrified; and so their remains were preserved in stone. Fossils are the imprints left of these ancient living organisms.

DINOSAURS
SHELLS

Ichthyosaurus

Snail shell – Below, a large ammonite. The hard shell of this now extinct mollusk was preserved in rock for millions of years.

Plant and insect fossils:
1. Alethopteris
2. Calamites
3. Lepidodendron
4. Meganeura
5. Eugereon Boeckingi
6. Eophrynus
7. Seymouria baylorensis

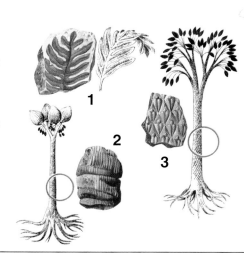

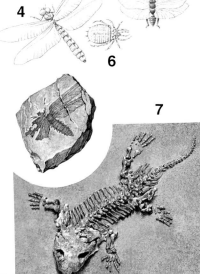

FREDERICK THE GREAT

Prussia was a small country at the beginning of the 18th century, but it soon became a powerful nation under the leadership of Frederick II. Frederick II, the son of Frederick William I, became king in 1740. He received a strict military education and was an enlightened ruler. Frederick II reformed the school system and abolished torture. He also introduced a civil code (1745–1751). Frederick the Great won Silesia from Austria and fought the allied forces of Austria, France, and Russia during the Seven-Year War from 1756 to 1763.

A portrait of Frederick II of Prussia, known as Frederick the Great.

1712: Born in Berlin.
1740: Succeeds his father to the throne.
1741–45: War against Austria; conquers Silesia.
1756–63: Seven-Year War.
1763–78: Rebuilds Prussia.
1786: Dies in Potsdam.

In 1730 Frederick, with the help of his friend Katte, tried to escape abroad to avoid a strict military education. His father accused him of treason, imprisoned him in the Küstrin Fort, and executed Katte (right).

Military genius – Frederick II renewed the recruitment system and supervised the training of soldiers. He also introduced the use of the bayonet. Frederick was a great strategist and tactician: his battles are considered some of the finest examples of military art. During one of Frederick's most famous victories in Rossbach (left), 20,000 Prussian soldiers defeated the French army, which had more than 40,000 soldiers.

Prussian soldiers:
1. Grenadier; 2. Artilleryman;
3. Dragon officer; 4. and 5. Hussars;
6. Cavalryman; 7. Infantryman

WEAPONS

1   2   3   4   5   6   7

FRENCH REVOLUTION

When Louis XVI took the throne in 1774, he was faced with a financial crisis: the clergy and nobles were exempt from taxes, leaving the burden to the middle class and peasants, who were demanding equal rights. A social and political upheaval arose from this discontent and led France from absolute monarchy to a constitutional government (1789), a republic (1792) and the dictatorship of Napoleon (1799). On August 26, 1789, the Constitutional Assembly approved the Declaration of the Rights of Man, stating that all citizens were equal before the law.

Guillotine

In June 1791 Louis XVI attempted to escape, but he was recognized and taken back to Paris, where he was forced to sign the new constitution in September. The king was condemned to death and decapitated on January 21, 1793. Queen Marie Antoinette suffered the same fate on October 16, 1793.

Capture of the Bastille

The people of Paris revolted and occupied the city. On July 14, 1789 (below), they captured the Bastille, a prison where the king's enemies were held without trial.

The French courageously fought in the name of liberty, equality and brotherhood.

LOUIS XIV
NAPOLEON

FRUITS

Orange

Some trees grow edible fruits that contain sugar, vitamins, and mineral salts needed for a nutritious diet. The oldest cultivated fruits are figs and dates, which were grown back in the days of the ancient Egyptians. Today new technologies let farmers raise strong, resistant trees and invent new varieties of fruit.

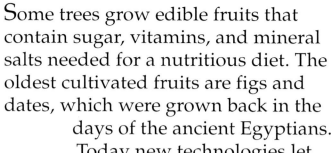

Apples – The apple is the fruit of the apple tree. There are many types of apples — Macintosh, Granny Smith, Golden Delicious — that ripen at different times of year.

Pears – They may change in size and color, but their shape is unmistakable. The pulp contains tiny hard grains.

Lemon

Citrus fruits
Oranges, tangerines, lemons, and grapefruits are some of the most popular citrus fruits. These fruits are rich in Vitamin C.

Tangerine

Persimmons
These orange fruits ripen in autumn when all the leaves on the tree have already fallen.

Figs – The part of the fig we call fruit is actually an *infructescence*, meaning a cluster of fruits contained within a receptacle. The skin can be green, black or reddish.

Nuts – Nuts, which are also fruits, are rich in oil and calories. Walnuts and hazelnuts have hard, wood-like shells, while chestnuts are enclosed in a prickly shell called the *husk*.

Hazelnut

Walnut
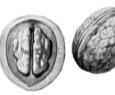

Grapes – There are many different varieties of edible grapes, but most of them are used to make wine. The clusters are pressed to produce a sweet, thick juice called *must*, which ferments and becomes wine.

Chestnut and husk

139

Cherries

Cherries – Cherries, which can be tart or sweet, have a pulp that ranges in color from yellow to dark red. Cherry trees, which can reach a height of 65 ft (20 m), provide valuable wood. Morello cherries are very tart.

Morello cherries (left) and cherries.

Plums – These fruits come in many varieties: red, yellow, green, and purple. They ripen in the summer and can be eaten fresh, dried, or stewed. They are also made into jam. Dried plums are called *prunes*.

Plums

Fruit can be used to make pies, cakes, ice cream, salads, candy, jams and jellies.

Peaches – These fruits ripen from the end of June to September. The pulp is juicy and tasty, and the skin is covered with fuzz.

Peach

Washing fruit – Chemical products called *pesticides* are used to protect fruit trees from diseases and parasites. Therefore, you must wash fruit very well or peel it before you eat it.

Apricots – The pulp of this small fruit has a delicate flavor. The apricot tree originally comes from Asia and belongs to the same family as the apple and the peach tree.

Apricot

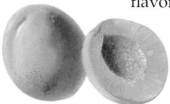

☞ FRUITS (EXOTIC)
NUTRITION

FRUITS – SOME EXOTIC VARIETIES

After America was discovered and trade developed between the colonies, fruits grown in tropical countries were imported to Europe. Today we can find exotic fruits such as coconuts, dates, avocados, and papayas at our local grocery store.

Coconut   Avocado

Dates

Papaya

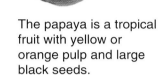

Pineapple

Pineapple
Beneath its tough skin that resembles a pine cone the pineapple has a tart, juicy pulp rich in sugars and vitamins.

The papaya is a tropical fruit with yellow or orange pulp and large black seeds.

FRUITS NUTRITION

Banana

Banana – This fruit is rich in sugar, Vitamin A, and mineral salts such as potassium. It is very nourishing and can be eaten all year round because banana trees produce fruits in every season.

GAMES

Games help children develop psychologically, but even adults enjoy card games, board games and outdoor fun. Hobbies such as gardening, do-it-yourself projects, stamp collecting, and cooking are enjoyed by old and young alike.

Paper dice you can make yourself

Outdoor games
Ring-around-the-rosy, hide and seek, jump rope, tag, kick ball, blindman's bluff, and hopscotch are all games you can play outdoors with friends.

Some card games, such as bridge, are rather complicated while others, like gin rummy, are much simpler. Both of these games are played in groups, while other card games, like solitaire, can be played alone. A standard deck has 52 cards (plus two jokers) divided into hearts, clubs, spades, and diamonds.

Chess pieces: 1 king, 1 queen, 2 bishops, 2 knights, 2 rooks, 8 pawns.

The checkerboard with checkers.

Checkers and chess – In the game of *checkers*, each player has 12 checkers (red or black). The checkers are placed on a checkerboard with 64 alternating light and dark squares. The aim is to capture or immobilize all your opponent's checkers and reach the last row on the board. *Chess* was invented in India and the Arabs brought the game to Europe in the 11th century. Each player has 16 pieces, white or black, that are moved according to precise rules. A player wins by declaring checkmate on his opponent's king.

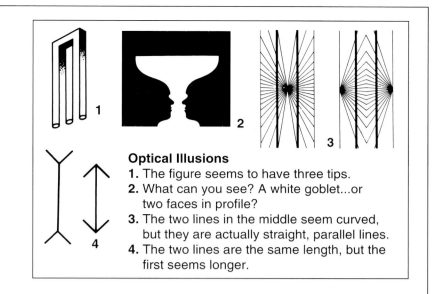

Optical Illusions
1. The figure seems to have three tips.
2. What can you see? A white goblet...or two faces in profile?
3. The two lines in the middle seem curved, but they are actually straight, parallel lines.
4. The two lines are the same length, but the first seems longer.

GARDENING
RECIPES
SHELLS
TOYS

Play the board game below. After throwing the dice, move forward or backward according to the instructions in the squares. Use buttons, beans, or coins as tokens.

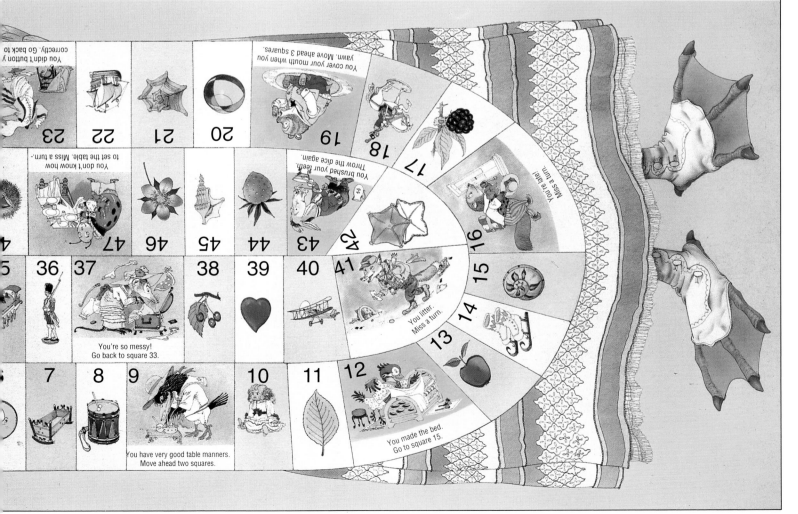

GANDHI, MAHATMA

Mohandas K. Gandhi was born of a rich family on October 2, 1869 in Porbandar, India. At the time, India was a part of the British Empire. Gandhi studied law in England where he was considered a second-class citizen because of his color and origins. This early experience with racism and colonialism led Gandhi to an interest in the principles of passive resistance and non-violence as described by Henry David Thoreau. He put these ideas into practice in South Africa and later in India, where he became leader of the nationalist movement to free the country from British control.

Mahatma Gandhi (1869-1948) fought for his fellow countrymen in India and South Africa, both former British colonies.

Non-violence – Gandhi preached non-violence and civic disobedience as a response to unjust laws. He tried to unite Muslims and Hindus, but he was unsuccessful at keeping India united. In 1947 the Muslim part of the country became the independent state of Pakistan. Gandhi was assassinated by a religious fanatic in 1948.

Martin Luther King, Jr. was inspired by Gandhi's ideas of non-violence.

Leader of Indian independence
Gandhi returned to India in 1914 and became a leader in the struggle for home rule. Although he was often jailed for his beliefs and actions, he convinced many of his followers that independence could be achieved through non-violence. India achieved independence in 1947. Although he never held office, Gandhi was considered India's political and spiritual leader and became known as Mahatma, or great soul.

HINDUISM
INDIA ☞

GARDENING

Gardening is the art and technique of growing vegetables, flowers and trees. Not everyone is lucky enough to have their own outdoor garden, but we can grow plants and flowers inside as well. Some plants must sit beside the window, while others require shade. Some plants need lots of water and others survive with very little. All plants need a constant temperature, however, so make sure you do not place them beside radiators or heaters or where there is a draft. Fertilizer will help them grow better.

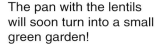

Here is what you need to grow lentils: lentils, a shallow pan, cotton balls and water.

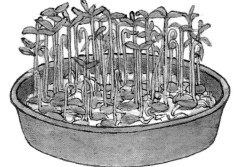

The pan with the lentils will soon turn into a small green garden!

The lentil garden – Cover the bottom of the pan with cotton balls, and soak the cotton in water. Then place the lentils on top. After a week you will see the first green sprouts appear. In a few days, the sprouts will grow 2 or 3 inches (5-6 cm).

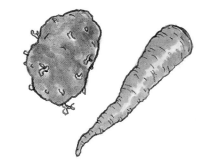

Here is what you need for *hydroponics* (plants grown in water): a large potato, a carrot, two containers and some water.

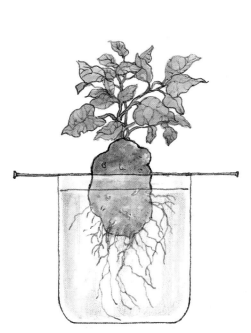

Potato and carrot – Fill two containers almost to the rim with water. Use two knitting needles to keep the vegetables raised from the bottom. Make sure two-thirds of the vegetables are covered with water. After a few days, the first roots and then the leaves will appear.

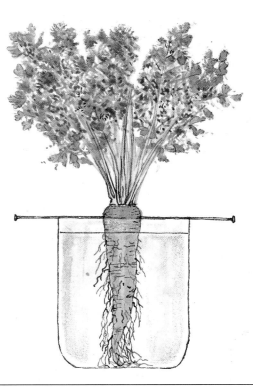

Dried flowers – Flowers can be picked and dried for various uses. You can dry them hanging upside down and make lovely flower arrangements. You can press the flowers and use them to make pictures. You can even make a *herbarium*: classify and identify the flowers and leaves and place them in a book. Petals of fragrant flowers (lavender, roses) can be used to make pot-pourri in sachets or clay jars.

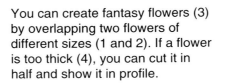

You can create fantasy flowers (3) by overlapping two flowers of different sizes (1 and 2). If a flower is too thick (4), you can cut it in half and show it in profile.

Bouquets – If you want to dry fresh bouquets, you must tie them together with a string, wrap them in newspaper, and hang them upside-down in a dark, dry, well-ventilated place so they will dry but keep their color.

How to dry flowers – Place dried flowers between the pages of a book (or better yet between two sheets of absorbent paper). Now place a weight on top. You can use several books or an iron.

Dried flowers can be used to decorate the cover of a notebook, the pages of a diary, or a wooden box. They can also be used to decorate bookmarks and greeting cards.

FLOWERS, GAMES, SEEDS, VEGETABLES

GIRAFFE

Giraffes live in the grasslands of central and southern Africa. They have long necks and their front legs are longer than their hind legs, which is why they have sloped backs. Their brownish red coat has patches that are larger on the body and smaller on the legs. The giraffe has a short, dark mane and a long tail with a thick tuft of dark hairs on the end. Giraffes are the tallest animals on Earth. An adult can reach 18 ft (5 m) in height. They defend themselves with their front hooves, and lions only attack a giraffe when it is cut off from the rest of the herd.

Funny face – A giraffe's head is small in proportion to the rest of its body. It has two horns covered with hair between its short, pointed ears. It has large expressive eyes and sharp eyesight that distinguishes almost every color.

Behavior – To determine who is the strongest, male giraffes fight by hitting each other with their heads and swinging their long necks. Females and their young watch the scene from a distance. Giraffes eat leaves that they pull out of trees with their tongues, which can be up to 18 in (45 cm) long.

Baby giraffes – Female giraffes give birth standing up; the baby giraffe falls almost 6 ft (2 m) to the ground. The baby giraffe can stand and walk only a few hours later. The mother licks her newborn clean while it suckles milk.

Legs – Giraffes have an awkward way of galloping because their front legs are raised and their neck must balance their weight. When they want to drink water, they must spread their front legs and bend their long neck to reach the water.

ANIMALS OF AFRICA, CAMOUFLAGE, ENDANGERED SPECIES, MAMMALS

GLASS

The glass is shaped while it is hot.

The oldest glass objects that have been found were made ca. 2000 B.C. in Egypt and Mesopotamia. Glass was first produced in the Far East and later in the Roman Empire. Potters in medieval Italy adapted the technique for making Chinese porcelain by mixing clay and powdered glass. Glass-blowing dates from the 16th century and gave rise to the art of stained glass, which reached its height during the Renaissance. Architects still use glass in modern buildings, especially in skyscrapers, where the material is treated to resist extreme temperatures and shocks.

Glass-blowing

This technique is still used today by artisans. The glass-blower dips the tip of a metal pipe into melted glass, then blows through the pipe. The hot glass inflates like a balloon and is shaped while it is still soft.

ARCHITECTURE,
GOTHIC CATHEDRALS ✓,
OPTICS, SKYSCRAPERS

A medieval church window decorated with religious scenes.

Below, a 19th-century glassworks: the glass was fired in the oven, then blown with special pipes to create cylindrical containers.

GREEKS

Independent city-states were formed after the decline of the Mycenean civilization at the end of the 2nd millennium B.C. The most important city-states were Athens in Atticus and Sparta in Laconia. In the 5th century B.C., the expansion of city-states in the Mediterranean led to wars with the Persians, who were defeated at Marathon, Salamine, and Platea. After a period of prosperity under Pericles (ca. 495–429 B.C.), Athens fell to Sparta at the end of the Peloponnesian War. In 338 B.C., Philip II of Macedon became ruler of Greece. The Romans conquered Greece in 146 B.C.

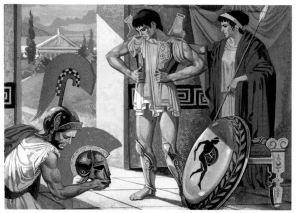

Spartan warrior – Strict discipline required boys from Sparta to endure strenuous physical exercise. From a very young age, Spartan children were put to the most gruelling tests of strength.

Greek artists painted terra-cotta vases with geometrical designs or mythological tales of gods and heroes.

The Iliad – This epic poem by Homer (8th century B.C.) describes the battle of Troy. One of the most exciting passages narrates the battle between Hector and Achilles at the gates of Troy.

Greek coins were often used as currency by the merchants of different states during the golden period of trade in the Mediterranean.

The word *philosophy* means love of knowledge. The first great Western philosophers were Greek: Pythagorus, Heraclitus, Socrates, Plato, and Aristotle.

Greek culture – Well-respected teachers from Athens taught poetry, music, dance, and gymnastics. Parchment rolls were used as books and students learned to write using wood sticks (*styluses*) on soft clay or wax tablets. Thanks to authors such as Aeschylus, Sophocles, and Euripides, a new type of literature called *tragedy* was developed and performed in the theater in the 5th century B.C.

Clothes – Women wore a loose, open tunic called a *peplos* or a closed gown called a *chiton* with a white cape (*himation*). They wore their hair in a bun, decorated with ribbons. Men wore different clothing depending on their social status and age. They wore a short woolen cloak, felt hat, and sandals, or a tunic, long or short, with a cloak held with decorative clasps on the shoulder.

ALEXANDER THE GREAT,
ARCHITECTURE,
AUTHORS AND POETS,
FASHION,
MYTHS AND LEGENDS,
PERSIA, SPORTS

GUTENBERG, JOHANNES

Johannes Gutenberg from Germany (ca. 1400–1468) invented the *printing press* that used movable metal characters around 1440. In 1455 he published a Bible, the first book ever printed with a printing press. Thanks to this invention, books, and therefore knowledge, were made available to people of all classes.

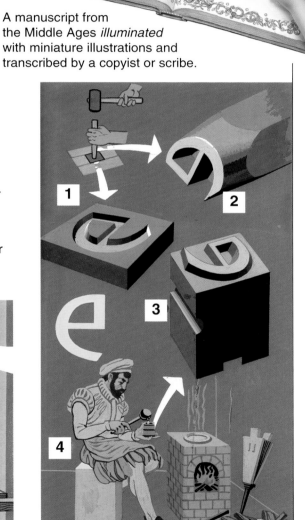

A manuscript from the Middle Ages *illuminated* with miniature illustrations and transcribed by a copyist or scribe.

Johannes Gutenberg

The Chinese – Already in the 3rd century B.C. the Chinese printed documents using clay seals. In 400, they invented a printing process using stamps carved out of wood blocks that were covered with ink and then pressed against paper.

BOOKS
CHINESE

Below: a 15th century print shop. The pages were prepared and then printed with ink using a printing press.
Details: 1. Preparing a matrix for metal characters; **2.** A sheet of paper ready for the press.

Above: 1. A punch is used to prepare the mold; **2.** Metal character; **3.** The letter is backwards so that it will be the right way around when printed; **4.** Metal is cast to create the characters.

HEDGEHOG

Hedgehogs live in Asia and Europe. They are nocturnal feeders that come out at dusk. They leave their burrow and rummage among leaves and grass in search of food. Hedgehogs eat seeds and fruit, but their favorite foods are worms and snails. Their appetite for slugs and beetles and other "pests" makes them popular among gardeners. In Europe gardeners leave out bowls of bread and milk to attract hedgehogs.

Hedgehog paws have small claws that enable them to catch their prey.

Quills – The common hedgehog has a short stocky body about 10 in (25 cm) long. Its back is covered with quills; its belly, snout and paws are covered with fur. These yellowish quills about 1 inch (2-3 cm) long are actually thick hairs that the hedgehog stiffens to protect itself.

Rolling up into a ball – An adult hedgehog can have as many as 5,000 needle-sharp quills to protect itself. It can also roll itself up into a ball when attacked. Baby hedgehogs too young to roll up into a ball are easy victims for predators. In cold climates hedgehogs hibernate in winter, but when the temperature is not too cold they interrupt their long sleep and spend some time awake and active.

According to legend, hedgehogs love apples and spear them with their quills!

Voices in the forest

Hedgehogs sometimes make high screeching sounds. Their excellent hearing and keen sense of smell help them search for food and identify enemies at a distance.

ANIMALS OF EUROPE,
HIBERNATION,
MAMMALS, RODENTS

HERBAL MEDICINE

Before synthetic drugs were produced in laboratories, diseases and illnesses were treated with herbs, flowers and roots. Herbalists still collect and prepare medicinal and aromatic plants. This specialty is called herbal medicine, an example of alternative healing, along with aromatherapy and homeopathy. Such methods are called holistic because they treat the symptoms as well as the cause of an illness.

Nettle is a natural diuretic with anti-inflammatory properties.

Algae are divided into three groups: brown, red and green. Many types are used as remedies.

Aromatherapy

Aromatherapy involves essential oils and other plant extracts. The oils are bottled and usually used for massage or for the bath.

The malva plant and flower

Homeopathy

Homeopathy – This specialty, founded by the German physician S. Hahnemann (1755–1843), is based on the idea that a sickness can be treated with tiny doses of the substance that causes the illness.

FLOWERS
MEDICINE
PLANTS (USEFUL)

An herbalist monk from the Middle Ages.

Plants are used in creams, ointments, lotions, essential oils and herbal teas.

HIBERNATION

Some mammals, such as bears, hide in a den and sleep all through the winter. But because their body temperature remains at a normal level, this is not considered true hibernation.

The dormouse (above) loses almost half its weight during hibernation.

In the cold winter months animals have a harder time finding food. Many animals, like swallows for instance, migrate to warmer areas while others hibernate until spring. Some animals suddenly fall into a deep sleep; others, like the squirrel, prepare a burrow. Many animals eat as much as possible before winter so they accumulate a store of fat that allows them to survive without eating until they wake up. Other animals wake up periodically to drink, eat, and eliminate wastes. When they are hibernating, their heart beat and physiological functions slow down so they can save energy. Even their body temperature drops to adapt to the surroundings.

AMPHIBIANS, BEARS, HEDGEHOG, MAMMALS, RACCOONS, SEASONS, SNAKES, SQUIRRELS

Estivation – Some desert animals become inactive during the hottest months: they slow down their bodily functions so they can survive without water. Frogs and crocodiles remain submerged in mud until it starts raining. Snails that live in the Sahara desert can survive for years without eating or drinking.

1. Tench
2. European pond turtle
3. Frogs
4. Ringed snake
5. Ladybugs
6. Snail
7. Slow worm
8. Lizard
9. Brown bear
10. Marmots
11. Hedgehog
12. Dormouse
13. Squirrel
14. Badger

HINDUISM

Hindus believe in one divine being that is adored under different forms and names. The Hindu religion (born around 1500 B.C.) venerates many gods and demigods. The three most important gods are *Brahma*, the creator of the universe, *Vishnu*, the protector and preserver of the universe, and *Shiva*, the god of its destruction. Hindus believe that the soul is reincarnated into different forms of life until it achieves *Nirvana*, perfect bliss in the final liberation from the cycle of rebirth.

Hindus consider cows to be sacred animals.

Vishnu and *Shiva* (left) are two of the most venerated gods.

Brahma (above) is often portrayed sitting on a sacred goose and having four crowned heads and four arms.

Daily rituals – Hinduism is not just a collection of religious beliefs but a way of being that influences all aspects of life. Hindus possess many portraits of their gods, which are considered expressions of holiness. Yoga is a daily ritual that purifies the body and the soul.

According to Hinduism, society is divided into rigid *castes* or classes.

Hindu temples – There are many Hindu temples in India: some have even been dug out of rock. An important characteristic is the tower, which rises up from the center of the temple. In some temples several smaller towers surround the largest one and are decorated with a great many statues of gods and goddesses.

The Hanuman Temple

☞ ARCHITECTURE, BUDDHISM, CHRISTIANITY, GANDHI, INDIA ISLAM, JUDAISM

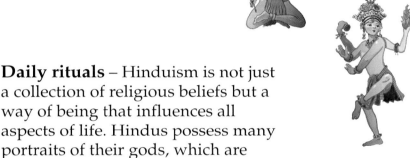

HORSES

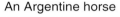

The small Sardinian donkey patiently carries out all the heaviest jobs: it plows fields and carries heavy loads on difficult trails.

Horses are members of the *Equus* family, which also includes zebras, mules and donkeys. They all descend from the eohippus, an ancient mammal from the Eocene epoch. These herbivorous animals share a long narrow skull, four long legs with hooves, a tail and a flowing mane. Domestic breeds are found on every continent.

We can judge a horse's age by checking the number, size and condition of its teeth. Adult horses have between 40 and 42 teeth.

Gaits – The three gaits of a horse are the walk, trot and gallop. When a horse gallops, all four feet are off the ground during each stride and the horse remains suspended in air for a fraction of a second.

An Argentine horse

Argentine horse – This strong horse is suited for heavy work. Argentine gauchos, or cowboys, ride them to follow the cattle herds.

An English thoroughbred (a type of saddle horse)

FARM ANIMALS, MAMMALS, STEPPE, ZEBRAS

A Clydesdale (a type of draft horse)

Burchell's zebra

Domesticated horses – The largest domesticated breed is the English Shire, and the smallest is the miniature pony. There are three main categories: draft horses for carrying heavy loads, harness horses for use with carts, and saddle horses for riding. A stallion is an adult male, and a mare is an adult female. A horse's height is measured in hands from the ground to the top of the shoulders. A hand is equivalent to 4 in (10 cm).

Zebra – The zebra has a black and white striped coat that acts as camouflage in the African savanna. Although zebras look alike, each one has a unique number, placement and size of stripes. Zebras live in herds and can run at speeds of 40 mph (65 km/h).

HOUSEHOLD APPLIANCES

The advent of electricity brought about great changes in daily life. Between the end of the 19th and the beginning of the 20th centuries, many homes had electric lights and running water for the first time. Later, phonographs, gramophones, radios, and telephones were installed. Television programs were first broadcast in the 1930s. Synthetic materials such as plastic (1909) and nylon (1930s) were invented. Robots and computers arrived around 1970.

The first electric iron (1881) had a heating plate that used the principle of electric resistance.

Early household appliances

The sewing machine was invented in 1846 by the American Elias Howe. In 1851 Isaac Singer perfected this invention and founded a company in New York that still bears his name. The electric vacuum cleaner was invented in 1901. The blender dates back to 1910, and the electric tea kettle and hair dryer were patented at the beginning of the century. Electric refrigerators were introduced around 1920.

Domestic conveniences
1. manual typewriter
2. toilet bowl with flushing system
3. running hot and cold water
4. gramophone (early record player)
5. vacuum cleaner
6. telephone
7. electric light
8. iron
9. sewing machine

Radio – Heinrich Hertz produced the first radio waves artificially in the late 1800s. Italian scientist Guglielmo Marconi, at 22 years old, sent a radio signal that was detected more than a mile away. Marconi received the Nobel Prize for physics in 1909. In 1924 he transmitted a radio wave from England to Australia.

Phonograph – Thomas Edison invented the first phonograph in 1877. It used a needle that ran in the grooves of a cylinder. The first record was made in 1887 by Emile Berlin. The early phonographs had to be cranked by hand.

Telephone – The first transmission of sound by electricity was made by the American Page in 1837. Bourseul in France (1854) and Reis in Germany pursued similar experiments, but Reis succeeded in sending only musical sounds. Alexander Graham Bell was the first to send a human voice over the wire and demonstrated his device in 1875.
Today, telephones are linked by cable, while intercontinental communications take place via satellite. *Cellular phones* with no cord communicate with a radio relay station. The *modem* is a device that connects computers through the telephone lines. The *fax* machine, which is used to transmit copies of printed documents, also uses the telephone line.

Television – Televisions work today thanks to an invention by Braun made in 1897: the picture tube, later improved and replaced by the cathode-ray tube. The TV antenna receives electromagnetic waves and sends the signals to the television. Inside the cathode-ray tube, an electron beam hits the screen, which illuminates and reproduces the images transmitted.

Computer – Personal computers experienced a boom in the seventies after the invention of tiny electronic components called *chips* that were able to contain a great amount of data.

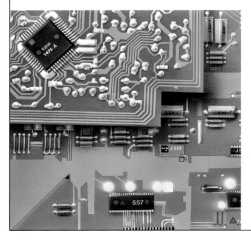

A chip made of semiconductor material (usually silicon) upon which integrated electrical circuits are printed.

COMPUTERS, ELECTRICITY, INFORMATION SCIENCE, SCIENTISTS AND INVENTORS

HUMAN ANCESTORS

primitive skulls

Homo habilis, who made stone tools, lived in East Africa about 2 million years ago. *Homo erectus* walked upright, made fires and hunted in groups. Then, *Homo sapiens* appeared. Among this group were the Neanderthals (about 60,00 years ago), who lived in caves, hunted big game with spears and buried their dead; then the Cro-magnon (about 35,000 years ago), our direct ancestor, who perfected hunting weapons and used tools made from bone. Human beings began living in villages around 13,000 years ago and began farming around 10,000 years ago.

By the time humans appeared, dinosaurs had already disappeared from the earth, but primitive people had to defend themselves from large mammals like mammoths and saber-toothed tigers.

Cro-magnons were probably the first to make cave drawings.

Village life
1. Farming. 2. Tanning hides. 3. Making pots out of clay and baking them in ovens. 4. Spinning and weaving wool. 5. Raising animals. 6. Celebrating religious rites and dancing.

(cont'd)

Hunting – Hunting large animals like the buffalo was done in groups with spears and traps. Primitive people learned to use all the parts of the animal: the meat was eaten, the fur was used for warmth, the hide for clothes and the fat was used for fuel. The bones were carved to make tools and also served as support in making tents and huts.

Capturing a buffalo.

ARTISTS
DWELLINGS
FASHION
PREHISTORIC INVENTIONS

Prehistoric children
Young boys learned to catch animals and shoot with a bow and arrow. Girls were taught how to weave baskets, make clay pots and pick wild fruits.

Village life
7. Fishing. 8. Building wooden boats. 9. Dying cloth.
10. Preparing cheese. 11. Building new huts of wood and straw.
12. Pressing grapes. 13. Casting metal. 14. Washing clothes.

THE HUMAN BODY

Our body is made up of parts that work together in perfect harmony, just like a machine. Each part carries out a precise function and interacts with the others. The human body is made up of more than 50 billion living organisms called *cells*. There are several types of cells. Cells that carry out the same function group together to form tissues (such as nerve tissue). Tissues group together to form *organs* (such as the heart, liver, and lungs). Organs that work together make up *systems* (such as the digestive system) and are controlled by the brain.

Heart – This fist-sized muscle works like a pump and sends blood to all parts of the body. The heart is divided into four chambers: the top ones are called *atriums* and the bottom ones are called *ventricles*.

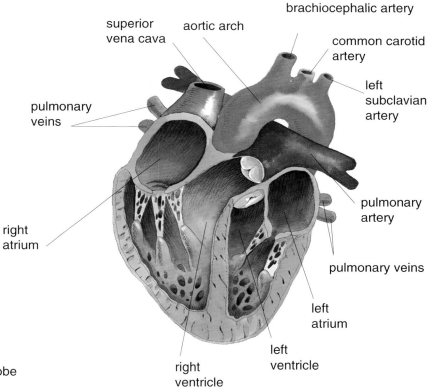

superior vena cava

aortic arch

brachiocephalic artery

common carotid artery

left subclavian artery

pulmonary veins

right atrium

pulmonary artery

pulmonary veins

left atrium

left ventricle

right ventricle

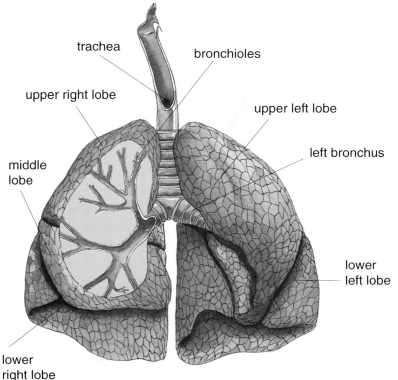

trachea

bronchioles

upper right lobe

upper left lobe

middle lobe

left bronchus

lower left lobe

lower right lobe

Lungs – Our body breathes about 1.5 gallons of air (7 liters) per minute. When we breathe, air enters the nose or mouth and passes through the *pharynx* and *larynx*. It enters the *trachea* and passes down the *bronchi* to the *bronchioles*. Here, tiny sponge-like sacs called *alveoli* are filled with capillaries: this is where the blood absorbs oxygen and releases carbon dioxide.

The Digestive System – This system — formed by the *mouth, salivary glands, pharynx, esophagus, stomach, small intestine, large intestine, liver,* and *pancreas* — digests food. Chewed food travels from the mouth down through the esophagus and reaches the stomach, where gastric juices turn the food into pulp. After two or three hours, food passes from the stomach into the intestine.

Intestine – The intestine is a tube that loops through the abdomen. The first part is called the *small intestine.* Here, *bile* and *pancreatic juice,* which are produced by the liver and pancreas respectively, help transform food into liquid. Then nutrients pass through the wall of the intestine and into the bloodstream. Undigested solid waste is eliminated through feces, which accumulate in the *large intestine* and are expelled through the rectum.

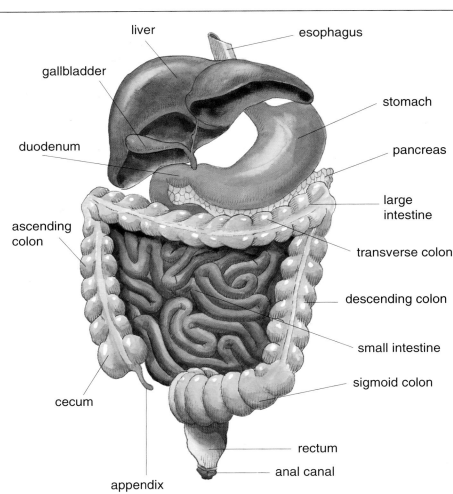

liver
esophagus
gallbladder
stomach
duodenum
pancreas
large intestine
ascending colon
transverse colon
descending colon
small intestine
sigmoid colon
cecum
rectum
anal canal
appendix

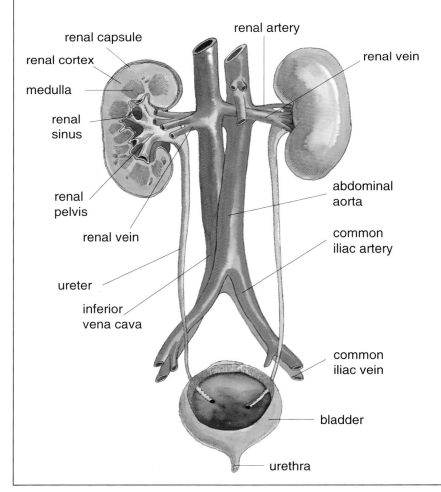

renal capsule
renal artery
renal cortex
renal vein
medulla
renal sinus
renal pelvis
renal vein
abdominal aorta
ureter
common iliac artery
inferior vena cava
common iliac vein
bladder
urethra

Urinary System – The urinary system is made up of the *kidneys, ureters, bladder,* and *urethra.* It eliminates the body's liquid wastes. *Kidneys,* which are about 6 in (15 cm) long and shaped like a bean, filter the blood and get rid of waste in the form of urine. Urine then accumulates in a little sac called the bladder before it is expelled by the urethra.

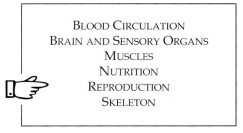

BLOOD CIRCULATION
BRAIN AND SENSORY ORGANS
MUSCLES
NUTRITION
REPRODUCTION
SKELETON

INDIA

Groups of farmers first settled down in the Punjab (northwest India and Pakistan), the fertile land of the five rivers, in the 4th millennium B.C. These groups were the  ancestors of civilizations that later developed along the great Indus and Ganges rivers. The dynasties that followed had to cope with constant invasions and partitions of their land. The Persians, ruled by Darius I (522–486 B.C.), annexed northwest India; Alexander the Great (327–325 B.C.) in turn reached the Indus Valley and took control of the Punjab. During the Gupta dynasty, in the 3rd century, arts and literature flourished in what is now considered the classic era of India. In the 4th century, the Gupta empire was broken up by the Huns, who threatened to destroy the unity of India.

Flooding – Indian land was rich and fertile. But frequent floods often destroyed crops.

Luxury – The *rajahs*, or princes, backed by the military caste, lived in ornate palaces (below). The *brahman* or priest caste was also very powerful.

Right: An Indian prince on horseback.

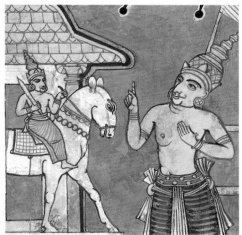

Spirituality – The Indian civilization has made important contributions to the worlds of religion and literature. Buddhism and Hinduism developed in India. Epic poems such as *Ramayana* and *Mahabharata* were written in India, and the oldest collection of stories in the world, *A Thousand and One Nights*, supposedly comes from India.

ALEXANDER THE GREAT,
BARBARIANS, BUDDHISM,
GANDHI,
HINDUISM,
PERSIA

INFORMATION SCIENCE

This is the study of electronic technologies for collecting, storing, processing and communicating information or data.

Apple Computer Inc.: a U.S. computer corporation founded in California by S. Wozniak and S. Jobs. They produced the *Apple* in 1977. After Apple II's success, the company began production of the *Macintosh* computer.

Artificial intelligence: an area of information technology that aims to produce computers that can think like human beings so that they can carry out sophisticated tasks otherwise done by humans.

BASIC: a computer programming language.

Bit: a basic unit of measurement for information stored in computer systems.

Byte: a group of eight bits treated as a single unit.

Clicking: to select an option on the computer screen by pressing a button on the mouse.

Codify: to organize data in a systematic way.

Compact Disc (CD): a plastic disc covered with reflective material. It stores digital data that can be read by optical devices (laser) that turn the data into audio, video, or computer signals. The *CD-ROM* (Compact Disc Read Only Memory) is a CD that can contain a huge amount of data due to greater data compression. It can also reproduce sounds and pictures.

Computer virus: a program that can damage or destroy a computer's memory if it enters the system.

CPU (Central Processing Unit): the box that contains all the electronic components used to make the computer work.

Cursor: a moving point on the screen that indicates where the next operation will take place or where a character can be inserted or changed.

Data bank: a large amount of information stored in files that can be accessed by computer.

Database: a collection of related data files that can be accessed with a specific program.

Digital: data codified according to the binary digit system.

Diskette: a magnetic disk used to store data. When the diskette is in the disk drive, information can be consulted, stored or modified.

E-mail (electronic mail): a service that lets people exchange documents or messages through a computer network like the Internet.

Fax: abbreviation for *facsimile*; a telecommunications process that lets you transmit documents and pictures across the telephone line, from one fax machine to another.

File: contains data grouped together under a single name. Files are kept on the hard drive or on diskettes.

Floppy disk: a flexible magnetic disk that is used by some computer systems to record and store data.

Hard drive: an internal information storage device that serves as the computer's memory.

Hardware: all the physical parts of the computer: microchips, hard drive, scanner, etc.

Hypertext: a system that lets the user access information according to pre-established paths or links, by clicking, for example, on underlined keywords.

IBM (International Business Machines): a U.S. company founded in 1911 by T. J. Watson. It began producing electronic calculators in the 1950s and later moved on to large mainframe computers. IBM began selling PCs, personal computers, in the 1970s.

Input: data entered in a computer.

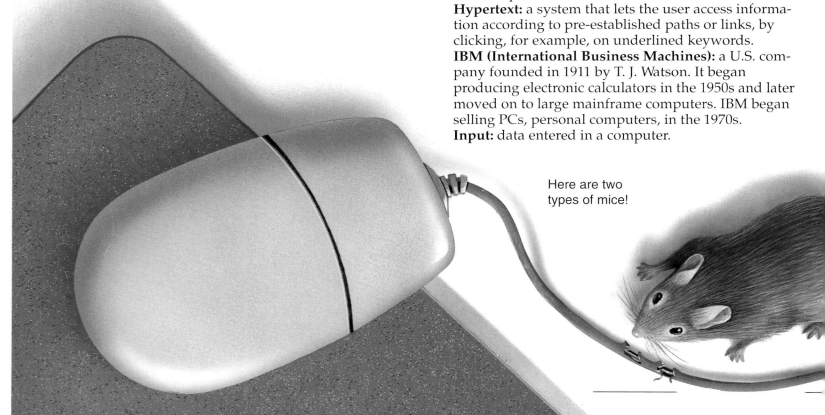

Here are two types of mice!

Interface: a device that connects the CPU to other pieces of hardware so that they can exchange data.

Internet: an information network (the *Information Highway*) made up of numerous data banks that offers access to all sorts of information and provides an E-mail service.

Keyboard: a device with alphanumerical keys used for typing or giving commands to the computer.

Megabyte: a unit of measurement of the computer's memory or storage capacity, equal to 1,048,576 bytes.

Memory: a fundamental component in the computer that records and stores information either permanently *(ROM)* or temporarily *(RAM)*.

Microchip: a tiny but very powerful electronic component used in computers.

Modem: a device that lets two computers connect with each other and transmit data over the telephone lines.

Monitor: the computer screen that displays images or texts.

Mouse: a device linked to the computer that moves over a flat surface to designate a point on the screen.

Multimedia: a data system that lets you simultaneously use several media: text, images, animation, sound.

Operating system: the basic software of a computer that lets it use application programs. DOS, OS, UNIX, and Windows95 are operating systems.

Output: data processed by a computer and sent to an output device (such as a printer).

Password: a secret word that must be typed in order to access a certain network, program or file.

Peripheral: a device connected to the computer through an interface. The printer, keyboard and screen are peripherals.

Printer: a machine that prints the documents prepared by the computer. Printers can be dot-matrix, ink jet, or laser.

Program: a sequence of instructions that tells a computer how to perform a specific task.

Programming language: a set of codified symbols used to write computer programs (*BASIC* and *COBOL* are computer programming languages).

RAM (Random Access Memory): the part of the computer memory that temporarily stores data.

ROM (Read Only Memory): part of the computer memory that permanently stores data. You can consult the data but it cannot be changed.

Scanner: an electronic device that reads text and images and stores them as data so that they can be reproduced.

Screen: see Monitor.

Software: the programs used by a computer. Each one has a specific use: word processing, accounting, drawing, etc.

Type: to write a text or command using the keyboard.

Video game: an electronic game.

Virtual Reality (VR): a technique that lets you simulate reality with devices (gloves, helmet, suit) provided with sensors and connected to a computer. When you use these devices, you can enter a virtual world and interact with it.

Voice processing: lets you communicate with your computer by talking.

☞ COMPUTERS

INSECTS

There are more than one million species of insects divided into *Apterygota* (without wings) and *Pterygota* (with wings). These two groups are in turn divided into 26 orders, including *Coleopterans* (beetles, ladybugs), *Hymenopterans* (bees, wasps, ants), *Lepidopterans* (butterflies and moths).

Bee

Wasp

The female wasp has a poisonous stinger that it uses to attack. In contrast, bees only sting when they feel threatened.

Dragonflies can fly for hours without stopping to rest. Their eggs are deposited on the bottom of fresh water ponds.

Anatomy – Insects are invertebrates. They have a head (1), thorax (2), abdomen (3), antennas (4), eyes (5), six legs, and often two pairs of wings. Their body is covered with a hard substance called *chitin*.

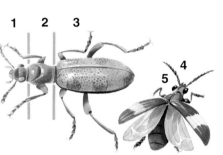

1   2   3

5   4

Ladybug – This insect is very useful to gardeners and farmers because it eats aphids harmful to plants.

Ladybug

Tsetse fly

Feeding – Insects eat all sorts of food: wood, nectar, blood, paper, other insects, etc. The structure of an insect's mouth depends on whether it bites, chews or sucks. Some have powerful jaws, while others have a long trunk.

Clothes-moth – This insect eats cloth. The females lay their eggs on the fabric so the larvae immediately find food when they hatch.

Diseases – Some insects transmit diseases: anopheles mosquitoes spread malaria, fleas spread infectious diseases, and tsetse flies in Africa spread the sleeping sickness.

Pollination – Insects carry pollen from the stamens of one flower to the pistil of another flower. At the bottom of the pistil is the ovary where the pollen fertilizes the eggs of the second flower to make seeds.

ANTS,
BEES, BUTTERFLIES,
FIELDS AND MEADOWS,
FLOWERS, SEEDS

ISLAM

The word *Islam* in Arabic means submission to Allah (God). Muslims, the followers of this religion, apply the laws that Mohammed, the Prophet, received from Allah. These laws are contained in a sacred book called the *Koran* that includes prophecies and practical rules for social and moral behavior. The Islamic calendar counts years starting from *Hegira*, the date when Mohammed fled from Mecca to Medina (622).

Arab artists only create abstract works of art because Islam prohibits the representation of living beings, humans or animals.

The Najaf-Al-Asraf mosque in Iraq.

ARABS, ARCHITECTURE, BUDDHISM, CHRISTIANITY, HINDUISM, JUDAISM, RICHARD THE LION HEARTED

Holy wars – According to the Koran, whoever dies fighting for Islam goes straight to Heaven. The followers of Mohammed therefore went on several holy wars, or *jihads*, to defend and promote Islam. They conquered lands in Asia, Africa, and Europe.

Mosques – These places of worship have a tall tower called a *minaret*. From this tower the *muezzin* calls the faithful to prayer five times a day. Muslims pray kneeling on the ground and facing in the direction of Mecca.

Each Muslim must go once in his life on a pilgrimage or *hadj* to Mecca, the holy city. This is where the *Kaaba*, the holy shrine containing the Black Stone (above), is found.

JAPANESE

According to legend, Jimmu Tenno, descendant of the Sun Goddess Amaterasu Omikami, founded the Japanese empire in 660 B.C. Japan stepped up its relations with China in the 6th century, adopting its imperial policy and the Buddhist religion (552). The Japanese Middle Ages (1185–1615) were characterized by the many battles and feudal skirmishes between the *shogun* and *bushi*, which were different warrior castes. All ports except Nagasaki were closed to trade in 1633; this period of isolation lasted until 1854.

Shogun – This hereditary title disappeared at the end of the feudal period. The *shogun*, or great general, had extensive military and civil powers.

Ladies of the court wore wide pants and several kimonos, one on top of the other.

Samurai – This warrior from the feudal days pledged allegiance to his lord, the *daimyo*. Samurai warriors wore light armor made of metal or leather plates tied together with cords that gave them freedom of movement (right and above).

CHINESE, DWELLINGS, FASHION

JEWS

According to the Bible, Abraham, leading a tribe of shepherds, settled in the land of Canaan (today's Palestine) around 2000 B.C. His son Issac and grandson Jacob continued the lineage. Deported from the kingdom of Israel, the Israelites went to Egypt where they were treated as slaves until Moses led them to freedom around 1290 B.C. Over the centuries, the Jews suffered terrible persecutions and were forced to abandon their lands several times. The present-day state of Israel was founded in 1948.

Menorah, a candlestick with seven arms.

Left and below: the Romans destroyed Jerusalem and its Temple in 70 A.D.

Nomadic people – Hebrew tribes traveled with their herds in search of pasture. When they reached the fertile land of Canaan, the *Promised Land*, they became sedentary farmers — farmers who stayed in one place.

Exodus – Around 1290 B.C. Moses led the Jews out of Egypt, where they were slaves, towards the Promised Land. The journey took more than 40 years and was called the *Exodus*, which means *departure*. When the Jews finally reached Palestine, they became a powerful population under the reign of three great kings named Saul, David and Solomon.

Anti-Semitism – Hostility against the Jews, who had been persecuted for centuries, reached its apex between 1933 and 1945 when the German Nazis committed horrendous war crimes and exterminated more than six million Jews in concentration camps *(the Holocaust)*.

JUDAISM,
MESOPOTAMIAN
CIVILIZATIONS,
PERSIA, ROMANS

169

JOAN OF ARC

Joan of Arc was called the *Maid of Orléans* because of her heroism. Joan was born to a peasant family in France in 1412. As a child she was convinced that God had chosen her to free France from the English invaders. She was given a small army by Charles VII, heir to the throne, and headed off to the city of Orléans, which was besieged by the English. Joan was so courageous she inspired her army to victory and freed the city in 1429.

Joan of Arc was a young peasant girl born in the town of Domrémy.

After the victory at Orléans, Joan was greeted by a cheering crowd.

Coronation of Charles VII (below) – The victory in Orléans gave the French army new courage. Under Joan's command it freed other cities before arriving in Rheims, where Charles VII was solemnly crowned king of France (1429).

Condemned to the stake – After the coronation of Charles VII, Joan set out to free Paris with the support of the army and her fellow countrymen. Joan was wounded and forced to retreat. In 1430 as she tried to lift the siege of Compiegne, Joan was captured by the forces of Burgundy, who were English allies. She was thrown in prison, tried for heresy and witchcraft, and condemned to death. Joan was burned alive at the stake in the square of Rouen on May 30, 1431.

Patron Saint of France – Charles VII won back Rouen in 1450 and opened an investigation into Joan's trial. Pope Calixtus III reversed the charges and declared Joan innocent in 1456. She was proclaimed the Patron Saint of France in 1920.

Joan was wounded in battle at the gate of Saint Honoré during the attack on Paris.

WOMEN

JUDAISM

Three thousand years ago, when ancient people were *polytheists* (meaning they worshipped many gods), the Jews believed in a single God who created the universe. One day on Mount Sinai, God gave Moses the *Tablets of Law* upon which the Ten Commandments were inscribed.

Star of David

Judaism is based on reading and commenting sacred texts under the guidance of *rabbis*, the scholars of Jewish law. The *Torah*, the central document of the Jewish faith, contains 613 rules that concern everyday life. Jews meet to pray in places of worship called *synagogues*.

Menorah – The seven-armed candlestick called the *menorah* is a symbol of the ancient state of Israel. Since the Temple of Jerusalem was destroyed, the most sacred object in the Jewish liturgy is the roll containing the *Sacred Scriptures*, or Torah.

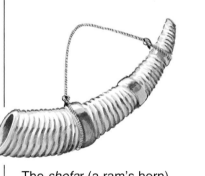

The *shofar* (a ram's horn) is blown during religious ceremonies such as *Rosh Hashana*, the Jewish New Year.

The Ark of the Covenant

God ordered Moses to build a wooden chest covered with gold (left) to hold the *tablets* bearing the Ten Commandments. The Ark was kept in a secret room in the innermost part of the Temple of Jerusalem.

Temple of Jerusalem

The Temple of Jerusalem was built by King Solomon around 1000 B.C. and later destroyed by Babylonian King Nebuchadnezzar. It was rebuilt and consecrated in 515 B.C., and enlarged by Herod the Great. The Temple was destroyed again in 70 A.D. by the Romans and only the *Wailing Wall* still exists today.

BUDDHISM
CHRISTIANITY
HINDUISM
ISLAM
JEWS

JULIUS CAESAR

Caesar was a Roman statesman and general (ca.100 B.C.–44 B.C.) who conquered territories ranging from Gaul, part of Brittany, as far as Egypt. In 59 B.C. he formed the *First Triumvirate* with Pompey and Crassus. When Crassus died, Pompey joined the Senate in plotting against Caesar. After many victorious battles against his enemies, Caesar was named dictator.

On March 15, 44 B.C., Julius Caesar was stabbed to death by a group of conspirators who feared that he would abolish the republic if he were crowned king.

In Rome, Caesar introduced grandiose projects, supervised administrative matters, and reformed the annual calendar. He was also an outstanding writer: he wrote *The Gallic Wars* (a commentary on events that took place from 58 to 52 B.C.) and *The Civil Wars* (about events that took place from 49 to 48 B.C.).

After Caesar's death, Cleopatra joined forces with Mark Antony, a Roman politician who was a member of the Second Triumvirate with Octavian (43 B.C.), to wage war on Rome. After the naval defeat in Actium (31 B.C.), Cleopatra committed suicide by letting herself be bitten by a poisonous snake.

Military victories – After the First Triumvirate was created, Caesar left Rome and set out to conquer Gaul. In 55 and 54 B.C. he organized two expeditions to Brittany, then repressed an insurrection led by Vercingetorix (right) in Gaul in 52 B.C. He returned victorious to Rome in 49 B.C. after defiantly crossing the Rubicon River with his army against the Senate's orders. In 48 B.C. he defeated Pompey at Pharsalus. Julius Caesar also helped Cleopatra regain the throne of Egypt.

EGYPTIANS
ROMANS
WOMEN OF HISTORY

KHAN, GENGHIS

The real name of Genghis Khan (ca.1155–1227) was Temujin. He was the son of a tribal leader of eastern Mongolia. In 1206 he reunited all the Mongolian tribes under his rule and was proclaimed *Genghis Khan*, which means Supreme Ruler. He died after a fall from his horse. After his death, wars of succession broke up his huge empire that stretched from the China Sea to the Caspian Sea and from the Persian Gulf to southern Siberia.

Conquests – Genghis Khan attacked Gansu and Manchuria. He broke through the Great Wall of China and besieged the city of Beijing, which he conquered in 1215. He also conquered Turkestan, Afganistan and all of Persia (1220–1221). His lieutenants Sabutain and Gebe raided the regions surrounding the Caspian Sea and took control of Georgia, the Caucasus and the Crimea. Genghis Khan died just when his empire had reached its peak of expansion.

Mongolian costumes during the time of Genghis Khan.

Genghis Khan chose Persian and Chinese officials to govern the empire because he respected their knowledge and culture.

CHINESE,
GREAT WALL OF
CHINA ✓

KNIGHTS

During the Middle Ages, knights and vassals lived in castles or fortified manors. During the induction ceremony, a young man was knighted after he pledged his devotion and loyalty and swore to protect his lord. Knights wore protective garments made of metal mesh. Starting in the 13th century, they wore shaped metal pieces that were connected with each other, including brassards (forearm guards), gauntlets (gloves), jambeaus (shin-guards), helmets, and cuisses (thigh guards). Knights wore a padded tunic underneath their suit of armor. Different suits of armor were used for jousting tournaments, parades, and battles.

Jousting tournaments were fake battles on horse. In the beginning they were used for battle training, then they became a form of entertainment for the King and his court.

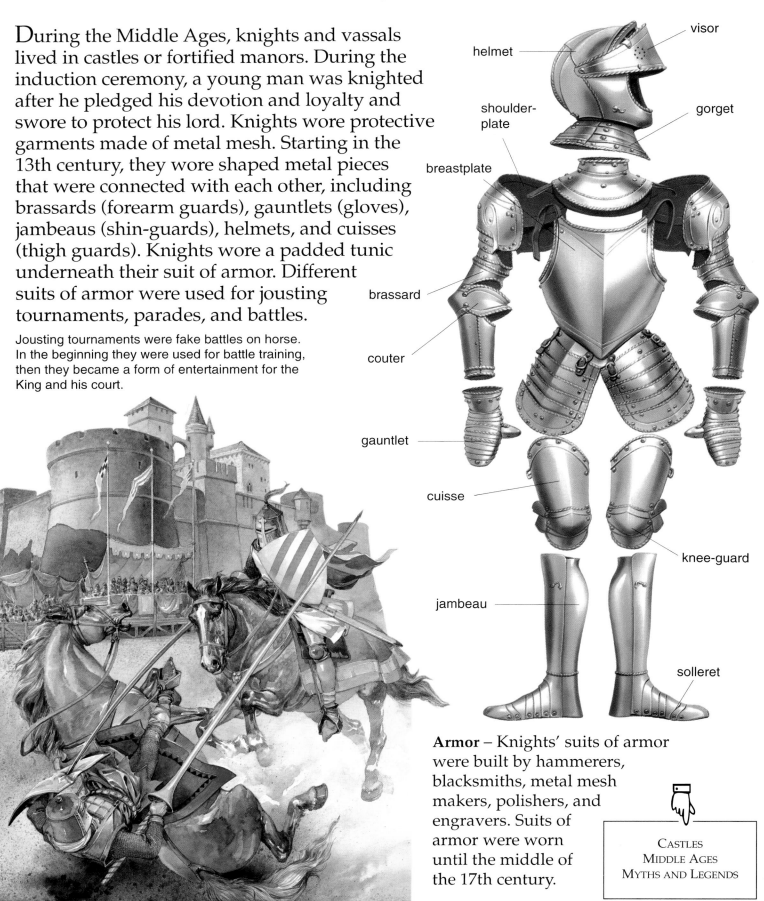

helmet · visor · shoulder-plate · gorget · breastplate · brassard · couter · gauntlet · cuisse · knee-guard · jambeau · solleret

Armor – Knights' suits of armor were built by hammerers, blacksmiths, metal mesh makers, polishers, and engravers. Suits of armor were worn until the middle of the 17th century.

CASTLES
MIDDLE AGES
MYTHS AND LEGENDS

LEONARDO DA VINCI

A self-portrait of Leonardo, born in the Tuscan town of Vinci in 1452.

Leonardo da Vinci (1452–1519) was first and foremost a Renaissance painter, but he was also known as a sculptor, military engineer, architect, musician, and inventor. He produced his early works in Florence, then worked for princes such as Ludovic the Moor, Duke of Milan. From 1515 to 1519, Leonardo da Vinci worked for the king of France, Francis I. He lived in the Cloux Castle near Amboise until his death.

Leonardo, who lived during a period of great turmoil, designed many war machines such as these early tanks.

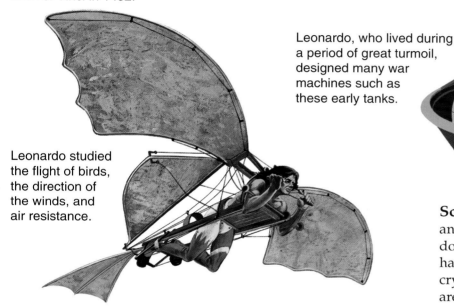

Leonardo studied the flight of birds, the direction of the winds, and air resistance.

Science – Leonardo studied anatomy, nature and the physical laws that govern it. His documents were written in a strange inversed handwriting, that seems to be some sort of cryptography. His drawings and manuscripts are contained in several anthologies: one of the most famous is the *Codex Atlanticus*.

Flying – Flying was Leonardo's dream. He designed many flying machines but was never able to build them because he didn't have an engine, the one thing that is indispensable for lifting a man off the ground.

Art – Leonardo's most famous painting is the *Mona Lisa* (1503–1506). Other masterpieces of his include *The Annunciation*, *The Lady with the Ermine*, *The Last Supper*, *The Battle of Anghiari*, and *The Virgin of the Rocks*.

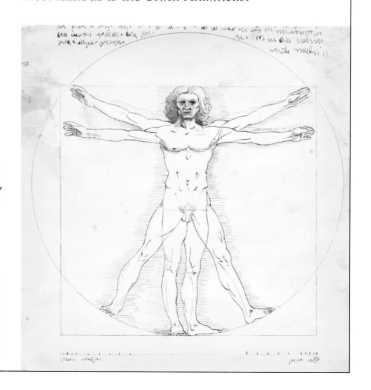

Leonardo understood the principle of the helicopter and designed a machine with a spiral propeller that could perform a vertical take-off.

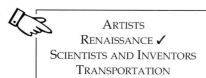

ARTISTS
RENAISSANCE ✓
SCIENTISTS AND INVENTORS
TRANSPORTATION

LINCOLN, ABRAHAM

Abraham Lincoln was born in 1809 in a log cabin in Kentucky. He was a self-taught man and became a lawyer in 1837. Lincoln, a Republican, was elected a member of Congress in 1847. He advocated *abolition* or the prohibition of slavery in the new Western territories. These ideas helped him win the election of 1860 and he became the 16th President of the United States.

The Civil War began in 1861. After a series of victories, the Confederate army of the South was defeated at Gettysburg, Pennsylvania in 1863. The Unionist troops from the North then won in numerous cities in the South, including Chattanooga and Savannah, Georgia in 1864. The Confederate army finally surrendered in 1865.

Secession – The economy in the North was mainly industrial, while in the South it was agricultural with slave labor. Lincoln's ideas on slavery contributed to the secession of the 11 Southern states that formed the Confederation. The Civil War between the North (the Union) and the South lasted 4 years. After the victory of the North, the states were reunited but tension between the two regions continued.

General Lee (above) surrendered on April 9, 1865 to General Grant.

A free country – Abraham Lincoln played an important role in United States history. He believed in freeing the slaves not only for humanitarian reasons but also for political and economic reasons. Lincoln laid the foundation for a free, modern nation.

Slavery was abolished in 1865 with the 13th Amendment to the U.S. Constitution.

Assassination – The political, economic, and social changes brought about by Lincoln (below) led to the secession of the Southern states (1861) and the Civil War. At the end of the war in 1865, Lincoln was assassinated by a fanatic, John Wilkes Booth.

HISTORY TIME LINES ✓
SLAVERY

LOUIS XIV

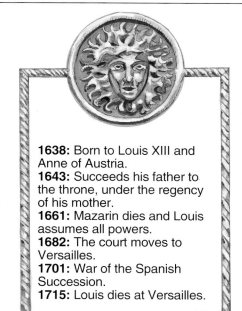

Louis XIV became king in 1643 when he was just 5 years old. His mother ruled on his behalf with the help of Cardinal Mazarin, advisor to the throne. When the cardinal died in 1661, Louis assumed all powers. The beginning of his reign was marked by several territorial conquests (Franche-Comté, Luxembourg, Strasbourg). At the end of the War of the Spanish Succession (1701–1714), however, France was left in ruin and England gained control of Europe.

A Louis XIV-style sofa.

1638: Born to Louis XIII and Anne of Austria.
1643: Succeeds his father to the throne, under the regency of his mother.
1661: Mazarin dies and Louis assumes all powers.
1682: The court moves to Versailles.
1701: War of the Spanish Succession.
1715: Louis dies at Versailles.

Louis XIV, also known as the *Sun King*.

Absolutism – When Louis XIV became king, he invested his throne with absolute powers: "I am the state!" he would boast. To better control the nobles, he obliged them to live at the royal court. His poor management and squandering of money caused a financial crisis: when the king died, the treasury of France was empty. The people's discontent would later end in revolution at the end of the century.

Versailles – In 1682 Louis XIV moved the court to Versailles, the splendid new palace built outside of Paris. The royal palace was surrounded by magnificent gardens, fountains, waterfalls and reflecting pools. Life at the court was lavish with many balls and outdoor festivities.

FRENCH REVOLUTION ☞

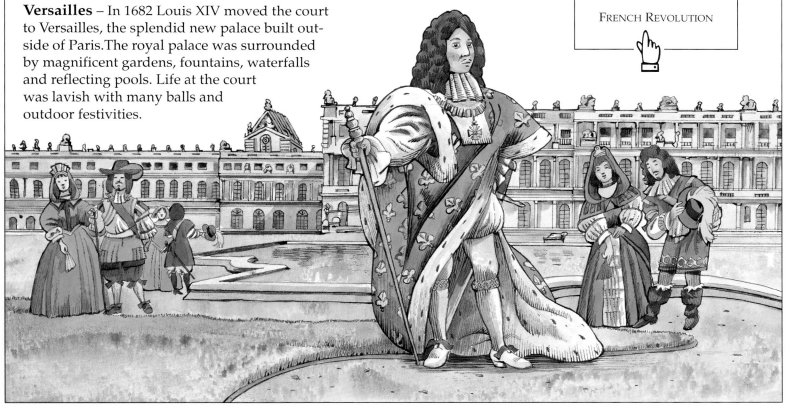

MAMMALS

Mammals are at the top of the evolutionary ladder. This class of vertebrates is made up of over 4,000 different species found around the world, with some mammals on every continent. Mammals are warm-blooded animals that breathe with their lungs and are covered with body hairs. Females have mammary glands that produce milk for their young.

Whale

Size – Mammals vary in size from one species to the next. The shrew, for example, is only 2 in (5 cm) long, while the whale can reach a whopping 100 ft (30 m). A lemur weighs about 2 oz (60 g) while a gorilla weighs over 500 lb (270 kg).

Humans are mammals: a baby grows inside its mother's body and after it is born it is breast-fed or fed milk from a bottle.

Fossils – Mammals are probably descendants of reptiles. Fossils found show that today's species of mammals started to evolve around the Eocene Epoch, about 65 million years ago.

Warm-blooded animals
The body temperature of mammals remains constant even if the surrounding temperature changes. This characteristic, shared by mammals and birds, is called *homeothermy*.

The kangaroo carries its baby in its pouch.

Marsupials – When they are born, these animals are not very well-developed and so must stay in their mother's abdominal pouch and suckle milk until they develop further. This order of mammals includes kangaroos, koalas and opossums.

Cats, dogs, monkeys and many other mammals are called placentals because the fetus is fed through the placenta inside the mother's uterus. Marsupials (kangaroo) and monotremes (platypus) are not placentals.

Suckling – A sow suckles her young for months before they are weaned (below). Whales, dolphins, narwhals, and sperm whales are all mammals that suckle their young.

ANIMALS OF AUSTRALIA, APES AND MONKEYS, BEARS, BOVINES, CATS, CLASSIFICATION OF LIVING THINGS ✓, DINOSAURS, DOGS, ELEPHANTS, FARM ANIMALS, GIRAFFE, HEDGEHOG, HIBERNATION, HORSES, MARINE MAMMALS, PETS, RACCOONS, RHINOCEROS, RODENTS, SQUIRRELS, TIGERS, WILDCATS, ZEBRAS

MAPS

Maps help us find our way about in unfamiliar territories. They also give us an idea of what a very large area looks like. Cartography is the science of making maps. To make them easier to read, all maps are made according to precise rules. For example, the territory is shown as you would see it from an airplane so that everything appears at the same distance. The *scale*, meaning the size of the drawing compared to the territory, is indicated on the map.

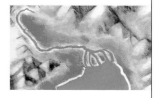

A detail of a physical map.

Political maps show each country in a different color.

Portuguese navigator Vasco da Gama (below) landed in the Indian port of Calicut in 1498.

Back in ancient times – The Egyptians used maps to determine boundaries that were periodically erased when the Nile River flooded its banks. Ancient maps were very inaccurate, however, because mapmakers thought the Earth was flat. The world was portrayed in a more precise way only in the 16th century, during the period of great explorations.

Above: an ancient map of the Americas taken from *Cosmographia universalis* (1541).

ARABS
EARTH
EXPLORERS
TIME ZONES

Symbols – Standard symbols are used to illustrate the physical and political details of the territory. A *key*, explaining the symbols, is found on the margin of the map.

Road map

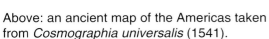
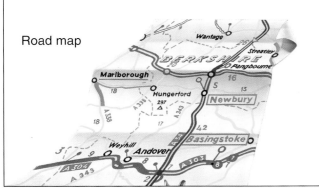

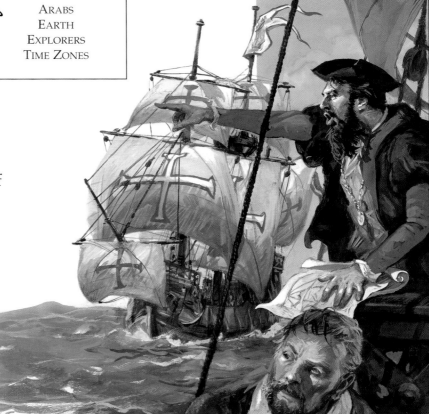

MARINE MAMMALS

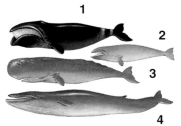

1. Right whale
2. California gray whale
3. Sperm whale
4. Blue whale

Whales, sperm whales, killer whales, and dolphins belong to the Cetacea order. They look like large fish (whales can be 100 ft/30 m long), but they are actually marine mammals. These mammals have flat, forked tails. Their rear limbs have disappeared and their front limbs have become pectoral fins. Some species of marine mammals, like sperm whales, can stay underwater for up to 75 minutes without breathing!

The young of marine mammals are suckled and stay with their mothers for a long time. Like all mammals, they have lungs and so must come up to the surface of the water to breathe oxygen.

fin whale

Dolphins – These mammals communicate with each other using a wide variety of sounds, some audible to humans and others at supersonic frequencies. Dolphins are very intelligent and playful animals that eat fish and mollusks.

sei whale

Killer whales – Killer whales are black with characteristic white markings behind the eyes, under the chin and on the belly. They hunt in small groups for dolphins, penguins, seals and even other whales. The male can be up to 30 ft (9 m) long.

killer whale

dolphin

Extinction – Whales used to be hunted for their blubber, teeth and flesh. But today many species of marine mammals are in danger of extinction and must be protected.

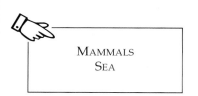

MAMMALS
SEA

MARSHLAND

Also called a swamp or bog, a marsh is a damp lowland region with reeds and aquatic plants growing in shallow water. Dragonflies and gnats fly directly above the water. Certain plants and animals are attracted to marshland. Many birds migrate to swamps and ponds to spend the winter. Many have webbed feet for swimming or long stilt-like legs for wading through water.

The white-tailed eagle has brown and white feathers and lives along the coast of seas, lakes and rivers.

Blue heron – Blue herons are wading birds that build nests in tall trees. In the spring the male engages in courting behavior to attract a female: he squawks, stretches his neck and clicks his beak.

eider

Storks – There are 17 species of storks. Many of them spend the winter in marshy areas in Africa. They are voracious omnivores. The African adjutant (far right) is native to Africa. It is 5 ft (1.5 m) tall.

1. shoveler
2. short-eared owl
3. night heron
4. osprey
5. mallard
6. reed sparrow
7. blackwinged stilt
8. great crested grebe
9. water rail
10. water vole
11. wild goose
12. common snipe
13. white-fronted goose
14. coot
15. European pond tortoise
16. blue heron

BIRDS, CROCODILES, MIGRATION, RAPTORS

MEDICINE

Primitive people used herbs and magic to try to cure sickness. In the 5th century B.C., Hippocrates laid the basis for modern medicine. Galen, in the 2nd century A.D., made discoveries by dissecting animals. By the 1600s, surgery and the understanding of the human body had greatly improved.

Right: Ancient surgical instruments (Egyptian, Roman, and Greek).

Above: Edward Jenner (1749–1823) discovered a vaccine for smallpox. Below: Jonas Salk discovered a vaccine for polio in 1955.

Progress – By the 9th century, the Arabs had developed a hospital system, but the first 'modern' hospitals appeared only 400 years ago. *Anesthesia* was discovered in 1842: patients would fall asleep after breathing ether. Unfortunately, surgery often failed because of infections. In 1865, Joseph Lister became the first surgeon to use a disinfectant.

BLOOD CIRCULATION, BRAIN AND SENSORY ORGANS, HERBAL MEDICINE, HUMAN BODY, MUSCLES, REPRODUCTION, SCIENTISTS AND INVENTORS, SKELETON

Louis Pasteur (1822–1895), a French chemist and biologist, laid the basis for bacteriology and created a vaccine for rabies in 1885.

French doctor Albert Schweitzer (1875–1965) founded a hospital in Africa, at Lambaréné (The Gabon). He received the Nobel Peace Prize in 1952.

Modern medicine

Use of synthetic drugs made in laboratories began in the 19th century. Christian Barnard, the South African surgeon, performed the first heart transplant in 1967. Today many organs can be transplanted: heart, lungs, kidney, bone marrow, cornea, etc.

MEDITERRANEAN CIVILIZATIONS

The Phoenicians founded the cities of Tyre, Sidon, and Byblos on the eastern Mediterranean coast. These excellent navigators and traders reached the Canary Islands and set up colonies in Spain and Africa. One of their many inventions is a purple dye, which was made from a shellfish called the *murex*.

Alphabet – Our alphabet derives from the Phoenicians. They replaced *ideograms* with pure *phonetic signs* that represented the sounds of spoken language. At the end of the 2nd millennium B.C., the Phoenician alphabet was made up of 22 consonant signs. The Greeks later developed it further and introduced vowels into the alphabet.

Above, a double-edged ax, the sacred symbol of the ancient people that lived on the island of Crete. The people of Crete were conquered by the Myceneans in 1450 B.C.

ALEXANDER THE GREAT
EGYPTIANS
MYTHS AND LEGENDS

According to Greek mythology, Thesus from Crete fought the Minotaur and managed to kill him.

MELVILLE, HERMAN

When American author Herman Melville (1819–1891) was a young lad, he worked on a whaling boat and traveled the seas. His masterpiece, *Moby Dick*, tells the story of the whale hunters off the coast of New England.

"Moby Dick tried to sink the boat, throwing it who knows where. Having missed its mark, it moved to the side, thrust its head beneath the keel and opened its huge mouth, almost as though it wanted to swallow the ship. When the jaws closed, the crew rolled to the stern and Captain Ahab fell into the water..."

MOBY DICK

"The day after, I went to the port and found out from the sailors that three whaling ships were ready to set sail for a three-year period: the *Devil Dam*, the *Tit-bit*, and the *Pequod* ... But once I boarded the *Pequod* I thought it was just perfect: not too large, but strong, sturdy, and agile. It was covered with thousands of hunting trophies. Whale jaws and bones decorated the walls and a huge whale mandible was used for the ship's rudder bar. I had already decided and sought out someone so I could enlist. A man was seated beneath the main mast. 'Are you the captain?' I asked hesitantly…"

"That captain was Ahab. He engaged in a courageous duel with Moby Dick, the white whale. Back then the whale's powerful jaws ripped off his leg..."

AUTHORS AND POETS,
CHILDREN'S
LITERATURE

MESOPOTAMIAN CIVILIZATIONS

The word Mesopotamia means *between two rivers*. This fertile land in western Asia that lies between the Tigris and Euphrates Rivers was the birthplace of ancient civilizations. The *Sumerian* civilization lived there around the 4th millennium B.C. The *Assyrian* civilization flourished in the Tigris Valley (where the city of Assur was erected) in the 2nd millennium B.C. and the *Babylonian* civilization developed in the Euphrates Valley (where the Tower of Babel was located). Babylonian king Hammurabi (1792–1750 B.C.) created the first code of laws and had them carved on a slab of black basalt (left). In the 8th century B.C. the Babylonians were defeated by the Assyrians, who were in turn conquered by Cyrus the Great of Persia in 539 B.C.

Sumerians – The Sumerians settled north of Mesopotamia near the Persian Gulf around the 4th millennium B.C. They were probably the first people to use the wheel. Sumerian war chariots terrorized enemy troops. This *Sumerian mosaic* (below) depicts soldiers wearing typical Sumerian leather helmets.

According to legend, the Tower of Babel (295 ft/90 m tall) was built to reach into Heaven. But God punished this arrogance by giving humans different languages so that they could not understand each other. Construction of the tower was abandoned.

Writing – The Sumerians invented cuneiform writing, using wedge-shaped signs pressed on a table of fresh clay. The Accadians (end of the 3rd millennium B.C.) developed this writing, and the Assyrian-Babylonians helped introduce it to other civilizations. Cuneiform writing, like Egyptian hieroglyphics, could not be considered a real alphabet because it was made up of *ideograms*, which are symbols used to express concepts.

A wooden wheel from a Sumerian chariot.

JEWS
PERSIA
PREHISTORIC INVENTIONS

THE MIDDLE AGES

The Middle Ages, also known as the Medieval Era, is said to begin in 476 with the fall of the Roman Empire and end in 1492 when Columbus discovered America. It is divided into the Early and Late Middle Ages (before and after the year 1000). A political, economic, and social system called *feudalism* developed during this period. The feudal lord gave his vassal a fief, which was the use of a piece of land, in exchange for his obedience and loyalty. Vassals in turn ruled over other minor vassals and serfs.

The castle was the center of activity during the Middle Ages. Above, Cinderella's castle in Disneyland.

Clothes were designed and made to last a lifetime. Some were so valuable they were inherited.

In the fields

The majority of peasants were serfs attached to the land they cultivated. They had no rights, only duties. The lord could give them away, along with the land they farmed.

serf

Artisans made up about half of the male population in the city. Those who practiced the same trade formed associations called *guilds*.

glass-blower

Protection

Protection – The castle was basically a tiny, self-sufficient village built to withstand a siege. In wartime, serfs and artisans would seek shelter within the castle walls and the feudal lord guaranteed their protection.

dyer

blacksmith

Medieval castle:
1. Loophole
2. Armory
3. Cellars and torture chamber
4. Storerooms
5. Castle kitchen
6. Cold storage room
7. Bedroom
8. Investiture hall
9. Chapel
10. Banquet hall
11. Bookkeeper counting gold coins
12. Scribe
13. Drawbridge

CASTLES
CHARLEMAGNE
FASHION
KNIGHTS

MIGRATION

Some species of insects, birds, fish, and mammals migrate in search of a more favorable climate and environment to survive and reproduce.

We can trace the migratory route of birds by attaching a ring around their legs.

Eurasian crane and bean goose
These are migratory birds. The Eurasian crane lives in Scandinavia and Central Europe, but is in danger of extinction. The bean goose, which has dark brown feathers and lives in the northernmost part of Eurasia, migrates south in the winter to coastal areas and river deltas.

Eurasian crane

bean goose

Migratory birds:	8. Scoter	17. Harrier
	9. Mute swan	18. Hawk
1. Tern	10. Coot	19. Swift
2. Curlew	11. Black-headed gull	20. Swallow
3. Heron	12. Turtledove	21. Stork
4. Skylark	13. Shearwater	22. Merganser
5. Pratincole	14. Arctic tern	23. Lapwing
6. Sheldrake	15. Goose	24. Bee-eater
7. Avocet	16. Plover	25. Night heron

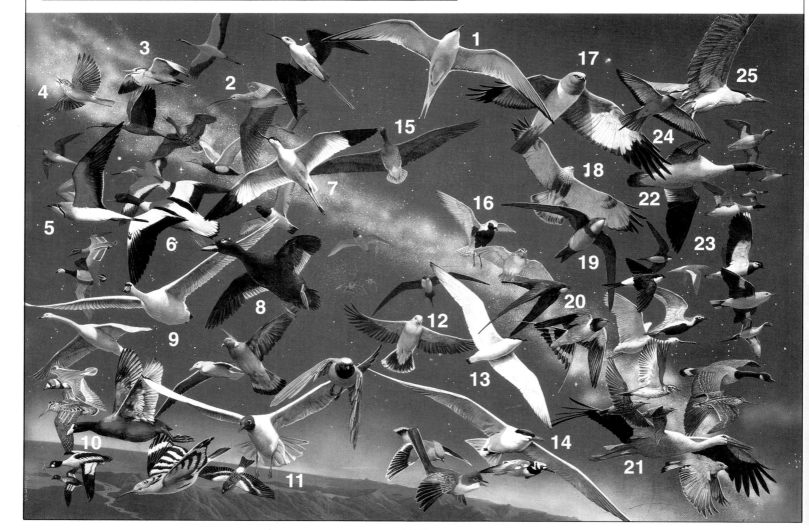

monarch butterfly

Butterflies
Some butterflies migrate huge distances. The monarch butterfly flies all the way from Canada to Mexico every winter.

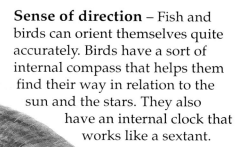

Sense of direction – Fish and birds can orient themselves quite accurately. Birds have a sort of internal compass that helps them find their way in relation to the sun and the stars. They also have an internal clock that works like a sextant.

swan goose

Swan goose – This bird has a long beak and a large bump on its forehead. Young geese grow very rapidly in just a few weeks. Also known as the Chinese swan, this bird is an excellent flyer and migrates in large flocks.

young larva

leptocephalus

elver

eel

Sardines migrate in large schools.

Salmon – This fish lives in large rivers during its youth then migrates towards the sea where it spends several years along the coast. It grows quickly and returns to breed in the fresh water river or stream where it was born. To do this, it must swim upstream, at times jumping 15 ft (5 m) into the air to get past dams.

A salmon swimming upstream.

Eel – This fresh-water fish is found in Europe and America. Once it has matured, it starts off on a long journey to reach the Sargasso Sea, in the north-east Antilles, where it breeds. The eggs hatch into larvae with a transparent body (*leptocephalus*) then become young eels called *elvers* that migrate towards river deltas and swim upstream where they will grow into adults.

The migratory route of eels.

Velella – This strange bluish jellyfish lives in the Mediterranean Sea and Atlantic Ocean, where a school of velellas 150 mi (250 km) long was once spotted. The velella travels long distances by raising a sort of transparent sail.

Birds, Butterflies, Fish, Marshland, Pelicans

MINERALS

Minerals are natural substances in a solid crystal state. Rocks are made up of several types of minerals, which together make up the Earth's crust. There are more than 2,000 known minerals, but only a few, like marble and quartz, can be found in their pure state.

Minerals are classified according to their color, hardness, *cleavage* (their tendency to break cleanly into smooth parts), and *malleability* (their capacity to be extended or shaped without breaking).

Classifications – One of the most common mineral classifications is the *Mohs Scale*, which is based on hardness: Talcum 1; Gypsum 2; Calcite 3; Fluorite 4; Apatite 5; Feldspar 6; Quartz 7; Topaz 8; Sapphire 9; Diamond 10. The pictures marked with an asterisk (*) are rocks.

Sulfur

Alabaster

Cinnabar

Fluorite

Flint*

Granite*

Clay*

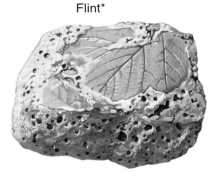
Travertine

Serpentine

Bauxite*

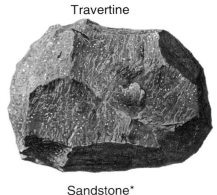
Sandstone*

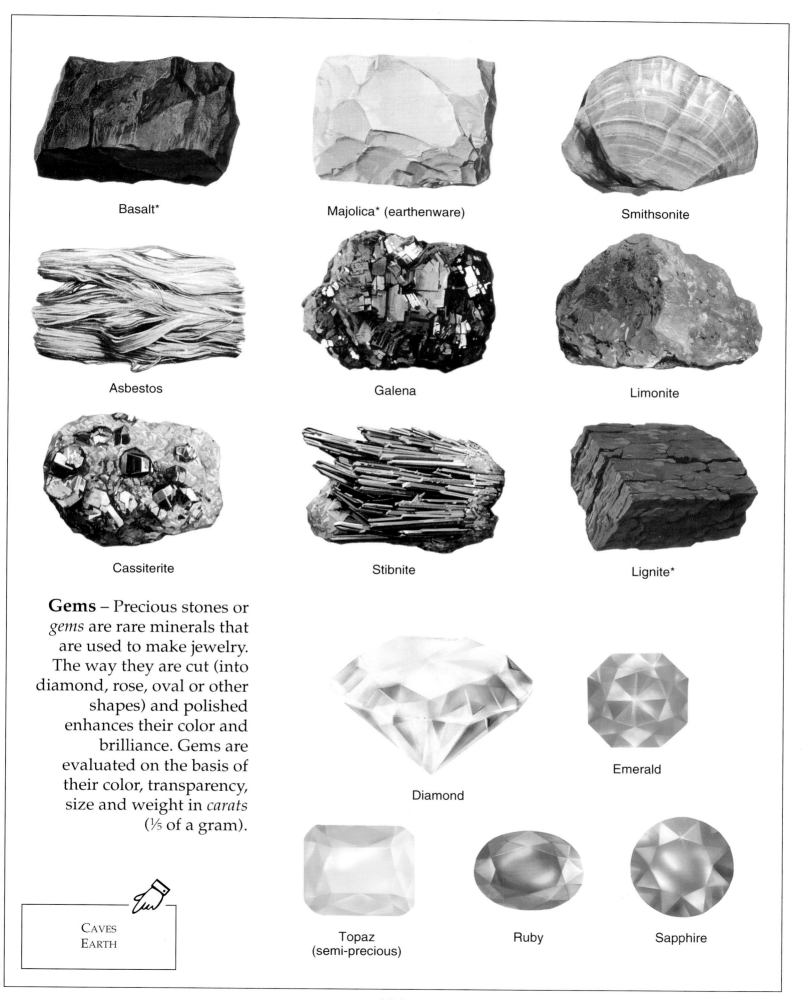

Basalt*

Majolica* (earthenware)

Smithsonite

Asbestos

Galena

Limonite

Cassiterite

Stibnite

Lignite*

Gems – Precious stones or *gems* are rare minerals that are used to make jewelry. The way they are cut (into diamond, rose, oval or other shapes) and polished enhances their color and brilliance. Gems are evaluated on the basis of their color, transparency, size and weight in *carats* (⅕ of a gram).

CAVES
EARTH

Diamond

Emerald

Topaz
(semi-precious)

Ruby

Sapphire

MONASTERIES

During the Middle Ages religious life centered around the monasteries. Monks lived and prayed in these communities. They also farmed and raised animals, grew medicinal herbs, and took care of the poor and ill. Some monks studied philosophy, grammar, rhetoric, mathematics, astronomy, and alchemy. Through these monks, culture was preserved and handed down through the centuries.

Libraries – The libraries of several monasteries contained valuable books saved from the destruction of barbarian invasions. In the silence of the *scriptorium*, scribes (above) copied books and decorated them with color miniatures.

The chapel was the heart of the monastery: monks met several times a day to pray.

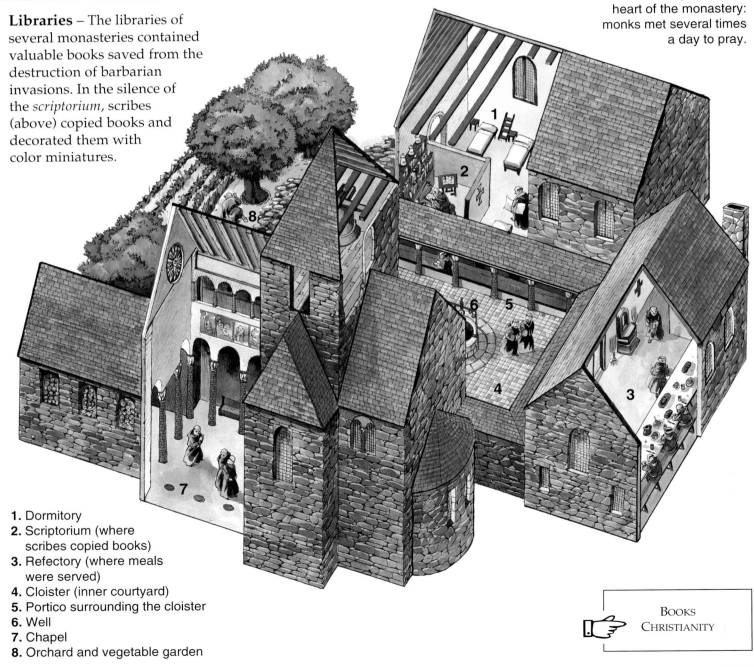

1. Dormitory
2. Scriptorium (where scribes copied books)
3. Refectory (where meals were served)
4. Cloister (inner courtyard)
5. Portico surrounding the cloister
6. Well
7. Chapel
8. Orchard and vegetable garden

BOOKS
CHRISTIANITY

MOON

The Moon is the Earth's natural satellite and is about 240,000 miles (380,000 km) away. It has always had a great influence over the Earth: tides are effected by the Moon's gravitational pull; in some countries farmers decide when to plant and harvest their crops according to lunar phases. In fact, the Moon has often been used to measure time. The Egyptian calendar was lunar, the Mayan and Chinese calendars were lunar-solar, and the Muslim calendar remains essentially lunar even today.

Before spaceships can reach the Moon, they must *orbit* or make at least one full rotation around the Earth.

The surface of the Moon – The Moon is covered with craters caused by the impacts of *meteorites*, which are large rocks hurtling through space. There are tall mountains and huge volcanic plains called *maria* or seas because that is what they were once thought to be. The temperature on the Moon varies greatly because the Moon has no atmosphere. The side that is lit by the Sun can reach almost 240°F (115°C), while the dark side plunges to -260°F (-160°C).

The surface of the Moon

Lunar phases – Depending on its position in the sky in relation to the Sun and the Earth, the Moon sometimes seems completely round (full moon). As the days go by, it moves towards the Sun and becomes less visible on Earth (waning moon) until it passes between the Sun and the Earth and disappears (new moon). Then a slim crescent moon appears and it expands until it becomes a large luminous sphere once again.

Moon landing
An American astronaut named Neil Armstrong was the first man to set foot on the Moon on July 21, 1969. This success was preceded by experiments with probes, radar, and a space lab that collected photographs, data and soil samples and sent them back to Earth. Today scientists are still studying the Moon (its geology, origin, etc.) but they have concluded that there is no life or atmosphere on the Moon.

According to Greek mythology, the Moon was a goddess called *Selene* who rode through the night upon a silver chariot.

ASTRONOMY
EARTH
SPACE TRAVEL

MOUNTAINS

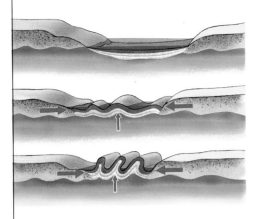

Land masses called *plates* collided during the Tertiary Era. They rippled and overlapped to form folds that were thousands of miles long (left). The oldest mountains (about 200 million years old) are smooth and rounded because they have been *eroded* or worn down by the wind, rain, snow, and ice. Newer mountains formed 50 million years ago have high, pointed peaks.

Records – The Rocky Mountains and the Andes (the world's longest mountain chain about 4,800 mi/ 7,600 km long) are the world's most important mountain chains that stretch through North and South America. The Himalayas, Alps, and Atlas Mountains cut across Asia, Europe, and northern Africa respectively. The tallest mountain peak in the world is Mount Everest (29,028 ft/8,848 m) in the Himalayas. Many tall peaks, such as Mount Kilimanjaro (19,340 ft/5,895 m) in Tanzania and Mount Fuji (12,385 ft/3,775 m) in Japan are volcanic mountains.

The faces of four American presidents (Washington, Jefferson, Teddy Roosevelt and Lincoln) are carved into the side of Mount Rushmore in South Dakota.

Above: a glacier.
The Hubbard Glacier in the Yukon/Alaska (about 94 mi/150 km) is the world's longest glacier.

Earthquakes – The Earth's crust is divided into several huge land masses, called *tectonic plates*. When these plates collide, they cause an earthquake that spreads through seismic waves. When they move apart, they can form a *fault*, like the San Andreas Fault in California, where the land moves 2 in (5 cm) every year. Since these plates are constantly moving, in a few million years, the position of the continents will have changed completely.

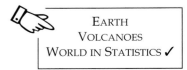

EARTH
VOLCANOES
WORLD IN STATISTICS ✓

MUSCLES

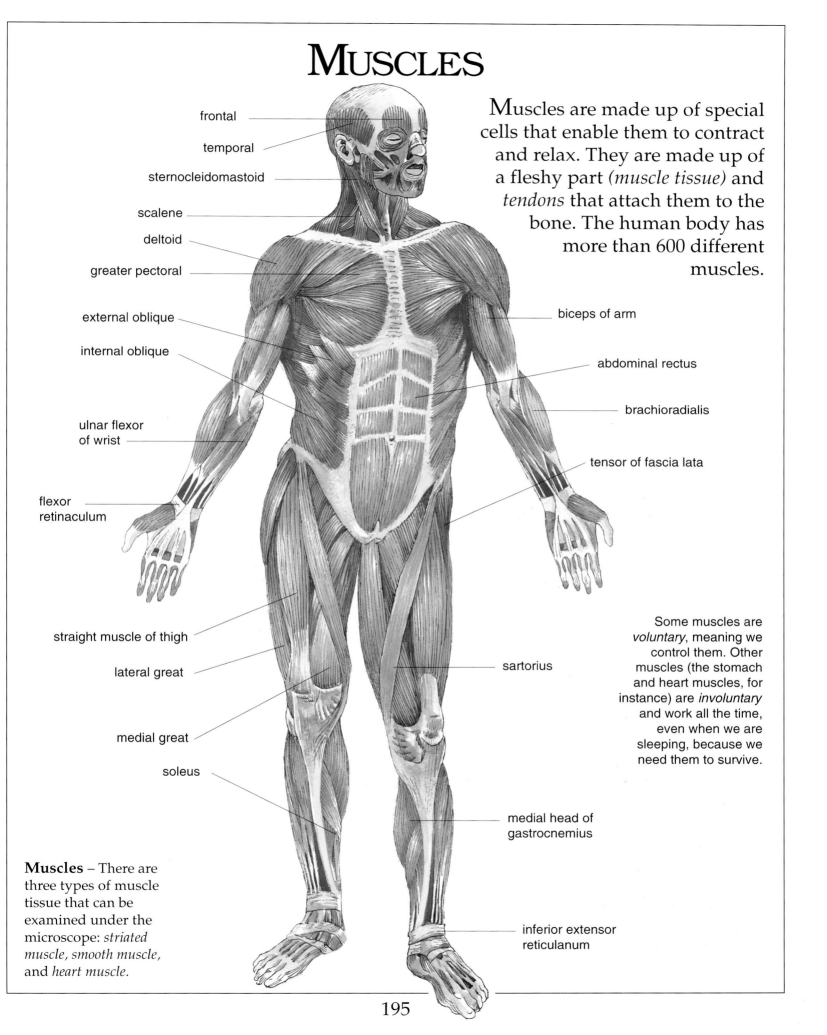

frontal

temporal

sternocleidomastoid

scalene

deltoid

greater pectoral

external oblique

internal oblique

ulnar flexor
of wrist

flexor
retinaculum

straight muscle of thigh

lateral great

medial great

soleus

Muscles are made up of special cells that enable them to contract and relax. They are made up of a fleshy part *(muscle tissue)* and *tendons* that attach them to the bone. The human body has more than 600 different muscles.

biceps of arm

abdominal rectus

brachioradialis

tensor of fascia lata

Some muscles are *voluntary*, meaning we control them. Other muscles (the stomach and heart muscles, for instance) are *involuntary* and work all the time, even when we are sleeping, because we need them to survive.

sartorius

medial head of
gastrocnemius

inferior extensor
reticulanum

Muscles – There are three types of muscle tissue that can be examined under the microscope: *striated muscle, smooth muscle,* and *heart muscle.*

195

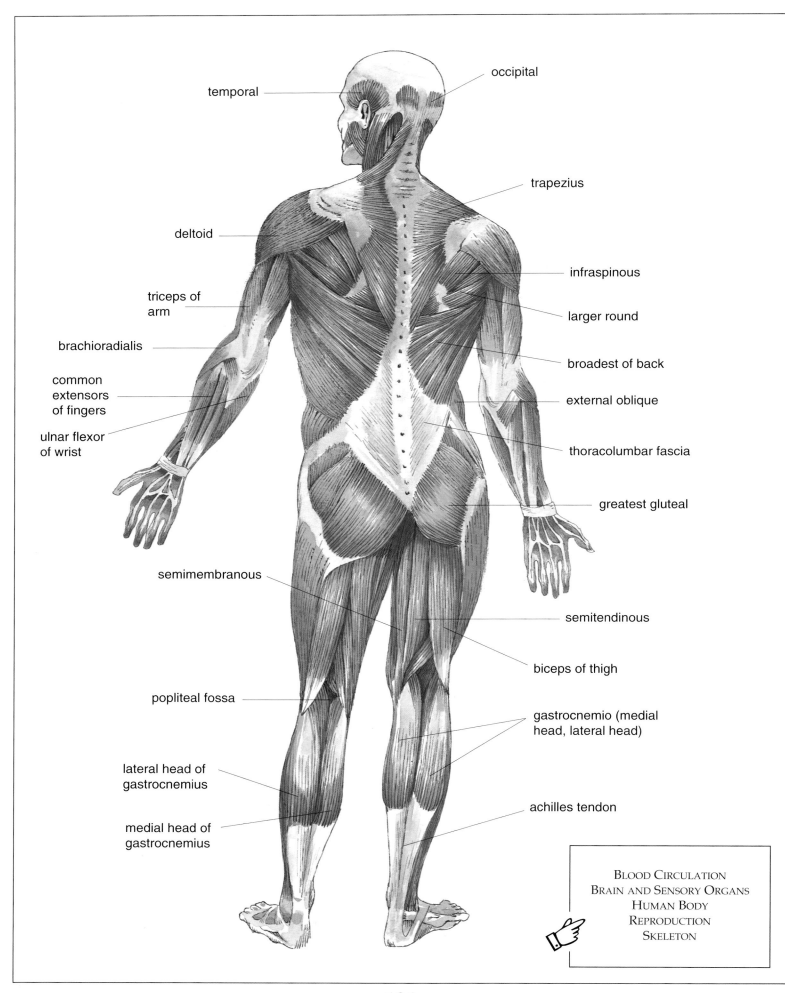

temporal

occipital

trapezius

deltoid

infraspinous

triceps of arm

larger round

brachioradialis

broadest of back

common extensors of fingers

external oblique

ulnar flexor of wrist

thoracolumbar fascia

greatest gluteal

semimembranous

semitendinous

biceps of thigh

popliteal fossa

gastrocnemio (medial head, lateral head)

lateral head of gastrocnemius

medial head of gastrocnemius

achilles tendon

BLOOD CIRCULATION
BRAIN AND SENSORY ORGANS
HUMAN BODY
REPRODUCTION
SKELETON

MUSHROOMS

Mushrooms are strange vegetables that have no chlorophyll. They grow rapidly in humid areas, under trees and in meadows. They have narrow, long filaments called *hypha* that live underground. The part we see above ground is only the fruit. Some mushroom cells contain a substance called *chitin* that is also found in the hard parts of anthropods (crustaceans, insects, spiders).

The part of the mushroom that appears above ground can grow overnight.

Poisonous mushrooms

Many mushrooms are edible, but some, such as the Amanita phalloides or death cap, are poisonous. That is why you should only pick and eat mushrooms you are familiar with!

parasol mushroom

tawny grisette

penny bun

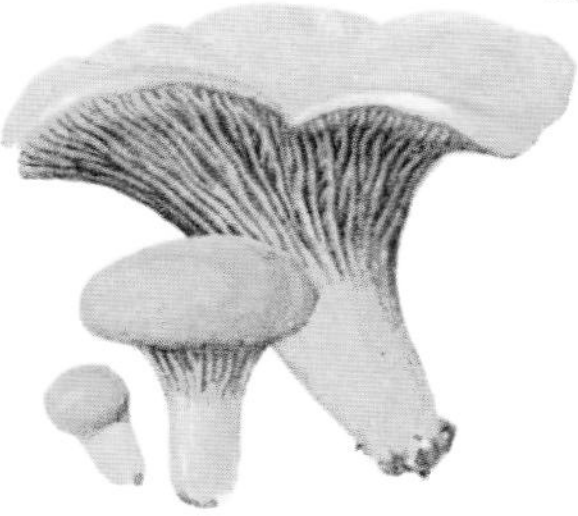

orange birch bolete

brown birch bolete

chanterelle

spindle shank

Warning! Fatal!
death cap

milk cap

Warning! Poisonous!
fly agaric

CLASSIFICATION
OF LIVING THINGS ✓,
NUTRITION

MUSIC AND MUSICIANS

Music dates back to prehistoric times when primitive people believed that it possessed magical powers. Music was used by ancient civilizations during social and religious ceremonies. Ancient Greeks used music to accompany poetry, dance, drama and gymnastic events. Early Christians developed the Gregorian chant (9th century). French troubadours wandered through western Europe in the 12th and 13th centuries singing their poems and stories. Opera originated in Italy in the 17th century.

The harp was played by Assyrians, Babylonians and Egyptians. It was first used by an orchestra in Monteverdi's opera *Orfeo* (1607).

Early records were made out of vinyl and turned at 78 revolutions per minute. They were replaced by forty-fives, then LPs (long-playing). Today we listen to compact discs.

Musical instruments

The first musical instrument was probably the drum. We classify all instruments into three groups: string, wind, and percussion. Today there are also instruments that produce music electronically.

Types of music – There are many kinds of music. Folk music derives from local traditions and differs in each country. Classical music originated in Europe in the 17th century. Pop and rock, which include ballads and fast dance music, emerged in the 1950s. Jazz and rhythm and blues have their roots in 20th century African-American music. Country and western music originated among poor white people in the American South in the early 1900s.

Johann Sebastian Bach (1685–1750)
A German composer and organist whose works include the six Brandenburg Concertos (1718–1721), *The Well-Tempered Clavier* (1722–1744), *The Art of the Fugue* (1748–1750) and *The Passion according to St. John* (1723).

J. S. Bach

George Frederick Handel
(1685–1759) – A German-born composer who moved to England in 1712. He wrote many operas and is chiefly remembered for his oratorios (semi-dramatic works for orchestra and voice). His most famous is the *Messiah* (1742).

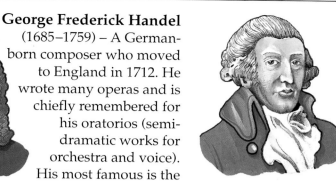

G. F. Handel

F. J. Haydn

Wolfgang Amadeus Mozart
(1756–1791) – An Austrian composer and child prodigy who started composing minuets at the age of four. Mozart died penniless at 35. His most famous works are *The Marriage of Figaro, Don Giovanni, The Magic Flute* and *Requiem*.

W. A. Mozart

Franz Joseph Haydn
(1732–1809) – An Austrian composer and teacher of Beethoven and Mozart. He wrote many string quartets and symphonies and represented the classical Viennese style.

L. van Beethoven

Franz Schubert (1797–1828)
An Austriain composer and a leading exponent of the romantic movement, he was the greatest composer of lieder, or German songs. He also wrote piano sonatas, chamber music and symphonies.

F. Schubert

Ludwig van Beethoven (1770–1827)
A German composer whose most important works are nine symphonies, especially the Third *(Eroica)*, Sixth *(Pastoral)*, and Ninth (with *Ode to Joy*). He also wrote many piano sonatas, including *Pathetique* and *Moonlight Sonatas*, and the opera *Fidelio*. Beethoven gradually lost his hearing and was totally deaf by 1819.

R. Schumann

Robert Schumann (1810–1856)
A leading German composer of the romantic period, he wrote sacred music, symphonies and chamber music.

Richard Wagner
(1813–1883)
A self-taught composer from the romantic period. His most famous opera is *Der Ring des Nibelungen*, a cycle of four operas based loosely on ancient German tales. He developed a genre he called music drama.

R. Wagner

Giuseppe Verdi
(1813–1901)
A great Italian opera composer who became famous in 1842 at La Scala in Milan with the opera *Nabucco*. Among his most famous operas are *Macbeth, Rigoletto, La Traviata, Il Trovatore, Aida, Otello* and *Falstaff*.

G. Verdi

Johannes Brahms (1833–1897)
A German composer and pianist, he was discovered by Schumann. A staunch defender of classical form, he helped renew the technique of composition. He wrote chamber music, symphonies, concertos and lieder.

DANCE, SYMPHONY
ORCHESTRA ✓

MYTHS AND LEGENDS

Since the dawn of time, humans have used myths to explain the creation of the Earth. The ancient Greeks believed in immortal gods and goddesses who lived on Mount Olympus. They personified natural elements and the vices and virtues of human behavior. Their adventures explained life and the mysteries of nature: for example, Uranus personified the sky, Athena personified war, and Aphrodite was the goddess of love.

Theseus, the son of Aegeus (king of Athens), managed to kill the Minotaur and escape from the labyrinth with the ball of string given to him by Ariadne, the daughter of Minos (king of Crete).

Mythological heroes
Besides the gods and goddesses on Olympus, ancient Greek myths told of *heroes*. These strong and courageous mortals founded cities and dynasties: Hercules was known for his twelve seemingly impossible labors, Jason and the Argonauts conquered the Golden Fleece, and Perseus killed Medusa, a monster whose head was crowned with writhing snakes.

1. Athena, the goddess of war
2. Apollo, the god of light, healing, music, poetry, prophecy and manly beauty
3. Zeus, the supreme god of Olympus

Arthur extracts the magical sword Excalibur.

Legends – Legends are stories handed down through the centuries that try to explain natural or historical events that are difficult to interpret. The legend of Narcissus is a good example. Narcissus was a handsome youth who fell in love with his own reflection in a stream. One day he was so mesmerized that he fell into the water and drowned. A flower later grew on the spot and was called *narcissus* or daffodil.

Merlin the Wizard

Knights of the Round Table – Many fantastic characters appeared in stories about King Arthur, including Queen Guinevere, Merlin the Wizard and Morgan le Fay, a healer and magician. The Knights of the Round Table, including the courageous Lancelot (below), accomplished legendary feats.

King Arthur – Legends of King Arthur of Britain have been told and retold for centuries: by the French, then the Celts and finally the English. According to the ancient story, young Arthur was crowned king after extracting the magic sword *Excalibur* from the stone. His court at Camelot was the setting for the Knights of the Round Table. When Arthur died, a hand emerged from the magical waters of a lake, and disappeared with Excalibur.

NAPOLEON BONAPARTE

A brilliant military strategist, Napoleon led the French army in Italy in 1796. He tried to create an empire overseas but was defeated by the English admiral Nelson in 1798. He returned to France, overthrew the government in power and became supreme ruler, assuming the title of First Consul. After declaring himself emperor in 1804, he began to reorganize the French legal and education systems. Abroad, he began the Napoleonic Wars, which lasted from 1800–1815.

Napoleon's coat of arms

Emperor – Napoleon was crowned emperor in 1804 in the Notre Dame Cathedral in Paris. During the coronation ceremony he took the crown from the hands of Pope Pius VII and placed it on his own head.

1769: Born in Corsica.
1793: Drives the British from Tolon.
1794: Brigadier general, arrested then released.
1796: First campaign in Italy.
1800: Becomes First Consul.
1804: Declares himself emperor.
1805: Loses Battle of Trafalgar.
1812: Loses battle in Russia.
1814: Exiled to the island of Elba.
1815: Returns to power, defeated at Waterloo.
1821: Dies in exile in St. Helena.

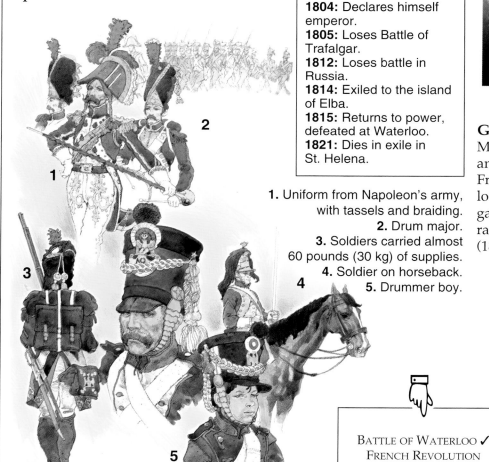

1. Uniform from Napoleon's army, with tassels and braiding.
2. Drum major.
3. Soldiers carried almost 60 pounds (30 kg) of supplies.
4. Soldier on horseback.
5. Drummer boy.

Napoleon on Horseback by J. Chabord

Great battles – Napoleon was victorious at Marengo (1800), Austerlitz (1805), Jena (1806) and Wagram (1809), thus establishing a French empire from Spain to Poland. But he lost the batttle at Aboukir (1798) and Trafalgar (1805), where he was defeated by Admiral Nelson. He also lost battles in Russia (1812), Leipzig (1813) and Waterloo (1815).

After the defeat at Waterloo, Napoleon was exiled by the English to St. Helena, a small island in the Atlantic Ocean, where he died in 1821.

BATTLE OF WATERLOO ✓
FRENCH REVOLUTION

NATIVE AMERICANS

When Christopher Columbus came to America, he called the native people there Indians because he mistakenly thought he had reached the Indies. Years ago settlers used to call these indigenous people redskins because some tribes painted their faces with red ochre. Today we use the term American Indians or Native Americans. Canadians also use the term First Nations. The economy of American Indians was mainly based on farming and hunting animals, especially the buffalo. Every part of the buffalo was used: the meat served as food, the hide was used for clothing, shields, and tents, and the buffalo tendons were used for thread and for making bows for arrows.

The Iroquois lived north of Lake Ontario, Lake Erie and and Lake Huron and also in the Saint Lawrence Valley.

Beliefs – Native Indians share a belief in The Great Spirit, the creator of all living things, whose vital force is called *mana*.

A totem pole (right), carved with human and animal shapes, was a symbol that represented a clan's ancestors. They were common among Indians in the northwest.

Below: a Cheyenne chief

Indian dwellings – Native Americans in the East lived in rectangular houses, while those in the West had tents, or teepees. Teepees were supported by about a dozen long poles that crossed at the top and were firmly planted in the ground in a circle. This structure was covered either with animal skins or birch bark, and an opening was left at the top so smoke could escape. Teepees were simply decorated: furry buffalo skins were laid out on the ground and used as beds.

Tribes – Each native tribe, or band, had a distinct culture, language, and set of traditions. The tribe was broken down into clans whose members were related. Clan members helped each other. Warriors had the right to join the council, which governed the tribe and made decisions.

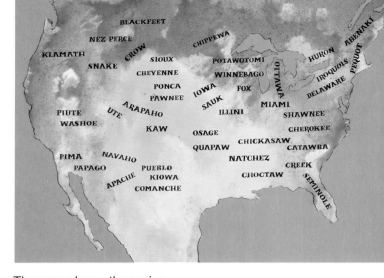

The map shows the major tribes in the United States and Canada.

AMERICA,
CHRISTOPHER
COLUMBUS,
WILD WEST

From top to bottom:
Sioux
Cheyenne
Apache
Sauk
Chicasaw
Iroquois

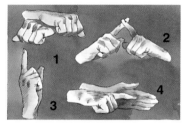

Sign language was used to communicate between different language groups. Here are some examples:
1. Prisoner.
2. Camp.
3. Wait for me.
4. Follow me.

Indian wars – When the American settlers began conquering the Western territories, some Native Americans went to war to defend their lands. Indian chiefs such as Red Cloud, Crazy Horse and Sitting Bull won a few battles (Fort Kearny, 1868; Little Big Horn, 1876), but the American army, led by Generals Sherman and Sheridan, was more powerful. After the Battle of Washita (1868) against the Cheyenne and the Battle at Wounded Knee (1890) against the Sioux, Native Americans were forced to live on reservations.

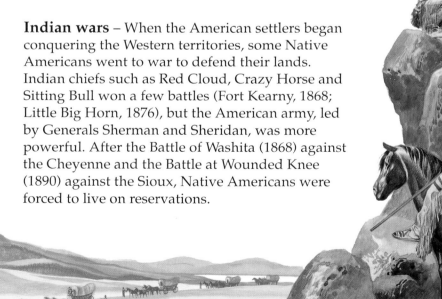

NEW WORDS

Animals communicate using sound and gestures, but we humans are the only creatures that use language. There are over 5,000 in the world, along with many dialects. Languages undergo constant change, and in the 20th century it has been English, more than any other language, that has added to the world's vocabulary. Here are some words commonly used around the globe. You will notice that many are from the entertainment industry.

Anchorman/anchorwoman: the person who reads the news on TV.

Art director: an artist in an advertising agency who supervises the artistic development of all advertising materials.

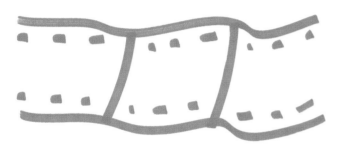

Audience: people who attend a live performance on stage, watch a TV program, or listen to a radio program.

Background: cultural and professional experience.

Best-seller: a very popular book.

Broadcast: a program transmitted by radio or television.

Budget: an amount of money set aside for a specific project.

Business: commercial, industrial or professional dealings.

Cable TV: television programs transmitted by cable to subscribers.

Cameraman: the person who operates the TV or movie camera.

Cartoon: an animated film with illustrated characters, not human actors.

Cast: actors and actresses engaged for a performance.

Comic strip: a sequence of illustrations that tell a story.

Commercial: advertising on television.

Compact disc/CD: a laser disc for reproducing recorded sound.

Copyright: the legal right granted to an author or composer for exclusive publication of a literary, musical, dramatic, or artistic work.

Design: an arrangement of parts, color, form, etc.; an artistic invention.

Designer: a person who creates something (like a fashion designer, industrial designer, etc.).

Editing: adaptation and preparation of a written text or film.

Fantasy: a book or film portraying imaginary characters such as elves, dragons, fairies.

Flashback: an interruption in a story that shows an earlier episode.

Flop: a failure.

Freelance: a person, especially a writer or artist, who sells his or her services to employers without a long-term commitment.

Gadget: a gift offered to increase sales.

Headline: the words in a print advertisement or newspaper that readers notice first.

Hi-fi: a stereo system.

Hit parade: a list of successful, best-selling records, books, etc.

Home video: a VCR system that lets you tape TV programs and view rented or purchased videotapes in your own home.

Instant book: a book written to exploit a current event.

Jet lag: tiredness and a disruption of daily body rhythms due to a change in time zones. This often occurs when you travel long distance.

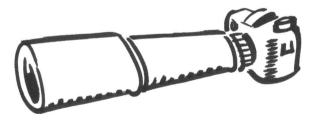

Know-how: knowledge needed to correctly perform a task.

Laser: stands for *l*ight *a*mplification by *s*timulated *e*mission of *r*adiation.

Marketing: a series of complex activities involved in the creation of products and services and their promotion with the customer.

Market research: information on a marketing problem/opportunity.

Music video: film sequences that accompany a song.

Network: a group of radio or television stations.

Scoop: an exclusive news item.

Share: a percentage of families watching a TV program or listening to a radio program.

Sitcom: a humorous radio or television series featuring a regular cast of characters. It stands for "situation comedy."

Soap opera: A serial on daytime television with stock characters and a complicated plot. In the early days of radio many of the sponsors were companies that sold washing detergent or soap.

Talk show: a television or radio show in which people are interviewed by a host and often answer questions from viewers or listeners.

Target: a goal to be reached in a sales campaign; the segment of consumers to which advertising is directed.

Testimonial: a famous person who publicizes a product and helps to guarantee its success.

Trailer: previews of a film coming to a movie theater.

Trend: a general tendency or current style (in business or fashion, for example).

Video game: an electronic or computerized game played by manipulating images on a display screen.

Videotape: a magnetic tape used to record visual images and associated sound for playback or broadcasting.

Zapping: using the remote control device of a television to rapidly change from one channel to another.

COMPUTERS
INFORMATION SCIENCE

NUTRITION

The body needs a varied, well-balanced diet. Foods are divided into proteins, fats, and carbohydrates (that include starches and sugar). Vitamins and minerals are also very important.

VITAMIN TABLE

Vitamin A: fruit, vegetables, eggs, liver, and butter. To prevent eye problems and ensure proper growth.

Vitamin B_1: whole grains, liver. To prevent circulatory problems.

Vitamin B_2: whole grains, eggs, and milk. To prevent skin disease and ensure proper growth.

Vitamin PP/B_3: meats and yeast. To prevent skin disease and stomach problems.

Vitamin B_5: found in almost all foods. To prevent stomach problems and nervous ailments

Vitamin B_6: meats, fish, fruit, and vegetables. To prevent skin disease and nervous ailments.

Vitamin B_9: raw vegetables, eggs, and milk. To prevent anemia.

Vitamin B_{12}: meats, eggs, and milk. To prevent anemia and nervous ailments.

Vitamin C: vegetables and fruit (citrus fruits). To prevent scurvy.

Vitamin D: cod liver oil, milk, vegetables. For healthy bones.

Vitamin E: vegetal and animal oils. To prevent sterility and nervous ailments.

Vitamin H: eggs and liver. To improve strength and skin.

Vitamin K: fresh vegetables. For normal blood clotting.

Vitamin PP: To prevent pellagra, a skin disease.

Liquids
You should drink approximately 8 glasses of water each day, preferably outside of meals.

Frozen and canned foods lose some of their nutritional value, so it is wiser to eat fresh foods.

FRUITS, FRUITS (EXOTIC), GRAINS, HUMAN BODY, MUSHROOMS, RECIPES, SKELETON, VEGETABLES

THE OCEAN DEPTHS

Latimeria – This fish (above) was named after M. Courtenay-Latimer, a woman scientist and the director of the East London Museum of Natural History in South Africa. She had the fish identified by ichthyologist J.L.B. Smith, who immediately realized the importance of her discovery. The Latimeria, which can be up to 5 ft (1.5 m) long, is a "living fossil," the only surviving example of prehistoric fish called Coelacanths.

The sun's rays cannot penetrate the ocean below a certain depth. Plants cannot grow here and even forms of animal life must adapt to the special conditions. The water pressure in the deep sea is up to one thousand times higher than it is on the surface. Many fish species produce their own light through bacteria or luminescent organs called *photophores* to attract their prey. Deep-sea fish are dark in color and often have curved, spiky teeth or strange bulging eyes.

1

Deep-sea fish – The argentine is a fish with bulging eyes that lives in the eastern tropical area of the Atlantic Ocean.

The viperfish lives in tropical and subtropical seas. A long mobile appendage projecting from its dorsal fin attracts prey to its mouth.

The gulper or pelican eel is often more than 6 ft (2 m) long). It has tiny teeth but a huge gaping mouth that hangs open to trap food.

The dragonfish can light up unexpectedly to disorient its enemy.

2

Here is the deep sea hatchetfish, also known as the "silver hatchet."

3

1. Argentine
2. Saber-toothed viperfish
3. Gulper or pelican eel
4. Scaly dragonfish

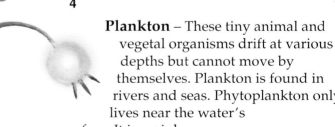

4

The anglerfish attracts its prey with a "lantern" hanging from its head.

Plankton – These tiny animal and vegetal organisms drift at various depths but cannot move by themselves. Plankton is found in rivers and seas. Phytoplankton only lives near the water's surface. It is mainly composed of single-cell algae and carries out photosynthesis. Depending on the depth, zooplankton is made up of organisms in larval form or minuscule crustaceans.

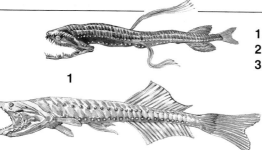

1. Photostomias
2. Deep-sea bristlemouth
3. Anglerfish

Strange fish – The photostomias belongs to the "mousetrap" genus: its jaws can hold very large prey. The deep-sea bristlemouth is practically transparent. The anglerfish can devour fish much bigger than itself. The tripod fish uses its stiff pelvic fins and a long tail fin to balance on the ocean floor while it holds its pectoral fins above its head.

Exploring the ocean depths Divers, who wear special diving suits that maintain normal air pressure inside, can go to a depth of 650 ft (200 m). In his book *Twenty Thousand Leagues under the Sea*, Jules Verne imagines exploring the deep sea aboard Captain Nemo's submarine, the *Nautilus*.

1. Deep sea crustaceans
2. Deep-sea barrel-eye
3. Lanterfish
4. Euphausid shrimp
5. Gigantactis
6. Anglerfish
7. Deep-sea bristlemouth
8. Black dragonfish
9. Plankton

tripod fish

SEA FISH

OCEANIA

Oceania is a large and diverse territory that includes the continent of Australia (explored around 1600), two large islands (New Zealand and New Guinea), and many small islands scattered in the Pacific Ocean that form Micronesia, Melanesia and Polynesia.

Many native groups still live in Oceania: Aboriginals in Australia, Maori in New Zealand, Papuans in New Guinea, and Polynesians, who live on several islands. Other inhabitants are descendants of European colonists.

In the map below, independent countries are shown in capital letters.

Music and dance are an important feature of Polynesian culture and tradition. Songs are accompanied by drums covered with sharkskin.

Sport – The Polynesians invented the sport of surfing years before it became popular in California. Variations of this sport are windsurfing, acrobatic surfing and belly-board surfing.

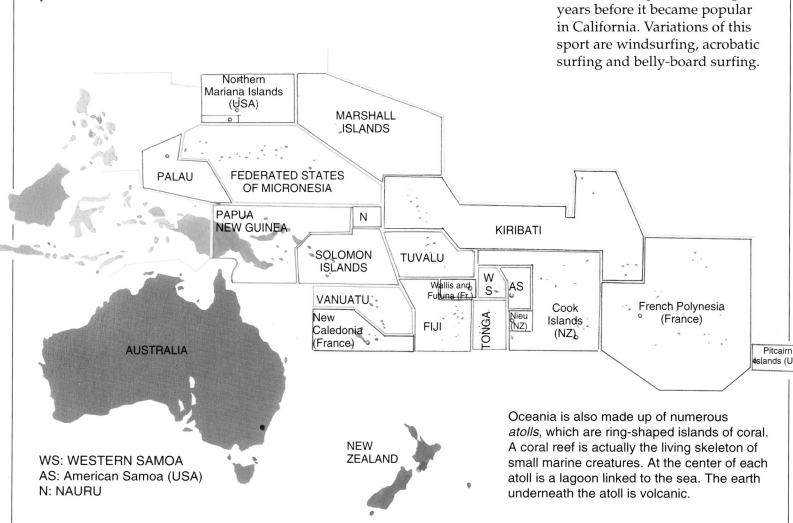

WS: WESTERN SAMOA
AS: American Samoa (USA)
N: NAURU

Oceania is also made up of numerous *atolls*, which are ring-shaped islands of coral. A coral reef is actually the living skeleton of small marine creatures. At the center of each atoll is a lagoon linked to the sea. The earth underneath the atoll is volcanic.

About 60,000 years ago, people from Southeast Asia began migrating to Polynesia. They settled in Melanesia and gradually spread out to other regions of Oceania. The Polynesian mythology is rich in epics and legends.

Polynesians are excellent fishers. They brave the high seas and sharks in several types of boats: outrigger canoes and sailboats with triangular sails.

People are preparing *kava*, the typical drink of the Pacific islands, made from pepper plant roots chopped and mixed with water or coconut milk.

Australia – This country was inhabited 40,000 years before the Europeans arrived. James Cook, an English explorer, claimed the east coast of Australia for Britain in 1770. Actual colonization began in 1778 when English convincts were sent here. Today, most of the population lives in the eastern part of the country. Australia is home to strange animals that are found nowhere else in the world—the kangaroo, platypus, koala and echidna.

Coconut leaves are used to weave carpets and to make screens that keep out the hot sun.

New Zealand – Formed by volcanoes, the country is still prone to earthquakes. New Zealand is made up of two large islands and other small ones. The majority of the population is of European descent (88%); the Maori and Polynesians, who arrived between the 9th and 12th centuries, make up around 11%. Today, New Zealand is the world's fourth leading producer of sheep.

Polynesia – This group of islands (of volcanic and coral origin) lies in the easternmost part of Oceania, separated from the coasts of North and South America by the Pacific Ocean. Some of the islands are territories ruled by France. The island of Hawaii belongs to the United States. Easter Island, famous for its huge stone giants, belongs to Chile.

Papua New Guinea – This country includes the territories of Papuasia, New Guinea and several small archipelagos. The predominant ethnic groups are the Melanesians and the Papuans. Population is concentrated in the coastal areas.

ANIMALS OF AUSTRALIA, ENDANGERED SPECIES, EXPLORERS, SPORTS

COUNTRIES IN OCEANIA

	COUNTRY	CAPITAL	AREA	POPULATION	LANGUAGE(S)	CURRENCY
	Australia	Canberra	2,973,472 sq mi (7,700,700 sq km)	18,322,000	English, native languages	Australian dollar
	Papua New Guinea	Port Moresby	178,276 sq mi (461,700 sq km)	4,295,000	Pidgin, Motu, English	kina
	New Zealand	Wellington	103,745 sq mi (268,680 sq km)	3,407,280	English, Maori	New Zealand dollar
	Solomon Islands	Honiara	10,985 sq mi (28,450 sq km)	399,000	English, Pidgin, others	Solomon Islands dollar
	Fiji	Suva	7,055 sq mi (18,272 sq km)	773,000	Fijian, Hindi, English	Fijian dollar
	Vanuatu	Port Vila	5,700 sq mi (14,760 sq km)	173,600	English, French, Bislama	vatu
	Western Samoa	Apia	1,100 sq mi (2,860 sq km)	209,300	Samoan, English	tala
	Kiribati	Tarawa	275 sq mi (717 sq km)	79,000	Gilbertese, English	Australian dollar
	Tonga	Nuku'alofa	290 sq mi (750 sq km)	105,600	Tongan, English	paanga
	Federated States of Micronesia	Palikir	272 sq mi (707 sq km)	100,000	English	US dollar
	Palau	Koror	176 sq mi (458 sq km)	16,660	Sonsorolese, Angaur, others	US dollar
	Marshall Islands	Majuro	69 sq mi (180 sq km)	54,000	Marshallese, English	US dollar
	Tuvalu	Funafuti	10 sq mi (26 sq km)	10,000	Tuvaluan, English	Australian dollar, Tuvaluan dollar
	Nauru	Yaren	8 sq mi (21 sq km)	10,000	Nauruan, English	Australian dollar

OPTICS

Discoveries in the field of optics in the 17th century led to a greater understanding of natural phenomena. Isaac Newton (1642–1727) showed that white light is made up of the colors of the rainbow: he called this range of colors the *spectrum*. The invention of the telescope allowed scientists to observe the sky and make progress in astronomy.

When Newton held a glass prism up to the light, he noticed the light split into the colors of the rainbow.

Eyeglasses – A monk from Florence, Alessandro della Spina, made the first pair of eyeglasses in the 13th century. In 1775 Benjamin Franklin invented the first bifocal lenses for correcting both near and far vision. The first contact lenses were invented in 1887 by Adolf Fick but were not perfected until 1948.

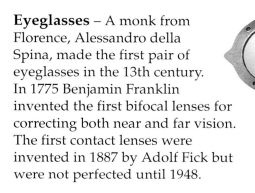

Telescope – Scientist *Galileo Galilei* (1564–1642) carried out many experiments in optics. He perfected the refracting telescope (below) used to observe faraway stars invisible to the naked eye. *Isaac Newton* improved the sharpness of the image of this instrument by changing the lens to one with a curved shape, thus inventing the reflecting telescope. Today we use radio telescopes that receive and analyze electromagnetic waves from space.

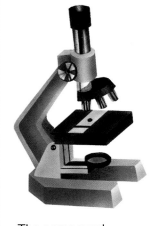

Microscope – Galileo invented a very simple microscope. The invention was later improved around 1590 by two Dutch eyeglass makers, Zacharias and Janssens, who invented the compound microscope, which had more than one lens. Another Dutchman, scientist Leeuwenhoek (1632–1723), devised microscopes that led to the discovery of single-celled organisms like bacteria.

The compound microscope uses light rays and several lenses to magnify objects up to 2,000 times. The electron microscope can magnify up to 1 million times.

☞ ASTRONOMY
GLASS
SCIENTISTS AND INVENTORS

PELICANS

Pelicans are aquatic birds found on all continents, near fresh and salt water. They are among the largest of all flying birds. Their plumage is primarily white, with some gray, black and brown in secondary feathers. While awkward on land, pelicans soar in graceful formations. They often fish in shallow water by forming semi-circles and beating their wings to herd schools of fish towards the shore where the pelicans scoop them up. Beneath their beaks, pelicans have a special pouch, made of skin, that expands to hold more food.

Different types – The most common pelican, found in Africa, has white and pink coloring with an orange bump on its forehead that swells during the mating season. The pink-backed pelican, also from Africa, is one of the smallest of the species. The Dalmatian pelican has silvery plumage and a tuft of curly feathers on its head. The spectacled pelican from Australia was given this name because its eyes are circled by hairless skin.

Pelicans build their nests in trees or on the ground.

☞ BIRDS MIGRATION

Pelicans are migratory birds that fly very long distances to reach countries with warm climates.

Only a few pelican species can dive into the water to catch a meal.

Young pelicans – A colony can range from 5 pairs to several thousand birds. Pelican eggs are bluish or yellowish and they hatch after 30 days. The baby birds grow white or brownish-black fuzz and start to fly with their parents after 12 to 15 weeks.

PERSIA

In around 1000 B.C., tribes settled in a part of the world known as Iran, better known as Persia. In 546 B.C., Cyrus II, king of Persia, overthrew the ruling tribe of the Medes, and went on to conquer neighboring lands as well, including Babylon and Lydia. The empire reached its peak under Darius I (521–486 B.C.). Alexander the Great defeated the last Persian king, Darius III, at Issus in 333 B.C.

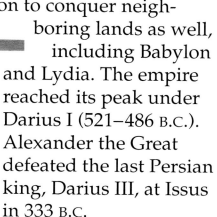

The city of Persepolis was the capital of the empire, beginning with Darius I. His palace was built on a raised terrace surrounded by walls and beautified by fountains and trees.

A column with carved bull heads at the Royal Palace of Susa. Below: a Persian warrior.

A bas-relief (below) shows a row of Persian soldiers who were members of the Imperial Guard.

The Persian coin, called *daricus*, was used throughout the Greek empire.
Above: a coin showing a ceremonial altar of fire.

Satrapies – Cyrus I divided the empire into *satrapies*, or provinces. There were twenty satrapies under Darius I. Heading each one was a *satrap*, a governor assigned full civilian, judicial and military powers.

ALEXANDER THE GREAT, EGYPTIANS, GREEKS, INDIA JEWS, MESOPOTAMIAN CIVILIZATIONS

PETS

Every child wants a pet to play with, but animals are not toys: they need tender loving care! You must keep their baskets, cages, or tanks clean, remember to feed them regularly, and make sure they are healthy. Many animals such as large dogs suffer if they are kept in cramped quarters, which means they should not live in small city apartments.

Dogs normally wear a leash when they are in public places. Some also wear a muzzle.

The cat – Cats are attached to their owners but are less openly affectionate than dogs. Because a cat has a strong personality and loves its freedom, people mistakenly think cats are aloof and indifferent.

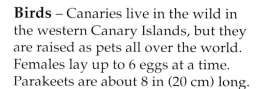

Birds – Canaries live in the wild in the western Canary Islands, but they are raised as pets all over the world. Females lay up to 6 eggs at a time. Parakeets are about 8 in (20 cm) long.

Water turtles – These animals are raised in fresh water tanks. Their jaws are lined with a sharp horny layer instead of teeth. Water turtles are about 3 in (6–7 cm) long.

Goldfish – These fish are about 2.5 to 3 in (6–7 cm) long. The water in their fish bowl must be changed every day.

The veterinarian – This is the doctor who takes care of farm animals and small pets. The vet vaccinates puppies and kittens, performs surgical procedures, and also teaches owners about health care for their pets and animals.

Rodents – These animals eat salad, carrots, grains, apples, and bread crusts. They are raised in cages and enjoy running on the wheel attached to the bars of the cage. Some examples of pet rodents are *Guinea pigs* (6–8 in / 15–20 cm) with silky long or short coarse fur; *hamsters* (3 in / 8 cm) shown here to the left; and *white mice* (2 in / 5 cm).

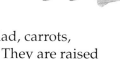

BIRDS
CATS
DOGS
FISH
MAMMALS
RODENTS

216

PHOTOGRAPHY

The birth of photography
The first photograph (above right) by Niepce was made using a pewter plate exposed to light in a camera obscura.

Nicéphore Niepce invented photography between 1820 and 1824 using a camera obscura, but he could not make the images clear and permanent. A few years later he and Louis Daguerre improved the procedure. They coated copper plates with silver, then exposed them to iodine fumes and then to light in a camera obscura. The images were fixed by soaking the plates in a salt solution. In 1835 William Talbot devised a way to print photographs on special light-sensitive paper. Finally, in 1903, the Lumière brothers designed a plate for color photographs.

The body of early cameras was made of wood.

camera obscura

Camera obscura
This device is the first camera. It was formed by a box with a tiny hole at the front and a white screen on the opposite side. The upside-down image of an object outside of the box was reflected upon the white screen. Sharper and brighter images were obtained with lenses.

CINEMA
INFORMATION SCIENCE

Camera – Small cameras were first built at the end of the 19th century, and rolls of film replaced plates. Today's most modern cameras let us record photos directly onto diskettes.

PIRATES

A black flag with skull and crossbones, called a Jolly Roger, fluttered above pirate ships that attacked merchant vessels on the high seas. Piracy has a long history dating from the ancient Etruscans and later the Vikings and Saracens. Piracy flourished in the 16th century with the discovery of the New World and an increase in maritime traffic.

The bloodcurdling screams of the pirates as they swooped down on merchant ships instilled terror in the hearts of sailors.

Treasure Island by Robert Louis Stevenson tells an exciting story of a treasure hidden by pirates.

Corsairs and buccaneers

Most pirates were simply outlaws whose only aim was to rob precious treasures. Corsairs, however, were pirates that stole on behalf of a sovereign who gave them a special letter of passage. Queen Elizabeth I made the corsair Francis Drake a knight. Buccaneers were adventurers who preyed upon Spanish ships in the West Indies in the 17th century. The most famous was Sir Henry Morgan.

ELIZABETH I
STEVENSON

PLANTS—SOME USEFUL VARIETIES

Since prehistoric times, people have used herbs, roots, fruits and vegetables for food, medicines and fibers. In fact, the earth provides us with a multitude of useful plants. In addition to those illustrated here, there are important grains such as rice, barley, millet and oats and beets, which give us sugar. Aromatic oils can be extracted from certain plants. The rind of the bergamot fruit, for example, is used in perfumes and baked goods.

hemp

Cotton – Fluffy white balls of cotton are harvested and the seeds extracted. The cotton is processed into thread to make cloth. Mexican Indians used the plant to weave clothes as early as 2400 B.C.

cotton

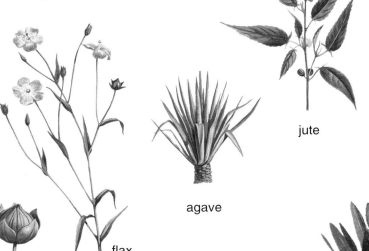

jute

agave

flax

Plant fibers – Many plants provide fibers that can be made into thread and cloth. Hemp and sisal (from the agave plant) are used for rope and mats. Jute is used for string and canvas.

Flax – The stem of the flax plant is soaked in water, dried, and then pressed with a roller to separate the woody part from the fibers. These short fibers are spun into thread to make linen.

sunflower

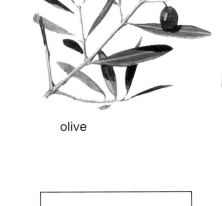

olive

peanut

Oil – The seeds from sunflowers and the cotton plant can be made into oil. Peanuts, olives and the fruit of certain palm trees can also be crushed to make oil.

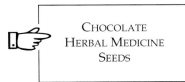

CHOCOLATE
HERBAL MEDICINE
SEEDS

PORTS

In ancient times huge torches were lit along the coasts to mark the entrance to a port. Today the lighthouse's flashing light warns sailors that the port is near. Natural harbors were chosen as the first ports. They were protected areas, usually with deep water, that provided shelter. Later, artificial ones were built, protected by man-made wharves.

Ports often include factories where freshly caught fish are cleaned, frozen, canned, salted and smoked (above).

Port structures

1. lighthouse
2. & 3. lights at the entrance to the port
4. breakwater pier
5. wharf
6. crane
7. cargo ship
8. tourist port
9. pleasure boats
10. cargo warehouses
11. port offices
12. shipyards with fueling station

Tourist ports – Tourist ports, such as Cape Cod in the United States and Portofino and Saint Tropez in Europe, are popular with vacationers with and without boats. The busiest commercial ports in the world are Rotterdam (Holland), Singapore and Kobe (Japan).

NAUTICAL SCIENCE ✓
SAILING SHIPS ✓
SEA
TRANSPORTATION

PRE-COLUMBIAN CIVILIZATIONS

These civilizations developed in America long before Christopher Columbus arrived in 1492. The first populations date back to 50,000 years ago, and probably originated in Asia. The *Olmech* and *Mayan* civilizations reigned in 2000 B.C. and were later conquered by the *Toltecs* and *Aztecs*. The *Incas* dominated Peru up until the arrival of the Europeans.

This ancient engraving shows Cortez communicating with Montezuma, the last Aztec emperor: his words are being translated by Marina, an Aztec woman who was his interpreter.

Aztecs – (left) This warrior population dominated Mexico, invading and conquering neighboring lands. Their capital Tenochtitlán, which means *among the cactuses growing on rocks*, was the wealthiest pre-Columbian city. The Aztecs made human sacrifices to appease their gods, and played many games, including *tlachtli*, or *juego de la pelota*. Their reign came to an end when Cortez captured the Aztecs' last emperor, Montezuma.

Mayas – The Mayas lived in Guatemala, Mexico, and western Honduras. Their society was divided into classes: *nobles*, *priests*, and *peasants*. The priests studied astronomy and mathematics and created an almost perfect annual calendar. The Mayan culture has left many traces, including numerous truncated pyramids.

Incas – The Incas, or *children of the sun*, dominated most of Peru. They had a well-developed social system with their administrative center in Cuzco. Francisco Pizarro finally conquered the Incas in 1533 and reduced them to slaves to work in the silver mines.

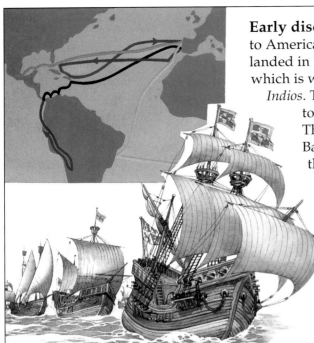

Early discoveries – The map shows explorations to America. Columbus' journey is shown in red. He landed in 1492 and thought he had reached India, which is why the inhabitants of America were called *Indios*. The orange line shows the route Cortez took in 1521 when he conquered the Aztecs. The black line shows the voyage of Vasco de Balboa, who was the first navigator to reach the Pacific Ocean (1513). The yellow line shows the route Pedro Cabral from Portugal took on his voyage to conquer Brazil in 1500. The blue line is the route Francisco Pizarro took to conquer the Incas (1533).

BOLIVAR, CHOCOLATE, CHRISTOPHER COLUMBUS, EXPLORERS, SPORTS

Cocoa, potatoes, corn, tobacco, tomatoes and pineapples were imported from America.

Cortez destroys the city of Tenochtitlán.

Massacres

The *Conquistadors* (Cortez, Pizarro, and other European adventurers) came to the New World in search of riches. Thanks to their firearms and horses, creatures the local people had never seen before, they conquered the native populations and took their treasures, mainly gold and silver.

Cocoa (above) comes from South America. Coffee (below) is native to Africa.

PREHISTORIC INVENTIONS

The discovery of fire by prehistoric people was of huge importance: fire was used for heat and light, for protection from animals and for cooking and preserving food. Already 40,000 years ago prehistoric people realized they could cross rivers and streams on top of floating trunks. They braided rush to make fishing nets (below). Hunters killed their prey using crude spears until the bow and arrow were invented. Later, primitive people learned how to cast metal, producing new and improved tools. Humans starting raising animals (goats and sheep) around 8000 B.C. The invention of the wheel marked a turning point in the history of transportation.

Primitive people made fishing hooks out of bone, then out of metal.

Primitive weapons

Ancient tools – Primitive people used to chip flint to make almond-shaped arrow heads and hand-held axes. Animal bones were also made into all sorts of tools such as fishing hooks and needles for sewing animal skins.

Agriculture and villages – Farming and growing wheat and other useful plants transformed the life of primitive people. The first farming settlements were founded between the 9th and 7th millennium B.C. Farmers used the plow to till the soil to make the ground more fertile before they sowed the seeds. They also built dams and canals to irrigate the fields. Some villages were built on piles or posts to protect the people from wild animals and flooding.

A prehistoric farming village.

Bronze casting phases (drawing found in a tomb in Thebes) **1.** Bronze is fused in a melting-pot; bellows are pumped by foot to raise the temperature; **2.** Curved wooden sticks are used to lift the melting-pot; **3.** Bronze is poured into molds; **4.** Other pieces of metal are carried to the spot to be fused.

Two-wheeled chariots date back to the days of the Sumerians and Egyptians. They were light and fast, so they were used in war for surprise attacks. Later, the chariot became an everyday means of transportation.

Metals – Most metals are not found in their pure state, but are hidden in mineral ores. That is why it took primitive people time to learn how to extract them. The traditional division of pre-history into the *Stone Age*, *Bronze Age*, and *Iron Age* reflects the progress made by humans in working with minerals and metals. They first used stone and copper, then found a way to fuse copper with tin to make bronze. Iron, which melts at a very high temperature, was discovered much later.

Right: a wheel used for prospecting minerals.

Invention of the wheel
The idea of the wheel probably came about by observing heavy objects being transported on logs. The early wheels were heavy solid wood disks which were eventually made lighter by adding holes. Lighter and faster wheels with spokes were invented later.

Water wheel (left) – Large wheels placed above streams were useful for sending water into irrigation canals in the fields. During the Middle Ages the water wheel was used to drive devices for prospecting minerals. Early flour mills were based on the same principle.

EGYPTIANS
HUMAN ANCESTORS
MESOPOTAMIAN CIVILIZATIONS
SCIENTISTS AND INVENTORS

RACCOONS

The raccoon has a well-developed sense of touch.

The Procyonidae family takes its name from its most famous member, the raccoon *(Procyon lotor)*. It lives in rural and urban areas of North and Central America. The raccoon has a distinctive black mask, round ears, grayish brown fur, agile paws and a bushy tail with five to seven black and white bands. It washes its food in water before eating.

Food – Raccoons are omnivorous. In the country they live near streams and ponds where they capture small reptiles, amphibians and worms. They also steal birds' eggs and consume plenty of vegetables.

Raccoons hibernate in the winter. They dig a burrow with their strong claws or seek shelter in a hollow of a tree trunk.

ANIMALS OF NORTH AMERICA, HIBERNATION, MAMMALS

The crab-eating raccoon lives in Central America.

Behavior – The raccoon likes to sleep on tree trunks (1). The female holds its young by the nape of the neck (2). The raccoon arches its back and keeps its head low when it walks (3). It sniffs its prey before eating it (4). The raccoon combs through the bottom of streams in search of prey (5).

RAPTORS

There are nearly 280 species of raptors, which are *birds of prey*. They include eagles, falcons, vultures, osprey, owls and hawks. They fly high over the land to search for a victim, then quickly swoop down and seize their prey with strong, sharp claws. The birds use their curved beak to tear the flesh into shreds.

The goshawk is between 20 and 24 in (50–60 cm) long and lives in the Northern hemisphere. The female is larger and stronger than the male.

1. Iceland gyrfalcon
2. falconet

The bald eagle, the national emblem of the United States, is a powerful and skilled hunter. It is protected by law in all states.

barn owl

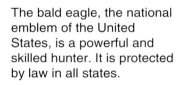

hawk owl

Records – The fastest raptor is the peregrine falcon. It flies at 168 mph (270 km/h) when it dives to catch its prey. Condors have the greatest wingspan— about 9 ft (3 m). The condor of the Andes is the heaviest bird of prey and weighs 20–25 lb (9–11 kg).

Hark owl and barn owl – These two raptors, up to 24 in (60 cm) in length, are skillful nocturnal hunters. They see very well in the dark and silently attack their sleeping prey. These owls live in hollows of large trees and eat small animals such as field mice. The barn owl also attacks hares, dormice and birds.

ANIMALS OF NORTH AMERICA, BIRDS, ENDANGERED SPECIES, MARSHLAND, STEPPE

Griffon vulture – Like all vultures, this bird eats animal carcasses. It has a hooked beak that tears flesh.

griffon vulture

Falconry – This type of hunting, which became very popular during the Middle Ages, was introduced to Europe by invaders from Asia. Raptors, and falcons in particular (which were hooded to stay calm), were trained to fly from a gloved hand and to swoop down on their victims.

RECIPES

Whether it is easy or complicated, each recipe must be carefully followed so the dish comes out perfectly. Make sure you have all the ingredients before you start. And remember to clean up the kitchen after you are done!

Sweeteners – Europeans used to sweeten their food with honey. They didn't discover sugar cane until the Middle Ages. The French began extracting sugar from beets in the late 1700s. The Chinese, however, had known about sugar for centuries, as had the Persians and Arabs from the Middle East.

Ladyfingers

A no-bake cake

Here is a delicious, easy-to-make dessert!

What you need: one package of ladyfingers, sugar, 1 jar marmalade, a measuring cup and glass, a cake pan with tall sides.

1. Mix 1 cup (250 mL) of water and 1 tablespoon (15 mL) of sugar in the glass. Dip the ladyfingers into the sweetened water, one by one.

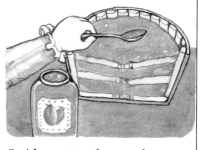

2. Line the bottom of the pan with some of the ladyfingers.

3. Line the sides of the pan with the remaining ladyfingers.

4. Cut off the tips of the ladyfingers and set them aside.

5. Alternate a layer of ladyfingers (soaked in the sugared water) with a layer of marmalade.

You can replace the marmalade with chocolate or vanilla pudding.

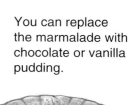

6. Make the last layer marmalade. Then place the cut-off tips of the ladyfingers on top.

7. Cover the cake pan with a dish; then place a pot on top so it presses down on the cake. Put the cake in the refrigerator and leave it there for one day.

8. Remove the cake from the refrigerator and remove the pan gently. Decorate it with fresh strawberries and a dab of marmalade in the center.

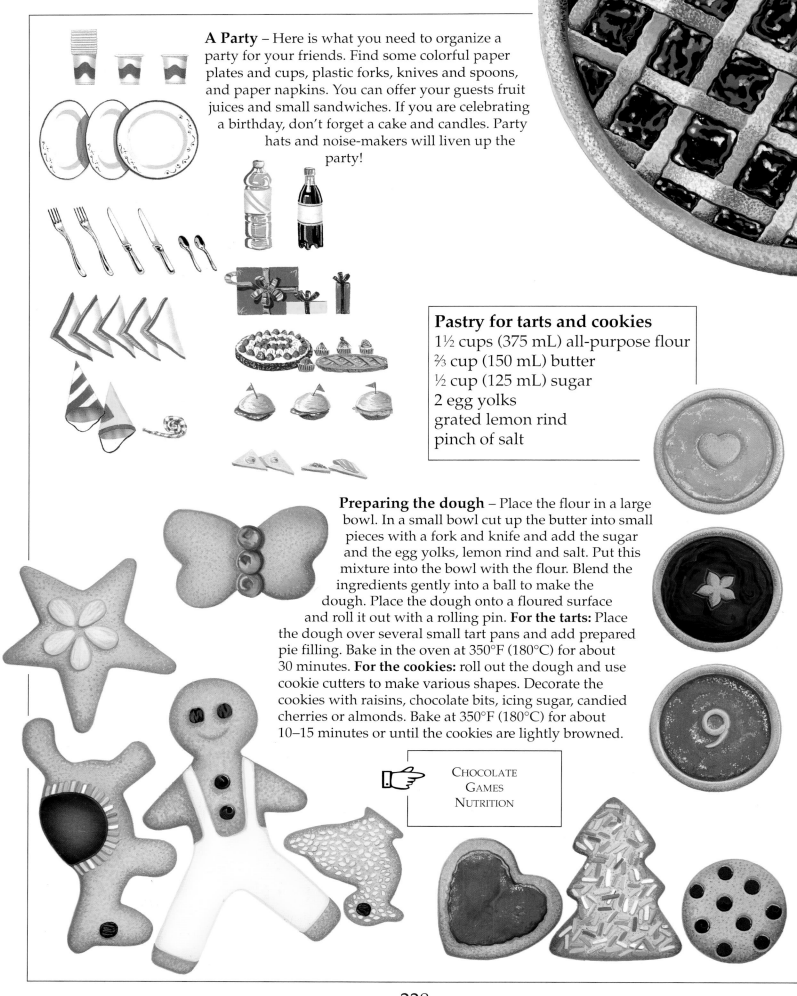

A Party – Here is what you need to organize a party for your friends. Find some colorful paper plates and cups, plastic forks, knives and spoons, and paper napkins. You can offer your guests fruit juices and small sandwiches. If you are celebrating a birthday, don't forget a cake and candles. Party hats and noise-makers will liven up the party!

Pastry for tarts and cookies
1½ cups (375 mL) all-purpose flour
⅔ cup (150 mL) butter
½ cup (125 mL) sugar
2 egg yolks
grated lemon rind
pinch of salt

Preparing the dough – Place the flour in a large bowl. In a small bowl cut up the butter into small pieces with a fork and knife and add the sugar and the egg yolks, lemon rind and salt. Put this mixture into the bowl with the flour. Blend the ingredients gently into a ball to make the dough. Place the dough onto a floured surface and roll it out with a rolling pin. **For the tarts:** Place the dough over several small tart pans and add prepared pie filling. Bake in the oven at 350°F (180°C) for about 30 minutes. **For the cookies:** roll out the dough and use cookie cutters to make various shapes. Decorate the cookies with raisins, chocolate bits, icing sugar, candied cherries or almonds. Bake at 350°F (180°C) for about 10–15 minutes or until the cookies are lightly browned.

☞ CHOCOLATE
GAMES
NUTRITION

REPRODUCTION

Reproduction takes place when an ovum cell from a woman unites with a spermatozoon cell from a man. Each cell contains 23 chromosomes that carry inherited genetic information. The spermatozoon encounters the ovum in the Fallopian tube of the woman and fertilizes it. From this union, the first cell of the new baby—the zygote—is formed, attaching itself to the wall of the uterus.

ovum

spermatozoon

urinary bladder

uterus

ovary

Fallopian tube

urethra

symphysis pubis

clitoris

rectum

vaginal opening

vagina

anus

anal sphincter

uterus

Fallopian tube

ovary

fimbria

cervix

vagina

Conception
Spermatozoa travel up the vagina to the uterus. When they reach the Fallopian tube, they meet the ovum. This is where fertilization takes place.

Spermatozoa – These cells, which are contained in a whitish liquid called semen, travel from the man's penis to the woman's vagina during sexual intercourse.

urinary bladder

vas deferens

symphysis pubis

Pregnancy
The fetus lives in the mother's uterus for nine months. It swims in amniotic liquid inside the amniotic sac, which acts as protection. The fetus takes its nourishment from the mother's blood by the placenta through the umbilical cord.

cavernous bodies

urethra

prepuce

urinary opening

scrotum

seminal vesicle

rectum

anal sphincter

anus

prostate

epididyme

testicle

vas deferens

BLOOD CIRCULATION, BRAIN AND SENSORY ORGANS, HUMAN BODY, MUSCLES, SKELETON

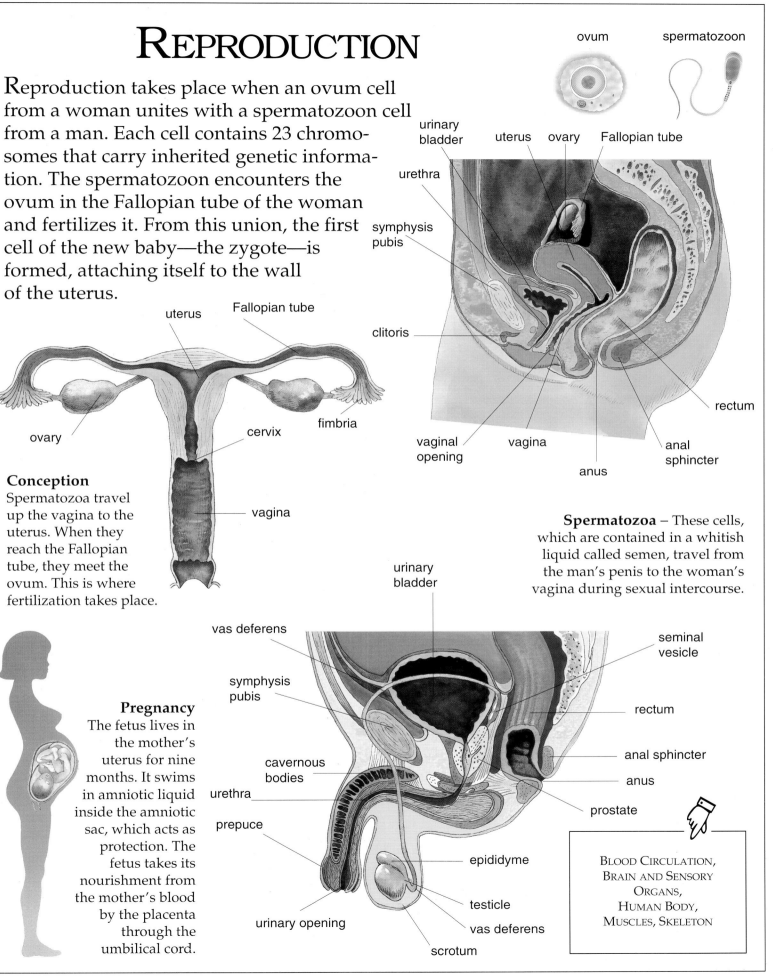

REPTILES

Reptiles were the first vertebrates to conquer land. The four major groups are the turtles, lizards, snakes and crocodiles. Although they have lungs, reptiles absorb more oxygen through their skin.

Reptile skin is covered with scales that can be either rough like that of crocodiles or smooth like that of snakes. The scales help protect reptiles from predators and from dehydration.

Snakes – These animals are the only reptiles without legs, but they slither quickly across the ground. During certain periods of the year snakes shed the skin that covers their scales.

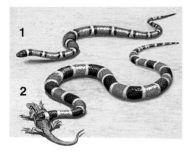

1. milk snake
2. coral snake

Lizards – These animals belong to the Squamata order. They have a long tail that can grow back if cut off. Lizards have a muscular forked tongue covered with a sticky substance that helps them to catch insects. The largest lizard is the Komodo dragon, which is over 9 ft (3 m) long and weighs about 280 lb (130 kg).

From top to bottom: green turtle, loggerhead turtle, hawksbill turtle.

Turtles and tortoises
These two animals belong to the order Testudinata. They have a shell divided into an upper part (shell or carapace) and bottom part (plastron). The two parts are joined together by flexible ligaments.

CAMOUFLAGE,
CROCODILES,
DINOSAURS,
ENDANGERED SPECIES,
EVOLUTION, SNAKES

Dinosaurs – These huge primitive reptiles made their appearance on Earth 225 million years ago and became extinct about 65 million years ago.

Tyrannosaurus rex

Characteristics – Reptiles are cold-blooded animals, which means that their body temperature varies with the temperature of the environment. They are more abundant in tropical and humid regions of the world. Typically, the female mates, deposits her eggs and leaves them to hatch on their own.

The longest snake is the reticulated python that measures up to 33 ft (10 m). The smallest reptile is one of the species of the gecko lizard, weighing only 2 grams.

RHINOCEROS

There are five species of rhinoceros, all with thick, almost hairless skin, stocky legs with three short toes, and a snout with horns. The African rhino is characterized by two horns, while most of the Asian rhinos have one. The black rhinoceros and white rhinocero both live in Africa, and despite their names, they are almost the same grayish color. The Asian species include the relatively small Sumatran rhino, the Javan rhino and the Indian rhino.

The gestation period of a rhinoceros lasts almost a year and a half. The baby rhino has no horn and weighs about 145 lb (65 kg) at birth. It grows 4 to 5 lb (2–3 kg) per day.

Mock battles – The white rino is a mild species and is more social than other rhinoceros. White rhinos engage in playful wrestling of horns when they meet.

The Indian rhinoceros has such thick skin that it is arranged in plates and resembles a suit of armor.

Black rhinoceros
This animal is better referred to as the hook-lipped African rhinoceros. Its upper lip is used to pull leaves into its mouth. It has very poor eyesight and cannot distinguish a man from a tree trunk, but its hearing and sense of smell are very keen.

 ANIMALS OF AFRICA MAMMALS

RICHARD THE LION HEARTED

Richard I (1157–1199) was named Lion Hearted for his courage. He was the son of Henry II and Eleanor of Aquitaine and in 1189 succeeded his father to the throne of England. Richard set off for the Third Crusades, but decided to return to England because his brother John Lackland was scheming to usurp the throne. During his journey home he was taken prisoner by Emperor Henry VI.

After a long period in prison and payment of a large ransom, Richard returned home in disguise and defeated his brother.

KNIGHTS
WOMEN OF HISTORY

Richard won back the city of Saint John of Acre (1191) during the Third Crusades.

The end – Richard traveled to France to fight Philip II of France, who had taken over several lands in Normandy. During a siege, Richard was fatally wounded by an arrow and died in 1199.

The Crusades – Christians considered Jerusalem the Holy Land, but it had been conquered by Muslims. The Catholic Church invited all European rulers to recover Jerusalem and the Holy Sepulcher from the Arab rulers. Several military expeditions were organized: the soldiers were called *crusaders* because they wore a cross. Seven crusades were organized between 1096 and 1270. Jerusalem remained in the hands of the crusaders from 1099 to 1187.

RODENTS

The female mouse has between 6 and 13 babies per litter and up to 50 litters per year. The young leave the nest after two weeks and can breed shortly thereafter.

The Rodentia is the largest order of mammals. Rodents, found all over the world, have a short life span, but they reproduce rapidly and adapt to any habitat. They are usually herbivorous, but some rodents also eat insects, birds and eggs.

Field mice, rats, squirrels, beavers, hedgehogs, hamsters, chinchillas, lemmings, gerbils and marmots all belong to this order.

The mouse (right) removes fleas with its teeth and carefully cleans its fur.

The mouse wraps its tail around the stem of a plant to keep its balance.

The harvest mouse is about 3 in (6 cm) long and hides in the fields.

The round nest is made of woven grass.

Teeth – Rodents have no canine teeth, but their scissor-like incisors grow back with use (up to 1 cm per week). They have molars and premolars at the back of the jaw that are used for chewing.

house mouse

black (or sewer) rat

Mice and rats belong to the same family. House mice *(Mus musculus)* are small and timid: they eat crumbs and food stored away. The black rat *(Rattus rattus)* is about 12 in (30 cm) long plus the tail. It is more aggressive and lives in sewers. Rats and other rodents transmit infectious diseases such as leptospirosis and bubonic plague.

Field mouse (right)
A common rodent in America and Europe, the field mouse causes serious damage to crops. It digs tunnels where it stores food supplies. It always follows the same path so it may escape more quickly.

When its territory is invaded, the brown rat (left) grinds its teeth, stands up on its hind legs and squeaks threateningly. The invader usually leaves without a fight.

Chipmunk
(1) This animal native to North America (2) holds its food tightly in its front paws and tucks food away in its cheeks (3).

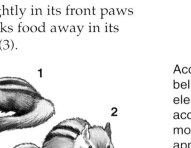

According to popular belief in India, the elephant god Ganesh is accompanied by a mouse when he appears on Earth.

The Country Mouse and the City Mouse is a fable by La Fontaine.

ANIMALS OF SOUTH AMERICA, HEDGEHOG, MAMMALS, PETS, SQUIRRELS, STEPPE, TUNDRA

Beaver – This rodent lives mainly in North American forests, near rivers and lakes. A beaver family cuts down down trees for food and for building dams to create ponds. They build huts in the ponds with access via an underwater tunnel. Their ears and nose have valves that shut under water. Their rear legs are webbed for swimming, and the flat tail acts as a rudder for changing direction.

Record-making rodents
The world's largest rodent, the capybara, lives in South America, reaches 3 ft (1 m) in length and weighs 145 lb (66 kg)! The smallest is the pygmy jerboa, similar to a hamster and gerbil, whose body length measures only 36 to 47 mm (1-2 in).

ROMANS

The poet Virgil tells the mythical story of the founding of Rome: Aeneas arrived in Italy on the Tiber River. His son Ascanius founded the city of Albalonga. His descendants, Romulus and Remus, were abandoned but saved by a female wolf that suckled them (right). After killing Remus in a quarrel, Romulus founded the city of Rome in around 753 B.C. Seven legendary kings succeeded Romulus and in around 509 A.D. Rome became a republic that lasted five centuries. The empire began with Octavian Augustus in 27 B.C., and more territory was added. In the year 395 the Roman Empire was divided into two parts: the Western and Eastern empires. The Western Roman Empire fell in 476 B.C., while the Eastern, or Byzantine, Empire lasted until 1453.

A Roman house (below)
1. vestibule
2. atrium with reflecting pool
3. workshop
4. frescoed walls
5. overhanging tile roof
6. small, narrow windows

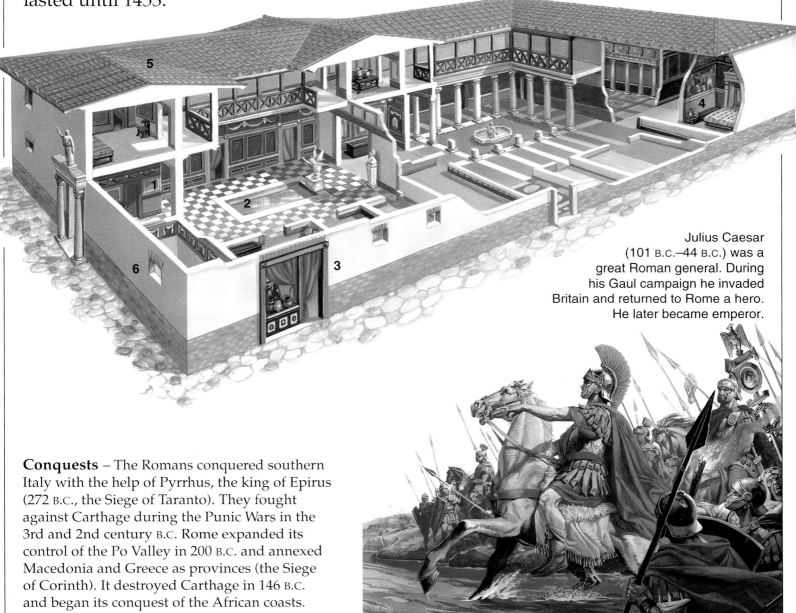

Julius Caesar (101 B.C.–44 B.C.) was a great Roman general. During his Gaul campaign he invaded Britain and returned to Rome a hero. He later became emperor.

Conquests – The Romans conquered southern Italy with the help of Pyrrhus, the king of Epirus (272 B.C., the Siege of Taranto). They fought against Carthage during the Punic Wars in the 3rd and 2nd century B.C. Rome expanded its control of the Po Valley in 200 B.C. and annexed Macedonia and Greece as provinces (the Siege of Corinth). It destroyed Carthage in 146 B.C. and began its conquest of the African coasts.

Children between 7 and 15 years of age woke up at dawn to go to school. They used wax tablets and a stylus for writing.

Left for posterity – The Romans left important public works such as the fourteen aqueducts that supplied the city of Rome with water. The first sewer system, installed 2,500 years ago, still functions. Certain roads that linked the entire Roman Empire are still in use today. The greatest legacy left by the Romans is their system of laws, still studied.

The Roman army (below)
1. Soldiers protected themselves with shields when they attacked the walls.
2. Tall towers were used in the attack.
3. The battering ram was used to break through walls.
4. A giant catapult was operated by two teams of soldiers.
5. A catapult launched large stone balls.
6. A ballista for hurling arrows.
7. A standard-bearer was a soldier who wore the colors of his unit.
8. A legate (Roman officer).

Roman baths – The public baths were important meeting places for the Romans, where they discussed politics and gossiped.

ARCHITECTURE, BARBARIANS, CHRISTIANITY, FASHION, JEWS, JULIUS CAESAR, MATHEMATICAL FORMULAS ✓

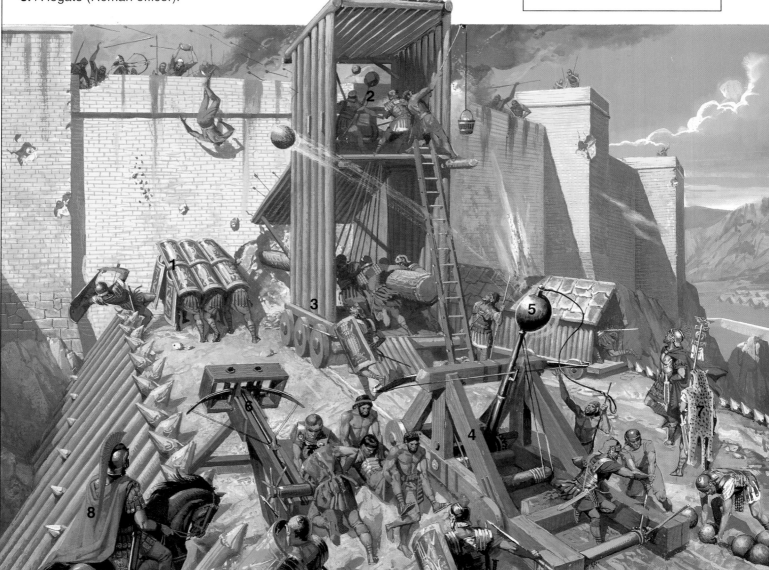

SCIENTISTS AND INVENTORS

A scientific discovery reveals the secrets of nature; an invention is the creation of something that did not previously exist. For example, gravity is a discovery, while the clock and steam engine are inventions.

The husband and wife team of Pierre and Marie Curie studied the effects of radiation. In 1898 they isolated the radioactive elements polonium and radium.

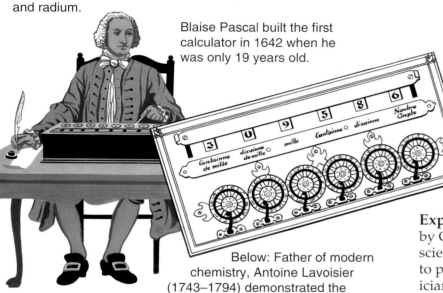

Blaise Pascal built the first calculator in 1642 when he was only 19 years old.

Below: Father of modern chemistry, Antoine Lavoisier (1743–1794) demonstrated the rule of conservation of matter: nothing is created, nothing is destroyed, everything is transformed.

Albert Einstein (1879–1955) revolutionized physics at the beginning of this century when he discovered the relationship between mass and energy.

Experimental method – This method, introduced by Galileo (1564–1642), paved the way for modern science, which is based on experimentation as a way to prove new theories. English physicist, mathematician and astronomer Isaac Newton (1642–1727) was the author of the laws on dynamics and discovered the law of universal gravitation (1687).

Roger Bacon (ca. 1214–1294) was a philosopher, monk and mathematician who conducted extraordinary experiments that earned him the name Doctor Mirabilis, or "Admirable Doctor." Unfortunately, he was imprisoned for his ideas.

Patent – The inventor does not sell a product but an idea. To patent the idea, he or she must apply to the government, explain the idea and prove that it is original. If successful, the inventor receives a patent and obtains copyright, which grants the inventor a percentage of the earnings derived from the invention.

Galileo (1564–1642) supported Copernicus' radical theory that the earth revolved around the sun, not the other way around. Galileo developed his own telescope and discovered four satellites of Jupiter.

George Stephenson (1564–1642) and his son Richard invented the first steam locomotive for passenger service.

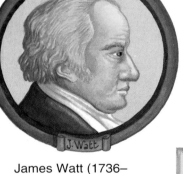

James Watt (1736–1819) perfected the steam engine so it could be used in industry.

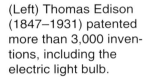

(Left) Thomas Edison (1847–1931) patented more than 3,000 inventions, including the electric light bulb.

Louis Pasteur (1822–1895) produced the first vaccine against rabies, a disease that is transmitted from animals to humans.

The Montgolfier brothers invented the hot-air balloon, called *montgolfière* in French, in 1783.

Karl Benz invented the first car with an internal-combustion engine in 1885.

☞ CINEMA, ELECTRICITY, ENERGY, HOUSEHOLD APPLIANCES, LEONARDO, MEDICINE, OPTICS, PREHISTORIC INVENTIONS, STEAM, TELLING TIME, TRANSPORTATION, TRAVEL IN THE OLDEN DAYS

What more can be invented? Today scientific research is seeking ways to improve the quality of life by studying new drugs and testing renewable and clean sources of energy that do not pollute the environment.

THE SEA

The Earth is called the *Blue Planet* because two-thirds of it is covered by water. It is in these waters that life first appeared in the sea about 3 billion years ago. The continents are separated by three oceans: the Atlantic, Pacific, and Indian Ocean. Smaller bodies of water between continents are called *seas*: the Mediterranean Sea is located between Europe, Asia, and Africa.

Red mullet

Angelfish

Jellyfish

Sea water – This liquid contains mineral salts, especially sodium chloride, or sea salt. Water evaporates more in tropical and equatorial zones, so salts are more concentrated in these areas: salinity in the Dead Sea reaches 30%.

Below: a walrus with its young. Today, all types of marine animals are threatened by pollution.

Shell (skeleton)
of a sea-urchin

Tides and currents – Tides are periodical changes in the level of sea water, which rises and falls due to the combined gravitational pull of the Moon and the Sun. The difference between high tide and low tide is called the *amplitude*. Ocean currents are large-scale movements of water in various directions that influence climate. They may be hot or cold, constant or periodical, at the surface of the water or far below it. The Gulf Stream is a warm current that starts out from the West coast of Africa and goes towards the Gulf of Mexico, then moves up towards Newfoundland and over to the West coast of Europe.

☞ EARTH, EVOLUTION, FISH, MARINE MAMMALS, OCEAN DEPTHS, PORTS, SEA FLOOR, SHARKS, SHELLS

THE SEA FLOOR

Cuttlefish
This mollusk, found throughout the Mediterranean Sea, has a flat body, two fins, and ten tentacles. It has an oval-shaped shell inside called the *cuttlebone*. It secrets a black liquid — a sort of ink — to defend itself from its enemies.

All sorts of creatures live on the sea floor, where the waves and tides constantly change the characteristics of this natural habitat. The forms of life that live on the sea floor depend on whether it is rocky, sandy, or muddy. Mollusks attach themselves to reefs, fish and crabs hide in crevices between rocks, and soles bury themselves in the sand as they wait for their prey.

A *nudibranch* or sea slug is a mollusk without a shell.

Scorpion fish – This fish, which lives along coral reefs, has colorful pectoral fins, but its quills are poisonous and can kill a swimmer in two hours.

Hippocampus – This animal is also called a sea horse because its head resembles that of a horse. It lives on the sea floor and hangs onto algae with its tail. It is about 6 in (15 cm) long. The female deposits her fertilized eggs in a pouch on the male's stomach. The eggs stay there until they hatch.

Sole – This fish lives on sandy sea floors where it is easily camouflaged. It has a flat body and resembles a flounder.

Ray – This cartilaginous fish has a flat body shaped like a disc or a diamond. Its eyes can be seen on top, while the mouth and gills are underneath.

Moray eel – This fish can reach about 3 ft (1 m) in length. Its dark, marbled skin has no scales.

Octopus
The octopus is a cephalopod mollusk and has no shell. It can measure from 2 to 220 in (5-540 cm). It has a beak-like mouth and eight tentacles with suckers. It sprays ink or uses camouflage to protect itself.

Lobster – This crustacean up to 20 in (50 cm) long lives on rocky coasts. Its flesh is considered a delicacy.

Hermit crab – This decapod crustacean lives in shells abandoned by other marine animals that it exchanges as it grows. It reaches up to 4 in (10 cm) long, and its right claw is larger than its left.

Actinia or sea anemone
This coelenterate animal has long stinging tentacles. It eats small animals and organic matter. It can survive out of water during low tide.

1. Cuttlefish
2. Rock gunnel
3. Sea snail
4. Hermit crab
5. Sea horse
6. Scorpion fish
7. Ray
8. Sole
9. Cowrie
10. Squid
11. Sea slug
12. Sea anemone
13. Parrot fish
14. Octopus
15. Limpets
16. Barnacles
17. Sea urchins
18. Lobster
19. Mussels
20. Coral
21. Moray eel
22. Clown fish
23. Grouper

FISH
SEA

SEASONS

The Earth makes two types of movements at the same time: 1) It rotates on its axis, making one full turn every 24 hours. This movement causes day and night. 2) The Earth also revolves around the Sun, one complete revolution taking 365 days, or one year. When the Northern Hemisphere is tilted *toward* the Sun, we receive more warmth and more hours of sunlight, giving us summer. The seasons are reversed in the Southern Hemisphere. When this part of the globe is tilted *away* from the Sun, the people there are experiencing winter—less warmth and fewer hours of sunlight.

Earth's orbit – The Earth rotates around the Sun along an elliptical route called an orbit that looks like a stretched oval (as shown in the figure above). It takes our planet 365¼ days to make one full revolution.

How seasons change – Seasons are the result of the Earth's tilt of 23½°. In winter the Suns's rays are slanted, so when they reach the Earth they are weak and not as warm. The day with the least amount of light is the winter solstice, which falls on December 21 in the Northern Hemisphere. The day with the most light is the summer solstice, June 21. The days with equal amounts of light are the spring equinox (March 21) and the fall equinox (September 23).

If the Sun did not exist, the Earth would be buried under a layer of ice so thick it would cover the base of the Eiffel Tower.

Leap year – Every four years is a leap year, one with 366 days. During leap year the extra day is in February, when there are 29 days rather than the usual 28. Imagine if you were born on February 29. You would have a birthday every four years!

When it is noon on an American child's watch, it is midnight for a child living halfway around the globe in China.

Night and day – It is easy to see why people from previous centuries believed that the Sun orbits the Earth, because we see the Sun rise in the east in the morning and set in the west at night. Actually, the Earth is spinning on its axis: when there is daylight in the part of the world facing the Sun, it is night in the other half of the globe. We only see stars sparkling at night because sunlight makes them invisible during the day.

Climate zones – The Earth is divided into five climate zones. There are two polar climates at the northern and southern tips of the globe that are marked by the Arctic and Antarctic Circles. Two temperate zones are located between the two poles and the Tropics of Cancer and Capricorn. The Equator has a torrid climate.

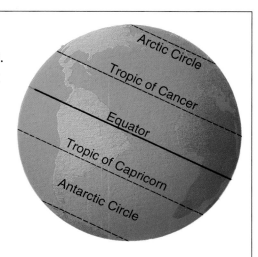

Arctic Circle
Tropic of Cancer
Equator
Tropic of Capricorn
Antarctic Circle

Different seasons – Due to the tilt of the Earth on its axis, one hemisphere, then the other, is tilted towards the Sun. When it is winter in Europe and the United States, it is summer in South America, South Africa and Australia. The four seasons are more evident in temperate zones. The tropics have basically two seasons only—a dry and a rainy season, while the Equator has generally the same hot weather all year round.

CAMOUFLAGE, EARTH, HIBERNATION, SUN

243

SEEDS

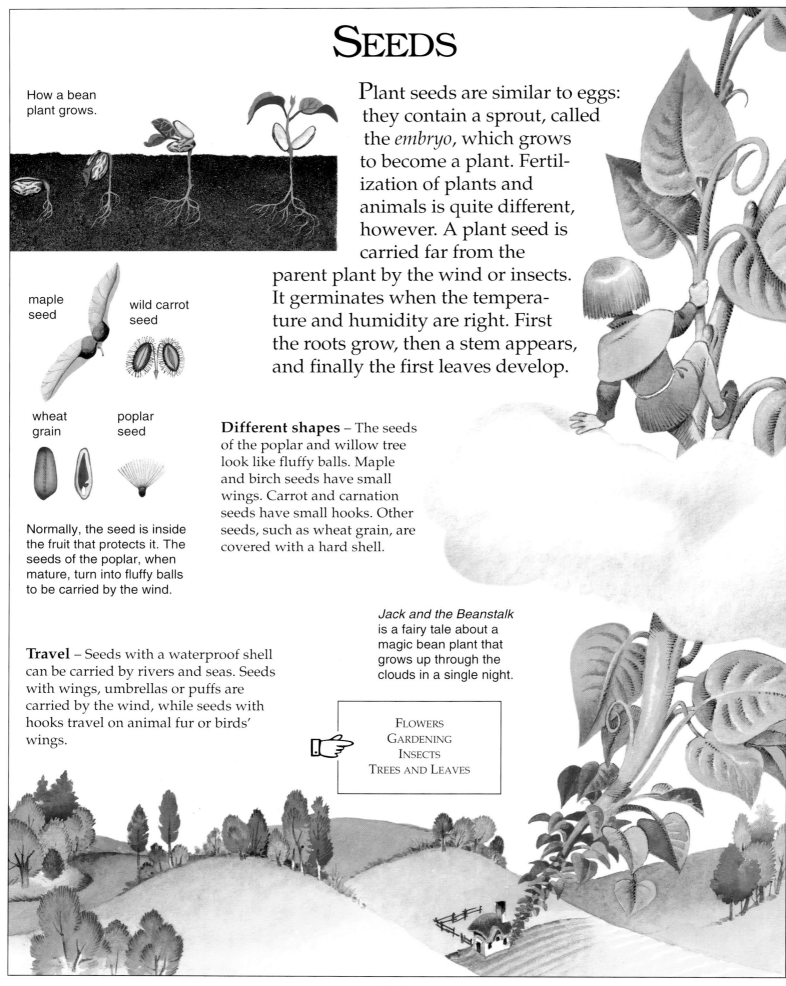

How a bean plant grows.

maple seed

wild carrot seed

wheat grain

poplar seed

Normally, the seed is inside the fruit that protects it. The seeds of the poplar, when mature, turn into fluffy balls to be carried by the wind.

Plant seeds are similar to eggs: they contain a sprout, called the *embryo*, which grows to become a plant. Fertilization of plants and animals is quite different, however. A plant seed is carried far from the parent plant by the wind or insects. It germinates when the temperature and humidity are right. First the roots grow, then a stem appears, and finally the first leaves develop.

Different shapes – The seeds of the poplar and willow tree look like fluffy balls. Maple and birch seeds have small wings. Carrot and carnation seeds have small hooks. Other seeds, such as wheat grain, are covered with a hard shell.

Jack and the Beanstalk is a fairy tale about a magic bean plant that grows up through the clouds in a single night.

Travel – Seeds with a waterproof shell can be carried by rivers and seas. Seeds with wings, umbrellas or puffs are carried by the wind, while seeds with hooks travel on animal fur or birds' wings.

FLOWERS
GARDENING
INSECTS
TREES AND LEAVES

SHARKS

Sharks have a slim body, fan-shaped fins, an asymmetrical tail and a dorsal fin. They are excellent predators, possessing superb eyesight, a keen sense of smell (that easily detects blood), and a mouth full of sharp, pointy teeth. Sharks must always keep moving or they will sink. The great white shark swims more than 250 mi (400 km) per day and is the largest predator fish. It weighs more than 550 lb (250 kg) and is more than 29 ft (9 m) long.

Sharks date back to about 350 million years ago, and they have maintained such prehistoric characteristics as a cartilaginous skeleton and numerous gills on the sides of their jaw.

blue shark

Dolphins, which are friendly to humans, are great enemies of sharks. They attack sharks in groups and butt them with their snouts.

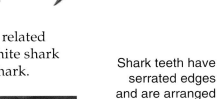

Lake Nicaragua shark

Blue shark – This shark, which is darker blue on its back and lighter in color on its sides, is about 20 ft (6 m) long. It lives in tropical and temperate waters.

The most dangerous sharks
The most voracious are tiger sharks, makos and the Lake Nicaragua shark, a predator related to the Atlantic shark. The white shark is also called a man-eating shark.

Shark teeth have serrated edges and are arranged in many rows.

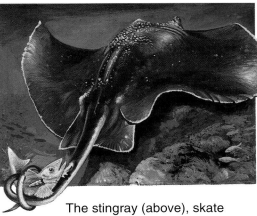

The stingray (above), skate and manta ray also belong to the shark family.

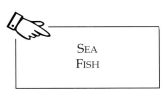

SEA FISH

SHELLS

Mollusks or shellfish have no bones in their bodies so they build a protective *shell* for protection. There are several types of shells. Some are formed by a single piece and are spiral or cone-shaped, while others, like oysters, are made up of two shells joined by a hinge.

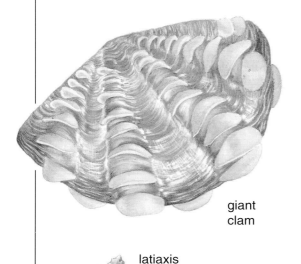
giant clam

murex

latiaxis

rim shell

triton

turret

sundial

How they live

Many mollusks live their entire lives attached to a rock or buried in the sand. Other mollusks, such as scallops, swim quickly underwater. There are tiny shells and huge ones, such as the giant sunset clams that live at great depths and whose shells are as large as a serving tray.

marble cone

bubble shell

abalone

spiny oyster

nautilus

The largest shell

The largest shell is the *tridacna gigante*, a giant clam that lives in the Indian and Pacific Oceans. This shell can weigh up to 440 lb (200 kg) and is up to 3.5 ft (1 m) wide.

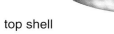
top shell

Shell collecting – If you want to start a shell collection, just go for a walk on the beach. Make sure you only gather empty shells without the mollusk still inside. Afterwards, rinse them in fresh water and let them dry. You can glue shells to cardboard and label them by name.

You can string shells together on a nylon thread to make a pretty necklace.

murex

cockle

wentletrap

patella

helmet shell

clam

mussel

miter

keyhole limpet

FOSSILS, OCEAN DEPTHS, SEA, SEA FLOOR

SKELETON

The skeleton that supports the body is composed of 206 bones connected to each other. The rib cage, formed by 12 pairs of *ribs* connected to the *vertebrae*, is very important because it protects the heart, lungs and other vital organs.

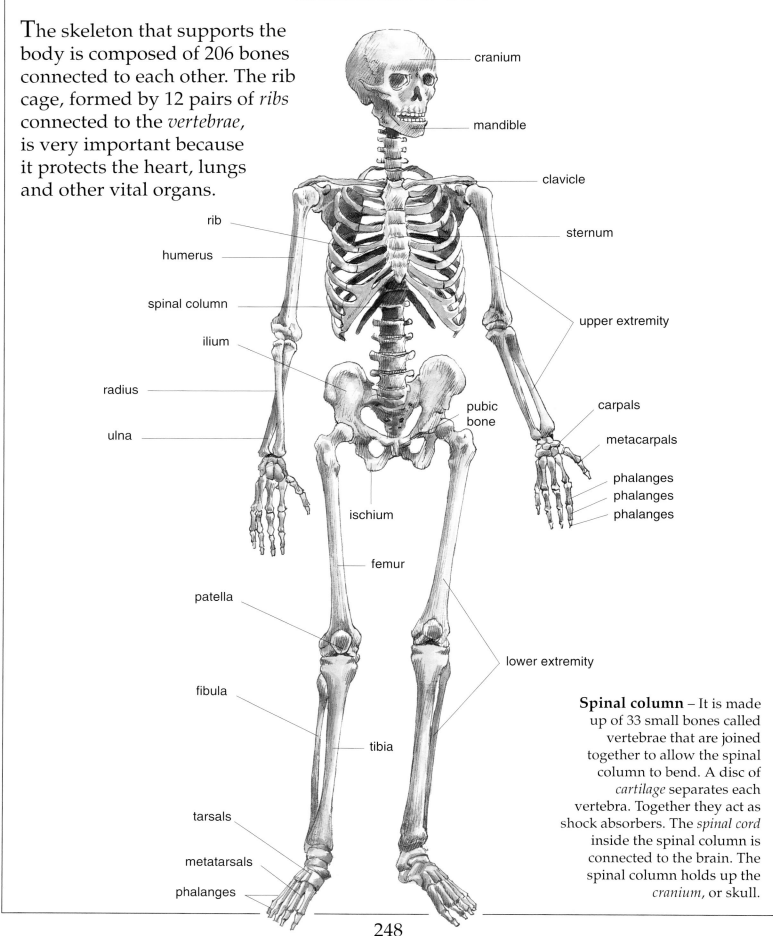

cranium

mandible

clavicle

rib

sternum

humerus

upper extremity

spinal column

ilium

radius

pubic bone

carpals

metacarpals

ulna

phalanges
phalanges
phalanges

ischium

femur

patella

lower extremity

fibula

tibia

tarsals

metatarsals

phalanges

Spinal column – It is made up of 33 small bones called vertebrae that are joined together to allow the spinal column to bend. A disc of *cartilage* separates each vertebra. Together they act as shock absorbers. The *spinal cord* inside the spinal column is connected to the brain. The spinal column holds up the *cranium*, or skull.

Our skeleton is like a coat stand that supports the body. The muscles attached to the bones allow the body to move.

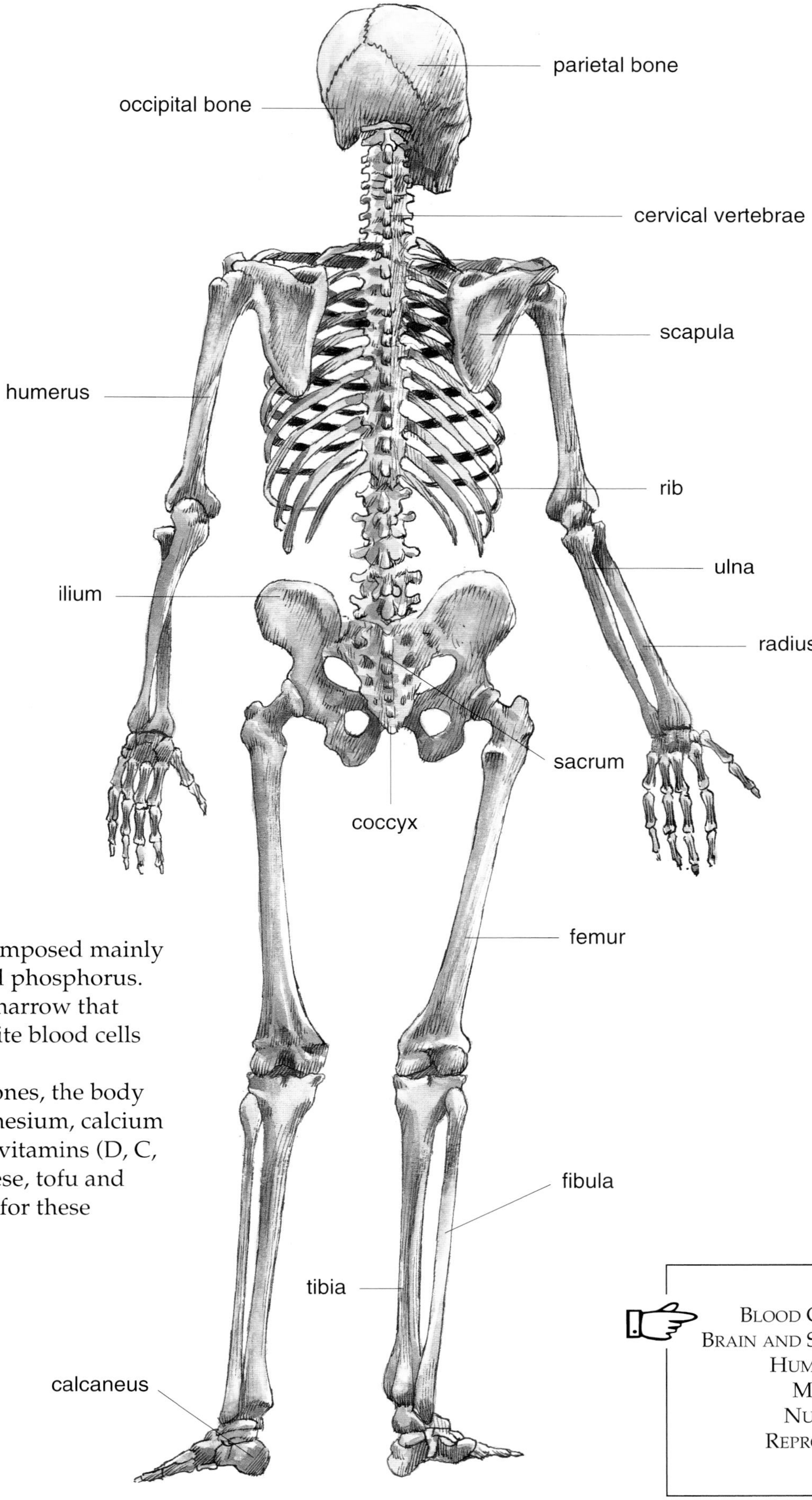

occipital bone

parietal bone

cervical vertebrae

scapula

humerus

rib

ulna

ilium

radius

sacrum

coccyx

femur

Bones – Bones are composed mainly of ossein, calcium and phosphorus. Some bones contain marrow that produces red and white blood cells and blood platelets.
For strong, healthy bones, the body needs minerals (magnesium, calcium and manganese) and vitamins (D, C, A and B$_{12}$). Milk, cheese, tofu and fish are good sources for these nutrients.

fibula

tibia

calcaneus

BLOOD CIRCULATION
BRAIN AND SENSORY ORGANS
HUMAN BODY
MUSCLES
NUTRITION
REPRODUCTION

SLAVERY

The settlement of the New World increased the practice of slavery, an institution already found in most parts of the world. About 12 million Africans were captured between 1550 and 1800 and transported by slave ships to the United States to work in mines and on tobacco, cotton (below left) and sugar plantations.

American author Harriet Beecher Stowe (1811–1869) achieved great success with her novel *Uncle Tom's Cabin* (above), published in 1852. The book was very influential in the mounting antislavery movement that began before the Civil War.

cotton flower and plant

Slave ships – A triangular pattern of trade developed in the 16th century: ships left Europe filled with trinkets and rum (1), which slave traders carried to the western coast of Africa. There they bartered the rum for slaves (2). The African slaves were transported to the West Indies to raise sugar. The sugar was sent to New England, where it was manufactured into rum (3), and the triangle continued. The U.S. and Britain finally made the international slave trade illegal in 1808.

Abraham Lincoln was elected President of the United States in 1860. At the end of the Civil War in 1865, Congress approved the 13th Amendment to the U.S. Constitution, which ended slavery.

HISTORY TIME LINES ✓
LINCOLN

SNAKES

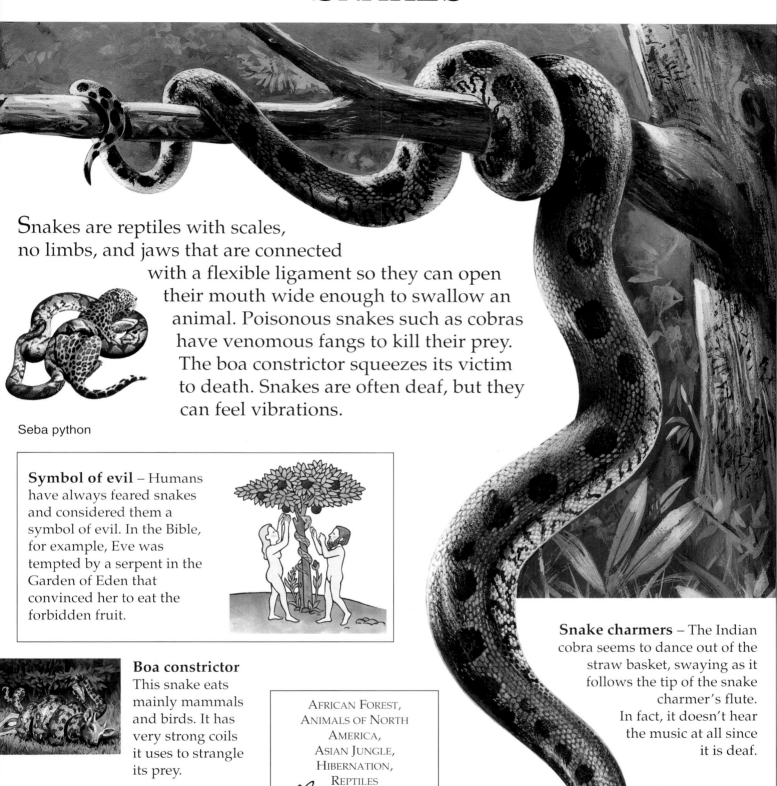

Snakes are reptiles with scales, no limbs, and jaws that are connected with a flexible ligament so they can open their mouth wide enough to swallow an animal. Poisonous snakes such as cobras have venomous fangs to kill their prey. The boa constrictor squeezes its victim to death. Snakes are often deaf, but they can feel vibrations.

Seba python

Symbol of evil – Humans have always feared snakes and considered them a symbol of evil. In the Bible, for example, Eve was tempted by a serpent in the Garden of Eden that convinced her to eat the forbidden fruit.

Boa constrictor
This snake eats mainly mammals and birds. It has very strong coils it uses to strangle its prey.

Poison – The poison apparatus consists of a gland that produces the venom, a duct that carries it, and the fang that injects the poison into the victim. The most poisonous snakes are the rattlesnake, black mamba, Indian cobra and coral snake.

AFRICAN FOREST, ANIMALS OF NORTH AMERICA, ASIAN JUNGLE, HIBERNATION, REPTILES

Snake charmers – The Indian cobra seems to dance out of the straw basket, swaying as it follows the tip of the snake charmer's flute. In fact, it doesn't hear the music at all since it is deaf.

The anaconda (left) reaches 22 ft (7 m) in length.

SOLAR SYSTEM

MERCURY

VENUS

EARTH

MARS

JUPITER

Nine planets revolve around the Sun: Mercury, Venus, Earth, Mars, Jupiter, Saturn, Uranus, Neptune and Pluto. Asteroids, which are small, irregularly-shaped celestial bodies, and comets (nebulous bodies with an incandescent halo and tail) also orbit the Sun. Our solar system is in a spiral galaxy called the *Milky Way*. This flat disc with a diameter of 100,000 light years has 100 billion stars and nebulosas (clouds of gas and dust). The Milky Way has two satellite galaxies called the Magellanic Clouds.

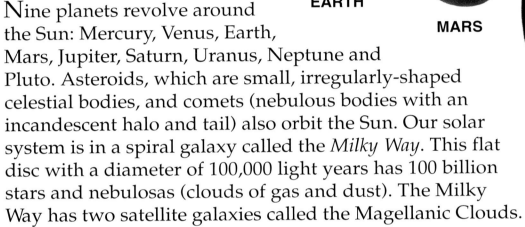

	Diameter (m/km)	Distance from Sun (millions mi/km)	Mass (Earth = 1)	Volume (Earth = 1)	Surface temperature	Length of year	Length of day	Number of satellites
MERCURY	3,032 mi 4,880 km	36 mi 57.9 km	0.055	0.056	+662°F +350°C	87.97 days	58.65 days	0
VENUS	7,519 mi 12,100 km	67.24 mi 108.2 km	0.815	0.86	+896°F +480°C	224.7 days	243.16 days	0
EARTH	7,926 mi 12,756 km	92.9 mi 149.6 km	1	1	+71.6°F +22°C	365.26 days	23 hr 56 min 4 sec	1
MARS	4,217 mi 6,787 km	141.7 mi 227.9 km	0.107	0.150	-9.4°F -23°C	686.9 days	24 hr 37 min 23 sec	2
JUPITER	88,700 mi 142,800 km	483.6 mi 778.3 km	318	1,319	-238°F -150°C	4,332 days	9 hr 50 min 30 sec	16

Mercury, Venus, Earth, Mars – Mercury is the planet closest to the Sun. Venus has a desert-like surface and a few mountain peaks. Earth is the only planet in the system with a breathable atmosphere. It has one satellite, the Moon. The atmosphere on Mars is extremely thin. This planet has two satellites called Deimos and Phobos.

Jupiter, Saturn, Uranus, Neptune, Pluto – Jupiter is the largest planet in our solar system – 317 times bigger than Earth. Saturn is surrounded by rings of ice and dust. Uranus and Neptune are similar: they are extremely cold planets because they are so far from the Sun. Pluto is the farthest planet from the Sun. It is considered a double planet with its satellite, Charon.

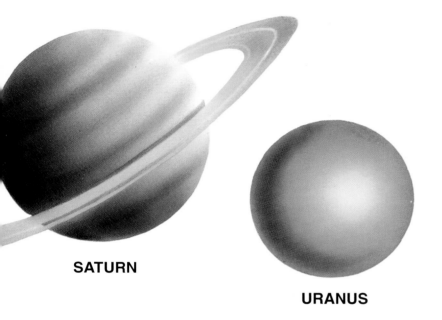

SATURN

URANUS

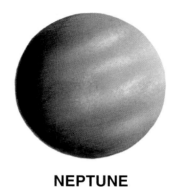

NEPTUNE

PLUTO

	Diameter (m/km)	Distance from Sun (millions mi/km)	Mass (Earth = 1)	Volume (Earth = 1)	Surface temperature	Length of year	Length of day	Number of satellites
SATURN	74,978 mi 120,660 km	887 mi 1,427 km	95	744	-292°F -180°C	10,759 days	10 hr 39 min	23
URANUS	32,200 mi 51,800 km	1,783 mi 2,870 km	15	67	-353.2°F -214°C	30,685 days	17 hr 14 min	15
NEPTUNE	30,800 mi 49,500 km	2,796 mi 4,497 km	17	57	-364°F -220°C	60,195 days	16 hr 3 min	8
PLUTO	1,480 mi 2,320 km	3,666 mi 5,900 km	0.002	0.01	-382°F -230°C	90,475 days	6 days 9 hr	1

SPACE TRAVEL

Space exploration began in 1957 when the Soviet Union launched *Sputnik I*, the first artificial satellite. The U.S. joined the race for space and launched its own program that culminated in 1969, when American astronaut Neil Armstrong set foot on the moon. The first space laboratories were launched soon after: the Soviet Union's *Salyut 1* was launched in 1971, but it ended in disaster when the cosmonauts aboard died during re-entry after spending 23 days in orbit. The shuttle missions began in 1981 with the first space vehicles that could be reused.

The first unmanned space labs collected useful data that was analyzed on Earth by scientists.

In 1959 the unmanned Soviet probe *Luna 2* (left) became the first spacecraft to strike the Moon. Its shape is similar to the rocket that Jules Verne imagined almost a century earlier.

An ancient dream – The dream of landing on the Moon is an ancient one that has led to many imaginings. Three such fantastic voyages are illustrated below: a kite pulled by swans, a ship transported by hot-air balloons and a space capsule shot from a cannon. This last notion comes from Jules Verne's book *From the Earth to the Moon*, written in 1865.

Artificial satellites

These satellites have no engine: they are launched into orbit around the Earth by rockets that break away and eventually disintegrate into space or fall into the ocean. Over the years these satellites have collected data on stars and planets in the solar system that even the most modern radiotelescopes could not have obtained. They continue to provide measurements and data for meteorology and geophysics, the scientific study of the Earth. Today, many satellites are used for telecommunications: they handle much of the data transmission for telephones, radio and television.

EARTH
MOON
SKY
SOLAR SYSTEM

Space travelers

Before humans were sent into space, several flights were made with animals aboard. The first was a dog, Laika, that the Russians launched into orbit aboard *Sputnik II*.

SPORTS

The five rings of the Olympics

According to recorded history, people played sports up to 6,000 years ago. Egyptians rowed boats on the Nile, people swam in Mesopotamia and played polo in Persia. In pre-Columbian America the Aztecs played *tlachtli*, a kind of basketball. Homer's *Iliad* mentions boxing, wrestling, running and javelin contests between Achean heroes. The very first Olympic games were played in Olympia, Greece, in 776 B.C. and lasted just one day with a single event called the *stadion* (a race of about 210 yards or 192 m). The *diaulo* (a race twice as long as the stadion) and *dolico* (a long-distance race) were added in 720 B.C. Winners were crowned with a laurel of olive leaves. Pythagorus, the famous mathematician, was an excellent boxer and won the Olympics in 588 B.C.

Basket ball

Volley ball

Ball games
According to the Latin poet Martial, playing ball was as difficult as playing the lyre. There were three types of balls in ancient Rome: the *follis* (a leather ball filled with air), the *pila trigonalis* (a small hard ball that resembled a tennis ball) and the *pila paganica* (a ball stuffed with feathers).

Soccer ball

American football is a combination of rugby and soccer rules. Players must penetrate the other team's territory and try to make a touchdown.

11 in (28 cm)

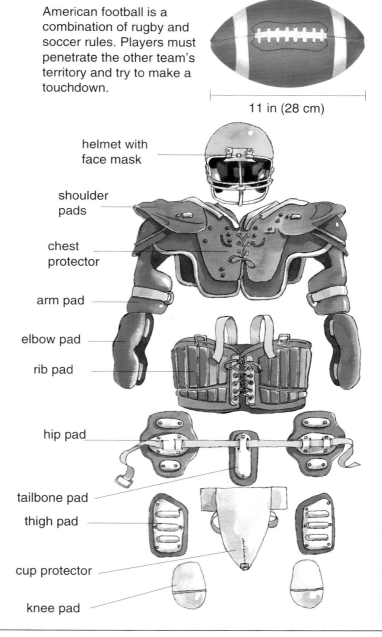

helmet with face mask

shoulder pads

chest protector

arm pad

elbow pad

rib pad

hip pad

tailbone pad

thigh pad

cup protector

knee pad

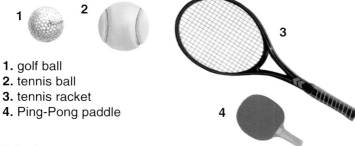

1
2
3
4

1. golf ball
2. tennis ball
3. tennis racket
4. Ping-Pong paddle

Modern games – Tennis was officially born in 1873 and was first called lawn tennis since it was played on grass. Table tennis, or ping-pong, was introduced in the same period. This sport was named after a brand of balls called Ping-Pong balls. The rules of golf were already well established in 1754.

A German gymnast organized the first diving competitions in 1830 and described the techniques in a manual. Diving was admitted to the Olympics in 1904. There are six main types of dives divided into two categories: springboard diving and platform diving.

Gymnastics – One of the most popular sports is gymnastics (from the Greek word *gymnasion*: a place where athletes exercised in the nude). There are six men's gymnastic events and four women's events. All use equipment except the floor exercises.

Left, a windsurfer. Right, a sail boat. Sailing can be done with many types of boats. Sailing competitions are called regattas.

GREEKS,
PRE-COLUMBIAN
CIVILIZATIONS, ROMANS

Swimming – Ancient Romans felt that not knowing how to swim was as serious as not knowing how to read, so all soldiers had to learn how to swim. Swimming meets, featuring only the breaststroke, began in 1800 in England. The crawl, or *free-style*, from Australia, was added around 1900. In *synchronized swimming* (for women only), the swimmers (soloists or in a team) perform synchronized movements to music.

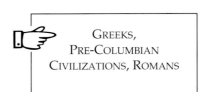

crawl or free-style

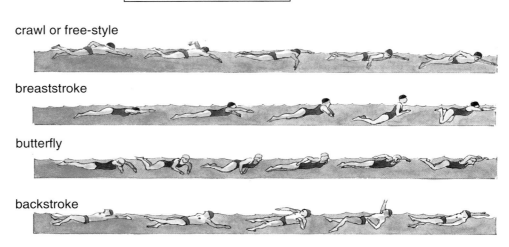

breaststroke

butterfly

backstroke

SQUIRRELS

This rodent, which belongs to the Sciurids family, has a bushy tail that acts as a parachute and helps the animal to keep its balance when jumping from one tree branch to another. Squirrels have four fingers on their front paws and five toes on their hind legs. They are active during daylight and do not hibernate. Flying squirrels, however, are nocturnal. Their coats vary in color from brown to gray. The common squirrel (*Sciurus vulgaris*) is found throughout Europe. The gray squirrel (*Sciurus carolinensis*) and chipmunk (*Tamias striatus*) live in North America, while the pygmy squirrel (*Myosciurus*) lives in Africa.

The gray squirrel is common in eastern parts of North America.

A squirrel raises its tail to frighten its opponent.

Defensive behavior.

Attack stance.

Habits – The mating season begins in spring and lasts through summer. The femals bears three to eight young in each litter. Waterproof winter nests made of leaves and twigs are often hidden inside of hollow tree trunks. Summer nests are soft and spongy.

A flying squirrel

Food – Squirrels eat flowers, fruit, sprouts and seeds. They carry food in their cheeks and accumulate provisions for winter.

ANIMALS OF EUROPE, HIBERNATION, MAMMALS, RODENTS

STEAM

An early pressure cooker.

A steam engine converts the energy of pressurized steam into mechanical energy. Greek scientist Heron built the first such machine (called *eolipila*) in 100 B.C., but the true pioneer of steam was French physicist Denis Papin. He designed the pressure cooker in 1679, an invention that inspired him to build the first steam-powered piston, and later a steamboat in 1707.

Papin's piston (above): Steam builds up inside the cylinder (1) when the water boils. The steam raises the piston in the cylinder (2). When it cools, the volume of the steam decreases and the cylinder is lowered (3).

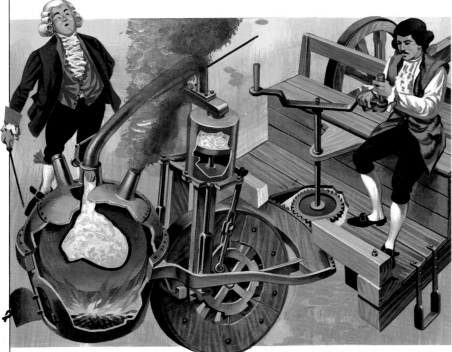

Cugnot's steam wagon (above), invented in 1770, is considered the first steam-powered vehicle. It was used in 1796 by the French army to tow canons.

SCIENTISTS AND INVENTORS, STEAM LOCOMOTIVE ✓, TRANSPORTATION, TRAVEL IN THE OLDEN DAYS

The Industrial Revolution – James Watt invented the modern steam engine in 1765, which launched the Industrial Revolution. By the 19th century, engineers were using steam to drive almost every device, even clocks. In 1825 in England inventors George Stephenson and son Robert made the first train trip by steam locomotive, their invention. In 1829 they won a contest with the locomotive *Rocket*, which went up to 29 mph (47 km/h).

STEPPE

The plains in central Asia are called *steppes*. The land is barren and desolate, and the only vegetation is grass and a few small bushes. The winter is long and cold; the summer is hot and short, with just a few showers. Many native animals, such as yaks and camels, have been domesticated. Large mammals migrate to escape the cold weather. Others, such as rodents, burrow underneath the ground and hibernate for long periods.

The Bactrian camel has been tamed for thousands of years.

Onagers, which are similar to donkeys, graze in the steppe. Their foot has just one toe with a hoof-like nail. There are also wild horses that have been tamed by local populations (below).

Eagle of the steppes
Thanks to its keen eyesight, this bird of prey (left) spots its victim from the sky, then swoops down and grabs it with its hooked claws. Other birds such as quails, little bustards and great bustards (which resemble peacocks) also live in the steppe. The mating dance of the great bustard is truly spectacular: the male opens its feathers like a large white flower.

Camels – These animals live in the steppes of central and southern Asia, not in the desert like the dromedary. Their two humps store fat, and their body accumulates great amounts of water.

ASIA
HORSES
RAPTORS
RODENTS

In the steppe	
1. eagle of the steppes	3. saiga
	4. bobak marmot
2. Przewalski's horse	5. little bustard
	6. great bustard
	7. manul

STEVENSON, ROBERT LOUIS

Scottish author Robert Louis Stevenson (1850–1894) became famous with his novel *Treasure Island*, which was followed by other adventure stories: *Black Arrow, The Lord of Ballantrae* and *The Strange Case of Dr. Jekyll and Mr. Hyde.*

EXCERPTS FROM *TREASURE ISLAND*

"In I got bodily into the apple barrel ... when a heavy man sat down with rather a clash close by ... I was just about to jump up when the man began to speak. It was Silver's voice, and, before I had heard a dozen words, I would not have shown myself for all the world, but lay there, trembling and listening, in the extreme of fear and curiosity; for from these dozen words I understood that the lives of all the honest men aboard depended upon me alone."

"There fell out the map of an island, with latitude and longitude, soundings, names of hills, and bays and inlets, and every particular that would be needed to bring a ship to a safe anchorage upon its shores ... and a hill in the centre part marked 'The Spy-glass.'"

"There were several additions of a later date; but above all, three crosses of red ink—two on the north part of the island, one in the south-west, and, beside this last, in the same red ink, and in a small, neat hand, very different from the captain's tottery characters, these words: 'Bulk of treasure here.'"

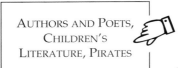

AUTHORS AND POETS, CHILDREN'S LITERATURE, PIRATES

An English sailing ship of the 17th century.

SUN

The Sun is a star around which the Earth and other planets in the solar system rotate. It is formed by a mass of incandescent gas with an average surface temperature of 11,000°F (6,000°C). Energy is produced at the center of the Sun through a series of atomic reactions called *fusion*: during this process four hydrogen atoms are combined to form one helium atom, generating an enormous amount of energy that travels throughout the entire solar system.

The Egyptians worshipped the Sun as a god named Ra, represented by a human body and a falcon head topped with a solar disc (above). The pharaohs considered themselves the children of Ra. In Greek mythology the sun god was Helios, who traveled through the sky on a fiery chariot.

Structure – The Sun is the closest star to the Earth, just 93 million miles away (150 million km)! Its diameter is 109 times that of the Earth's. The photosphere is the visible surface of the Sun, while the corona is the outer-most halo of light. Sunspots are caused by cooler gases on the surface. These spots are surrounded by tongues of incandescent material called *prominences*.

Age – Compared to other stars, the Sun is very young: it is just 5 billion years old, which is considered a middle-aged star. It takes about 30 million years for light from the core to reach the Earth! Its life cycle will terminate when it has depleted all the fuel it needs for fusion: that is when the Sun will die.

The Sun is a star that radiates heat and light.

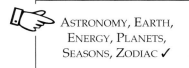

Astronomy, Earth, Energy, Planets, Seasons, Zodiac ✓

SWIFT, JONATHAN

AN EXCERPT FROM *GULLIVER'S TRAVELS*

" ... for when I awaked , it was just day-light. I attempted to rise, but was not able to stir: for as I happened to lie on my back, I found my arms and legs were strongly fastened on each side to the ground; and my hair, which was long and thick, tied down in the same manner ... I felt something alive moving on my left leg, which advancing gently forward over my breast, came almost up to my chin; when bending my eyes downwards as much as I could, I perceived it to be a human creature not six inches high, with a bow and arrow in his hands, and a quiver at his back. In the mean time, I felt at least forty more of the same kind ... "

Gulliver was sent to the court of the Emperor of Lilliput, who asked him to help fight Blefuscu, the neighboring island.

Irish-born author Jonathan Swift (1667–1745) wrote many satirical works. *Gulliver's Travels*, the most famous, is a classic enjoyed by children and adults.

AUTHORS AND POETS
CHILDREN'S LITERATURE

TELLING TIME

The oldest instrument for telling time was the sun dial. A rod called a *gnomon* threw a shadow on a stone slab engraved with numbers: as the hours passed, the shadow moved. About 3000 B.C. the Egyptians devised a water clock that measured time by the flow of water. The hourglass, invented in the 14th century, measured time by letting sand trickle from the upper glass chamber to the lower one. People also used candles to measure time.

hourglass

mechanical clock

Mechanical clocks

Mechanical clocks were introduced in 1200 and often placed on top of buildings and bell towers. Some clocks, such as the Moorish Clock in Venice, had figures that moved when the hour struck. Pocket watches first appeared in 1400 and were often decorated with enameling and precious gems. The first practical pendulum clock was designed by Christian Huygens and led to grandfather clocks. Wristwatches became popular in the 1920s.

The calendar – Ancient Egyptians divided the sky into 12 equal parts (above) and gave each part the name of a constellation. This division of the sky into the zodiac is the basis for our 12-month calendar.

Merkhet

Merkhet – This ancient Egyptian instrument, formed by a bar and a plumb string, was used to measure the hours according to the movements of the stars.

One of the first chronometers

Modern clocks – The first electric clock was built around 1840. Street clocks still run on electricity: a motor controls the movement of the hands. Harwood, an Englishman, invented the self-winding watch in 1922. The digital watch was patented in 1971.

TIGERS

The tiger, the largest cat, is found only in Asia. It has a brawny, muscular body, long sharp claws, strong teeth and yellow eyes. Its orange coat and black stripes help to camouflage it in the forest. This extremely agile feline can jump 20 ft (6 m) and leap to heights of 6 ft (2 m). Tigers are excellent swimmers. An adult tiger needs to eat about 18 lb (8 kg) of meat per day. It is the only carnivore that will occasionally attack a human for food. All species, except the royal tiger, are endangered and risk extinction.

The male tiger marks its territory with urine and by scratching tree bark with its claws.

White tigers – Their color ranges from white to ivory with blackish-brown stripes. This species lives in the wild in the Rewa Forest, India.

The Siberian tiger (above) is the largest feline.

Cubs – Tigers have between 2 and 4 cubs after a gestation period of 95–110 days. Tiger cubs suckle milk for the first 6 weeks, then follow their mothers while the adult female hunts. The young begin to hunt at 6 months and capture their first prey when they are a year old. They are unable to attack a buffalo, however, before 3 years of age.

Prey – Tigers do not have great endurance. They run only for about 650 ft (200 m). The tiger prefers to take its prey by surprise. It pounces with a quick leap and kills its victim by biting it on the neck or throat. Once the tiger has eaten its full, it covers the remains of the prey with leaves and dry branches. Then it falls asleep nearby to protect the carcass from jackals and hyenas.

ASIAN JUNGLE
CAMOUFLAGE
ENDANGERED SPECIES
MAMMALS
WILDCATS

TIME ZONES

When you travel around the world, you have to keep adjusting your watch according to the time zone you are in. Think of Phileas Fogg, the main character in Jules Verne's book *Around the World in Eighty Days*. He won the bet because after he had traveled around the world, he could set his watch back 24 hours, the number of time zones that divide the Earth.

Meridians and parallels
The surface of the globe is divided into many imaginary vertical lines called *meridians* and horizontal lines called *parallels of latitude*. The equator is the largest parallel of latitude that divides the Earth into two hemispheres.

EARTH
MAPS

Traveling east and west – The Earth is divided into 24 time zones, representing the 24 hours in a day. It is the same time everywhere within a zone. The Greenwich meridian in England was used as a reference (the international standard meridian, zero longitude) to count time zones (below). When you travel east you must add one hour to your watch for each time zone that you go through. Likewise, when you travel west, you must subtract one hour for each meridian. Therefore, if it is 8:00 p.m. in London, it is 3:00 p.m. in New York.

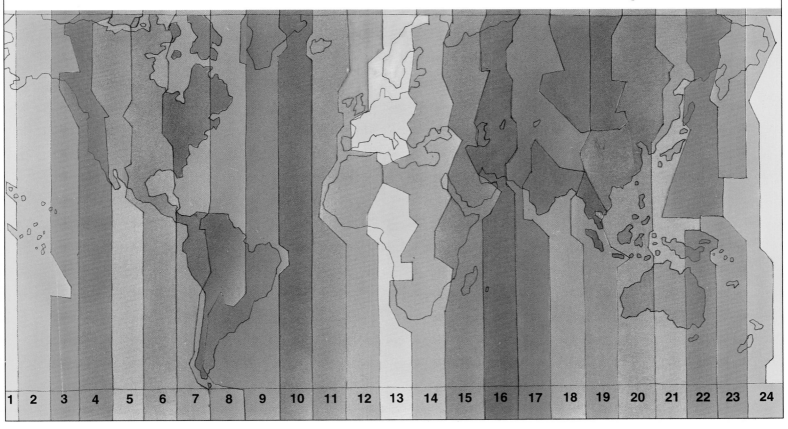

| 1 | 2 | 3 | 4 | 5 | 6 | 7 | 8 | 9 | 10 | 11 | 12 | 13 | 14 | 15 | 16 | 17 | 18 | 19 | 20 | 21 | 22 | 23 | 24 |

TOYS

Egyptian, Greek, and Roman children played with wooden or terra-cotta animals and mechanical toys such as wagons or dolls with jointed arms and legs. A wooden statue of a slave making bread was found in an Egyptian tomb: when she was pushed with a finger, she moved back and forth as though she were really kneading the dough! Toys became more sophisticated as technology improved. The first automatons were built in 1700. Gears hidden underneath their clothes made them move and play instruments. Music boxes that played simple melodies when their lids were opened were invented thereafter.

Egyptian toy

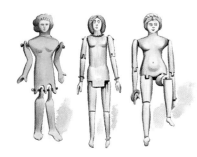

The toy on the left is a Greek doll made of terra-cotta. The other two are Roman dolls made of wood.

1. Cow with moving head.
2. Ram on two wheels.
3. Wagon with oxen and driver.
These mechanical toys in wood and terra-cotta were made by ancient civilizations in Asia.

Toys are also educational: they encourage children to use their imagination and to develop motor coordination.

Today's toys – Dolls made of cloth or porcelain, rocking horses, and tops – all these "old" toys have been replaced by plastic dolls, robots, electronic games and computers. Toys have developed along with technology, creating a close tie between make-believe and reality, which helps children develop and learn. When children play, they come in contact with the world around them and learn to communicate with others through a more complex language.

Locomotives, trains, and cars – At the end of the 19th century children started playing with steam locomotives powered by alcohol. These little trains worked just like the real ones! The first toy cars date back to the beginning of the 20th century. These toys have since become valuable collector's items.

1
2
3

1. Fire engine
2. Steam locomotive
3. Racing car

GAMES

STATION

TRANSPORTATION

Transportation went through a veritable revolution in the 19th century: steam was used to power ships, trains, and road vehicles and the first internal-combustion engines were invented. Means of transportation have developed and improved over the years. Today, each new car model is tested to ensure passenger comfort and safety before it is sold on the market. Car manufacturers have also become more aware of the damage that car exhaust fumes cause to the environment and are testing cars that use clean sources of power such as electricity and solar energy.

Bicycles – Baron Carl Drais invented the *draisienne* (above) in 1818. In 1839, a Scottish blacksmith named MacMillan added lever-controlled pedals that were pushed up and down. The *velocipede*, a bicycle with a front wheel much larger than the back wheel, was introduced in 1855 and became very popular. The first bicycle with a chain transmission made its debut in 1879.

Panhard (1892)

Renault (1898)

Ford Model T (1908–1927)

The Volkswagen Beetle became popular after World War II.

Cars – The first internal-combustion engines were designed by Otto and Langen (1876) and installed on G. Daimler cars in 1880. Rudolph Diesel improved the engine in 1897. Renault was the first car manufacturer to use a gearbox in 1898, and Michelin introduced rubber tires in 1895. In the beginning, cars noisily chugged along at just 10 mph (15 km/h) and were often preceded by a man who waved a red flag to warn pedestrians to get out of the way! Ford was the first company to mass produce an automobile, the Model T, in 1908. Today cars are produced by computer-controlled assembly lines.

Trains – The first passenger steam train ran between Manchester and Liverpool, England, in 1831. Locomotives were powered by steam engines that were eventually replaced by diesel engines and later by electric engines. Today there are high-speed trains such as the *TGV* in France and the Japanese *bullet train* that links Tokyo and Osaka (above).

Flying machines

The desire to fly inspired many of Leonardo da Vinci's designs, but he lacked the technical means to build them. In 1783 the Montgolfier brothers took the first flight aboard a hot-air balloon. The hot-air balloon was later replaced by airships called *dirigibles* (left) that were inflated and propelled with light gases.

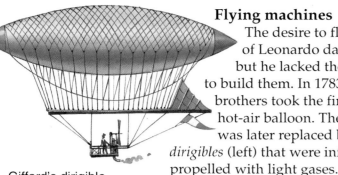

Giffard's dirigible (1851)

Caproni CA 33 bomber plane, Italy (1915)

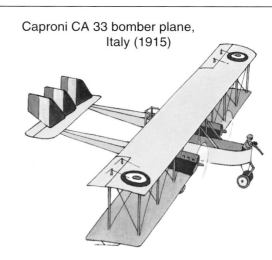

B17F bomber plane, U.S. (1941)

Russian MIG 15 fighter plane (1947)

Airplanes

Airplanes – In 1903, the Wright brothers became the first to fly a biplane equipped with two propellers and a combustion engine. This event marked the dawn of the aviation era. Airplanes quickly improved: Charles Lindbergh flew non-stop from New York to Paris aboard his plane *The Spirit of Saint Louis* in 1927, covering 3,600 mi (5,750 km) in 33½ hours.

The Boeing 747, made in the U.S. (1969), can carry nearly 500 passengers.

Military aviation

Airplanes were first used in battle during World War I. The use of planes for military purposes gave a great boost to the science of aeronautics.

North American X15 rocket plane, U.S. (1959)

Ships – The first steamboats were built around 1800, and by 1820 they could already cross the Atlantic Ocean. Ships were then made with metal hulls and wooden blades were replaced with metal propellers. Thus began the era of the great steamships like the *Normandie* and the *Queen Mary*.

The Normandie, France (1935)

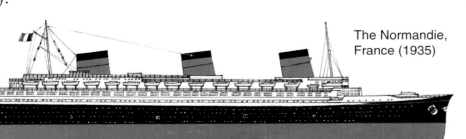

☞
ASSEMBLY LINE ✓,
COMPUTERS, ENERGY,
ENGINES, LEONARDO DA VINCI,
STEAM LOCOMOTIVE ✓,
PORTS, SAILING SHIPS ✓,
SCIENTISTS AND INVENTORS,
STEAM, TRAVEL IN THE OLDEN
DAYS, WORLD WARS

TRAVEL IN THE OLDEN DAYS

The desire to visit other places and meet other people is an ancient one.

Unfortunately, travel was not always easy. Until quite recently, it took considerable time to cover even short distances, and passengers had to cope with danger and hardships.

Steamboats – The *Clermont* (above), which was built in 1807 by Robert Fulton, was the first steamboat for passengers. It sailed along the Hudson River between Albany and New York.

The stagecoach carried from 6 to 8 people. Baggage was placed on the roof.

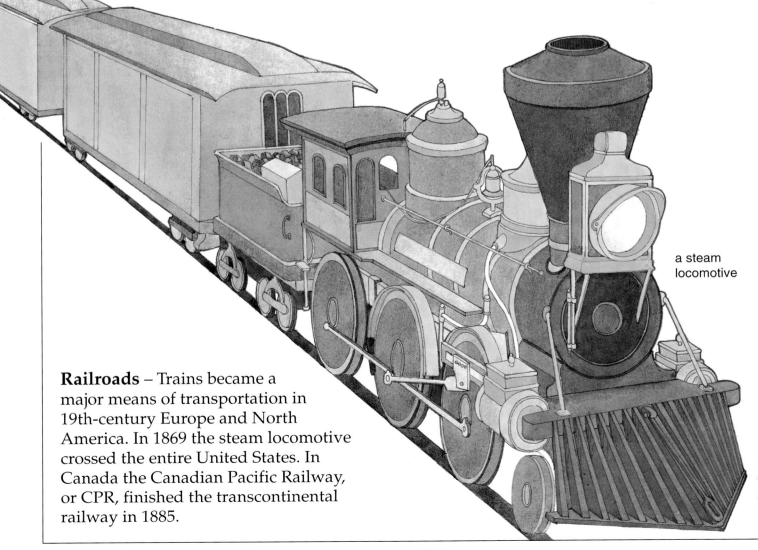

a steam locomotive

Railroads – Trains became a major means of transportation in 19th-century Europe and North America. In 1869 the steam locomotive crossed the entire United States. In Canada the Canadian Pacific Railway, or CPR, finished the transcontinental railway in 1885.

Hot-air balloon – The Montgolfier brothers flew the first hot-air balloon over Paris in 1783 (right). The first dirigible, or steerable airship, was built by Henri Giffard in 1852. This was followed by von Zeppelin's airship in 1900.

Elephants are still a means of transportation in India, but they are used mostly in religious ceremonies.

Velocipede – This early bicycle was popular around 1870. It had a very large front tire and a much smaller back one.

Brougham – This carriage was built for Lord Brougham in 1839. It became a huge success and was considered quite fashionable.

SCIENTISTS AND INVENTORS, STEAM, STEAM LOCOMOTIVE ✓, TRANSPORTATION

TREES AND LEAVES

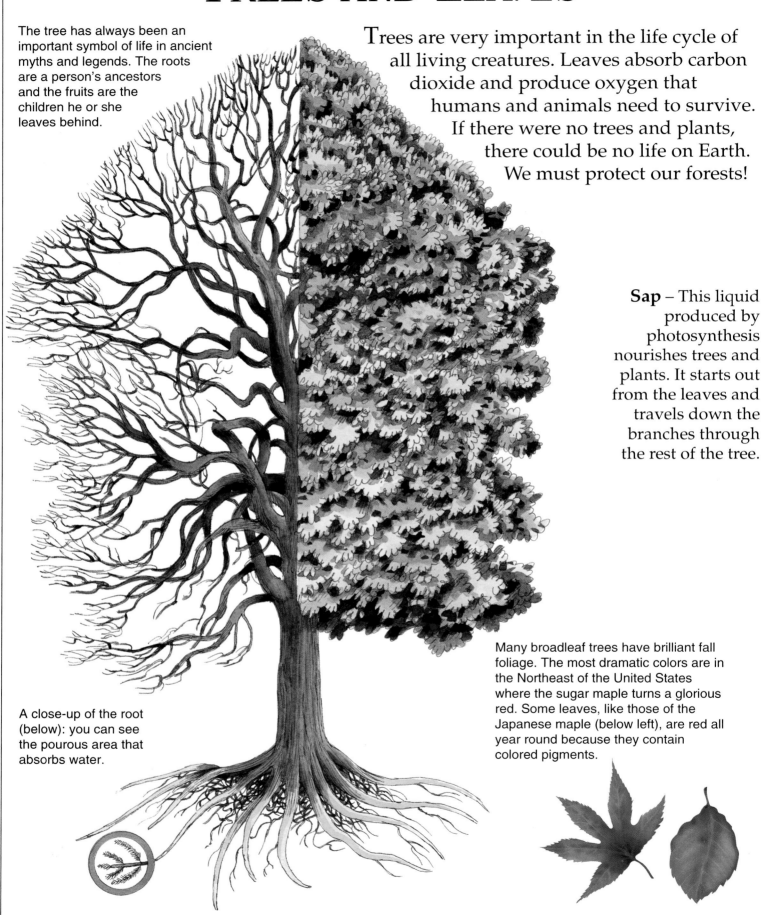

The tree has always been an important symbol of life in ancient myths and legends. The roots are a person's ancestors and the fruits are the children he or she leaves behind.

Trees are very important in the life cycle of all living creatures. Leaves absorb carbon dioxide and produce oxygen that humans and animals need to survive. If there were no trees and plants, there could be no life on Earth. We must protect our forests!

Sap – This liquid produced by photosynthesis nourishes trees and plants. It starts out from the leaves and travels down the branches through the rest of the tree.

A close-up of the root (below): you can see the pourous area that absorbs water.

Many broadleaf trees have brilliant fall foliage. The most dramatic colors are in the Northeast of the United States where the sugar maple turns a glorious red. Some leaves, like those of the Japanese maple (below left), are red all year round because they contain colored pigments.

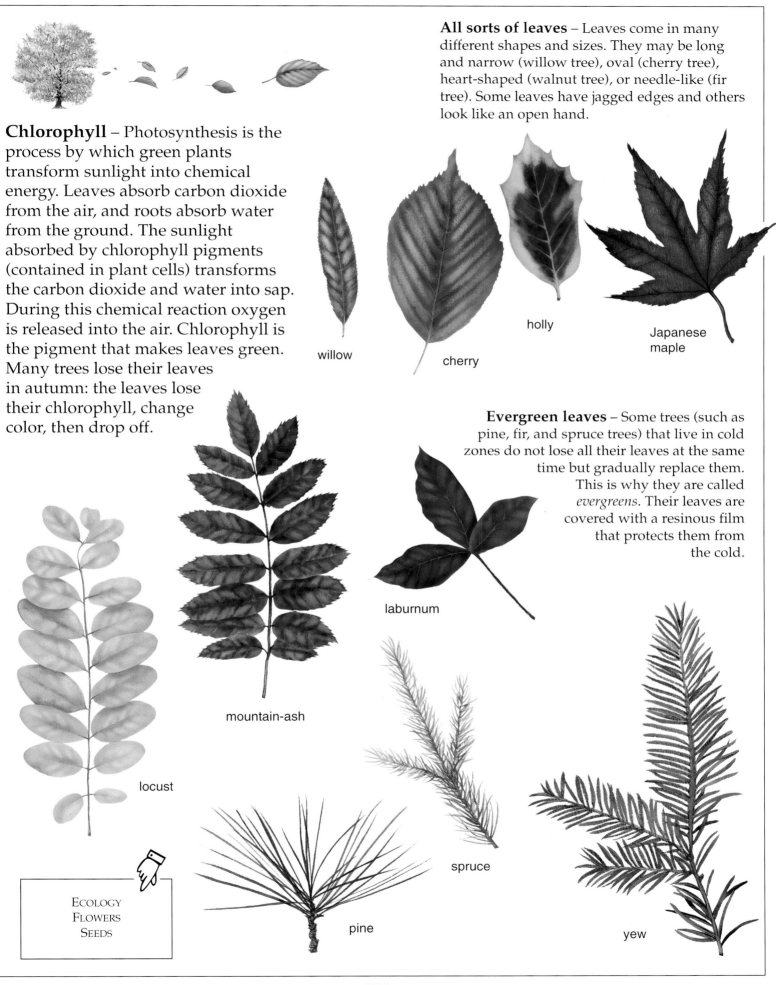

Chlorophyll – Photosynthesis is the process by which green plants transform sunlight into chemical energy. Leaves absorb carbon dioxide from the air, and roots absorb water from the ground. The sunlight absorbed by chlorophyll pigments (contained in plant cells) transforms the carbon dioxide and water into sap. During this chemical reaction oxygen is released into the air. Chlorophyll is the pigment that makes leaves green. Many trees lose their leaves in autumn: the leaves lose their chlorophyll, change color, then drop off.

All sorts of leaves – Leaves come in many different shapes and sizes. They may be long and narrow (willow tree), oval (cherry tree), heart-shaped (walnut tree), or needle-like (fir tree). Some leaves have jagged edges and others look like an open hand.

willow

cherry

holly

Japanese maple

Evergreen leaves – Some trees (such as pine, fir, and spruce trees) that live in cold zones do not lose all their leaves at the same time but gradually replace them. This is why they are called *evergreens*. Their leaves are covered with a resinous film that protects them from the cold.

mountain-ash

laburnum

locust

ECOLOGY
FLOWERS
SEEDS

pine

spruce

yew

273

TUNDRA

The tundra, a cold and treeless land whose soil is frozen most of the year, is found in the arctic regions of Europe, Asia and North America. Winter lasts ten months here. During the short summer the surface ice melts and low-lying vegetation grows: moss, lichens and shrubs. Animals of the tundra have thick fur to withstand the cold. They include small rodents, called lemmings, as well as ermines, arctic foxes, reindeer and caribou and the massive muskox.

caribou (Canadian reindeer)

The arctic hare changes the color of its fur according to the season: it is white in winter and reddish-brown in summer.

Birds of the tundra – Many birds such as Canadian geese, grebes, the long-tailed duck, the long-tailed seagull, the snowy owl and the white partridge live in the tundra.

1. caribou
2. wolf
3. long-tailed seagull
4. white partridge
5. snowy owl
6. arctic fox
7. Canadian goose
8. muskox

snow bunting

☞ ANIMALS OF THE POLAR REGIONS, BIRDS, CAMOUFLAGE, EUROPE, RODENTS

Reindeer – These ruminants with large antlers are raised for their milk and soft hide. Reindeer are also useful for pulling sleds.

Vegetables

In summer, vegetables are grown in gardens and farmers' fields, but greenhouses allow us to enjoy them year round. Vegetables contain large amounts of vitamins and minerals, both essential for healthy growth. It is preferable to eat raw vegetables because cooking makes them lose many of their nutrients.

There are many types of salad greens. Popular varieties are romaine lettuce (above left) and radicchio (above right), which were both grown in ancient Rome and Egypt.

Legumes – Green and yellow beans, peas, lentils and lima beans are legumes with many vegetable proteins. They are an important part of a vegetarian's diet.

peas

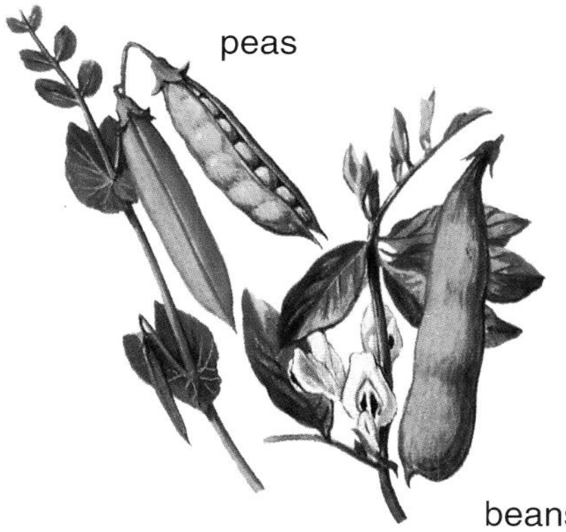

beans

Onions – These vegetables are bulbs that grow underground. Onions contain an oil that, when evaporates, irritates the eyes, thus making us cry when we slice them.

onions

zucchini

squash

Squash and zucchini
These vegetables grow on plants that crawl along the ground. The yellow flowers of the zucchini are edible also.

Eggplants and peppers
The eggplant, native to Asia, has either purple, pale green or white skin. Peppers can be mild, like the large green, yellow and red ones pictured here, or hot, like the small red or green chili peppers.

eggplant

sweet and hot peppers

Potatoes and tomatoes
Both of these plants are native to South America. The potato is a starchy tuber, which is a fleshy underground stem. The tomato is widely cultivated for its fleshy, usually red, fruit.

potatoes

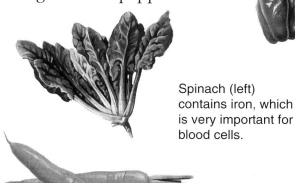

Spinach (left) contains iron, which is very important for blood cells.

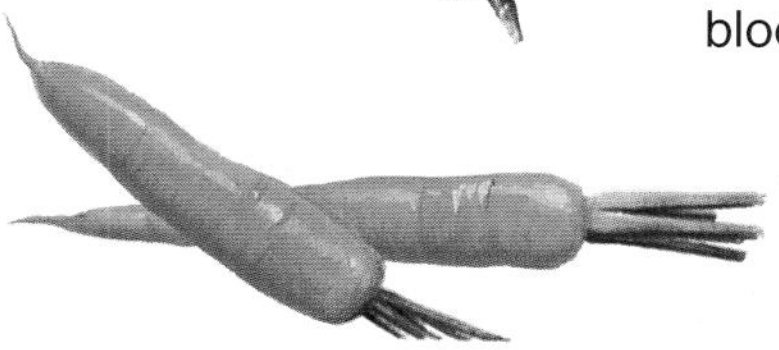

Carrots (above) are rich in Vitamin A.

tomatoes

NUTRITION
GARDENING

VOLCANOES

The Earth's crust is formed by plates that are constantly moving. Consequently, cracks sometimes form in the Earth's crust, and molten rock, an incandescent liquid found beneath the Earth's crust, bubbles out through the cracks. The volcanoes that result look like mountains, but they are formed by *lava* released during a volcanic eruption.

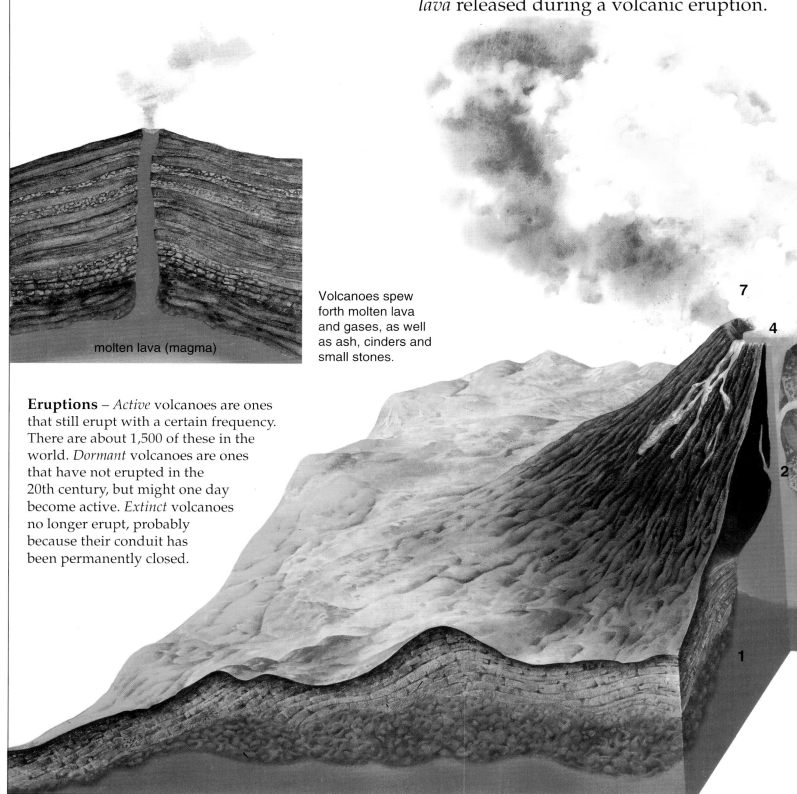

molten lava (magma)

Volcanoes spew forth molten lava and gases, as well as ash, cinders and small stones.

Eruptions – *Active* volcanoes are ones that still erupt with a certain frequency. There are about 1,500 of these in the world. *Dormant* volcanoes are ones that have not erupted in the 20th century, but might one day become active. *Extinct* volcanoes no longer erupt, probably because their conduit has been permanently closed.

Guallatiri (Chile) 19,882 ft (6,060 m)

Tupungatito (Chile) 19,685 ft (6,000 m)

Cotopaxi (Ecuador) 19,393 ft (5,911 m)

Kilimanjaro (Tanzania) 19,340 ft (5,895 m)

Elbrus (Russia) 18,510 ft (5,642 m)

Lascar (Chile) 18,346 ft (5,592 m)

Popocatepetl (Mexico) 17,887 ft (5,452 m)

Ruiz (Colombia) 17,716 ft (5,400 m)

Sangay (Ecuador) 16,736 ft (5,230 m)

Guagua Pichincha (Ecuador) 15,696 ft (4,784 m)

Purace (Colombia) 15,600 ft (4,755 m)

Types of volcanoes – Volcanoes are classified into six types in order of their explosiveness: 1) In the Icelandic type there is a flow of molten basaltic lava from parallel cracks. 2) In the Hawaiian type the lava flows from the summit. 3) The Strombolian type has small bursts of activity. 4) The Vulcanic type involves moderate explosions of ash. 5) Pelean volcanoes form hot, fluid pools of lava. 6) The Plinian type is a violent eruption that blasts out of the magma column.

Lava can reach a temperature of 3,000°F (1,500°C).

Lava may be thick or fluid, in which case it can travel at speeds of 50 mph (80 km/h).

Volcano structure
1. Magmatic reservoir, where magma forms.
2. Conduit, the crack through which the magma travels.
3. Cone, formed by the escaping lava.
4. Crater, an opening at the top of the volcano.
5. Lateral conduit.
6. Solid crust of sedimentary rock.
7. Cloud of gas and ashes.

Vesuvius, the Plinian type of volcano, erupted in 79 A.D. and buried the Roman cities of Ercolanum and Pompeii beneath a river of lava and a cloud of hot ash.

EARTH
MOUNTAINS

WALT DISNEY

Disney characters © Disney Enterprises, Inc./Used by permission from Disney Enterprises, Inc.

Walter Elias Disney and his brother Roy founded The Disney Brothers Studio in 1923, which became Walt Disney Productions in 1929. Today, The Walt Disney Company produces full-length animated cartoons as well as feature films with live actors. The company also publishes books and magazines and operates four world famous theme parks.

Walt Disney was born in Chicago in 1901 and died in Burbank, California, in 1966. His cartoon characters continue to provide enjoyment for children and adults the world over.

Mickey Mouse was created by Walt in 1928. These comic strips appeared in many newspapers.

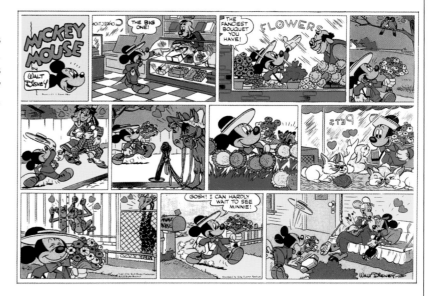

© Disney Enterprises, Inc.

Mickey Mouse – It seems that a real mouse kept Walt Disney company while he worked late in his office in Kansas City. This little creature acted as the inspiration for Mickey Mouse, who first went by the name of Mortimer. Mickey's appearance has gradually evolved over the years.

The evolution of Mickey Mouse.

© Disney Enterprises, Inc.

Mickey Mouse with his girlfriend Minnie.

© Disney Enterprises, Inc.

Donald Duck (right) was created in 1934. He was joined by his girlfriend Daisy Duck and his nephews Huey, Dewey and Louie.

Theme parks – Walt Disney's great dream to create a fantasy world came true in 1955 when Disneyland was inaugurated in Anaheim, California. Walt Disney World opened near Orlando, Florida, in 1971, followed by Epcot and Disney-MGM Studios.

© Disney Enterprises, Inc.

Mickey Mouse and friends

Disney stories have always starred heroes and villains: nasty Big Bad Pete, lovable Horace and Clarabelle, stingy Uncle Scrooge and absent-minded Goofy. Other famous characters are the dog Pluto, genius inventor Gyro Gearloose, the Beagle Boys, space alien Eega Beeva, grandma Duck and gluttonous Gus Goose.

© Disney Enterprises, Inc.

In Europe also

Disneyland® Paris, built near Paris, France, opened its doors in 1992 so that European children could also enjoy the magical world of Disney. Visitors can ride a spaceship, join a crew of pirates, and enter an enchanted castle. Plenty of shows and parades feature the famous Disney characters. A new attraction, Space Mountain, was inaugurated in June 1995. All Disney theme parks are constantly adding new attractions, so you can have fun and discover new things every time you visit!

1. Main Street, U.S.A.
2. Frontierland
3. Adventureland
4. Fantasyland
5. Discoveryland
6. Festival Disney

Left: A drawing of Disneyland® Paris.

279

Left:
*Snow White
and the Seven
Dwarfs* (1937).
Right:
*Lady and the
Tramp* (1955).

Left:
*The Jungle
Book* (1967).

Animated films – *Steamboat Willie*, the first film with Mickey Mouse, was shown in 1928 in New York City. Other famous animated films include *Pinocchio* (1940), *Fantasia* (1940), *Dumbo* (1941), *Bambi* (1942), *Cinderella* (1950), *Alice in Wonderland* (1951), *Peter Pan* (1953), *Sleeping Beauty* (1959), *101 Dalmatians* (1961), *The Sword in the Stone* (1963), *The Aristocats* (1970), *Robin Hood* (1973), *The Rescuers* (1977), *The Fox and the Hound* (1981), *The Black Cauldron* (1985) and *The Rescuers Down Under* (1990).

Other famous Disney films include *The Little Mermaid* (1989), *Beauty and the Beast* (1991), *Aladdin* (1992) and *The Lion King* (1994), left.

Innovative techniques
Disney produced *Who Framed Roger Rabbit* in 1988 with cartoon characters and live actors appearing together on the screen. In 1995 *Toy Story* appeared, a film made entirely by computer.

CINEMA,
FAMOUS TALES
AND AUTHORS

Right:
Pocahontas
(1995).

WASHINGTON, GEORGE

By 1773 there were thirteen English colonies in America. The people who lived there had to pay taxes to England but were not represented in the London Parliament. A revolt broke out when a new tea tax was passed, resulting in the famous Boston Tea Party. In 1774 the colonists formed the Continental Congress, and war broke out the following year. General George Washington led the colonists against the British army.

On July 4, 1776, the Declaration of Independence was made, but Washington fought for five more years. A peace treaty was finally signed in 1783.

George Washington's portrait is on the one-dollar bill.

First President – George Washington (1732–1799) came from a family of wealthy farmers in Virginia. He was placed at the head of the American troops fighting England in 1775. He won many battles and received aid from France. Washington presided over the Federal Convention in Philadelphia (1787) and was elected the first U.S. President in 1789. He was re-elected in 1792.

AMERICA, HISTORY
TIME LINES ✓

George Washington crossed the icy Delaware River on Christmas night of 1776.

WEAPONS

The Chinese invented gunpowder and used it to make fireworks. Gunpowder eventually reached Europe in 1300. In the first half of the 16th century, Henry VIII, Henry II, and Charles V introduced artillery (*cannons, mortars, pistols, muskets,* and *carbines*) in the armies of England, France, and Spain. The *long cannons* of Venetian galley ships were decisive in the victory against the Turks at Lepanto (1571).

Riflemen on horseback (above). Firearms were extensively used during the Thirty Years' War, 1618–1648.

Foot soldiers (above) handled heavy tasks, while specialist bombardiers carried out precision maneuvers.

Military aviation – Airplanes were used in combat for the first time during World War I. Their machine guns were synchronized with the propellers. War maneuvers were coordinated via radio, and many pilots became renowned for their courage. The most famous pilot was Manfred von Richthofen, otherwise known as the Red Baron.
During World War II many decisive battles were won due to fleets of fighter planes equipped with more and more accurate and powerful weapons.

The RAF (Royal Air Force) fought the Luftwaffe (German Air Force) during the Battle of England between August and September 1940. Air battles took place mainly between the English *Spitfire* and the German *Messerschmitt* fighter aircraft.

CHINESE
FREDERICK THE GREAT
WORLD WARS

WILDCATS

Large cats such as tigers, leopards, lions, and cheetahs, as well as the domestic cat, belong to the feline family. Felines first appeared about 40 to 45 million years ago. They have muscular bodies covered with thick fur that is often spotted so they blend in with their surroundings. Wildcats are carnivores with sharp claws and molars and pointy canines to tear meat from bones.

Different coats

The jaguar, who lives in Central and South America, has a reddish coat with round spots. The black panther, on the other hand, is a type of leopard from Africa and Asia and has spots that are barely visible on its dark fur coat. It spies its prey from trees and carries it up to the branches after the kill.

a jaguar and a black panther

Lion – Lions live in groups called *prides* in African savannas and brush. Lionesses hunt and capture the prey, while the males, with their distinctive thick manes, defend the pride's territory. A male lion leaves the pride at three and a half years of age to create a new group.

The ocelot or American tiger cat

Cheetah – This feline has a slim body and yellowish-red fur covered with black spots. It is a very fast runner: it can reach speeds of 45 mph (75 km/h) and can sprint as fast as 60 mph (100 km/h), over short distances up to 1,600 ft (500 m).

ANIMALS OF AFRICA,
ANIMALS OF SOUTH AMERICA,
ASIAN JUNGLE, CAMOUFLAGE,
CATS, ENDANGERED SPECIES,
MAMMALS, TIGERS

Marbled cat
This nocturnal feline hunts in the forests of Java and Myanmar (Burma). It has a long tail and brownish-gray fur with irregular spots.

Cheetah

WILD WEST

A Colt 45, the most famous revolver in the West.

The western part of the United States became the promised land for those seeking riches and fortune. People from all over North America made the voyage to the vast territories west of the Mississippi. Both native-born Americans and European immigrants left crowded cities to make the long and dangerous trip. Trains and wagons were held up by bandits, and the region earned the title the Wild West. The first gold nugget was discovered in 1848 in California, an event that started the Gold Rush, which attracted thousands of new pioneers and settlers.

Many movies and books have been inspired by the frontier stories of the Wild West.

Above: Monument Valley, on the border of Arizona and Utah.
Below: The town sheriff in a gunfight in front of a saloon: a scene that has been re-enacted hundreds of times in Westerns.

AMERICA
HISTORY TIME LINES ✓
NATIVE AMERICANS

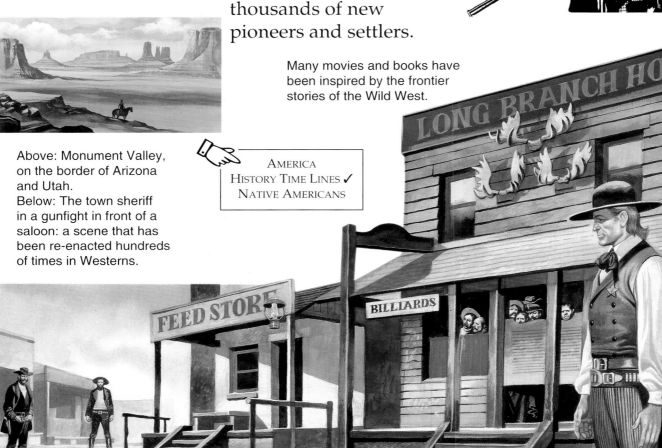

WOMEN OF HISTORY

Queen Victoria (1819–1901) became queen of England in 1837 and ruled at the height of the British Empire.

History books feature such famous women as Cleopatra, the ambitious queen of Egypt (68 B.C.–30 B.C.) and Marie Antoinette, the ill-fated sovereign of France guillotined in 1793. Emily Dickinson, Emily Brontë and Jane Austen are 19th-century authors who are still widely read today. Famous scientists include Marie Curie (1867–1934), who received the Nobel Prize for her work. Some women fought for social causes: Helen Keller (1880–1968), who was deaf and blind, overcame her disabilities and inspired many people. Rosa Parks (1913–1995), an African-American, helped spark the Civil Rights Movement. Other famous women excelled in the arts: actress Sarah Bernhardt (1844–1923), dancer Isadora Duncan (1878–1927), painter Georgia O'Keefe (1887–1986) and opera singer Maria Callas (1923–1977) are just a few.

Famous Women in the Middle Ages – Hildegard of Bingen (1098–1179), a German nun celebrated for her mystic visions, wrote poetry and music and was also interested in the natural sciences. Saint Clare (1193–1253), inspired by Saint Francis of Assisi, founded the religious order the Poor Clares. Matilda of Canossa (1046–1115) supported Pope Gregory VII against Holy Roman Emperor Henry IV, who stood in the snow for three days outside the Castle of Canossa to beg the Pope's forgiveness. Eleanor of Aquitaine (1122–1204), pictured above, was first the wife of Louis VII of France and then of Henry II of England. She ruled England while her son Richard the Lion Hearted was away fighting in the Crusades.

Elizabeth I (1533–1603), left, turned England into a major European power on the seas and in trade.

Florence Nightingale (1820–1910) served as an army nurse during the Crimean War. She improved the sanitation and care in the army hospital at Scutari, where she was known by the soldiers as the Lady of the Lamp for her nightly rounds.

☞ ALCOTT
CATHERINE THE GREAT
ELIZABETH I
HISTORY TIME LINES ✓
JOAN OF ARC

Sally Ride became the first American woman in space in 1983. She was flight engineer aboard the shuttle *Challenger*.

British pilot Amy Johnson, left, flew solo from London to Australia in 1930. During one of her stops in the 19-day trip, she had to repair her plane's wings with a shirt.
Amelia Earhart, probably the most famous woman aviator, disappeared in 1937 while trying to fly around the world.

Feminism – In the 19th century women began seeking equality. Women in England and America launched the women's suffrage movement; one goal was to obtain the right to vote, which was not achieved for women in these two countries until the 1920s. Women's liberation took on different aims in the second half of the 20th century: in western countries women have fought for equal pay while in Africa a goal has been to eliminate the bride-price. In the Middle East, feminists seek a more liberal dress code and in some places the right to drive a car.

Mother Teresa, a Catholic nun, has dedicated her life to helping the poor and sick of India. In 1979 she was awarded the Nobel Peace Prize.

WORLD WARS

During World War I, which began in 1914 and ended in 1918, the *Allies* (Russia, France, England, and later Italy) fought against Germany and the Austro-Hungarian empire. The United States' entrance in the war in 1917 on the side of the Allies ensured their victory.

The Fokker E, a German fighter plane (WWI)

Franz Ferdinand (heir to the Austrian throne) and his wife were assasinated on June 28, 1914 in Sarajevo by a Serbian student. This was the spark that triggered World War I.

World War II – In 1939, Germany invaded Poland under the leadership of Adolf Hitler. France and England then declared war on Germany. Italy, ruled by Benito Mussolini, became Germany's ally in 1940. Once Germany had invaded and occupied France, only England remained to stop the German forces.

The Mitsubishi A6M Zero, a Japanese fighter plane (WWII)

The phases of the war

The German Air Force could not bring England to its knees and the English fleet maintained its control of the seas. In 1941, Germany declared war on Russia, but after a few early victories, the German army was defeated and forced to retreat. The Russians marched on Berlin on May 8, 1945. In the meantime, the Nazis persecuted the Jews: millions of innocent men, women, and children died in Nazi concentration camps.

World War II airplanes:
1. Spitfire (England)
2. Messerschmitt BF 110 (Germany)
3. Hawker Hurricane (England)
4. Junkers JU 87 Stuka (Germany)
5. Messerschmitt BF 109 (Germany)
6. Junkers JU 88 (Germany)
7. Heinkel HE 111 (Germany)

CHURCHILL
EUROPE
TRANSPORTATION
WEAPONS

The British Spitfire fighter plane (WWII)

In 1945, the United States launched the first atomic bomb on Hiroshima and the second on Nagasaki to force Japan, which was Germany's ally, to surrender. Japan surrendered on September 2, 1945.

The German Messerschmitt BF 109 (WWII)

Pearl Harbor – On December 7, 1941 Japanese kamikaze pilots made a surprise attack on the American fleet at Pearl Harbor, Hawaii. The U.S. therefore declared war on Japan and Germany, sending troops and money to the war effort. This was the decisive element that helped the Allies win the war (right).

ZEBRAS

This African mammal is a member of the Equid family, like the horse. It has a characteristic black and white striped coat. Although zebras all look identical, each one has a unique combination of stripes. This highly sociable animal lives in herds, and some species run with antelopes. The zebra eats plants and often migrates to escape the drought. It lives in the plains regions with bushes and trees and in the arid mountainous areas of Africa.

A special snout – The stripes on the head of the Grant's zebra are interrupted by a dark brown area on the snout. This species is widespread on the plains of Africa.

Species – There are only three zebra species alive today: the *Grevy's zebra* of Northeast Africa is the largest. The *plains* or *Burchell's zebra* is the most prevalent species and the one most similar to the horse. The *mountain zebra* found in Namibia and in the southern Cape mountains is becoming more and more rare.

ANIMALS OF AFRICA
CAMOUFLAGE
HORSES
MAMMALS

Zebras are very fast and can reach speeds of 44 mph (70 km/h). However, they don't have much stamina.

Baby zebras – Newborns are able to stand immediately after birth. In general, the adult female reproduces every 11–12 months, giving birth to one foal.

Visual Dictionary

ASSEMBLY LINE

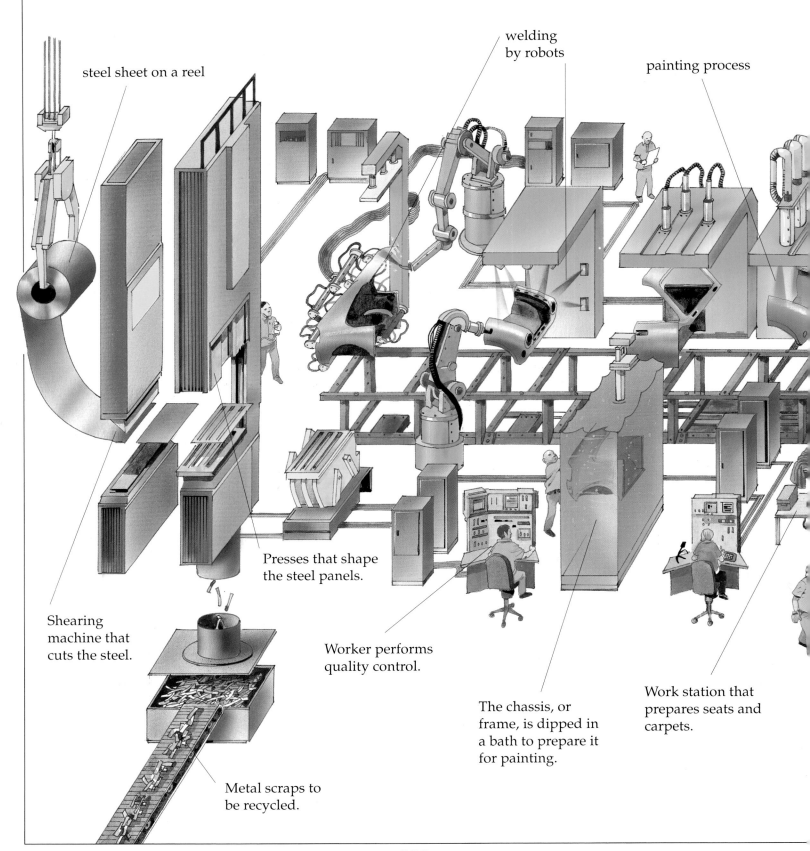

steel sheet on a reel

welding
by robots

painting process

Presses that shape
the steel panels.

Shearing
machine that
cuts the steel.

Worker performs
quality control.

The chassis, or
frame, is dipped in
a bath to prepare it
for painting.

Work station that
prepares seats and
carpets.

Metal scraps to
be recycled.

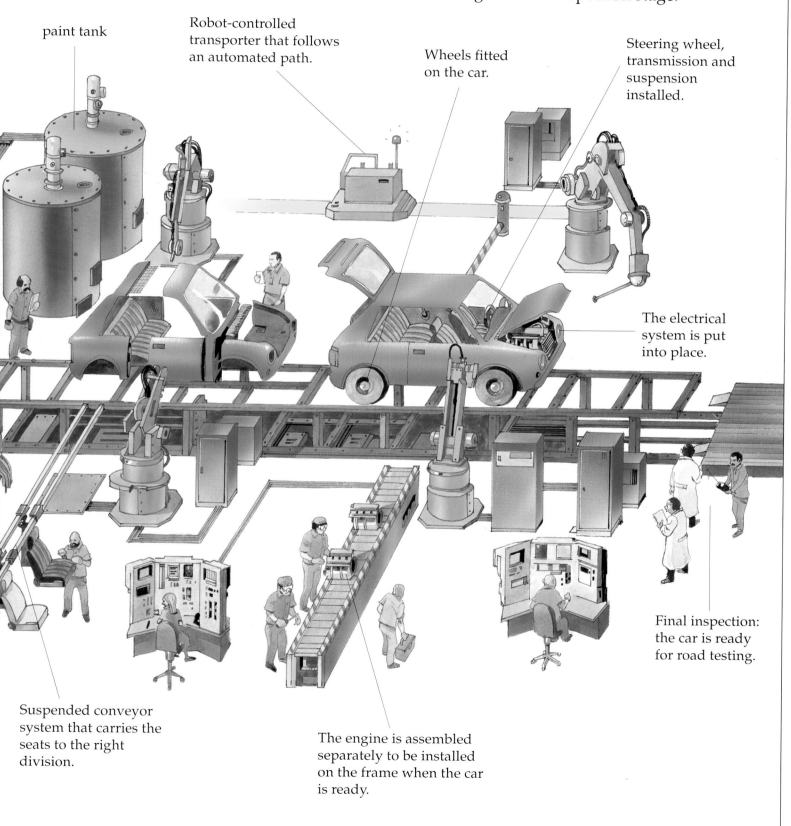

Robots – These automated machines do the heaviest and most repetitive work on the assembly line; they are used in the molding station, body shop, painting station and during the final inspection stage.

paint tank

Robot-controlled transporter that follows an automated path.

Wheels fitted on the car.

Steering wheel, transmission and suspension installed.

The electrical system is put into place.

Final inspection: the car is ready for road testing.

Suspended conveyor system that carries the seats to the right division.

The engine is assembled separately to be installed on the frame when the car is ready.

GOTHIC CATHEDRAL

Gothic – An architectural style that flourished during the Middle Ages, in western Europe, from the 12th to the 16th century. Gothic churches are characterized by pointed arches, vaults, and flying buttresses. The cathedrals featured magnificent stone sculptures, bas-reliefs and spires.

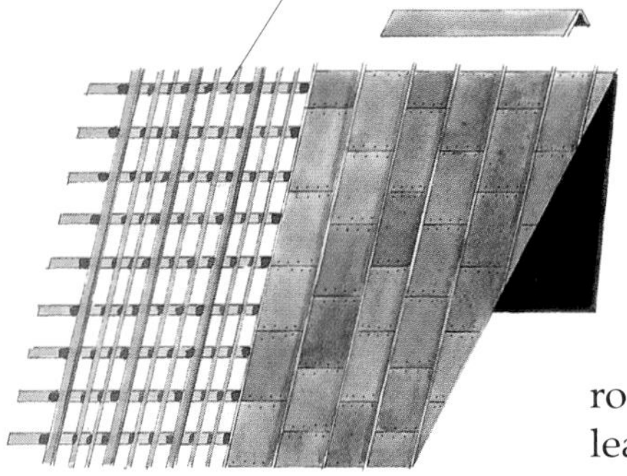

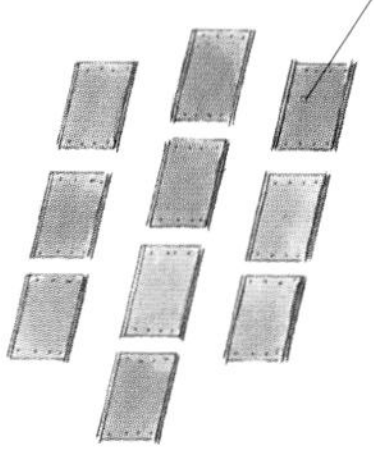

wooden beams

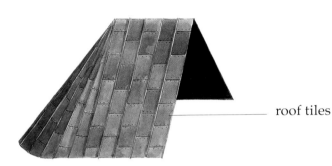

roof tiles

roof tiles of lead or copper

Examples of Gothic style are the cathedrals of Rheims, Chartres, Cologne, Salisbury, Notre-Dame, Canterbury and Milan.

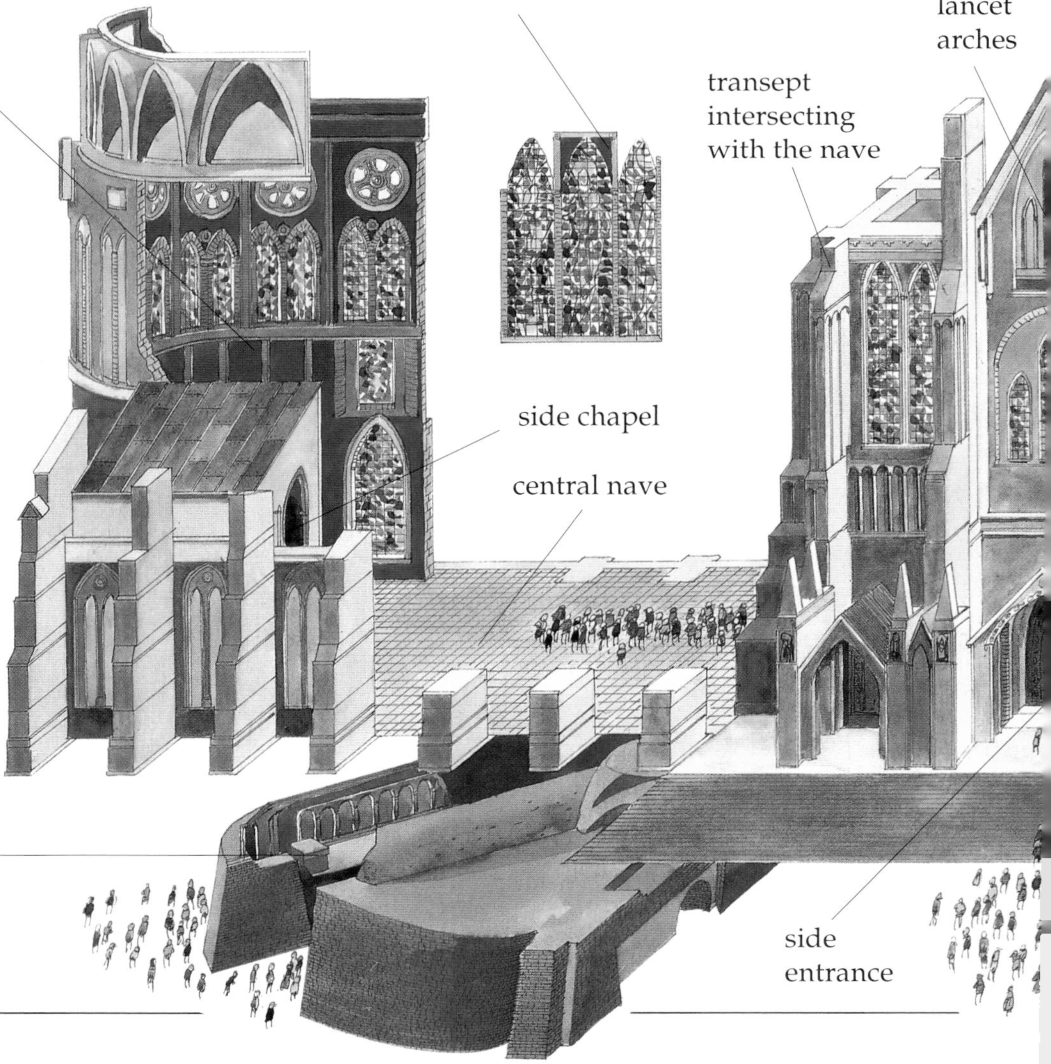

stained-glass windows

lancet arches

apse

transept intersecting with the nave

Many artisans and workers, under the guidance of the master builder, constructed cathedrals that required decades to complete. The craftsmen worked in stone (carvers, masons and stonelayers), wood (joiners, sawyers and carpenters) and glass.

side chapel

central nave

underground crypt with relics of saints

side entrance

Reformation – The Roman Catholic Church and the Orthodox Church of Constantinople broke apart in 1054. Today the Christians in Greece, Russia, the Middle East, and in Slavic countries are Orthodox Christians. The Church of Rome's authority began to collapse during the height of Gothic art, and rebellions began in Germany. In 1517 the monk Martin Luther (1483–1546) introduced the reformation movement of Christianity, which was later called Protestantism. This led to the foundation of many churches in northern Europe and North America: the Anglican, Lutheran, Calvinist (started by John Calvin, 1509–1564) and the Methodist churches.

John Calvin

Martin Luther

bell tower

niches

spires

wooden beams

wooden beams

main door

rose window

steps

ROMANESQUE CHURCH

Romanesque – A style of art and architecture that began in France and northern Italy in the late 9th century and spread across Europe in the 11th and 12th centuries. Romanesque churches are characterized by thick walls, semi-circular arches and columns.

Roof – Tiles cover the pyramidal tower roof.

Truss – The triangular structure that supports the roof and is made of two sloping beams called rafters, connected by a horizontal beam called a truss-rod.

Apse – The part of the church where the altar is located. The semi-domed ceiling above the apse is called the basin.

altar

Presbytery
The section of the church reserved to the clergy, and the area where the main altar is located. It is often raised off the ground and enclosed by a railing.

Balustrade – A railing formed by a series of small columns.

underground crypt

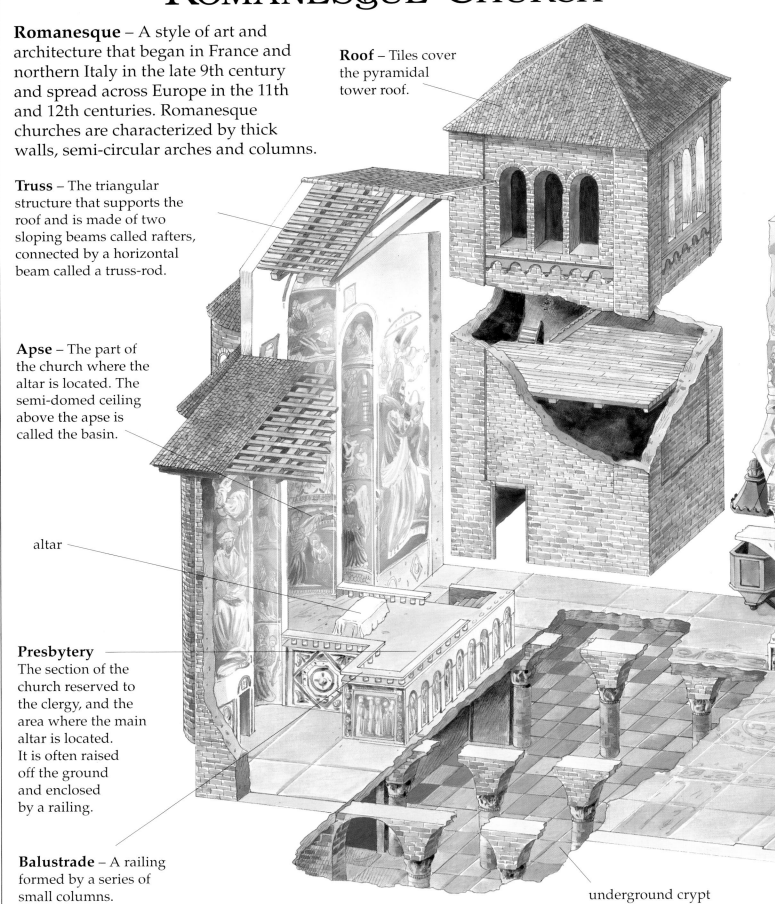

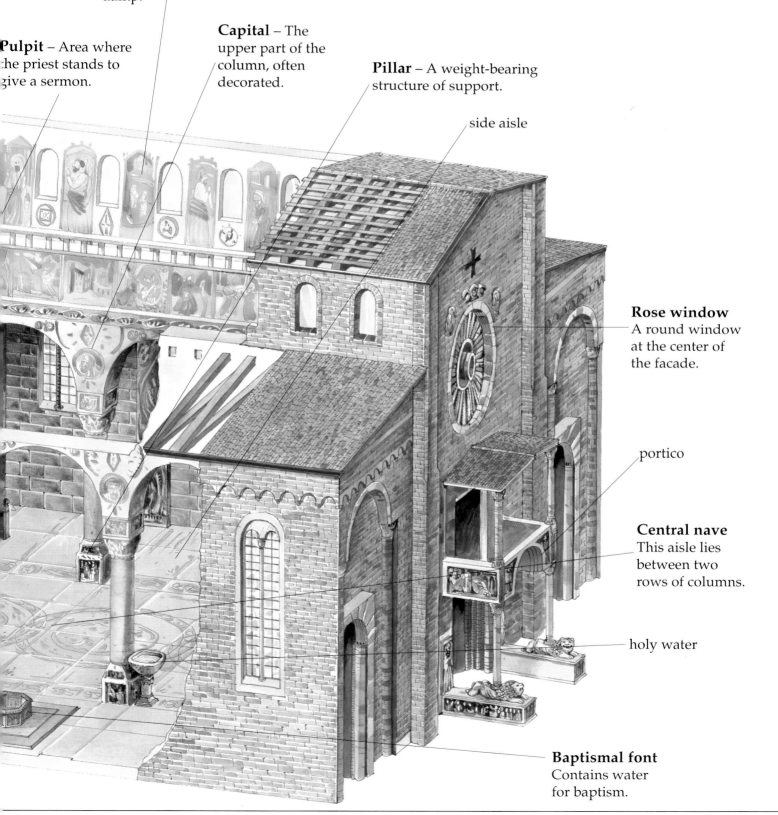

Simple style – The Romanesque style is very simple, spare and understated. The most beautiful Romanesque churches in Italy are San Miniato in Tuscany and Sant'Ambrogio in Milan.

Frescoes – Painted murals made when the plaster is still damp.

Capital – The upper part of the column, often decorated.

Pillar – A weight-bearing structure of support.

Pulpit – Area where the priest stands to give a sermon.

side aisle

Rose window A round window at the center of the facade.

portico

Central nave This aisle lies between two rows of columns.

holy water

Baptismal font Contains water for baptism.

295

CONSTELLATIONS

Sagittarius (the Archer): the ninth constellation of the zodiac (1); in the southern sky and visible low on the horizon on summer evenings.

Capricorn (the Goat): the tenth constellation of the zodiac (2); in the southern sky and visible on summer evenings.

Aquarius (the Water Bearer): the eleventh constellation of the zodiac (3); in the southern hemisphere, near the equator and visible on summer and autumn nights.

Pisces (the Fish): the twelfth constellation of the zodiac (4); in the southern sky and visible on summer and autumn nights.

Aries (the Ram): the first constellation of the zodiac (5); in the northern sky and visible on autumn and winter nights.

Taurus (the Bull): the second constellation of the zodiac (6); in the northern sky and visible on autumn and winter nights.

Orion (the Hunter): a constellation that crosses the celestial equator (7) and is made up of four stars, three of which are very bright: Betelgeuse, Rigel and Bellatrix.

Cygnus (the Swan): a constellation in the northern sky (8) that is shaped like a cross and crossed by the Milky Way.

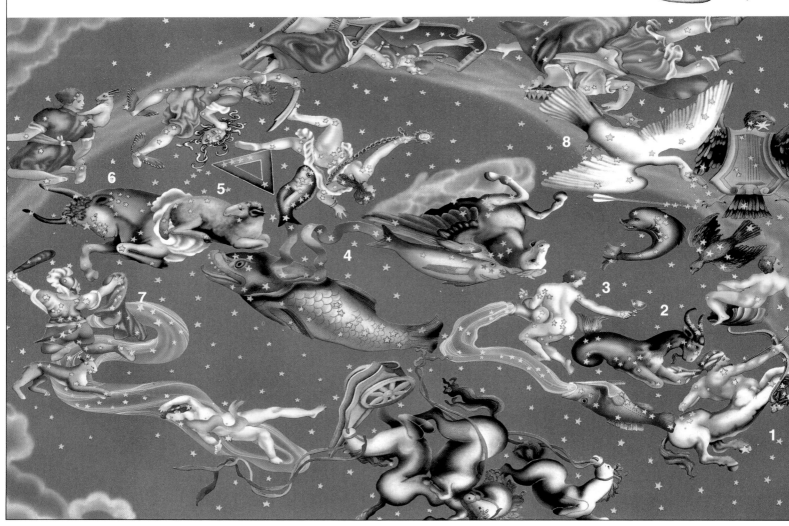

Gemini (the Twins): the third constellation of the zodiac (9); in the northern sky and visible on autumn and winter nights.

Libra (the Scales): the seventh constellation of the zodiac (13); in the southern sky and visible on spring and summer nights.

Cancer (the Crab): the fourth constellation of the zodiac (10); in the northern sky and visible on winter and spring nights.

Scorpio (the Scorpion): the eighth constellation of the zodiac (14); in the southern sky and visible on summer nights.

Leo (the Lion): the fifth constellation of the zodiac (11); in the northern sky and visible on winter and spring nights.

Ursa Major (the Great Bear): the seven brightest stars form the Big Dipper (15).

Virgo (the Virgin): the sixth constellation of the zodiac (12); on the edge of the celestial equator and visible on spring nights.

Ursa Minor (the Little Bear): the seven brightest stars form the Little Dipper (16), which includes Polaris, the North Star. Like Ursa Major, it is in the northern sky and is visible every night of the year.

SKYSCRAPERS

Reinforced cement and steel
Skyscrapers are very tall buildings especially designed to take advantage of limited space in large cities. The Chicago School introduced this architectural trend in 1880. These buildings are at least 12 to 15 stories high (164 ft or 50 m).

New York City Skyline

1. The twin towers of the World Trade Center, the world's second tallest building (110 stories).
2. A helicopter hovering over the city.
3. Citicorp Center sits on huge pillars nine stories tall. The top of the building is shaped like a clarinet mouthpiece.
4. Chrysler Building, 77 stories.
5. Empire State Building, 102 stories.
6. Circle Line ferry
7. Tugboats (New York lies at the mouth of the Hudson River).

STEAM LOCOMOTIVE

Steam-powered trains

The first steam-powered trains appeared around 1830 and had 8 to 14 cars. The locomotive was driven by the engineer and fireman. The train also had a conductor and ticket-collector. Cooks and waiters prepared and served meals. Sometimes there was even a barber on board. Mailmen from the postal service also traveled on these trains.

Smokestack – Puffs of smoke produced by the boiler come out of the smokestack.

Boiler – The steel tank to hold the boiling water.

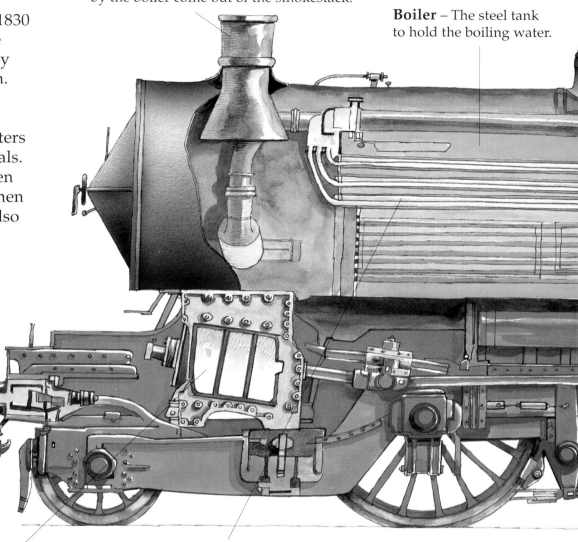

Cylinders – The boiling steam reaches the cylinders and drives the pistons that turn the wheels.

Pipes – Pipes containing the hot gases from the furnace. The steam from the boiler passes through the pipes to increase the power of the steam on the pistons.

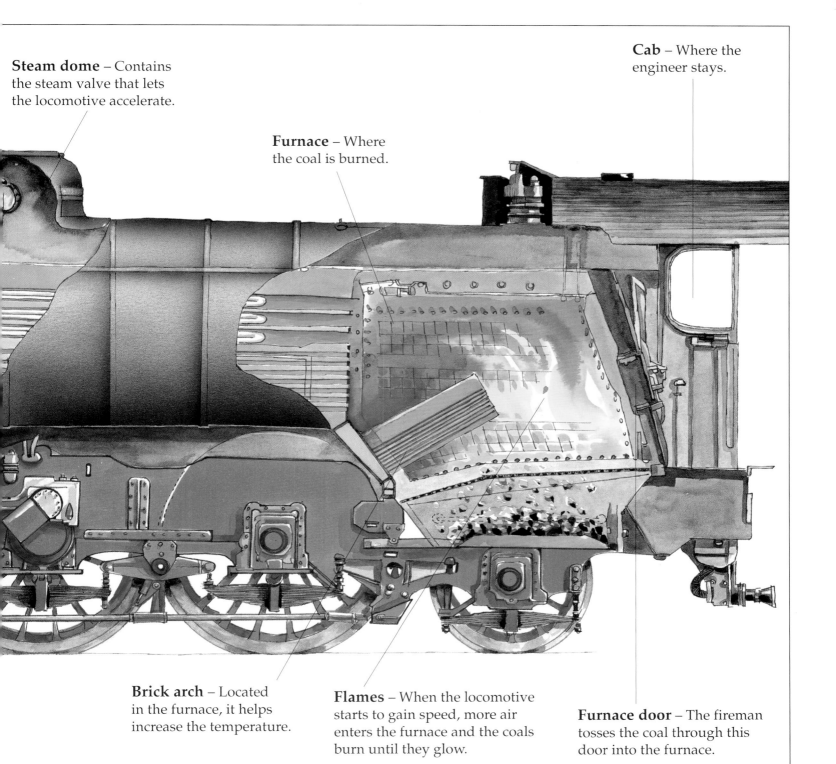

Steam dome – Contains the steam valve that lets the locomotive accelerate.

Furnace – Where the coal is burned.

Cab – Where the engineer stays.

Brick arch – Located in the furnace, it helps increase the temperature.

Flames – When the locomotive starts to gain speed, more air enters the furnace and the coals burn until they glow.

Furnace door – The fireman tosses the coal through this door into the furnace.

Above: a sectional view of the locomotive.

Left: A 685 steam locomotive from Italy.

Speed – The fireman would light the fire in the furnace several hours before departure to heat the water in the boiler that turned into steam. When the steam pressure was high enough, the engineer would open the steam valve and the steam would reach the pistons and then the wheels. The locomotive would start chugging slowly, then accelerate. It could reach a speed of about 100 mph (160 km/h).

Battle of Waterloo

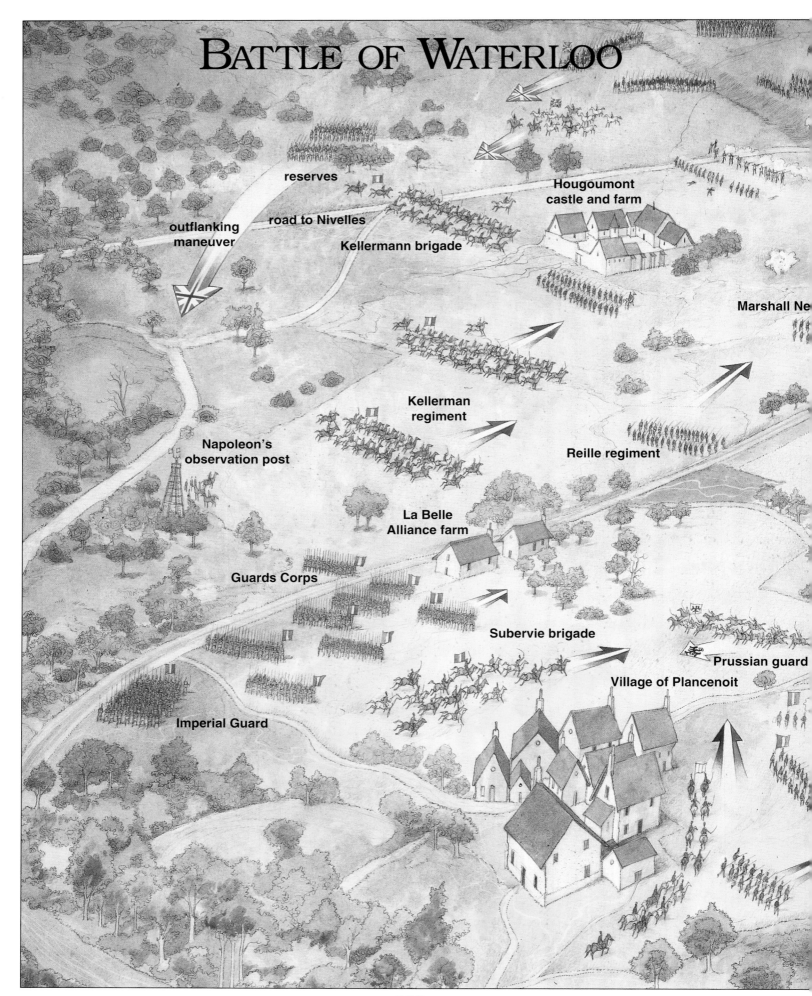

reserves

outflanking maneuver

road to Nivelles

Kellermann brigade

Hougoumont castle and farm

Marshall Ne

Napoleon's observation post

Kellerman regiment

Reille regiment

La Belle Alliance farm

Guards Corps

Subervie brigade

Prussian guard

Village of Plancenoit

Imperial Guard

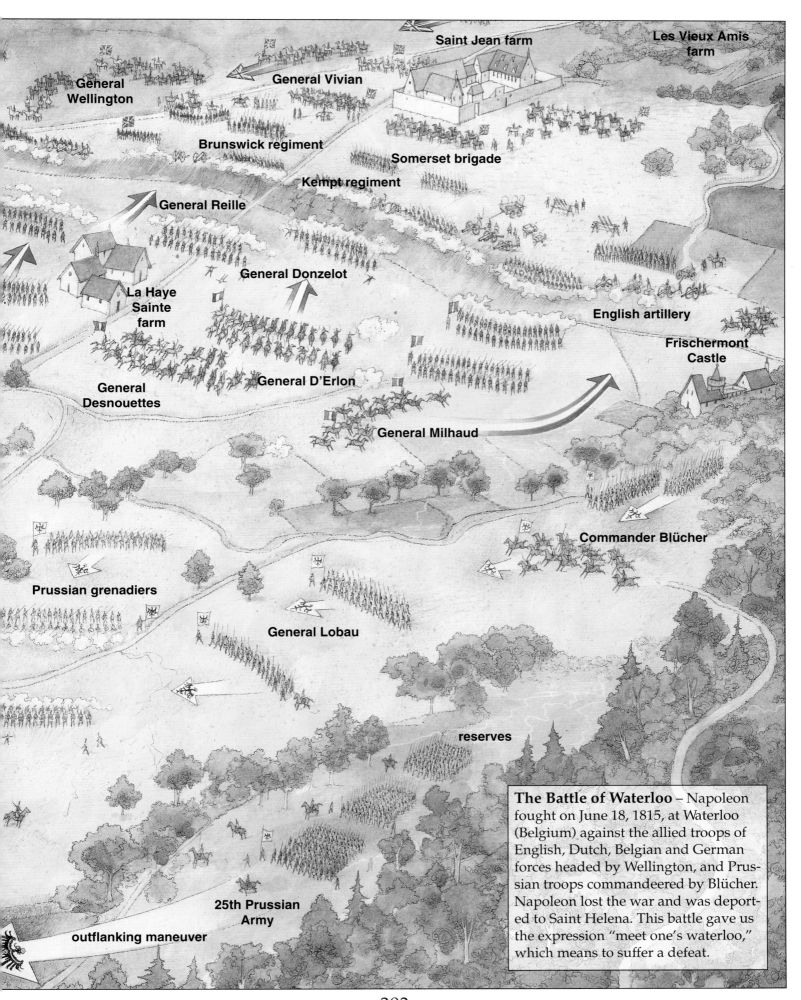

Saint Jean farm

Les Vieux Amis farm

General Vivian

General Wellington

Brunswick regiment

Somerset brigade

Kempt regiment

General Reille

General Donzelot

English artillery

La Haye Sainte farm

Frischermont Castle

General Desnouettes

General D'Erlon

General Milhaud

Commander Blücher

Prussian grenadiers

General Lobau

reserves

25th Prussian Army

outflanking maneuver

The Battle of Waterloo – Napoleon fought on June 18, 1815, at Waterloo (Belgium) against the allied troops of English, Dutch, Belgian and German forces headed by Wellington, and Prussian troops commandeered by Blücher. Napoleon lost the war and was deported to Saint Helena. This battle gave us the expression "meet one's waterloo," which means to suffer a defeat.

THE GREAT WALL OF CHINA

The Great Wall of China (about 4,000 mi or 6,400 km in length) was built by Chinese emperor Shih Huang Ti (229–221 B.C.) to protect China's northern borders.

1. Regiment flags
2. Drums used to incite the troops
3. Crenelated wall
4. Inner wall
5. Cavalry of the foreign invaders
6. Catapults used to attack the towers
7. Horses in front of the walls
8. Invaders trying to scale the wall
9. Carrier pigeons with messages
10. Watchtower with small openings
11. Guards ready to defend the wall
12. Soldiers arriving from the village
13. Tall observation towers
14. Smoke signals
15. Storehouses and stockpiles
16. Walled village
17. Pagoda
18. Barracks and armories
19. Peasant homes
20. Farmland

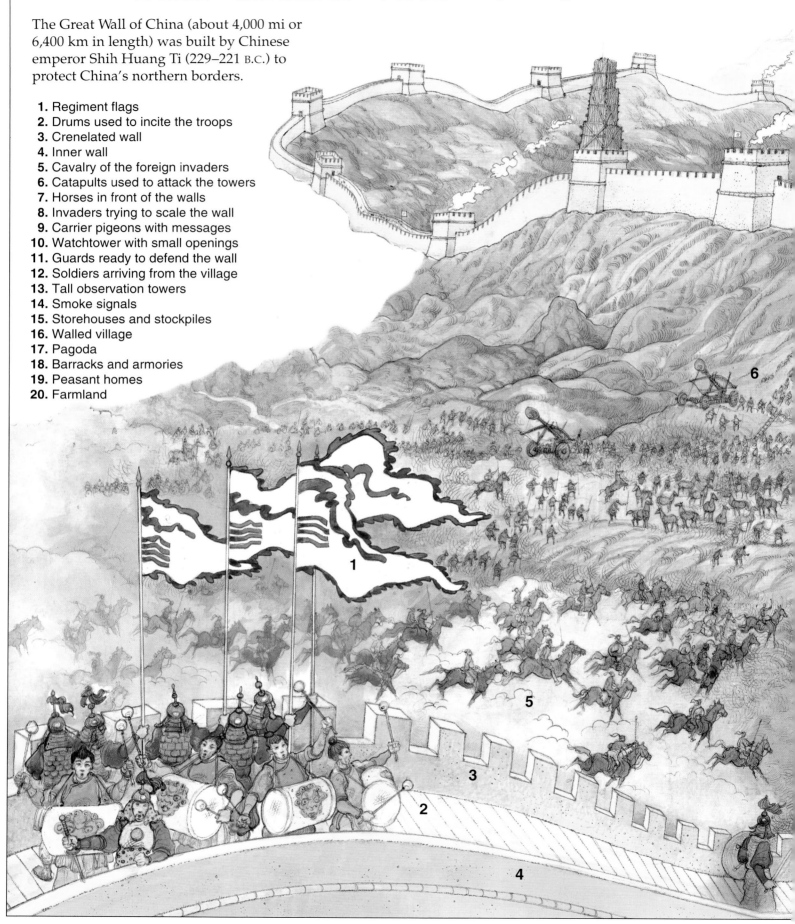

NAUTICAL SCIENCE

Nautical Science – This is the art of navigation. Besides engineering and building ships, nautical science also involves sailing maneuvers such as tying knots. There are special knots for tying, docking and maneuvering. Some knots are so difficult that only the most expert sailors know how to tie them.

timber hitch

one turn

overhand knot

square knot

slip knot

two half hitches

reef knot

sheepshank knot

strangle knot

whip knot

sheet bend

double sheet bend

lark's head knot

palm and needle whipping

clove hitch

fisherman's knot

bowline

stevedore knot

figure-of-eight knot

common whipping

bowline in the bight

one round turn

Signaling – Before there were radios on board, sailors used to communicate with lights or flags. The flags, which were hung from the ship's flagpole, corresponded to a number or letter of the alphabet. Certain flags also sent coded messages. These flags are still used today.

MAY DAY – This phrase actually comes from the French phrase *M'aidez*, which means *help me*. When a ship sends the MAY DAY radio message, that means it is in danger.

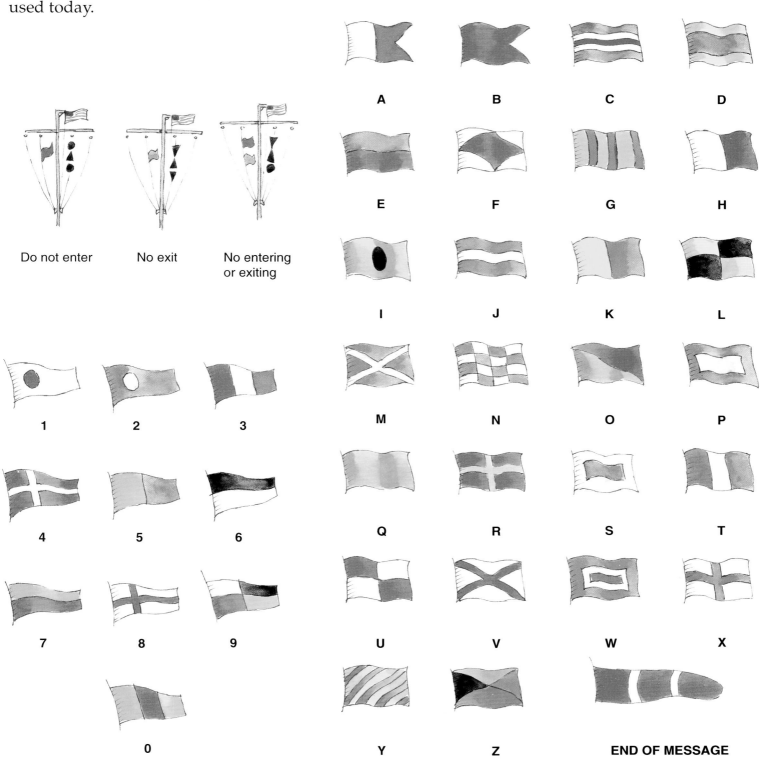

Do not enter

No exit

No entering or exiting

1

2

3

4

5

6

7

8

9

0

A

B

C

D

E

F

G

H

I

J

K

L

M

N

O

P

Q

R

S

T

U

V

W

X

Y

Z

END OF MESSAGE

NEW YORK CITY

New York was founded by the Dutch in 1624, who called it New Amsterdam. Today the city has seven million inhabitants spread across five boroughs: Manhattan, Queens, Brooklyn, the Bronx and Richmond. New York is an important cultural, financial and artistic center and is the home to many important institutions such as Columbia University, the Rockefeller Foundation and the United Nations.

Manhattan boasts many libraries, art galleries and museums such as the Metropolitan Museum and the Museum of Modern Art, which New Yorkers call the MOMA. The Metropolitan Opera and Carnegie Hall are world famous.

1. New York is the most ethnically diverse of all American cities. The population includes large numbers of Afro-Americans, Puerto Ricans, Asians, and European immigrants.
2. A hot-dog stand.
3. Typical New York food: an American breakfast of bacon and eggs, a giant pretzel and a bagel.
4. Yankee Stadium.
5. Bronze statue of Alice in Wonderland in Central Park.
6. Street signs in Greenwich Village.
7. Dragon in Chinatown.

8. Hell's Kitchen, a neighborhood where many Irish used to live.
9. The Statue of Liberty.
10. Policeman on horseback in Central Park.
11. Skaters and bicyclists ride along-side taxis and limousines on Fifth Avenue.
12. Mimes performing on the street.
13. Ice rink at Rockefeller Center.
14. FAO Schwarz toy store.
15. Empire State Building.
16. Aerial view of Central Park.
17. Statue of Balto, the heroic sled dog, in Central Park.

18. Workers on a skyscraper under construction.
19. Museum of Natural History.
20. *The Female Clown* by Toulouse-Lautrec (at the MOMA—Museum of Modern Art).
21. Camel ride at the zoo in the International Wildlife Conservation Park.
22. *Starry Night* by Vincent van Gogh at the MOMA.
23. Cisitalia car (1946) at the MOMA.
24. Ferry from LaGuardia Airport.

GREEK GODS

This family tree shows how the gods and goddesses of Mount Olympus descended from Uranus (the Sky) and Gaea (the Earth). Zeus (lord of the thunderbolt and son of Cronus and Rhea) was the supreme god of Olympus.

Crius

Prometheus

Climene

Iapetus

Mnemosyne

Atlas

Helios

Thea

Asteria

Cronus

Hyperion

Phoebe

Ceos

Rhea

Oceanus

Tethys

Eurynome

Uranus

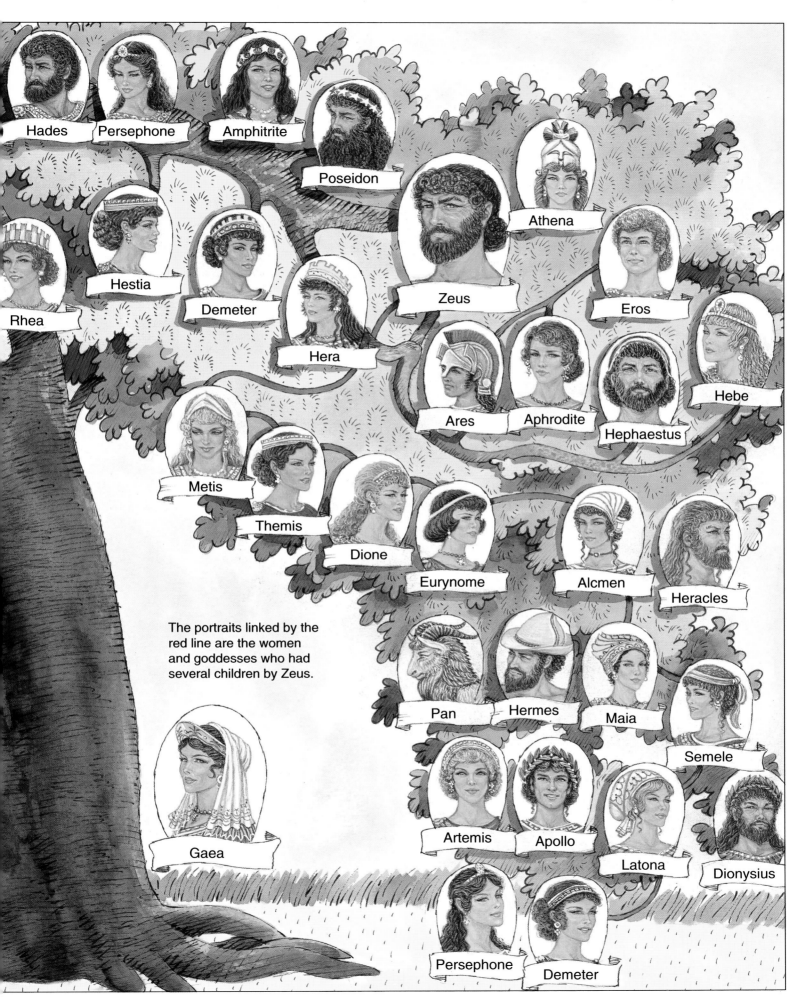

Hades Persephone Amphitrite

Poseidon

Athena

Hestia

Rhea

Demeter

Hera

Zeus

Eros

Hebe

Ares Aphrodite

Hephaestus

Metis

Themis

Dione

Eurynome

Alcmen

Heracles

The portraits linked by the red line are the women and goddesses who had several children by Zeus.

Pan Hermes Maia

Semele

Gaea

Artemis Apollo

Latona

Dionysius

Persephone

Demeter

SYMPHONY ORCHESTRA

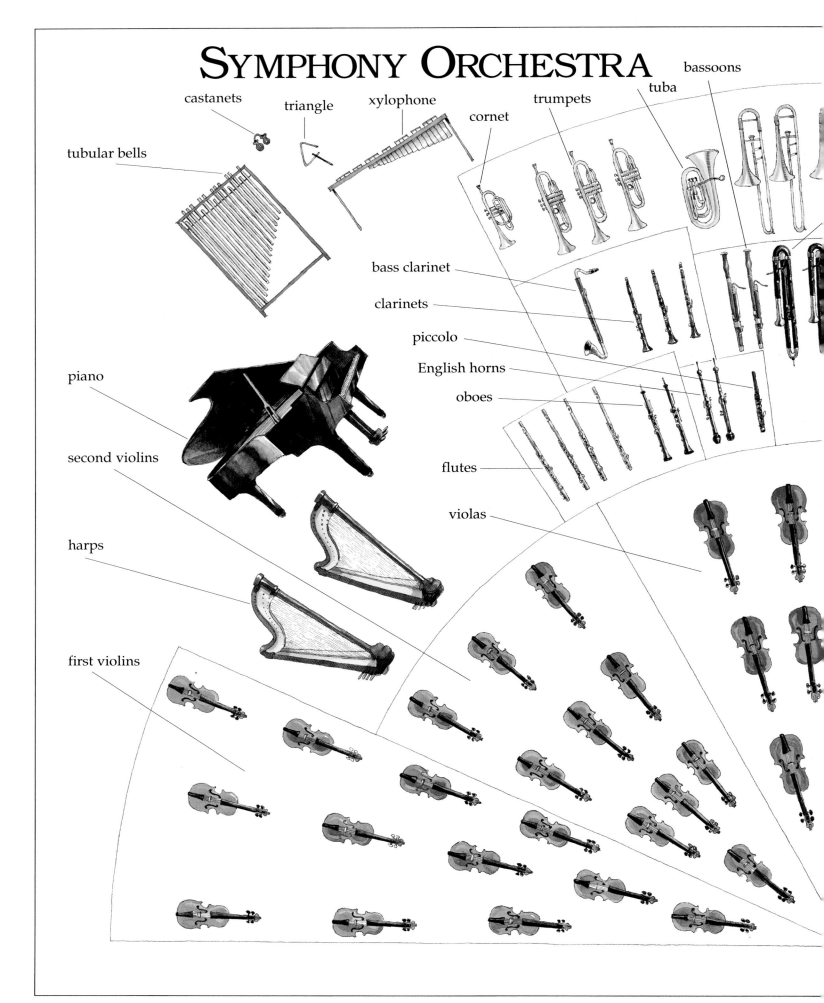

castanets

triangle

xylophone

cornet

trumpets

tuba

bassoons

tubular bells

bass clarinet

clarinets

piano

piccolo

English horns

second violins

oboes

harps

flutes

violas

first violins

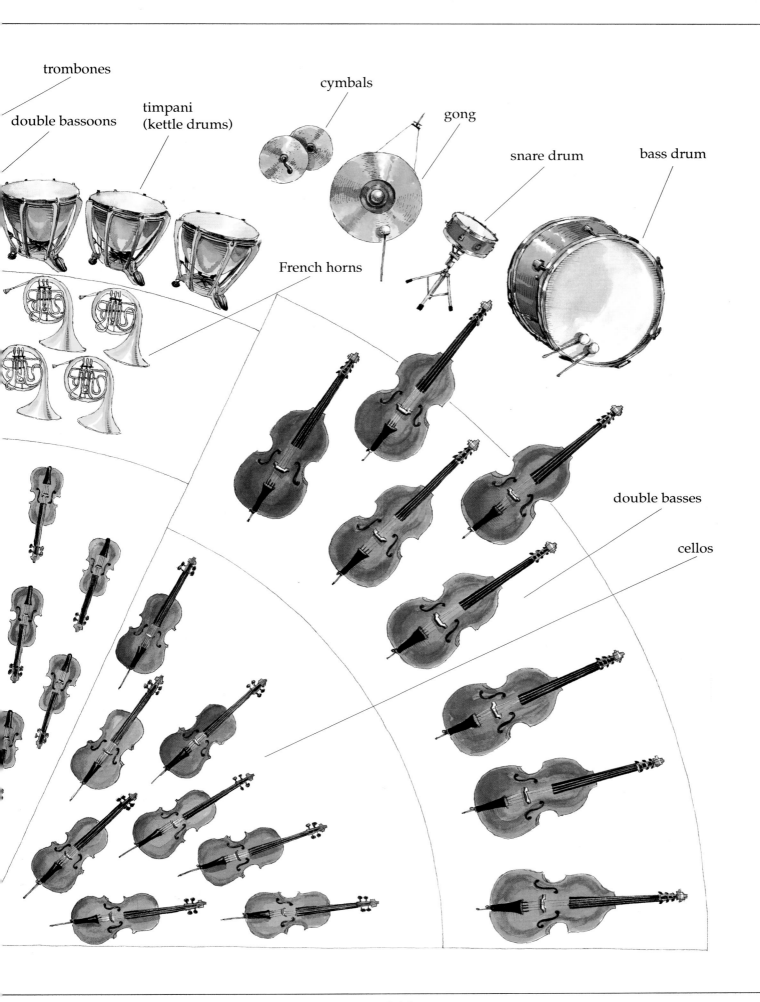

trombones

double bassoons

timpani
(kettle drums)

cymbals

gong

snare drum

bass drum

French horns

double basses

cellos

RENAISSANCE

Flourishing culture – The Renaissance is a cultural and historical period that began in Florence in the early 1400s and had spread across Europe by the late 1500s. During this period there was a great interest in classical Greek and Roman civilizations. All the arts—literature, painting, sculpture, architecture—flourished.

Artists – The Renaissance is known for such famous men as Leonardo da Vinci and Michelangelo, as well as the painter Botticelli, the writer Dante and the architects Brunelleschi and Palladio.

The illustration shows Florence in the second half of the fifteenth century, during Leonardo da Vinci's day.

1. Giotto's bell tower
2. Cathedral
3. The Brunelleschi dome
4. A dyer's shop, with cloth hung out to dry
5. Towers of private homes
6. Banner of the Medici family
7. Medieval home
8. Loggia (open gallery with roof)
9. Renaissance building
10. Paved street
11. Blacksmith's shop, with forge and bellows
12. Silvermith's shop
13. Tailor's shop
14. Artist showing his wares to two rich merchants
15. Casting furnace with crucible
16. Sculptor's studio with equestrian statue
17. Sectional view of home: a sculptor's studio on the first floor, a banquet hall on the second floor, a bedroom with canopied bed on the third floor, and an attic with sacks of grain.

SAILING SHIPS

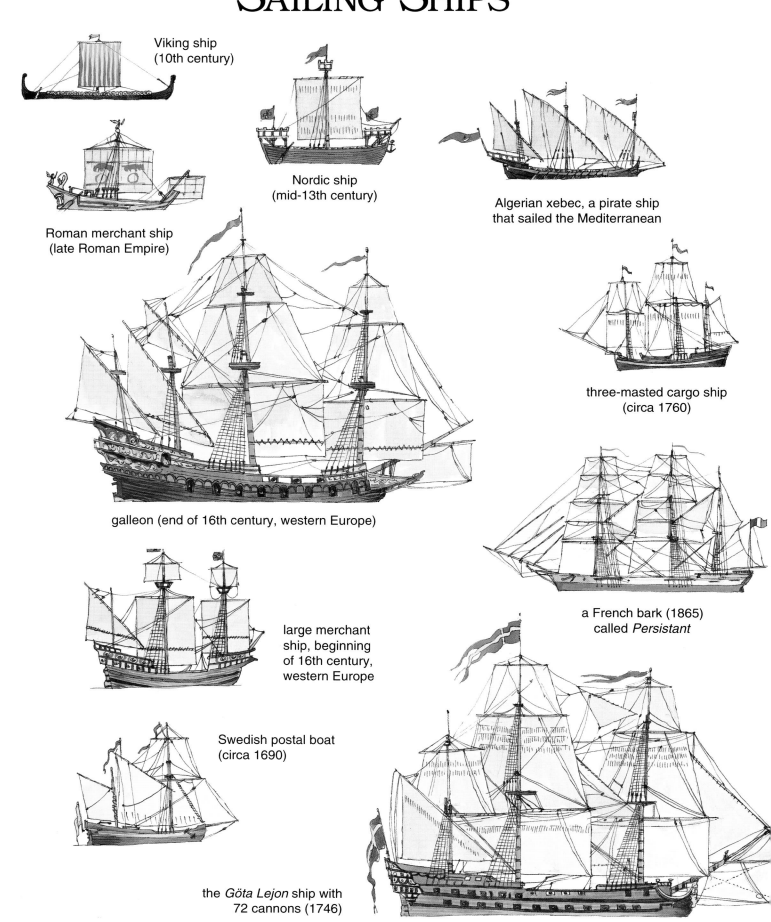

Viking ship
(10th century)

Nordic ship
(mid-13th century)

Algerian xebec, a pirate ship
that sailed the Mediterranean

Roman merchant ship
(late Roman Empire)

three-masted cargo ship
(circa 1760)

galleon (end of 16th century, western Europe)

large merchant
ship, beginning
of 16th century,
western Europe

a French bark (1865)
called *Persistant*

Swedish postal boat
(circa 1690)

the *Göta Lejon* ship with
72 cannons (1746)

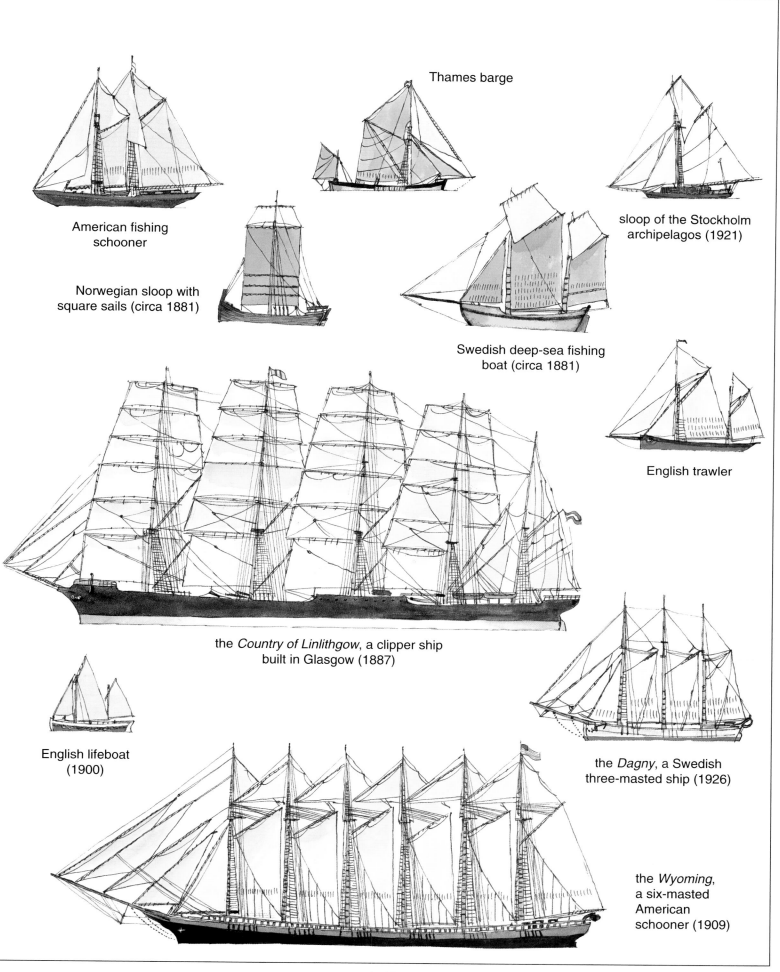

American fishing
schooner

Thames barge

sloop of the Stockholm
archipelagos (1921)

Norwegian sloop with
square sails (circa 1881)

Swedish deep-sea fishing
boat (circa 1881)

English trawler

the *Country of Linlithgow*, a clipper ship
built in Glasgow (1887)

English lifeboat
(1900)

the *Dagny*, a Swedish
three-masted ship (1926)

the *Wyoming*,
a six-masted
American
schooner (1909)

317

INUIT VILLAGE

Eskimos – The Inuit have long been called *eskimos*, from an Algonquian word for *raw-meat eaters*. The ancestors of the Inuit came from Central Asia about 4,000 years ago. Traditionally, they were nomads or semi-nomads that hunted and fished. The illustration shows a traditional Inuit village.

Hunting – The Inuit hunted polar bears, caribou, walruses, whales and seals. The animal bones were used to make needles, harpoons and other weapons. The skins were used to make clothing and to cover boats and tents. The tents served as shelter during the summer. During the winter the people lived in stone and sod houses, or in *igloos* made of ice and snow.

Beliefs – Like Native American Indians, the Inuit believed that all living creatures had a soul. After capturing an animal, a hunter performed a ceremony so as not to offend the creature's spirit. A shaman, or medicine man, was the intermediary between the living and the spirit world. He also used herbs to treat illness.

Today – There are nearly 100,000 Inuit who live in Greenland, northern Canada, Alaska and Siberia. While many still lead a life of hunting and fishing, present-day Inuit have adopted some modern ways. Snowmobiles, not sled dogs, are the main means of transportation.

Traditional Inuit village
1. Summer home
2. Houses made of stone and sod
3. Rack for drying meat
4. House under construction
5. Whale ribs
6. Women gathering blueberries
7. Hunting a bird with a net
8. Woman scraping skins
9. Sunken entrance to a home
10. Hunters with harpoons
11. Dead seals
12. Woman braiding leather
13. Sled dogs
14. Sled
15. Soapstone stove
16. Umiak
17. Kayak
18. Ice

319

Viking – *Viking* comes from the Norwegian word *vikingr*, meaning *he who travels by sea*, but it later became a synonym of pirate. The Vikings lived in Scandinavia between 800 and 1100. They were divided into clans, which are family groups related to each other.

Daily life – Homes had low, long, thick walls especially designed to provide shelter from the cold. The windows were small and the roof looked like an overturned boat. This design allowed the wind to blow over the roof without meeting resistance, just like the keel of a ship that flows through water.

Clothing – Viking men wore woolen pants, a tunic and a cape and a wool or fur hat, depending on the season. The men always had a sword tucked under their belt. Women wore wool or linen ankle-length tunics that were often decorated with heavy chain necklaces or buckles made of hammered metal.

A Viking village
1. *Thing*, or assembly hall
2. *Knorr*, a merchant ship run aground
3. Kettle with resin for sealing the ship
4. Boards used to build the ship
5. Wedge system used to obtain boards from tree trunks
6. *Karv*, a coastal cargo ship
7. Sail reinforced with leather strips
8. Entrance to the fjord
9. *Drakkar*, a war ship
10. Dragon head that decorated the ship's prow
11. Woodcutters
12. Ship ribs
13. Shipyards
14. Carpenter
15. Ship planking
16. Stern decoration
17. Viking home

ZODIAC

About 3000 B.C. Babylonian priests observed that the sun, moon and planets seemed to move around the earth on a yearly path that passed through 12 constellations. They established a calendar dividing the year into twelve signs of the zodiac.

Horoscope – Like the Babylonians priests, astrologers today believe that the movements in the sky can help them to predict events and to study someone's destiny. Astrologers calculate the exact position of the moon and planets at the time of someone's birth, then analyze a person's personality and future.

ARIES (March 21 – April 20): fire sign. Traits: energetic, courageous, easily becomes enthused about something but often underestimates difficulties.

TAURUS (April 21 – May 20): earth sign. Traits: calm, contemplative, able to cope with problems but is often possessive.

GEMINI (May 21 – June 21): air sign. Traits: intelligent, curious, intuitive, creative but tends to be unfocused and superficial.

CANCER (June 22 – July 22): water sign. Traits: sensitive and affectionate, romantic and creative but sometimes timid and a bit absent-minded.

LEO (July 23 – August 22): fire sign. Traits: ambitious and courageous, knows what he/she wants and is fascinating but is often self-centered.

VIRGO (August 23 – September 22): earth sign. Traits: neat, thoughtful, reliable, logical but sometimes too introverted.

LIBRA (September 23 – October 22): air sign. Traits: idealist, fascinating, loves beautiful things but is often frivolous and superficial.

SCORPIO (October 23 – November 21): water sign. Traits: magnetic, mysterious, intelligent and analytical but often jealous and possessive.

SAGITTARIUS (November 22 – December 20): fire sign. Traits: loyal, spontaneous and optimistic but often impatient.

CAPRICORN (December 21 – January 19): earth sign. Traits: hard-working, tenacious, possesses a sense of duty but is sometimes aloof and not very affectionate.

AQUARIUS (January 20 – February 18): air sign. Traits: independent, original, loves freedom and ideals but is sometimes vain.

PISCES (February 19 – March 20): water sign. Traits: sensitive, kind, affectionate and creative but is often weak-willed and a waster of time.

CLASSIFICATION OF LIVING THINGS

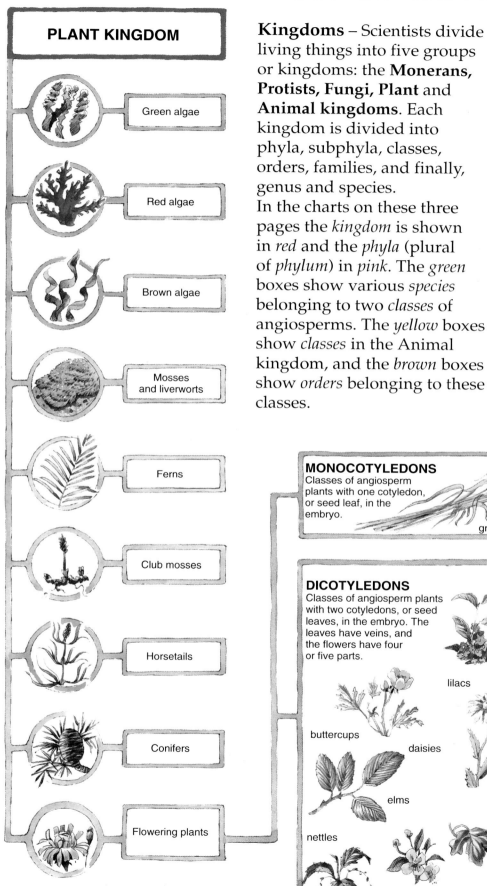

Kingdoms – Scientists divide living things into five groups or kingdoms: the **Monerans, Protists, Fungi, Plant** and **Animal kingdoms**. Each kingdom is divided into phyla, subphyla, classes, orders, families, and finally, genus and species.

In the charts on these three pages the *kingdom* is shown in *red* and the *phyla* (plural of *phylum*) in *pink*. The *green* boxes show various *species* belonging to two *classes* of angiosperms. The *yellow* boxes show *classes* in the Animal kingdom, and the *brown* boxes show *orders* belonging to these classes.

Giant sequoia:
Some are 6,000 years old.

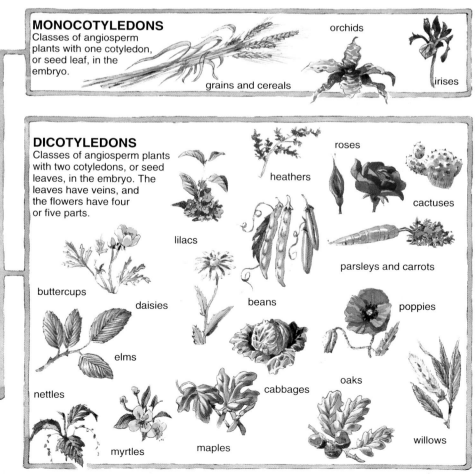

MONOCOTYLEDONS
Classes of angiosperm plants with one cotyledon, or seed leaf, in the embryo.

orchids

grains and cereals

irises

DICOTYLEDONS
Classes of angiosperm plants with two cotyledons, or seed leaves, in the embryo. The leaves have veins, and the flowers have four or five parts.

roses

heathers

cactuses

lilacs

parsleys and carrots

buttercups

daisies

beans

poppies

elms

oaks

nettles

cabbages

myrtles

maples

willows

323

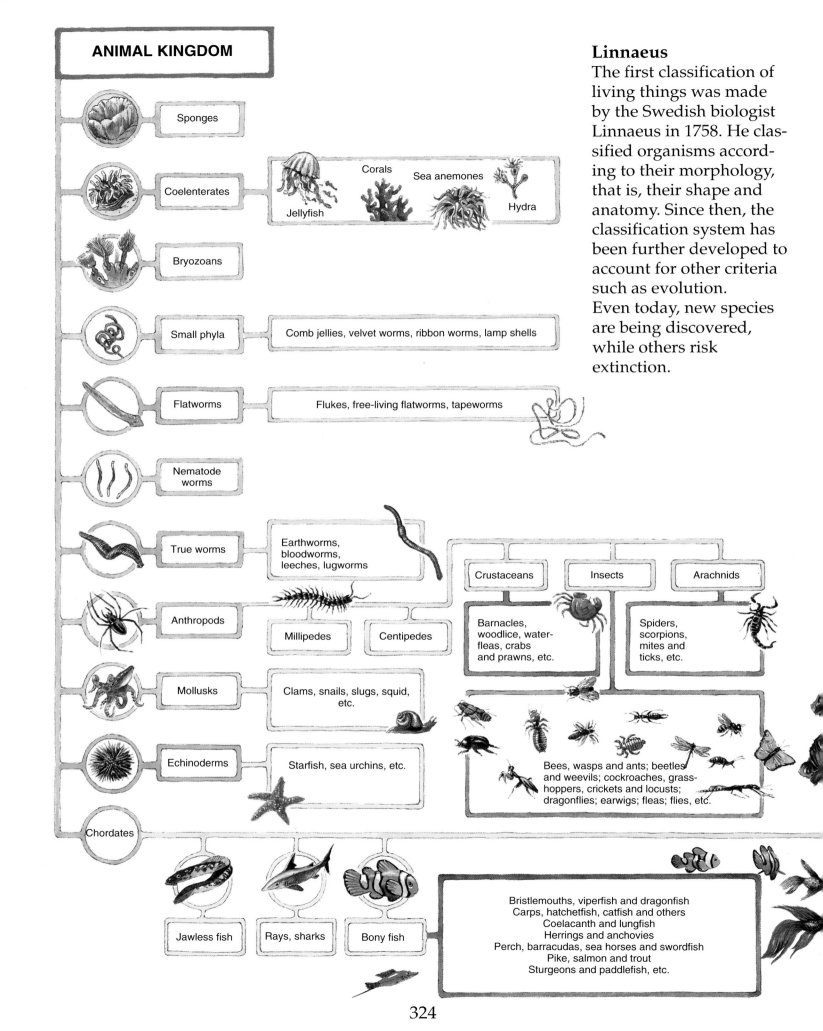

ANIMAL KINGDOM

Sponges

Coelenterates — Jellyfish, Corals, Sea anemones, Hydra

Bryozoans

Small phyla — Comb jellies, velvet worms, ribbon worms, lamp shells

Flatworms — Flukes, free-living flatworms, tapeworms

Nematode worms

True worms — Earthworms, bloodworms, leeches, lugworms

Anthropods — Millipedes, Centipedes

Crustaceans — Barnacles, woodlice, water-fleas, crabs and prawns, etc.

Insects — Bees, wasps and ants; beetles and weevils; cockroaches, grasshoppers, crickets and locusts; dragonflies; earwigs; fleas; flies, etc.

Arachnids — Spiders, scorpions, mites and ticks, etc.

Mollusks — Clams, snails, slugs, squid, etc.

Echinoderms — Starfish, sea urchins, etc.

Chordates — Jawless fish, Rays, sharks, Bony fish — Bristlemouths, viperfish and dragonfish / Carps, hatchetfish, catfish and others / Coelacanth and lungfish / Herrings and anchovies / Perch, barracudas, sea horses and swordfish / Pike, salmon and trout / Sturgeons and paddlefish, etc.

Linnaeus

The first classification of living things was made by the Swedish biologist Linnaeus in 1758. He classified organisms according to their morphology, that is, their shape and anatomy. Since then, the classification system has been further developed to account for other criteria such as evolution. Even today, new species are being discovered, while others risk extinction.

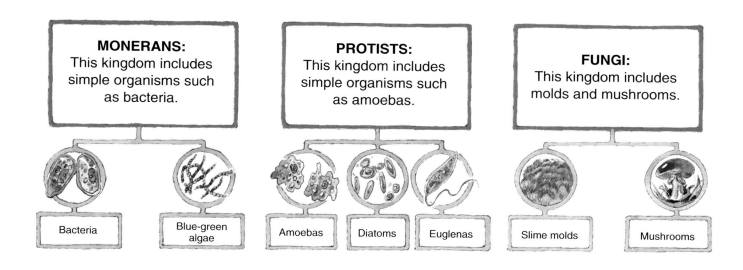

MONERANS:
This kingdom includes simple organisms such as bacteria.

Bacteria

Blue-green algae

PROTISTS:
This kingdom includes simple organisms such as amoebas.

Amoebas

Diatoms

Euglenas

FUNGI:
This kingdom includes molds and mushrooms.

Slime molds

Mushrooms

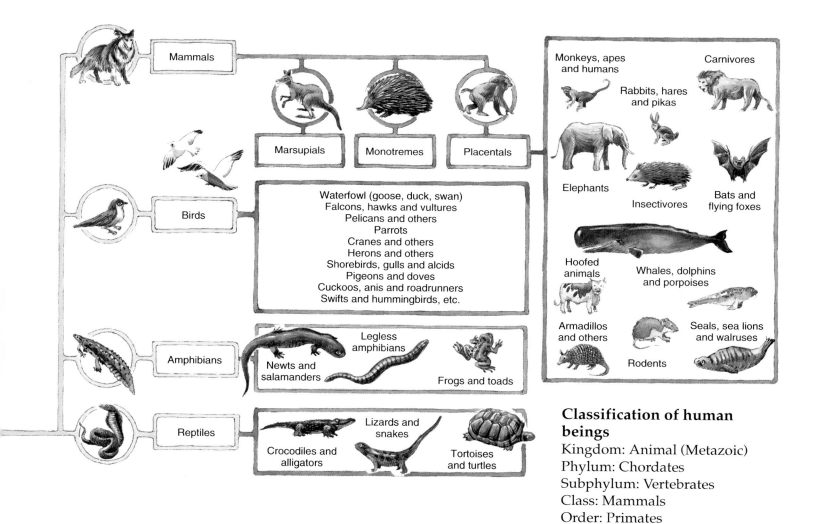

Mammals

Marsupials

Monotremes

Placentals

Monkeys, apes and humans

Carnivores

Rabbits, hares and pikas

Elephants

Insectivores

Bats and flying foxes

Hoofed animals

Whales, dolphins and porpoises

Armadillos and others

Rodents

Seals, sea lions and walruses

Birds

Waterfowl (goose, duck, swan)
Falcons, hawks and vultures
Pelicans and others
Parrots
Cranes and others
Herons and others
Shorebirds, gulls and alcids
Pigeons and doves
Cuckoos, anis and roadrunners
Swifts and hummingbirds, etc.

Amphibians

Legless amphibians

Newts and salamanders

Frogs and toads

Reptiles

Lizards and snakes

Crocodiles and alligators

Tortoises and turtles

Classification of human beings

Kingdom: Animal (Metazoic)
Phylum: Chordates
Subphylum: Vertebrates
Class: Mammals
Order: Primates
Family: Hominids
Genus: *Homo*
Species: *Sapiens*

HISTORY TIME LINES

THE UNITED STATES

1607 First permanent English settlement in Jamestown, Virginia.
1620 Pilgrims land on Plymouth Rock.
1630–1733 The thirteen original colonies are founded.
1754 French and Indian War starts.
1773 Boston Tea Party.
1774 First Continental Congress sends *Declaration of Rights and Grievances* to King George.
1775 Paul Revere's Ride/American Revolution begins.
1776 Declaration of Independence signed on July 4th.
1787 The Constitution signed.
1789 George Washington becomes first President.
1791 Bill of Rights added to the Constitution.
1803 Louisiana Purchase adds vast territories west of the Mississipi.
1812 War with Britain begins.
1821 The first public school is founded in Boston.
1823 Monroe Doctrine against European interference in Western Hemisphere.
1846–1848 Mexican War.
1849 California Gold Rush.
1861 Civil War begins.
1865 Abraham Lincoln assassinated.
1869 First transcontinental railroad completed.
1881 President Garfield fatally shot by assassin.
1906 San Francisco earthquake.
1917 U.S. enters World War I.
1920 Women receive the right to vote.
1929 The U.S. Stock Market collapses and the Depression begins.
1933 President Roosevelt launches the New Deal.
1941 U.S. enters World War II.

1946 First meeting of United Nations General Assembly.
1950 Korean War Begins.
1954 Supreme Court bans racial segregation in schools.
1959 Alaska and Hawaii become states.
1961 Bay of Pigs invasion in Cuba triggers crisis between U.S.S.R. and U.S.
1963 John F. Kennedy assassinated.
1964 American involvement in Vietnam War escalates after Tonkin resolution.
1967 Thurgood Marshall is sworn in as first African-American member of the Supreme Court.
1968 Martin Luther King, Jr., and Robert Kennedy assassinated.
1972 Watergate scandal unfolds.
1973 Richard Nixon resigns as President, American soldiers leave Vietnam.
1976 Jimmy Carter elected President; Bicentennial celebrations.
1981 Ronald Reagan nominates Sandra Day O'Connor, first woman on the Supreme Court.
1990 Iraq's invasion of Kuwait triggers Persian Gulf War.
1992 Bill Clinton is elected President.
1996 Bill Clinton is re-elected President.

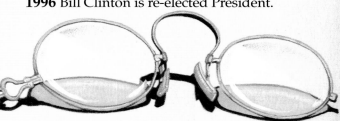

THE THIRTEEN ORIGINAL COLONIES

New Hampshire, Massachusetts, Rhode Island, Connecticut, New York, New Jersey, Pennsylvania, Delaware, Maryland, Virginia, North Carolina, South Carolina, Georgia.

CANADA

ca. 1000 Viking explorer Leif Ericsson lands on the shores of Canada in what is now Newfoundland and Labrador.
1497 John Cabot reaches coasts of Nova Scotia.
1534 Jacques Cartier explores Gulf of St. Lawrence.
1608 Samuel de Champlain establishes French colony in Quebec.
1663 Canada becomes the royal colony of New France.
1755 Britain expels the Acadians from Nova Scotia.
1763 New France is ceded to Britain.
1774 French rights guaranteed by the Quebec Act.
1837–1838 Uprisings in Upper and Lower Canada.
1867 The British North America Act establishes Canada as a dominion with Quebec, Ontario, Nova Scotia and New Brunswick as founding provinces.
1870 Manitoba becomes a province.
1871 British Columbia joins the Dominion.
1873 Prince Edward Island is added.
1897 Gold Rush begins in the Klondike.
1905 Saskatchewan and Alberta become provinces.
1934 The Dionne quintuplets are born.
1940 Unemployment Insurance is introduced.
1949 Newfoundland joins Canada.
1965 Canada gets a new flag with the maple leaf.
1967 Montreal hosts Expo 67, a world's fair.
1968–1984 The Trudeau years, named for Prime Minister Pierre Elliott Trudeau.

1969 The Official Languages Act recognizes English and French as official languages.
1975 The CN Tower, the world's tallest free-standing structure, is built in Toronto.
1976 The Summer Olympics are held in Montreal.
1976 The separatist Parti Québécois elects René Lévesque premier of the province.
1982 Constitution Act is passed.
1991 North American Free Trade Act signed.
1992 Toronto Blue Jays win the World Series.
1992 Ban on cod and salmon fishing in Newfoundland.
1993 Kim Campbell becomes first woman Prime Minister.
1993 Agreement signed to divide up the Northwest Territories in 1999 to give 350,000 sq km of land in the Arctic to the Inuit; area called Nunavut Territory.
1996 At the Olympics, Donovan Bailey breaks the world's record in the men's 100-meter sprint and wins a gold medal for Canada.

PROVINCES (10) AND TERRITORIES (2)

Alberta (capital: Edmonton)
British Columbia (capital: Victoria)
Manitoba (capital: Winnipeg)
New Brunswick (capital: Fredericton)
Newfoundland (capital: St. John's)
Nova Scotia (capital: Halifax)
Ontario (capital: Toronto)
Prince Edward Island (capital: Charlottetown)
Quebec (capital: Québec)
Saskatchewan (capital: Regina)
Northwest Territories (capital: Yellowknife)
Yukon Territory (capital: Whitehorse)

MATHEMATICAL FORMULAS

Measuring – The Imperial system of weights and measures (inches, feet, miles, gallons, etc.) is still common in the U.S., but the rest of the world has generally converted to the **metric system**.
Various tools help us measure: 1) A *thermometer* measures temperature. (Water freezes at 32°F or 0°C and boils at 212°F or 100°C.) 2) The *goniometer* measures angles. (A right angle is 90 degrees.) 3) Ships measure speed in *knots*, which are nautical miles per hour. 4) A *barometer* measures air pressure and changes in the weather. 5) Light is measured in *kilowatts*. 6) The huge distance between planets is measured in *light years*.

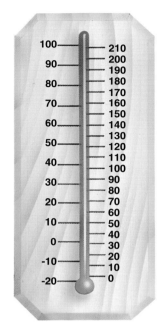

Celsius (°C)   Fahrenheit (°F)

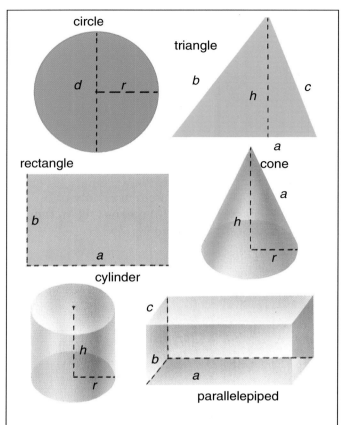

Roman numerals

1	I	18	XVIII	70	LXX
2	II	19	XIX	80	LXXX
3	III	20	XX	90	XC
4	IV	21	XXI	100	C
5	V	22	XXII	101	CI
6	VI	23	XXIII	150	CL
7	VII	24	XXIV	200	CC
8	VIII	25	XXV	300	CCC
9	IX	26	XXVI	400	CD
10	X	27	XXVII	500	D
11	XI	28	XXVIII	1000	M
12	XII	29	XXIX		
13	XIII	30	XXX		
14	XIV	40	XL		
15	XV	49	XLIX		
16	XVI	50	L		
17	XVII	60	LX		

Arabic numerals (1, 2, 3, etc,) have replaced Roman ones, but we still see Roman numerals in titles: Elizabeth I, Pope Paul VI, John Carter III.

Area and Volume

Square
Side *l*
Perimeter = 4 *l*
Area = l^2

Rectangle
Sides: *a, b*
Perimeter = 2 x (*a* + *b*)
Area = *a* x *b*

Cube
Side *l*
Surface = 6 x l^2
Volume = l^3

Parallelepiped
Sides: *a, b, c*
Surfaces = 2 x (*a* x *b*) + (*b* x *c*) + (*a* x *c*)
Volume = *a* x *b* x *c*

Triangle
Height *h*; Sides: *a, b, c*
Perimeter = *a* + *b* + *c*
Area = 1/2 x *a* x *h*

Cone
Height *h*; Radius *r*, Apothem *a*
Lateral surface = π x *r* x *a*
Volume = π/3 x r^2 x *h*

Pyramid
Height *h*
Volume = 1/3 x (area of base) x *h*

Circle
Radius *r*
Diameter *d* = *r* x 2
Circumference = *r* x 2 x π
Area = π x r^2

Sphere
Radius *r*
Surface = 4 x π x r^2
Volume = 4/3 x π x r^3

Cylinder
Height *h*; Radius *r*
Lateral surface = 2 x π x *r* x *h*
Volume = π x r^2 x *h*

Decimal system	Binary system	Mathematical symbols	
		+	add
0	1	−	subtract
1	10	+/-	more or less
2	11	x	multiply
3	100	÷	divide
4	101	=	equal to
5	110	≠	different from
6	111	≈	approximately equal to
7	1000	>	greater than
8	1001	<	less than
9	1010	≥	greater or equal to
	1011	≤	less than or equal to
	1100	%	percent
		√	square root
		π	Greek pi (3.1416)
		°	degree
		'	minute, foot
		"	second, inch

Binary system

This numerical system is used in computer science and technology. It lets you turn any information into a long sequence of binary numbers. The binary system uses only two numbers: 0 and 1. Zero (0) means OFF in the computer, and 1 (one) means ON.

Metric conversion

1 inch = 2.54 centimeters
1 centimeter = 0.39 inches

1 foot = 0.30 meters
1 meter = 3.28 feet

1 mile = 1.61 kilometers
1 kilometer = 0.62 mi

1 pound = 0.45 kilograms
1 kilogram = 2.20 pounds

1 pint = 0.56 liters
1 liter = 1.75 pints

1 gallon = 3.79 liters
1 liter = 0.26 gallons

Demographic growth

Since humans first walked the earth, population growth was limited by infant mortality, epidemic and wars. Starting in the 1800s, thanks to improvements in the quality of life (social progress, trade, medical breakthroughs and healthy habits), the earth's population started to grow. Today there are almost 6 billion people on the planet, and that number will continue to grow at mind-boggling speed. There is a population boom in Third World countries in Africa and Asia, while *zero growth rate* (the number of deaths are equal to the number of births) has been achieved in several European countries.

550	1600	1650	1700	1750	1800	1850	1900	1950	2000

THE WORLD IN STATISTICS

The world's highest mountains
1. Everest, Nepal/Tibet (29,028 ft/8,848 m)
2. K2, Kashmir/China (28,250 ft/8,611 m)
3. Kanchenjunga, Nepal/Sikkim (28,208 ft/8,598 m)
4. Lhotse, Nepal/Tibet (27,890 ft/8,501 m)
5. Makalu I, Nepal/Tibet (27,790 ft/8,470 m)
6. Dhaulagiri I, Nepal (26,810 ft/8,172 m)
7. Manaslu I, Nepal (26,760 ft/8,156 m)
8. Cho Oyu, Nepal (26,750 ft/8,126 m)
9. Nanga Parbat, India (26,660 ft/8,126 m)
10. Annapurna I, Nepal (26,504 ft/8,078 m)

North America's highest mountain: McKinley (20,320 ft/6,194 m)
Europe's tallest mountain: Mont Blanc (15,771 ft/4,810 m)

Deforestation around the world
1. Areas covered by rainforests one century ago.
2. Areas now covered by rainforests. Notice how much of the Amazon forest has been reduced.

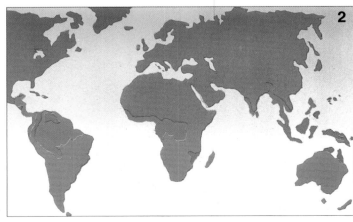

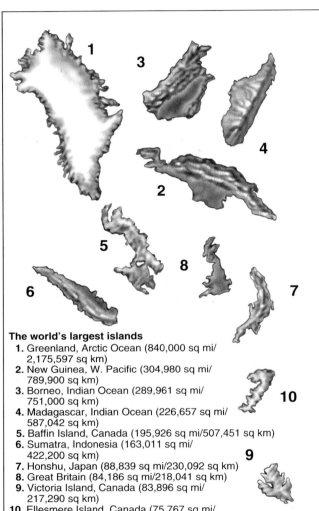

The world's largest islands
1. Greenland, Arctic Ocean (840,000 sq mi/ 2,175,597 sq km)
2. New Guinea, W. Pacific (304,980 sq mi/ 789,900 sq km)
3. Borneo, Indian Ocean (289,961 sq mi/ 751,000 sq km)
4. Madagascar, Indian Ocean (226,657 sq mi/ 587,042 sq km)
5. Baffin Island, Canada (195,926 sq mi/507,451 sq km)
6. Sumatra, Indonesia (163,011 sq mi/ 422,200 sq km)
7. Honshu, Japan (88,839 sq mi/230,092 sq km)
8. Great Britain (84,186 sq mi/218,041 sq km)
9. Victoria Island, Canada (83,896 sq mi/ 217,290 sq km)
10. Ellesmere Island, Canada (75,767 sq mi/ 196,236 sq km)

The world's longest rivers
Nile, East Africa (4,145 mi/6,671 km)
Amazon, Peru/Brazil (4,007 mi/ 6,448 km)
Yangtze-Kiang, China (3,915 mi/ 6,300 km)
Mississippi-Missouri-Red, U.S. (3,710 mi/5,970 km)
Yenisey-Angara-Selenga, Mongolia/Russia (3,442 mi/5,540 km)

The world's oceans in area
Pacific Ocean
64,000,000 sq mi/ 165,760,000 sq km

Atlantic Ocean
31,815,000 sq mi/ 82,400,000 sq km

Indian Ocean
25,300,000 sq mi/ 65,526,700 sq km

Dictionaries

DINOSAURS

Adasaurus: *(Upper Cretaceous period, Asia, 6.5 ft/2 m long, carnivore)* A light, agile predator with a bird-like build.

Albertosaurus: *(Cretaceous period, North and Central America, 26 ft/8 m tall, herbivore)* Similar to, but smaller than the Tyrannosaurus, with a long snout and teeth that curved inwards.

Algae: Primitive, chiefly aquatic plants. Huge lakes dried up during the Carboniferous period, which meant many aquatic plants had to transform when they came into contact with air in order to survive. Some plants adapted quite well and grew very tall.

Stegosaurus (lizard with roof): lived during the Jurassic period.

Allosaurus: *(Jurassic period, Africa, North America, and Australia, about 39 ft/12 m long)* This dinosaur used to walk upright on its hind legs. It captured its prey with its short forelimbs that had razor-sharp claws.

Ammonites: *(Mesozoic era)* Fossilized mollusks with a snail-like shell that used to live in the sea.

Ankylosaurus: *(Cretaceous period, North America, up to 36 ft/11 m long)* A dinosaur with bony plates covering its head and back. A round bone at the tip of the tail made it look like a club. Its snout had a bony beak.

Chirostenotes (slim hands): lived during the Upper Cretaceous period.

Aragosaurus: *(Lower Cretaceous period, Spain, herbivore)* A huge quadruped with a long neck and tail and heavy body. This dinosaur was discovered in 1987.

Archaeopteryx: *(Jurassic period, Germany, 3.5 ft/1 m long)* This dinosaur, an ancestor of today's birds, was covered with feathers. Although it could not soar, it could beat its wings to fly.

Brachiosaurus (lizard with arms): lived during the Jurassic period.

Diplodocus (with double tip): lived during the Jurassic period.

Archaeornithomimus: *(Upper Cretaceous period, China and North America)* An ancient dinosaur that looked like an ostrich. It had strong hind legs and forelimbs with curved claws.

Archaeosigillaria: Ancient club mosses, which were among the tallest plants during the Carboniferous period.

Avimimus: *(Upper Cretaceous period, Asia, 5 ft/1.5 m long)* Dinosaurs that most resembled birds and stood on two legs. They had a long neck and tail, small head, toothless beak, and probably wings with feathers.

Brachiosaurus: *(Jurassic period, North America, 80 ft/25 m long, herbivore)* This dinosaur, which weighed up to 50–60 tons, had a very long neck and tail.

Brachylophosaurus: *(Upper Cretaceous period, North America, about 22 ft/7 m long)* A primitive dinosaur that had a duckbill, a small crest on its snout, and a spike on its head.

A battle between a Tyrannosaurus and a Stegosaurus, which protected itself with the bony plates on its back and tail.

PRE-CAMBRIAN ERA (Origin of the Earth)		
4.5 billion years ago to 530 million years ago		
PALEOZOIC ERA		
245 to 530 million years ago	Cambrian	
	Ordovician	
	Silurian	
	Devonian	
	Carboniferous	
	Permian	
MESOZOIC ERA		
65 to 245 million years ago	Triassic	
	Jurassic	
	Cretaceous	
CENOZOIC ERA		
65 million years ago to today	Tertiary	Paleocene
		Eocene
		Oligocene
		Miocene
		Pliocene
	Quaternary	Pleistocene

333

Brontosaurus: *(Lower Cretaceous period, North America, up to 67 ft/21 m long, herbivore)* This name, which means *thunder lizard*, was given to this quadruped dinosaur because it supposedly made a great deal of noise when it ran. It had a small head, a long neck, and a huge body. It weighed more than 20 tons and was later called Apatosaurus.

Avimimus (bird imitator): *lived during the Upper Cretaceous period.*

Brontotheres: *(Tertiary period, 9.5 ft/3 m tall)* This ancestor of the rhinoceros had a tough hide like a suit of armor and a forked horn on its snout.

Calamites: Treelike plants from the Mesozoic era that dinosaurs used to eat.

Camptosaurus: *(Jurassic and Cretaceous periods, North America and Europe, 22.5 ft/7 m long, herbivore)* A biped-quadruped dinosaur with much larger hind legs than forelimbs. It had clawed toes resembling hooves.

Polacanthus (many spines): *lived during the Lower Cretaceous period.*

Cenozoic: The fourth and most recent geological era of the earth that began 65 million years ago. It includes the Tertiary and Quaternary periods. Continents and the seas came to look as they do today and huge mammals appeared. Humans also appeared in this era.

Tyrannosaurus rex (king lizard): *lived during the Cretaceous period.*

Ceratosaurus: *(Jurassic period, America and Africa, up to 19 ft/6 m long, carnivore)* A large biped with sharp tusks and dangerous claws, a thick tail and strong paws.

Chassternbergia: *(Cretaceous period, North America, herbivore)* A large quadruped dinosaur with armor-like skin.

Chirostenotes: *(Cretaceous period, North America, about 6.5 ft/2 m long, carnivore and herbivore)* A small, lightweight dinosaur with a toothless beak and three long, slim toes with claws.

Cicadale: A plant that was widespread during the dinosaur era and still can be found today.

Coelacanth: A fish that swam in the sea millions of years ago when life first appeared on earth. Some species still exist today.

Coelophysis: *(Upper Triassic period, North America, up to 10 ft/3 m long, carnivore)* This dinosaur had a small head, snake-like neck, and long tail.

Ankylosaurus (lizard with welded armor): *lived during the Cretaceous period.*

Compsognathus: *(Jurassic period, France and Germany, 2 ft/60 cm tall, carnivore)* A small, fast predator with sharp teeth and a long neck and tail. This is one of the smallest dinosaurs ever discovered.

Conchoraptor: *(Upper Cretaceous period, Mongolia, less than 5 ft/1.5 m long, carnivore or possibly herbivore)* A bird-like biped dinosaur with large eyes, a parrot-like beak, and a short, strong head.

Brachylophosaurus (lizard with small crest): *lived during the Upper Cretaceous period.*

Corythosaurus: *(Upper Cretaceous period, North America, herbivore)* A large biped-quadruped dinosaur with a curved crest that resembled a two-pointed hat.

Cro-Magnon: *(Pleistocene epoch)* An early form of humans, named after the caves in France where the first five fossils were found. They were about 5 ft 9 in/1.8 m tall and wore animal skins.

Crocodiles: These aquatic reptiles with large jaws appeared during the Triassic period. Crocodiles, which are carnivores, still exist today and are related to dinosaurs.

Saltopus (hopping foot): *lived during the Upper Triassic period.*

Deinonychus: *(Cretaceous period, America and Asia, about 10 ft/3 m long, carnivore)* Its name means *terrible claw*: its second toe, in fact, had a long, hooked claw.

Dimorphodon: *(Jurassic period)* A large flying reptile that had a stumpy neck and snout and a long tail.

Apatosaurus (deceptive lizard): lived during the Upper Jurassic period.

Dinosaur: This word was created in 1841 from the Greek words *deinos* (terrible) and *sauros* (lizard). Dinosaurs were reptiles that only lived on land and were divided into two orders: saurischian (with reptile pelvis) and ornithischian (with bird pelvis).

Diplodocus: *(Jurassic period, North America, about 86 ft/27 m long, herbivore)* A quadruped with an extremely long neck and whip-like tail.

Syntarsus (welded haunches): lived during the Upper Triassic period.

Dodo: A large bird discovered in 1500 on the Mauritius Island in the Indian Ocean. It became extinct two centuries ago. It had short wings and hooked beak and could not fly.

Dromaeosaurus: *(Upper Cretaceous period, North America, 6 ft/1.8 m long, carnivore)* This dinosaur had a retractable claw on its second toe.

Echinodon: *(Jurassic period, America and England, 2 ft/60 cm long)* A tiny herbivorous dinosaur.

Eohippus: *(Eocene epoch)* An ancestor of the horse just 14 in/35 cm tall.

Equisetum: A plant from the Carboniferous period that grew to a huge size during the dinosaur era. It exists in miniature forms today.

Era: The longest division of geologic time. It includes one or more periods.

Eucentrosaurus: *(Upper Cretaceous period, North America, 12 ft/6 m long, herbivore)* A dinosaur that had a long horn on its snout.

Euparkeria: *(Triassic period, found all over the world, 3 ft/1 m long)* This was not a dinosaur, but may be the ancestor of most of the reptiles from the Mesozoic era.

Compsognathus (graceful jaw): lived during the Upper Jurassic period.

Evolution: Changes that gradually took place in animals or plants after they first appeared on the earth.

Extinction: The disappearance of an animal or plant species. A species becomes extinct when more individuals die out than are born. Extinction can also be quick and wipe out entire groups of living creatures, which is what happened to the dinosaurs at the end of the Cretaceous period.

Parasaurolophus (next to the Saurolophus): lived during the Upper Cretaceous period.

Palteosaurus (flat lizard): lived during the Upper Triassic period.

Ferns: These plants, which appeared during the Carboniferous period, reached an amazing height and were much different than they are today.

Fossil footprints: Evidence in a certain area of the presence of animals that lived many years ago. Through these footprints we can discover how these animals walked, learn the shape of their feet, and study the habits of dinosaur herds.

Fossils: The remains or traces of plants and animals that lived millions of years ago and have been preserved intact by soil, mud, or sand.

Allosaurus (different lizard): lived during the Jurassic period.

Ginkgo biloba: An Asian plant that reaches 96 ft/30 m in height and has yellow fan-shaped flowers. It is considered a living fossil because it existed during the dinosaur era.

Glyptodon: *(Tertiary and Quaternary period, North and South America, 16 ft/5 m long)* A huge dinosaur that survived for many years, even after carnivores from Asia had arrived, due to the jointed bony plates that covered and protected it.

Hominids: This group includes primitive humans that appeared at the end of the Cenozoic era.

Homo sapiens: A word used to indicate all human fossils, from Cro-Magnon on; the group to which all modern humans belong.

Ichthyosaurus: *(from the Triassic to the Cretaceous periods)* These were not dinosaurs but marine reptiles that looked like dolphins.

Corythosaurus (helmet head): *lived during the Upper Cretaceous period.*

Iguanodon: *(Cretaceous period, America, Europe, Asia, 29 ft/9 m long)* This dinosaur had something that was never found on other dinosaurs: the thumb on its front paw turned into an 8-inch (20 cm) spur.

Maiasaurus: *(Cretaceous period, North America, 29 ft/9 m long, herbivore)* This dinosaur was given this name, which means *good mother lizard*, because its fossils were found in nests near its young.

Mammoth: *(Quaternary period, Europe, Asia, North America)* This extinct animal was no taller than the African elephant. Even though they share an ancestor, the elephant does not descend from the mammoth. The mammoth was covered with long hair and had curved tusks it

Chassternbergia (of Charles Sternberg): *lived during the Upper Cretaceous period.*

used for digging beneath the snow in search of moss and lichens. It died out at the end of the glaciations 12,000 years ago.

Archaeopteryx (ancient feathers): *lived during the Jurassic period.*

Megathere: *(Quaternary period, America, 16 ft/5 m tall)* A slow-moving mammal with grasping front paws. It had a furry body and ate leaves.

Mesozoic: Also known as the Secondary era, it went from 245 to 65 million years ago. It includes the Triassic, Jurassic and Cretaceous periods and is characterized by the predominance of reptiles.

Deinonychus (terrible claw): *lived during the Cretaceous period.*

Minmi: *(Cretaceous period, Australia, 6.5 ft/2 m long, herbivore)* A quadruped that had an armor-like skin and bears the name of the place it was discovered: Minmi Crossing.

Neanderthal: *(Beginning of the Pleistocene epoch)* An early form of humans named after the place in Germany where the first fossils were found. They were about 5 ft/1.5 m tall and looked like chimps.

Mammoth: an extinct mammal similar to the elephant.

Ornithischians: *(Upper Triassic period to the Cretaceous period, found on all continents)* These herbivorous dinosaurs, similar to today's birds, had a snout with a beak and an extra bone in their jaw.

Ouranosaurus: *(Lower Cretaceous period, Africa, 22 ft/7 m long, herbivore)* A biped-quadruped dinosaur with a fin-like flap of skin that traveled from its neck to the tip of its tail.

Oviraptor: *(Cretaceous period, Mongolia, 6 ft/1.8 m long)* A herbivorous dinosaur that was also a predator. It had paws with three fingers and long sharp claws.

Ouranosaurus (courageous lizard): *lived during the Lower Cretaceous period.*

Paleozoic: The Primary era that went from 530 to 245 million years ago. During this era tall mountains formed, volcanoes erupted, and the sea flooded large portions of land. Fish and amphibians appeared at this time. This era is divided into the Cambrian, Ordovician, Silurian, Devonian, Carboniferous and Permian periods.

Pangea: Only one continent, Pangea, which means *all the earth*, existed during the Triassic period when dinosaurs first appeared.

Parasaurolophus: *(Cretaceous period, America, up to 32 ft/10 m in length, herbivore)* A biped-quadruped that had a long bony tube on its head that probably was used to amplify sounds.

Pithecanthropus: A group of hominids from the Quaternary period. They were apelike and had a large

Thecodont (hollow teeth): *lived from the Permian to the Triassic periods.*

cranium, which meant their brain was more developed than that of apes. These creatures probably knew how to use stone tools.

Plates: Fat and bony, they covered the backs of dinosaurs and acted like armor to protect them from enemies. Plates also helped to capture the heat of the sun.

Precambrian: The first geological era. It went from 4.5 billion to 530 million years ago and is divided into the Archean and Proterozoic periods. During this time crystals formed and the first living organisms appeared.

Prehistoric Age: The period of history when humans first appeared but no written historical documents exist.

Pteranodon (smooth feather): *winged reptile of the Mesozoic era.*

Eucentrosaurus (lizard with horn): *lived during the Upper Cretaceous period.*

Primates: An order of higher mammals that includes simians (apes and monkeys), prosimians such as lemurs, and humans. They have five fingers and toes and a large brain. They appeared during the Cenozoic era.

Protoceratops: *(Cretaceous period, China, 6 ft/1.8 m long, herbivore)* This dinosaur had a bony collar around its head and a parrot-like beak.

Pteranodon: *(Jurassic period)* A flying reptile with a long beak and horny crest on its head.

Denversaurus (lizard from Denver): *lived during the Upper Cretaceous period.*

Pterosaurus: Flying reptiles that were not dinosaurs. Their wings were formed by a membrane that stretched from the fourth digit on their forelimbs to their tail. Some pterosaurus were furry.

Saltopus: *(Upper Triassic period, Scotland, 2 ft/60 cm long, carnivore)* A biped predator that weighed less than 2 lb (1 kg). It is probably the oldest European dinosaur known.

Saurischians: *(Upper Triassic period to the Cretaceous period)* Herbivorous and carnivorous dinosaurs with a reptile-like pelvis.

Stegosaurus: *(Jurassic period, North America, up to 29 ft/9 m long, herbivore)* This quadruped had a double row of bony plates on its back.

Thecodont: *(From the Permian to the Triassic periods; found on all continents)* Small animals that were the ancestors of Pterosaurus, crocodiles and dinosaurs.

Coelophysis (hollow shape): *lived during the Upper Triassic period.*

Triceratops: *(Cretaceous period, North America, 29 ft/9 m long, herbivore)* A quadruped with two long horns on its head and one on its snout. Its neck was protected by a bony collar.

Tyrannosaurus rex: *(Cretaceous period, America and Asia, 38–48 ft/12–15 m long, predator)* A fierce dinosaur that had razor-sharp teeth and powerful claws.

Adasaurus (Ada's lizard): *lived during the Upper Cretaceous period.*

Velociraptor: *(Cretaceous period, Asia, 5 ft 9 in/1.8 m long, predator)* Aggressive biped with a hook on the second digit of its front paws.

FAMOUS TALES AND AUTHORS

Aesop: according to legend, Aesop was a Greek slave and storyteller who lived in the 6th century B.C. In his fables animals behave like humans. Each fable has a moral, or lesson. His most famous fables are: *The Crow and the Fox, The Fox and the Grapes, The City Mouse and the Country Mouse, The Tortoise and the Hare, The Wolf and the Lamb* and *The Stag at the Stream.*

Afanasiev, Alexander (1826–1871): a Russian author who wrote *Popular Russian Fairy Tales* and *Popular Russian Legends.*

Aladdin: the story of Aladdin is included in *The Thousand and One Nights.* When Aladdin rubs a magic lamp, a genie appears and satisfies his every wish.

Dragons often protect treasures. They have wings on their backs and breathe out fire.

Ali Baba: a character mentioned in *The Thousand and One Nights* who discovers the magical phrase that opens the door to a cavern where forty thieves have hidden a treasure. The magical phrase is "Open Sesame!" Ali Baba finds the treasure and becomes rich.

Alice: the heroine of Lewis Carroll's book *Alice's Adventures in Wonderland.* Alice falls into a rabbit hole and ends up in Wonderland where she meets the White Rabbit, the Mad Hatter and the evil Queen of Hearts.

The Thousand and One Nights tells a story about a magical flying carpet.

Andersen, Hans Christian (1805–1875): a Danish writer of fairy tales and the author of *The Princess and the Pea, The Little Mermaid, The Tin Soldier, The Ugly Duckling* and *The Emperor's New Clothes.*

Around the World in Eighty Days: in this book by Jules Verne, Phineas Fogg, an English gentleman, bets he can travel around the world in eighty days.

Jack climbs the magical beanstalk and discovers the giant's castle.

With his faithful servant Passe-partout, he returns just in time to London and wins the bet.

Arthur: the legendary king of Britain first mentioned in the 12th century. Arthur, the son of King Uther Pendragon, gains the throne with the help of Merlin the Wizard. He marries Guinevere and founds the kingdom of Camelot and the Round Table, whose knights dedicate their lives to the search for the Holy Grail.

Beauty and the Beast: in this fairy tale by Charles Perrault, Belle is forced to live with the Beast to fulfill a promise made by her father. Even though the

Castles with handsome princes and beautiful princesses appear in many fairy tales.

Beast is hideous, Belle is touched by his kindness and falls in love with him. The Beast turns into a handsome prince when love overcomes the spell that made him into a beast.

"A giant! A giant!" comes the cry of alarm, and everyone runs.

Knights swore to fight injustice and to defend the weak.

Captain Hook: an evil pirate and Peter Pan's enemy. A crocodile bit off his hand, which was replaced with a hook.

Carroll, Lewis: a pen name of the English author Charles Lutwidge Dodgson (1832–1898). He wrote *Alice's Adventures in Wonderland* and *Through the Looking Glass*.

Cinderella: this fairy tale by Charles Perrault tells the story of a young girl who is mistreated by her stepmother and nasty stepsisters. The prince throws a ball and invites all the girls in the kingdom. The fairy godmother turns Cinderella's rags into a splendid gown and a pumpkin into a carriage. She tells Cinderella she must be home before midnight. The prince falls in love with Cinderella, but the girl runs away at midnight and loses a glass shoe in the process. The desperate prince searches far and wide for Cinderella. All the girls in the kingdom try on the shoe, but only Cinderella's tiny foot can slip into the shoe. When the prince finally finds her, he asks Cinderella to marry him.

An ogre is a type of giant that hates humans.

Cooper, James Fenimore (1789–1851): an American writer and author of *The Last of the Mohicans*.

Curse: a sentence or exclamation used to cast an evil spell on someone.

The tin soldier falls in love with a ballerina.

David Copperfield: a book written in 1850 by Charles Dickens about the cruel childhood of a boy in England during the Industrial Revolution.

Dickens, Charles (1812–1870): an English author who wrote *Oliver Twist, David Copperfield, A Christmas Carol* and *A Tale of Two Cities*.

Treasure Island tells the story of Jim and a mysterious map.

Don Quixote: the comic hero of a story written by Cervantes (1547–1616). Don Quixote swears to fight injustice all over the world, so he starts out as a wandering knight on a comic and tragic journey where he attacks a windmill because he thinks it is a giant. Sancho Panza is Don Quixote's servant.

Dragon: like the dwarf, the dragon guards hidden treasures. It breathes fire and smoke. It often has a pair of small wings and a long tail. According to legend, Saint George (a symbol of Good) killed the dragon. In paintings dragons are often shown devouring their tails.

Elf: also called a sprite or nymph. Elves are tiny and mischievous creatures.

Emperor's New Clothes, The: a fairy tale by Hans Christian Andersen about two swindlers who present a vain emperor a fabric that is supposedly invisible to stupid people. The emperor is thrilled: he will be able to distinguish his intelligent subjects from the stupid ones! The two swindlers pretend to weave the fabric but the loom is empty. The courtiers praise the fabric as though they could really see it. No one dares to point out the trick, for they are afraid they will appear stupid. The two thieves present the imaginary suit of clothes to the emperor. He tries it on and wanders nude about the streets of the city so his subjects can admire him. Finally an innocent child exclaims, "The emperor has no clothes!"

Only the kiss of a girl will break the spell of the Frog Prince.

Fable: a brief story in prose or verse that is usually about objects or animals (representing human vices and virtues). There is a moral, or lesson, to be learned at the end of the tale.

Fairy tale: a story where humans meet supernatural beings such as wizards, fairies and gnomes.

Fairy: a supernatural and often extremely beautiful creature who is able to grant any wish. Fairies are often friendly to humans, but sometimes they are cruel and spiteful. In fact, it is difficult to tell the difference between a fairy and a witch. If you meet a fairy, you should never call them by name but call them kind folks or neighbors.

Frankenstein: in this book by Mary Shelley (1797–1851), Doctor Victor Frankenstein creates a huge monster made from the parts of different dead bodies. The monster has human feelings, but his terrifying appearance frightens everyone he meets.

Frog Prince, The: in this fairy tale a witch casts a spell on a handsome prince and turns him into a frog. The spell will be broken only after a girl falls in love with the frog and kisses it.

An elf or sprite lives in the forest and loves to play pranks on people.

Ghost: a supernatural being that returns to Earth after death because it has left unresolved situations in this world. Ghosts are often transparent and can pass through walls. In stories they often appear in ancient castles and make strange noises.

Giant: these beings, which are extremely tall and strong, frighten humans. They may be evil or kind. There are giants in Greek mythology, in the Bible, in epic poems, and in fairy tales.

Merlin the Wizard was an advisor to King Arthur.

Gnome: this small creature has a long beard and sometimes a hunched back. He dwells in the earth and guards its treasures. A gnome can make himself invisible. He is kind to humans but spiteful with people who offend him.

Grimm, Jacob and Wilhelm (1785–1863; 1786–1859): German brothers who wrote a famous book called *The Tales of the Brothers Grimm*. The stories include *Hansel and Gretel* and *Snow White*.

Gulliver: in his book *Gulliver's Travels*, Irish author Jonathan Swift (1667–1745) tells the story of Lemuel Gulliver, who landed on the island of Lilliput inhabited by tiny people. On a second voyage, Gulliver ends up on an island of giants. On his third trip he visits a flying island inhabited by strange scientists, and on the fourth he discovers a country with talking horses.

Hansel and Gretel: in this fairy tale by the Brothers Grimm, a brother and sister are sent to the woods to gather berries because there is no more food at home. They find a house made of candy and cookies in the woods and start to

Even a magical trunk can carry fairy tale characters!

eat it. An old woman comes out of the house and invites them in: she is a witch and puts them in a cage so she can bake them and eat them later. Gretel pushes the witch into the oven and the old woman burns to a crisp. Hansel and Gretel happily return home with the witch's treasure.

Jack and the Beanstalk: in this English fairy tale, Jack finds a magic bean. After he plants it, the beanstalk grows so high it reaches the clouds. Jack climbs up the beanstalk and finds a castle with a giant. Jack steals a bag of coins, a hen that lays golden eggs, and a talking harp. The giant chases after Jack, but the boy quickly climbs down the beanstalk and cuts it down with a hatchet. The giant falls through the clouds and dies.

A fairy uses a magic wand to cast a spell.

Kipling, Rudyard (1865–1936): an English author born in India where he worked as a journalist. He wrote *Kim*, the *Just So Stories*, *Captain Courageous* and *The Jungle Book*.

Knights of the Round Table: in the legends of King Arthur, the king and his knights gather around a round table so all would be equals.

La Fontaine, Jean de (1621–1695): a French poet famous for his twelve books of fairy tales inspired by Aesop's and Phaedrus's fables. The stories are about animals that behave like humans. Each fable has a moral.

Lancelot: a knight of the Round Table who falls in love with Queen Guinevere, the wife of King Arthur.

Legend: a mythical story handed down from one generation to another.

Little Mermaid, The: in this fairy tale by Hans Christian Andersen, a little mermaid, the daughter of the king of the sea, falls in love with a prince she saves during a shipwreck. She gives a witch her voice so she can see him again: her fish tail turns into legs so she can search for her prince on land.

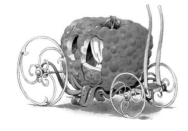

Cinderella goes to the ball in a pumpkin that has been turned into a carriage.

Dwarfs, trolls, elves and gnomes are all small creatures that appear in fairy tales.

The witch warns her that if she cannot earn the prince's love, she will turn into sea foam. The prince marries another, and the little mermaid is about to disappear into the sea forever, but a miracle occurs. Due to her kindness, she turns into a wind sprite.

Little Red Riding Hood: in this fairy tale by Charles Perrault, a little girl goes to visit her sick grandmother. She meets the bad wolf in the forest who runs to her grandmother's house and gobbles her up! When Little Red Riding Hood knocks on the door, the wolf pretends to be the grandmother, then gobbles up Red Riding Hood, too! A hunter shoots the wolf, then cuts open its stomach. Granny and Red Riding Hood pop out of the wolf, safe and sound.

The evil stepmother turns into a witch and offers Snow White a poisoned apple.

Little Women: a book by Louisa May Alcott about the four March sisters: Meg, Jo, Beth and Amy.

London, Jack (1876–1916): the pen name of John Griffith, an American author of adventure books such as *The Call of the Wild, White Fang* and *Martin Eden.*

Magic: the use of charms and spells to transform objects and change events. White magic is used to do good deeds, while black magic is used to obtain power. Fairies, witches and wizards use magic in many fairy tales.

Melville, Herman (1819–1891): an American writer who made many sea voyages that gave him ideas for adventure stories. His most famous is *Moby Dick.*

Moby Dick: the book by Herman Melville about Captain Ahab's hunt for the white whale, Moby Dick. The narrator of the story is Ismael, a whaler aboard the captain's ship.

Moral: an ethical lesson and indication of correct behavior. The lesson is often taught in a fable.

Sinbad tells his adventures to the Caliph of Baghdad.

Myth: a fanciful explanation of great events in life.

Never-Never Land: the home of Peter Pan.

Ogre: an ugly giant that eats human flesh, especially that of children.

Oliver Twist: a book by Charles Dickens about Oliver, an orphan forced to work in a factory who then joins a band of thieves and finds his real family in the end.

Perrault, Charles (1628–1703): a French writer and the author of *Little Red Riding Hood, Sleeping Beauty, Puss in Boots, Cinderella* and *Beauty and the Beast.*

Peter Pan: a book by J.M. Barrie (1860–1937). Peter Pan is a boy who refuses to grow up. He can fly and lives in Never-Never Land with a fairy named Tinkerbell. His enemy is Captain Hook, a nasty pirate. Wendy, Michael, and John, three children who are friends of Peter Pan, also join him on the island of Never-Never Land.

"And they lived happily ever after" is the ending to many fairy tales.

Phaedrus (1st century B.C.): a Roman poet who popularized Aesop's fables. He translated them from the original Greek into Latin.

Pied Piper of Hamelin: Robert Browning (1812–1889) wrote a poem about a magical piper who arrives in the town of Hamelin that has been invaded by mice. The music from his magical flute causes the mice to follow him to a river where they drown. When the townsfolk refuse to pay him, the piper plays his flute to attract all the children of the town. The children disappear, never to be seen again.

Pinocchio: Carlo Collodi (the pen name of Carlo Lorenzini 1826–1890) wrote this story about a puppet that wants to become human. Every time Pinocchio tells a lie his nose grows and grows. After several adventures, the Blue Fairy grants his wish and Pinocchio turns into a real little boy.

Thumbelina, at the end of her voyage, marries the King of the Elves.

In a fairy tale by La Fontaine, a magic hen lays golden eggs.

Princess and the Pea, The: this fairy tale by Hans Christian Andersen is about a prince who wants to marry a real princess. When a young woman arrives and claims to be a princess, the Queen Mother hides a pea in the bed and covers it with several mattresses. The morning after, the girl complains she couldn't sleep...only a real princess could have such sensitive skin!

Puss in Boots: in this fairy tale by Charles Perrault, the youngest son of a miller inherits a cat. The clever animal uses several tricks, and in the end he even helps his master marry the king's daughter.

Wizards and magicians often use crystal balls to predict the future.

Robin Hood: a legendary English outlaw who may have actually existed. He stole from the rich to give to the poor. He lived in Sherwood Forest (14th–15th century) with his band, the Merry Men, that included Friar Tuck and Little John.

Robinson Crusoe: in this book written by English author Daniel Defoe (1660–1731), Robinson, an English sailor, is shipwrecked on a desert island where he lives for many years. His only companion on the island is Friday, a native.

Rumpelstiltskin: in this fairy tale by the Brothers Grimm, a gnome helps a poor girl spin straw into gold for the king. In exchange, he makes her promise to give him her firstborn. The king marries the girl, and when their first child is born, the gnome comes to claim it. The girl is able to send him away by guessing his name: Rumpelstiltskin.

The genie in the lamp grants all of Aladdin's wishes.

Scott, Walter (1771–1832): a Scottish author who wrote many historical novels. The most famous is *Ivanhoe*, which tells a tale of battles between the Normans and Saxons during the period of King Richard the Lion Hearted.

Sinbad the Sailor: in a story of *The Thousand and One Nights*, Sinbad travels the world during seven adventuresome voyages.

Sirens: in Greek mythology, sirens are dangerous mermaids who lived on an island in the Mediterranean Sea. Their sweet singing lured sailors to their destruction on the rocks surrounding the island.

Geppetto, Pinocchio's father, loves him even though the little puppet misbehaves.

Sleeping Beauty: a fairy tale by Charles Perrault. All the fairies except one are invited to Princess Aurora's baptism. The uninvited fairy casts a spell in revenge so when Aurora grows up to be a lovely young girl, she pricks her finger on a spinning wheel spindle and falls fast asleep. After one hundred years, a prince kisses her and she awakens.

Snow White: a fairy tale by the Brothers Grimm about a beautiful girl with skin as white as snow. Snow White lives with her evil stepmother. Each day the stepmother asks the magic mirror, "Mirror, mirror on the wall. Who is the fairest of them all?" One day the mirror replies that Snow White, who has grown up, is the prettiest in the kingdom. The jealous queen orders a hunter to take Snow White into the forest and murder her, but he is filled with pity and sets her free. Snow White finds the home of the Seven Dwarfs in the forest, who ask her to stay. The Evil Queen turns herself into an old hag, finds Snow White and gives her a poisoned apple. The Seven Dwarfs weep over her glass coffin when a handsome young prince comes and kisses her. Snow White awakens and the prince asks her to marry him.

The City Mouse and Country Mouse is a fable by La Fontaine.

Sorcerer/Sorceress: like the wizard, he or she uses magic, but it is usually black magic. The sorcerer uses evil spirits and charms to commit foul deeds.

Spell: a magic word or formula used to bewitch people.

Sprite: a tiny creature similar to an elf or fairy.

Stevenson, Robert Louis (1850–1894): a Scottish author who wrote *Treasure Island, Kidnapped*, and *The Strange Case of Dr. Jekyll and Mr. Hyde*.

Superheroes: cartoon and comic strip characters with superhuman powers they use to either help or harm humanity. The most famous are Superman, Flash Gordon, The Fantastic Four, Batman, Spiderman and Wonder Woman.

Superman: a comic strip hero that inspired several films. Superman flies "faster than a speeding bullet." He uses his powers to fight evil and injustice. He is invulnerable but fears only one thing: Kryptonite, a green mineral from Krypton, a faraway planet. Superman hides his real identity under the guise of Clark Kent, reporter.

Alice meets the evil Queen of Hearts in Wonderland.

Talisman: an object, often a stone or ring, that acts like a charm to protect someone from evil.

Tarzan: a character created from novels by Edgar Rice Burroughs (1875–1950), Tarzan appeared in many comic strips and films. Abandoned in the forest as 5a child and raised by chimpanzees, Tarzan becomes a powerful hero.

Thousand and One Nights: a collection of ancient Arab stories (12th–16th centuries) that include *Ali Baba, Aladdin and the Magic Lamp, Sinbad the Sailor* and many others.

The Little Mermaid falls in love with a prince she saves during a shipwreck.

Three Little Pigs, The: in this fairy tale the first pig builds a house of straw, the second pig builds one of wood, and the third little pig wisely builds a solid brick house. When the Big Bad Wolf arrives, he blows the straw house down with one puff. The first little pig escapes and hides with his second brother in the wood house, but the wood house cannot withstand the wolf's huffing and puffing. Only the brick house of the wise little pig is able to resist the wolf. The wolf tries to climb down the chimney but the three little pigs light a fire in the fireplace and the wolf runs off howling with a burnt tail and is never seen again.

With a pair of magic boots Tom Thumb can cover seven leagues with just one step.

Thumbelina: in this story by Hans Christian Andersen, a little girl as tall as a thumb sleeps in a nutshell. She is kidnapped by a toad, but escapes and finds herself lost in a forest. A mole asks her to marry him. She agrees, but before the wedding she finds an injured swallow in a tunnel. She lovingly cares for the bird and nurses it back to health. When the swallow regains its strength it takes her to a land filled with flowers where

Thumbelina meets the King of the Elves, who asks her to marry him.

Tin Soldier, The: the leading character of a fairy tale by Hans Christian Andersen. The tin soldier falls in love with a tin ballerina. A gust of wind makes him fall off a windowsill. A group of children pick him up and place him in a paper boat. The tin soldier falls into the sea and is swallowed up by a fish. The fish is caught, brought to market, and bought by the cook of the home where he used to live. The tin soldier meets his beloved ballerina again, but another gust of wind knocks both into the fire.

Jiminy Cricket gives Pinocchio some very wise advice!

Tolkien, J.R.R. (1892–1973): an English author and Oxford University professor who wrote *The Hobbit* and a trilogy called *The Lord of the Rings*. These fantasy adventures were set in Middle Earth, a land of hobbits and other imaginary creatures.

Tom Sawyer: the main character of Mark Twain's book *The Adventures of Tom Sawyer*. Tom is a mischievous child who often gets himself into trouble. His friend is Huckleberry Finn, the subject of another book by Mark Twain.

The fox praises the crow in order to steal the cheese the bird is holding in its beak.

Treasure Island: in this book by Robert Louis Stevenson, a young boy named Jim finds a treasure map. He and Dr. Livesey and Captain Smollet set

In The Princess and the Pea, *only the real princess can feel a pea beneath a pile of mattresses.*

out to sea in search of the mysterious island. Long John Silver, an old sailor with a wooden leg, convinces the crew to stage a mutiny. In the end Jim's friends find the treasure.

Puss in Boots is so clever that he helps his master marry the king's beautiful daughter.

Troll: A mythical, bearded creature that usually lives in a cave or under a bridge.

Twain, Mark (1835–1910): the pen name of Samuel Langhorne Clemens, an American author who write *The Adventures of Huckleberry Finn* and *The Adventures of Tom Sawyer.*

Ugly Duckling, The: in this fairy tale by Hans Christian Andersen, a strange egg is hatched by a duck. When the egg

opens, a clumsy, ugly duckling emerges. All the animals on the farm make fun of him, so he decides to run away, but he is laughed at everywhere he goes. After a cold and difficult winter, spring finally arrives. The ugly duckling has grown up to be a gorgeous white swan.

Unicorn: a mythical animal that resembles a white horse with a single horn on its head. Greeks and Romans believed it existed and it is even mentioned in medieval legends. The unicorn is a tireless hunter of snakes and is immune to their poison. According to legend, its horn possesses magical powers.

Vampire: this creature leaves its coffin at night in search of human blood to drink. The most famous vampire is Count Dracula, who lived in a castle in Transylvania.

Verne, Jules (1828–1905): a French author who wrote nearly sixty books inspired by technological progress. *Voyage to the Center of the Earth, From the Earth to the Moon, Twenty Thousand Leagues under the Sea, Around the World in Eighty Days, The Mysterious Island* and *The Children of Captain Grant* are some of the titles.

Only the wisest of the Three Little Pigs builds a brick house.

Werewolf: a mythical being who can change from a person to a wolf when the moon is full.

Winnie the Pooh: a teddy bear featured in several books written by English author A.A. Milne (1882–1956). The author's son also appears in the character of Christopher Robin.

Witch: a being, especially a woman, who can turn herself into other forms. A witch's magical power was thought

The seven dwarfs welcome Snow White to their tiny house.

to come from the devil. In legends, witches come down from mountain peaks on evenings when there is a full moon so they can stir up trouble.

Wizard: an expert in magic who usually casts spells to do good.

Witches usually fly on broomsticks!

Wizard of Oz: the main character in the book *The Fantastic Wizard of Oz* by American L. Frank Baum (1856–1919). The story features Dorothy and her dog Toto, who are carried from Kansas to Oz by a tornado. There they meet a scarecrow who wants a brain, a tin man who wants a heart and a cowardly lion who wants courage.

Animals of the forest help
the elves, fairies and witches
organize a concert for the
King of the Elves' birthday.

HEALTH AND MEDICINE

Abdomen: the lower part of the trunk (the area between the chest and pelvis). The diaphragm separates the abdomen from the thoracic cavity. The abdominal cavity is covered by a watery membrane called the peritoneum.

Abscess: a swollen area filled with pus, usually caused by infection.

Acne: a breakout of pimples, usually on the face and back, caused by an inflammation of the oil glands of the skin. Acne in young people is usually linked to hormone imbalances.

Alcoholism: an addiction to the consumption of alcoholic beverages.

Allergy: hypersensitivity to an agent (allergen) that is usually harmless (such as dust, pollen or food). Symptoms include hives, eczema, rhinitis, stomach and intestinal problems, conjunctivitis, asthma and hay fever.

Amnesia: total or partial memory loss.

Anemia: a decrease of hemoglobin or red blood cells. Can be caused by hemorrhage, hemolysis (breakdown of red blood cells) or a lack of iron.

Anorexia: 1. Loss of appetite; **2.** Anorexia nervosa: a psychological illness where the person has an obsessive desire to lose weight and refuses to eat. This condition is most often found in teenagers and young women.

Too much exposure to the sun can cause skin cancer.

White meat (chicken, veal, rabbit) has less fat and is more digestible than red meat (beef and pork).

Always remember to brush your teeth after eating sweets to prevent cavities!

Antibiotic: a drug that destroys or limits the growth of bacteria. Antibiotics were originally made from plants (penicillin was made from mold, for example), but today they are artificially made.

Adenoids: enlarged lymphatic tissue of the pharyngeal tonsil. Adenoids can become inflamed and make breathing difficult.

AIDS (Acquired Immune Deficiency Syndrome): a disease caused by a virus called HIV. AIDS is transmitted through sexual relations, transfusions of infected blood and infected hypodermic needles. AIDS ultimately causes death by weakening the body's ability to ward off infections.

Anesthesia: this word means a loss of sensitivity. Anesthetics are given to relieve pain during surgery or other painful medical procedures. They may be in the form of drugs, such as novocaine, or alternative medical practices such as acupuncture.

Our body movements are controlled by the brain.

There are five senses: the sense of touch, taste, hearing, smell and sight.

Antibodies: protein substances made by lymphatic tissue in response to foreign bodies (antigens). They attach themselves to antigens and permit the body's defense mechanisms to recognize and destroy or neutralize bacteria, viruses or other foreign bodies.

Aorta: the main artery of the body that supplies blood with oxygen to the circulatory system. It starts out from the left ventricle and branches into the two iliac arteries that supply blood to the legs.

Appendix: tissue about 3 in (8 cm) long that extends from the large intestine. Appendicitis is an inflammation of the appendix. Its symptoms are pain in the right lower part of the stomach, fever and vomiting.

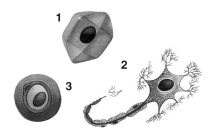

1. skin cell; 2. nerve cell; 3. ovum.

Arteriosclerosis: an alteration of the arteries that leads to thickening and a loss of elasticity of the artery walls. The disease is caused by high blood pressure and aging.

Artery: a blood vessel that carries blood from the heart to the rest of the body. Except for the pulmonary arteries (that carry blood without oxygen from the heart to the lungs), all arteries carry blood rich in oxygen. Arteries often take the name of the part of the body where they carry the blood (the femoral artery travels along the femur, for instance).

Arthritis: inflammation of the joints.

Articulation: the joint between one or more bones.

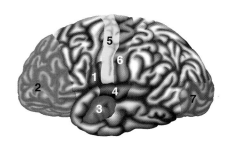

Areas of the brain and their functions.
1. language; 2. reasoning; 3. smell and taste; 4. hearing; 5. movement; 6. touch; 7. sight.

Asthma: a lung disorder characterized by difficult breathing and wheezing. It is caused by a bronchial spasm.

Astigmatism: an abnormal condition of the eye where images appear deformed (the retina does not focus the image due to an abnormal curvature of the cornea).

Bacteria: one-celled microorganisms lacking chlorophyll. Bacteria are among the oldest life forms: they have been found in fossils that date back to more than 3 billion years. Bacteria are classified on the basis of shape. They are round (cocci), comma-shaped (vibrios), rod-shaped (bacilli) or spiral (spirochetes). Bacteria can withstand unfavorable conditions such as dehydration and very cold or hot temperatures. They are found in the soil, water and air. Although some bacteria cause disease, they are essential to life on earth; for example, certain bacteria are used in industry to ferment milk.

Bile: a brownish green liquid secreted by the liver. Bile passes through the biliary ducts into the gallbladder and then the duodenum to help digest fats.

Bread, rice and pasta are carbo-hydrates that give the body energy.

Biopsy: the removal of a small piece of living tissue from an organ or other part of the body for diagnosis.

Blood group or type: there are four blood types: A, B, AB and O. During transfusions the donor's red blood cells must be compatible with the recipient's antibodies. Type O blood can be given to almost anyone. A person with type AB can receive blood from any of the four types. However, if blood type A is transfused into someone with blood type B (or vice versa), the red cells will be destroyed by the recipient. Blood tests can also show a hereditary factor called Rh, which can be Rh positive or negative.

Blood pressure: the pressure of blood circulating in blood vessels. Two measurements are taken: systolic (or

The ancient Egyptians treated fractures by immobilizing the broken bone with splints.

maximum) pressure and diastolic (or minimum) pressure. A person suffers from hypotension when blood pressure is too low and hypertension when it is too high.

Blood: a fluid made up of plasma, red and white blood cells and platelets.

Bone: the connective tissue of the skeleton. Bones are composed of mineral salts (calcium and phosphorus) and ossein. Bones can be short (the heel bone), long (the femur) or flat (the sternum).

Vegetables provide fiber the intestine needs to eliminate food.

Brain: in humans the largest part is called the cerebrum, consisting of a right and left hemisphere responsible for thought and speech. The second part of the brain, the cerebellum, controls movement and balance. The third, the brainstem, controls breathing and other body functions.

Very loud sounds damage the eardrums (tympanic membrane) and can cause deafness.

Bronchitis: inflammation of the mucous membrane in the bronchial tubes.

Bulimia: uncontrollable overeating. Sometimes the person binges on food, then vomits. This disease often alternates with attacks of anorexia.

Burn: a wound to the tissue caused by heat, acid, electricity, radiation or a chemical substance. A burn can range from a first degree (the most severe) to a third degree burn.

Caesarean section: a surgical procedure where the fetus is removed through a surgical incision of the abdomen and uterus. This operation is necessary when natural childbirth is not possible.

Cancer: an abnormal and malignant growth of cells. Cancer can spread to other parts of the body to create metastases. Surgery, chemotherapy and radiation are common treatments.

Capillaries: a system of tiny blood vessels that connect an arteriole (the end of an artery) with a venule (the beginning of a vein). Oxygen and nutrients pass from the blood to the cells through capillary walls, which are similar to membranes. The blood collects waste and carbon dioxide from the cells.

Cartilage: flexible tissue that connects and supports but has no nerves or blood vessels.

CAT (computerized axial tomography): a radiographic technique where a computer produces a three-dimensional image of a particular part of the body. A CAT scan is useful for examining the brain.

Cataract: a condition in which the lens of the eye becomes more and more opaque, resulting in blurred vision.

Cavities: erosion of the hard tooth enamel caused by decay.

Personal hygiene promotes good health.

Water accounts for 60% of our body weight.

Cell: a basic unit found in all living organisms. It is able to reproduce itself and is surrounded by a cell membrane.

Chicken pox: a contagious viral disease that mainly affects children. It forms red spots that can form blisters, which may leave scars.

Cholesterol: a molecule found throughout the body, especially in the brain, blood, bile and adrenal glands. It is needed to make hormones. Cholesterol is manufactured in the body by the liver and also comes from food, especially animal fats. Too much cholesterol can produce arteriosclerosis.

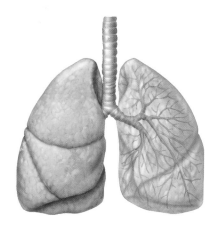

Polluted air can harm our lungs.

Cirrhosis: a chronic liver disease caused by alcoholism.

Colic: a pain (usually in the abdomen) caused by violent muscle spasms.

Childhood is the period from birth to 12 years of age.

Colon: the main part of the large intestine that goes from the cecum to the rectum. It is divided into ascending, transverse, descending and sigmoid colon. The colon excretes feces and also re-absorbs liquids.

Coma: a state of deep unconsciousness and loss of sensitivity marked by a lack of response to stimuli.

Conjunctivitis: inflammation of the conjunctiva (the mucous membrane inside the eyelid that also covers the front of the eye).

Contagion: transmission of an infectious disease from one person to another in a direct or indirect way (through an object, for example).

Blood is made up of a yellowish liquid (plasma) that contains white and red blood cells and platelets.

Cornea: the transparent front part of the eye. The cornea is divided into five layers. Light passes through these layers to reach the retina. Keratotomy is a surgical procedure where corneal tissue is removed; this operation can be used to correct myopia.

Coronary blood vessels: arteries and veins that carry blood to and from the heart. The left and right coronary arteries branch out from the aorta. Coronary veins take blood from the capillaries of the heart to the right atrium.

Cramp: a violent, painful muscle spasm that can be caused by overuse of a muscle.

Cyst: a closed sac lined with skin tissue and containing fluid or semi-solid material.

Diabetes: a disease caused by the body's lack of or insufficient amount of insulin. Diabetes causes high levels of sugar in the blood. There is juvenile-onset diabetes (which requires insulin injections) and adult-onset diabetes.

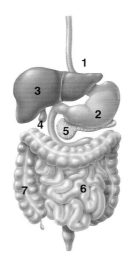

1. *esophagus;* 2. *stomach;* 3. *liver;* 4. *gallbladder;* 5. *pancreas;* 6. *small intestine;* 7. *large intestine.*

Dialysis: purification of the blood with the elimination of urea and other waste products of the body. This process is performed by a machine when a person suffers from kidney failure.

Drug: 1. a medicine; 2. a narcotic drug like alcohol, nicotine, cocaine and heroin that can lead to addiction, where the body becomes dependent on the substance. Drug abuse can cause irreversible brain damage.

Dysentery: frequent diarrhea, with inflammation of the colon.

Dyslexia: difficulty in reading and spelling caused by disorders to the central nervous system. A person with this disability may see letters reversed.

Spinach has a large amount of iron which the body needs. A lack of iron causes anemia.

Electrocardiogram (ECG): a graphic recording (produced by an electro-cardiograph) of the heart's electrical activity. The ECG reveals cardiac abnormalities.

Electroencephalogram (EEG): a graphic recording (produced by an electroencephalograph) of brain-wave activity.

Embolus: a solid, liquid, or gaseous foreign object that can obstruct a blood vessel and create an embolism (a blood clot).

Grains (rye, wheat, rice, corn, barley, oats) are rich in starch and protein.

Epilepsy: a neurological disorder marked by convulsions or seizures. There are two main types of epilepsy, the minor form lasting only a few seconds.

Erythrocytes: red blood cells.

Fetus: the unborn child from the end of eight weeks of pregnancy until birth.

Fever: a defense mechanism of the body that increases body temperature.

Gastritis: inflammation of the lining of the stomach.

Genitals: reproductive organs.

Germ: any microorganism that can cause illness.

Gland: an organ that produces substances the body needs. An endocrine gland secretes hormones directly into the blood, while the exocrine type secretes through ducts (sweat and oil glands, for example).

Human joints connect two or more bones. Like mechanical joints, they allow movement.

Glaucoma: abnormally high pressure in the eye. Glaucoma can damage the optic nerve and cause sight problems.

Hair: the longest hairs on the human body are on the scalp. Hair color and characteristics differ from one person to another. Hair grows about 5 in (12 cm) per year.

Heart attack: blockage of a heart artery that causes a dead tissue area in the heart muscle. The symptoms are a severe pain in the chest and sometimes also in the arms and throat.

Heart: the muscular organ located between the lungs and at the center of the rib cage. The heart is formed by a layer of muscle (myocardium) lined with an internal membrane called the endocardium and covered by an external membrane called the

Fish has very little fat and is an ideal food. It is also rich in phosphorus, which helps our memory.

pericardium. It is divided into two upper chambers (atrium) and two lower chambers (ventricles) that are separated by valves. The heart receives blood from coronary blood vessels and works like a pump: when it contracts and releases, it pumps blood all through the body.

Hematoma: a collection of blood that escapes from vessels and is trapped in skin tissues or an organ (after a trauma, for instance).

Hemorrhage: loss of a large amount of blood (caused by a wound, for example).

Hemorrhoids: enlarged veins in the lower rectum or anus that cause pain during bowel movements.

A doctor's bag holds basic medical equipment.

Hepatitis: an inflammation of the liver caused by a bacterial or viral infection, parasites, alcohol, drugs, poison or a transfusion of the wrong type of blood. Type A is usually caused by infected food or water. Type B is contracted through infected blood or non-sterile needles. Other types of hepatitis have been recently identified.

Herpes: a viral infection that causes blisters on the skin. The infection can break out on the lips in the form of a cold sore, or on the genitals. Herpes zoster (or "shingles") affects nerve cells.

Hormone: a substance secreted by endocrine glands or produced by tissues. Depending on the gland that excretes them, hormones regulate many body functions.

The vocal cords in the larynx vibrate like guitar strings.

Immunity: the body's natural or acquired resistance to infection, which occurs after recovery from an infectious disease or after a vaccination.

Infection: an invasion of microscopic agents such as viruses, molds and bacteria. When attacked by these agents, the immune system comes to the rescue to protect the body.

Inflammation: redness and painful swelling; this is the body's response to irritation or injury.

Muscles often work in pairs: one contracts and the other stretches.

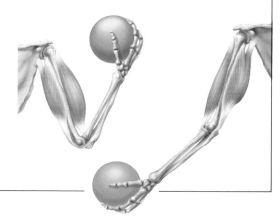

Influenza: a viral infection of the respiratory system. Symptoms are fever, sore throat, muscle pains, headache, cold and nausea.

Insomnia: sleeplessness that may be caused by physical or psychological reasons.

Citrus fruits (lemons, oranges, grapefruit) are rich in vitamin C, which helps the body fight infection.

Insulin: a hormone secreted by the islands of Langerhans in the pancreas. Insulin regulates the metabolism of sugar and its concentration in blood. Diabetes occurs when insulin is insufficient.

Intestine: the part of the digestive system from the stomach to the anus. It is a tube about 23 ft (7 m) long, divided into the duodenum, where bile and pancreatic juices flow that are needed for digestion; the small intestine, a long winding narrow section where nutrients are absorbed; the large intestine, where liquids are reabsorbed; and the rectum, where feces are excreted.

IQ (intelligence quotient): a numeric expression of a person's intellectual level.

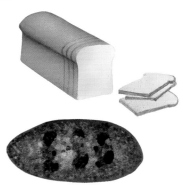

Whole wheat bread (rich in fiber) helps prevent constipation.

Jugular: the large vein in the neck that collects blood from the head and sends it to the clavicle (the "collarbone").

Kidney: a bean-shaped organ about 5 in (12 cm) long. The body's two kidneys filter waste products from the blood and eliminate them in the urine.

Larynx: the voicebox located between the pharynx and trachea (windpipe).

Leukemia: cancer of the blood.

Leukocytes: white blood cells that protect the body.

Ligament: a band of fibrous tissue that binds joints together and connects bones and cartilage.

Liver: the largest gland in the body weighing about 3 lb (1.5 kg). The liver is found in the upper right part of the abdomen. The portal vein carries nutrient-filled blood from the stomach and intestine to be used in the liver. The liver regulates the metabolism of protein, sugar and fats and the production of plasma and bile. It also eliminates toxins.

Be careful about picking wild mushrooms. Some are edible, while others are poisonous.

Lung: Every living animal needs oxygen. In humans oxygen is supplied by the lungs, two respiratory organs. Lungs have blood vessels, bronchi (air passages) and bronchioli (small airways) that open into alveolar sacs where carbon dioxide leaves the blood and oxygen is taken in. A person has pneumonia when this exchange of gases cannot take place because the alveolar sacs are filled with liquid.

Dairy products contain protein, fats, mineral salts (especially calcium) and vitamins.

Lymphatic system: the part of the circulatory system that protects the body from germs. White blood cells in the lymph nodes attack and kill bacteria and other foreign particles.

Measles: an acute and highly contagious viral disease that occurs mainly in young children. It is marked by small red spots and respiratory problems. There is a vaccine for measles.

Melanoma: a type of skin cancer.

Membrane: a thin layer of tissue that covers or lines organs or an area in the body.

Meningitis: an inflammation of the brain or spinal membranes (meninges) caused by viruses or bacterial infections. Meningitis can be contagious.

Menopause: the end of menstruation, which normally occurs when a woman is between 45 and 55 years old. Ovulation stops, and the production of the hormones gonadotropin and

Certain herbal teas made from flowers can help calm coughs.

estrogen gradually decreases. Therefore, a woman in menopause can no longer have children.

Menstruation: the flow of blood (for about 4 days) that takes place every 28 days (the normal menstrual cycle) during the reproductive life of women. The mucosal lining of the uterus thickens in preparation for a fertilized egg. If fertilization does not occur, the

Herbalists used plants for medicinal purposes before modern drugs were discovered.

lining is shed. The blood vessels that break during this process cause a small hemorrhage. The first menstruation is called the menarche.

Mucosa: the mucous membrane that lines and covers organs and areas that lead to the outside of the body, such as the nose and mouth.

Mumps: a contagious viral infection of the salivary glands. This disease is common in children.

Muscle: tissue with fibers that are either smooth or striated. Muscles are voluntary (striated muscle) or involuntary (smooth muscle). An exception is the heart muscle: even though it is involuntary, it is not smooth. Muscles contract if stimulated by motor nerves. Fibers that contract inside a flexible sheath cause the muscle to move. Involuntary muscles let the body carry out vital functions, while voluntary muscles control all movements and activities.

Orange juice helps ward off colds and flus.

Myopia: nearsightedness, or the difficulty of seeing things at a distance. Myopia is often hereditary. It can be caused by excessive length of the eyeball or an abnormal curvature of the cornea.

Nerves: bundles of nerve fibers (neurons) covered by a thin membrane. Each bundle has sensory fibers and motor fibers. Motor nerves carry instructions from the brain to the muscles. Sensory nerves carry information to the brain from sense receptors. Nerves are divided into cranial and spinal nerves.

Optometry: the practice of eye examinations; if a person has problems with eyesight, the optometrist will prescribe suitable corrective lenses.

The first operations with anesthesia took place in 1842 after ether was discovered.

Organ: Each organ of the body has a precise function and is coordinated with other organs. For example, the heart is an organ, and so is the skin.

Otitis: inflammation of the ear.

Ovary: one of a pair of female sexual organs located in the lower part of the abdomen. Each ovary contains about 50,000 eggs that gradually decrease in number until menopause.

Ovulation: this monthly process occurs when a follicle breaks open and releases an egg (ovum) that travels through the fallopian tube to the uterus. Ovulation occurs halfway through the menstrual cycle (normally, the 14th day from the first day of menstruation); it is a woman's fertile period when pregnancy can take place.

Tea and coffee are stimulants. People drink herbal teas (like chamomile) to help them relax.

Pacemaker: an electronic device inserted under the skin that sends electrical signals to stimulate the heart muscle.

Pancreas: a gland about 5 in (15 cm) long located behind the stomach. It is both an exocrine gland (it secretes juices that help digest fats and protein) and an endocrine gland because it releases insulin into the blood.

Pelvis: the lower part of the torso formed by the hip bones, sacrum and tailbone (coccyx).

Penicillin: an antibiotic discovered by Alexander Fleming in 1928.

Penis: the outer reproductive organ of a man. It contains the urethra, a tube that urine and sperm pass through.

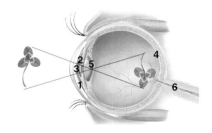

Parts of the eye: **1.** *cornea;* **2.** *iris;* **3.** *pupil;* **4.** *retina;* **5.** *lens;* **6.** *optic nerve.*

Pertussis (whooping cough): a childhood disease that affects the respiratory system.

Phalanges: the bones of the fingers and toes. Also called phalanxes.

Plasma: the clear, yellowish fluid in which blood is suspended. Plasma is made up mostly of water, along with proteins (albumin, globulin, and fibrinogen) and organic substances (uric acid, urea, sugar, fats, etc.).

Platelets: disc-shaped blood cells that have no color. There are from 200,000 to 400,000 platelets in every cubic centimeter of blood. Platelets are very important in blood clotting.

experience their first menstruation, their breasts start to develop and pubic hair starts to grow. Boys between 12 and 13 will notice their voice deepen, their testicles become larger and body hair appears.

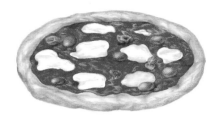

A lot of convenience or "junk food" has empty calories. Pizza is an exception!

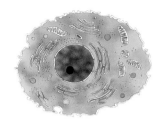

The cell is a fundamental unit found in all living things (except viruses).

Pharynx: a tube-like structure that connects the nasal cavities and mouth to the throat.

Phobia: an abnormal fear of situations and things (such as claustrophobia, a fear of closed places, or aracnophobia, a fear of spiders).

Physiotherapy: treatment of patients to restore normal functions after illness or injury, especially after damage to muscles.

Pituitary gland: a tiny endocrine gland near the hypothalamus in the brain. It controls all the other endocrine glands and also produces hormones for growth and sexual reproduction.

Perfumes generally contain 10–25% scent, and the rest is alcohol.

Pregnancy: the period during which the fetus grows from conception to childbirth (usually 280 days). The zygote (fertilized egg) implants itself in the uterus wall and grows, protected by the placenta.

Presbyopia: farsightedness, or difficulty in seeing things close up, is a condition that often begins in middle age.

Prognosis: a clinical prediction of how a disease or condition will develop.

Prostate: a gland the size of a chestnut that is found underneath a man's bladder.

Psoriasis: a chronic skin disease. The affected parts (scalp, elbows, knees and sacrum) are covered with itchy red patches.

Puberty: the period of adolescence that coincides with sexual maturation. During puberty, girls 10 to 12 years old

Pulse: a regular, rhythmic beating found on surface arteries that matches each beat of the heart. The average pulse rate of an adult is between 60 and 80 beats per minute.

Pupil: a circular opening at the center of the iris. The pupil changes in size: it dilates or contracts in response to changes in light that hits the retina.

Radiology: the use of x-rays to show parts of the body (fractured limbs, for instance).

Rejection: a response of the immune system to microorganisms or foreign material such as a transplanted organ.

Retina: the end of the optic nerve that receives images and transmits them to the brain, which then interprets them.

Many parents used to tell children that the stork delivered babies!

Placenta: a blood-rich organ that connects the fetus to the uterus wall. Nutrients and oxygen pass through the umbilical cord to the fetus. The placenta is expelled at the end of childbirth.

Fruit is often sprayed with pesticides, so rinse your apple before eating it.

Rheumatism: a disorder that brings pain to muscles, bones and joints. It causes inflammation and swelling in the affected areas.

Rickets: a childhood disease caused by a lack of vitamin D. It causes bone defects such as knock-knees.

Rubella (German measles): a contagious viral infection that often affects children. If a woman catches rubella during the first three months of pregnancy, birth defects may result.

Saliva: a liquid secreted by the salivary glands. It contains water, mucin, the enzyme ptyalin and salts. Saliva disinfects and helps in digestion.

Scarlatina (scarlet fever): a contagious childhood disease marked by a red rash.

Scoliosis: an abnormal curve of the spinal column.

Licorice extract is used in sweets and also in medicine.

Skeleton: the bones and cartilage that support the body.

Skin: a membrane that covers the entire body and is our largest organ. Skin protects us from microorganisms and keeps the body temperature stable through body hairs and sweating. It has a sensory function and secretes sweat. The skin is made up of two main layers: the thin outer layer is the protective epidermis, and the thick under layer is the dermis (connective tissue with blood vessels).

Sperm: the male seed produced by the testicle.

Spinal column (vertebral column or spine): the backbone, which is divided into bone segments called vertebrae: cervical vertebrae (7), thoracic vertebrae (12), lumbar vertebrae (5), sacrum (5) and coccyx. The spinal column protects the spinal cord and acts as fundamental support for the body.

Cans are airtight so that bacteria cannot grow. This preserves the food.

Spleen: a dark red, oval-shaped organ weighing about 200 g (7 oz) that is located on the left-hand side of the body between the stomach and diaphragm. It destroys old or damaged red blood cells and acts as a reservoir of healthy ones.

Sterility: the inability to produce children.

Sterilize: 1. to eliminate all living microorganisms through heat, chemicals, ultraviolet rays or other methods; **2.** to make an organism infertile.

False teeth were once made of gold and ivory.

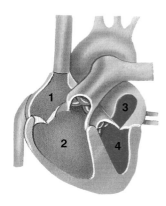

*Parts of the heart: **1.** right atrium; **2.** right ventricle; **3.** left atrium; **4.** left ventricle.*

Stomach: a sack-shaped organ of the digestive system located between the esophagus and the small intestine. The stomach receives partially digested food from the esophagus that is mixed with gastric juices (hydrochloric acid and pepsin). This semi-liquid mass passes through the pylorus to the small intestine.

Stress: in medicine, stress is defined as a strain caused by physical, chemical or emotional factors that can lead to physical illness.

Sweat (perspiration): liquid produced by the sweat glands. Sweat is made up of 99% water, salts, and waste products. Sweat eliminates toxins and also helps control body temperature. When it evaporates, the skin is cooled.

The stethoscope is used to listen to sounds produced in the body, especially by the heart.

Symptom: a phenomenon or feeling that suggests that something may be wrong with the body. For instance, itching, dizziness or pain are symptoms that can be used to help diagnose an illness.

Tartar: a hard calcified deposit on the teeth caused by dental plaque.

Testes: the pair of male reproductive organs that descend into the scrotum at puberty.

Tetanus: an infection caused by a bacteria found in the soil and whose spores are found in rust.

Humans are omnivorous, which means they eat foods that come from animals (meat, dairy products) and plants (vegetables).

Thyroid: an endocrine gland shaped like a half-moon and found in the neck in front of the larynx. It is activated by the pituitary gland and secretes a hormone that controls metabolism and growth.

Tonsils: two masses of lymphatic tissue on both sides of the back of the throat. Tonsillitis is an infection or inflammation of the tonsils.

Tooth: embedded in the jaw, a tooth is made up of pulp (which contains blood vessels and nerves), dentine and enamel (the hard outer layer).

Trachea (windpipe): a tube in the neck that carries air to the lungs. Tracheitis is a swelling of the windpipe.

Egg whites are rich in protein, while the egg yolk contains protein, fats, vitamins and salts.

Sugar provides a quick burst of energy, but eating too many sweets is harmful.

Transfusion: placing blood from a donor into the bloodstream. Transfusions are needed where there is a hemorrhage or anemia. Tests must first be made on donor blood to prevent infections. Transfusions can only be made between compatible blood groups or types.

Transplant: the transfer of an organ or tissue from one body part to another or from a donor.

Trauma: a contusion, lesion, or wound caused in a violent way (such as a brain concussion caused by an accident).

Tuberculosis: an infectious disease that affects the lungs. Today, tuberculosis rarely occurs in countries with modern medical care.

Tumor: a growth or enlargement of tissue with an uncontrolled growth of cells. Tumors are different from other inflammations or swellings because the cells in tumors are abnormal. A tumor can be malignant (untreated, the abnormal cells will travel to other places in the body and ultimately cause death); or it can be benign (centered in one place in the body and relatively easy to remove).

Ulcer: a lesion (wound or injury) on the skin or mucous membrane caused by inflammation. A duodenal ulcer is a lesion in the first part of the small intestine, and a peptic ulcer is a lesion in the stomach.

Ultrasound: a technique based on recording the reflection of high-frequency sound waves. It is used to visualize the shape of internal organs and to diagnose defects.

Urine: liquid that eliminates body waste. It is secreted by the kidneys.

Uterus: the hollow, pear-shaped female reproductive organ about 3 in (7 cm) long. It holds the fertilized egg during the development of the fetus.

Vaccination: an injection of weakened bacteria to protect the body against infectious disease. A polio vaccine, for example, provides immunization against this disease.

Vagina: in females, the passage leading from the external genitals to the uterus.

If you brush your teeth in the morning and evening and after every meal, you'll help prevent cavities.

Vein: a blood vessel in the circulatory system. It carries blood to the heart after tissues have absorbed the nutrients and oxygen from the blood.

Vertebra: any one of the 33–34 bones of the spinal column. Ligaments join them together and a disc of cartilage is found between one vertebra and another.

Virus: a microorganism visible under an electronic microscope. It can only grow inside living cells.

Zygote: a fertilized cell formed by the union of two gametes for sexual reproduction.

Blood circulation resembles these toy trains. The tracks are like veins and arteries, and the stations are like the organs in the body.

LUNGS

BRAIN

HEART

INTESTINE

KIDNEYS

LIVER

MYTHOLOGY

**Most of the gods and goddesses are listed under their Greek names.
The Roman names are in parentheses.**

Achilles: his mother, Thetis, held him by the heel and dipped him into the river Styx to make him immortal. Achilles' heel remained the only vulnerable part of his body and was precisely the spot where Paris shot him with a poisoned arrow.

Adonis: an extremely handsome young man loved by Aphrodite. Ares, who was jealous, had him torn to pieces by a boar. He descended to the underworld, where Persephone fell in love with him.

Aeëtes: King of Colchis and father of Medea, he was guardian of the Golden Fleece. Jason and the Argonauts succeeded in returning to Greece the Golden Fleece, once the coat of a flying ram sent by Zeus to save Prince Phrixus of Thessaly.

Aegeus: the king of Athens who in his youth secretly married Princess Aethra of Troezen. The king returned to his kingdom, never realizing that he had left behind his sandals and sword and that the princess had borne him a son named Theseus. When Theseus grew up, he brought the sandals and sword to Aegeus, who was overjoyed to meet his son. Theseus left to kill the Minotaur and promised his father that if he succeeded, he would replace the black sails of his ship with white ones. He forgot to change them, so when Aegeus, standing on top of a cliff waiting for his son, saw the black sails, he thought Theseus had been killed. Aegeus threw himself into the sea in sorrow. Since then the sea has been called the Aegean Sea.

Aeneas: the son of Anchises, a mortal, and the goddess Aphrodite. He participated in the Trojan War and was saved by his mother. After many adventures narrated by Virgil in the *Aeneid*, he reached Lazio and married Lavinia, the daughter of the king. The Romans are his descendants.

Aeolus: guardian of the winds. Zeus chose Aeolus to keep the winds in a cave and to let them out only one at a time.

Aesculapius: the Roman name for Asclepius.

Agamemnon: a king and the brother of Menelaus, he was commander of the Greek army during the Trojan War.

Ajax: a Greek hero who fought in the Trojan War. He and Odysseus rescued the slain body of Achilles. The dead soldier's weapons were to be awarded as a prize to one of the two men. When Ajax learned that he would not be the winner, he committed suicide in desperation. On the spot where he died, a flower sprang up, the hyacinth.

Alcmena: the queen of Tiryns and mother of Heracles.

Amazons: fierce women warriors who fought on horseback.

Amphitrite: the daughter of the sea god Nereus, she married Poseidon, the god of the sea.

Anchises: the father of Aeneas, he carried his aged father on his shoulders as they fled the burning city of Troy.

Andromache: the loyal wife of Hector and daughter-in-law of Priamus.

Andromeda: the daughter of King Cepheus and Queen Cassiopeia of Ethiopia. Her father tied her to a rock in sacrifice to a sea monster that was destroying the region. Courageous Perseus, returning home after killing the Medusa, came to her aid. He cut off the sea monster's head, freed Andromeda and later married her.

Achilles   Hades   Adonis   Antaeus   Ares   Ariadne

Poseidon gave the city of
Athens a horse. Athena gave
the city an olive tree, which
became a symbol of peace.

Antaeus: the gigantic son of Poseidon and Gaea, Mother Earth, he was unbeatable as long as he stayed in contact with his mother (meaning when his feet touched the ground). To defeat him, Heracles raised him in the air and strangled him.

Antigone: the daughter of Oedipus and Jocasta, the rulers of Thebes, she accompanied her blind father into exile.

Aphrodite (Venus): the goddess of beauty born from sea foam. She was the wife of Hephaestus, the god of fire, but she loved Ares, the god of war, and gave birth to Eros, the god of love.

Apollo: the god of music and prophecy and the son of Zeus and Latona. Apollo was also the brother of Artemis, the goddess of the moon and the hunt. At the famous oracle at Delphi, he revealed prophecies through the priestess Pythia.

Arachne: a skillful spinner and disciple of Athena. She was turned into a spider by Athena, who became jealous of her skill and condemned her to spin for eternity.

Ares (Mars): the god of war and son of Zeus and Hera. During the Trojan War he fought with the Trojans while his sister Athena defended the Greeks.

Argonauts: these heroes, named after their ship *Argo*, accompanied Jason to conquer the Golden Fleece, the skin of a sacred ram that was being protected by a terrible dragon.

Argus: The monster with a hundred eyes who guarded the cow Io on orders from Hera. Argus was killed by Hermes, who received orders from Zeus to free Io. Argus is also the name of Odysseus' faithful dog who died of joy when his master returned home.

Ariadne: the daughter of King Minos of Crete, she fell in love with Theseus, the hero who came from Athens to kill the Minotaur. Ariadne helped Theseus to kill the monster and leave the cave by holding a string at the entrance to the Minotaur's labyrinth.

Artemis (Diana): the goddess of the hunt and sister of Apollo. Artemis was the daughter of Zeus and Leto. She represented the moon while Apollo was the sun. Her most famous temple was in the city of Ephesus.

Ascanius: the son of the Trojan hero Aeneas, he followed his father Aeneas when they fled Troy and arrived with his father in Italy, where he founded the city of Alba Longa.

Asclepius: the god of medicine who received the gift of healing from Apollo, his father. Snakes were his symbol. This first great doctor of Greece was killed when he accepted gold for raising the dead. Zeus hurled a thunderbolt at him.

Atalanta: the daughter of the King of Arcady, who abandoned her because he wanted a son. She was raised by a bear and became a great hunter. Atalanta was the only woman who participated in a hunt organized to kill the terrible boar of Calydonia. She wounded the beast and her proud father finally recognized her as his daughter. She promised she would only marry the man who could beat her in a race. Hippomenes succeeded: during the race

he dropped three golden apples given to him by Aphrodite. Atalanta bent down to pick up the apples and lost the race.

Athena (Minerva): the goddess of wisdom and the daughter of Metis and Zeus. She sprang fully grown from her father's head. During the Trojan War she protected Achilles and Odysseus, who later counted on her help to return to Ithaca.

Atlas: the giant condemned by Zeus to hold Earth on his powerful shoulders. He was given this punishment because he fought beside Cronus in the war against Zeus.

Atreus: the father of Agamemnon and Menelaus, the two Greek commanders who fought against Troy. In *The Iliad*, they are called Atrids.

Bacchus: the Roman name for Dionysus, the god of wine.

Baucis: the wife of Philemon, a humble peasant. The couple offered hospitality to Zeus, who granted them a wish in return. They asked to die together. Baucis and Philemon became two trees with intertwined branches.

Bellerophon: he achieved many feats riding Pegasus, the winged horse that only he could tame. His pride grew to the point that he wanted to ride his magic horse to Olympus. He was punished for his arrogance and the gods made him fall back to Earth. He died a lame beggar in a distant land.

Briseis: the slave loved by Achilles. When the Greek assembly decided Briseis had to be returned to King

Harpy

Artemis

Atalanta

Athena

Bellerophon

Calchas

Agamemnon, Achilles refused to fight. He only took up arms again after the death of Patroclus and after Briseis was returned.

Cadmus: the son of King Agenor of Tyrus and the brother of Europa, the young girl kidnapped by Zeus. He stopped searching for his sister when Apollo ordered him to found the city of Thebes. Cadmus organized an expedition, but a dragon killed all his fellow soldiers. Athena advised him to plant all of the dragon's teeth. Cadmus did what he was told and armed men rose out of the ground and started to fight each other. Cadmus later married Harmonia. The couple lived together until old age, then were turned into snakes by Zeus.

Calchas: the high priest of Apollo and seer who gave the Greeks advice during the Trojan War.

Cassandra: daughter of King Priamus of Troy, she received the gift of prophecy from Apollo. She rejected the advances of Apollo, however, and he punished her by having no one believe her prophecies.

Cassiopeia: Queen of Ethiopia, she boasted that she was more beautiful than the goddesses of the sea. Poseidon punished her by sacrificing her daughter Andromeda to a sea monster. The girl was saved by Perseus, the son of Zeus, but during the ensuing battle Cassiopeia was turned to stone. Zeus took pity on her and made her a constellation in the sky.

Castor: the mortal son of Leda and King Tyndareus. Leda had been seduced by Zeus in the form of a swan.

She laid two blue eggs, one containing Pollux, the immortal half brother.

Centaur: a creature half man and half horse. The centaurs fought Heracles and the Lapiths, who drove them out of Thessaly. These brutal creatures lived in the mountains and forests and ate raw meat.

Ceos: a giant and one of the Titans. Ceos was the son of Uranus and Gaea.

Ceres: the Roman name for Demeter.

Charon: he ferried dead souls across the river Styx. The corpses were buried with a coin in their mouth so they could pay the passage.

Chimera: a monster with the head of a lion, the body of a goat and the tail of a snake. She was killed by Bellerophon.

Chiron: the only kind centaur, Chiron taught many of the Greek heroes. Achilles and Jason were among his students. Heracles killed him with an arrow whose tip was tinged with the poisoned blood of the Hydra of Lerna.

Circe: a sorceress and queen of the island of Aeaea. She turned Odysseus' companions into swine.

Climene: The wife of Iapetus and mother of Atlas and Prometheus.

Clytemnestra: the sister of Helen of Troy. She married Agamemnon, whom she murdered with the help of her lover, Aegisthus. She was later slain by her son Orestes.

Cronus (Saturn): the god of time. He was a Titan and the father of Zeus. After he defeated his father Uranus, he became the lord and master of the world and married Rhea. To prevent his children from overthrowing him, as he had done to Uranus, he would eat them as soon as they were born. Rhea saved Zeus, who defeated Cronus once he became an adult. Zeus rescued the devoured children who were still alive inside their father's stomach.

Cupid: the Roman name for Eros, the god of love. He was the son of Aphrodite (Venus).

Cyclopes (plural of Cyclops): a race of giants with just one eye. They made Zeus' thunderbolts. The most famous Cyclops, Polyphemus, was blinded by Odysseus.

Daedalus: a skillful architect and builder of the great palace of Cnossus in Crete, where he built the labyrinth where King Minos kept the Minotaur. Daedalus was later imprisoned with his son Icarus inside the labyrinth. They escaped by flight with wings Daedulus had made from feathers and beeswax.

Danaë: the daughter of King Acrisius, her father was angry that he had no son as heir. When an oracle told him that he would die one day by his daughter's son, he put Danaë into a sealed chamber with an opening in the roof. Zeus appeared to her in the form of a golden shower, and they had a child, Perseus. The king then put his daughter and grandchild into a chest and threw it into the sea. They were saved by a fisherman. Years later, the oracle came true when Perseus accidentally killed his grandfather.

Charon   *Cassandra*   *Circe*   *Cronus*   *Deianira*   *Demeter*

Danaüs: king of Libya, he had fifty daughters with different women. He left home with his daughters because he feared his brother King Aegyptus and his fifty sons. Danaüs reached Argos, in Greece, and the people there made him king.

Daphne: the nymph Apollo loved. She tried to escape Apollo's attentions and invoked the help of Mother Earth, who turned her into a laurel tree. From that day on, the laurel tree became Apollo's favorite plant.

Deianira: the wife of Heracles, she was kidnapped by Nessus, the centaur. Heracles shot a poisoned arrow at the centaur. Before he died, Nessus gave some of his blood to Deianira, telling her it would ensure her husband's love forever. Years later, Deianira gave Heracles a tunic dipped in the blood, hoping that this would discourage her husband from falling in love with another. Her husband suffered greatly from the poison and returned to Mount Olympus to be with the gods. His distraught wife committed suicide.

Delphi: the sacred place where the oracle told the future. It was guarded by the dragon Python, who was destroyed by the god Apollo, who made Delphi his sanctuary.

Demeter (Ceres): the sister of Zeus and goddess of wheat and farming. Hades, the king of the underworld, kidnapped her daughter Persephone. Since she could not have her daughter back, Demeter convinced Zeus to allow Persephone to spend at least some of the year on earth, giving us the seasons spring and summer.

Diana: the Roman name for Artemis, the goddess of the forest and protector of young mothers.

Dido: daughter of the King of Tyrus, she was forced to flee after her brother, Pygmalion, murdered her husband. She founded Carthage in Africa, where she fell in love with Aeneas. When she failed to convince him to stay, she killed herself.

Dionysus (Bacchus): the son of Zeus and Semele and the god of wine and fertility. His mother died, consumed by divine fire, after wanting to see Zeus in all of his splendor. Persecuted by Hera, Zeus' wife, Dionysus wandered throughout Africa and Asia and had many devotees, especially women, who followed him in frenzied processions.

Dioscuri: the Heavenly Twins, Castor and Pollux. They were half brothers, one mortal, the other immortal. When they both fell in battle, Pollux went to Mount Olympus (home of the gods) and Castor went to Hades, the underworld. They missed one another so much that finally the gods allowed them to stay together, spending half their time in Olympus, the other half in Hades.

Dryad: a nymph whose life was bound up with that of a tree; often called a wood nymph in English.

Egeria: a Roman nymph of the springs who inspired fair laws.

Electra: the daughter of Agamemnon and Clytemnestra. After her father was killed, she and her brother Orestes made a pact to revenge the death of their father.

Endymion: the son of Zeus and a nymph. He was so handsome that Selene, the moon goddess, fell in love with him and rewarded him with magical sleep and eternal youth.

Erinyes (the Furies): terrible goddesses of the underworld born from drops of blood from Uranus. They avenged the most horrible crimes, especially those against families.

Eris: the goddess of discord who caused trouble everywhere she went. Furious for not being invited to the wedding of Thetis and Peleus, she threw a golden apple as a prize for the most beautiful goddess. It created a quarrel among the guests and became known as the "apple of discord."

Eros (Cupid): the son of Aphrodite. This handsome boy with wings was the god of love. Eros carried a bow and arrow and took perfect aim at the hearts of gods and mortals.

Europa: Chosen by Zeus to be the first queen of Crete, the island where he had been born. She had three sons: Minos, Radamanthus and Sarpedon.

Eurydice: one of the Dryads and the wife of Orpheus.

Eurystheus: the King of Mycenea who ordered Heracles to accomplish the twelve labors so he could enter Olympus.

Fates: the Roman name for the Moirae.

Fortuna: the goddess of fortune, she was often shown blindfolded, holding a cornucopia in one hand and a rudder in the other. This image symbolized her control over the lives of mortals.

Dido

Dionysus

Dioscuri

Oedipus

Hephaestus

Helen

Furies: the Roman name for the Erinyes, the Furies.

Gaea: Mother Earth. She was the wife of Uranus and the mother of the Titans.

Galatea: a sea nymph and daughter of Nereus. She was loved by the Cyclops Polyphemus.

Ganymede: the most handsome mortal. Zeus had him kidnapped by an eagle and taken to Olympus to become cupbearer to the gods.

Gorgons: three terrible sisters named Stheno, Euryale and Medusa. The last one was deadly: she had snakes for hair and her glance could turn humans into stone.

Graces: the three goddesses of beauty, daughters of Zeus, they represented everything that is desirable. Their names were Aglaia (brilliance), Euphrosyne (joy) and Thalia (bloom).

Graeae: also called the Gray Sisters, they shared one eye and one tooth. They lived in the realm of the night where the sun never shone. They were the Gorgons' sisters.

Hades (Pluto): he became the lord of the underworld after he and his brothers, Zeus and Poseidon, defeated their father Cronus. He kidnapped and married Persephone. Hades is also the name of the world of the dead.

Harmonia: the daughter of Ares and Aphrodite, she married King Cadmus of Thebes and became queen. All the gods and goddesses attended her wedding.

Harpies: ugly birds with women's heads.

Hebe: the daughter of Zeus and Hera. Hebe was the handmaiden of the gods. She was the symbol of eternal youth and became the wife of Heracles when he joined the gods in Olympus.

Hector: the firstborn son of Priamus and the most valiant Trojan warrior. He was killed by Achilles.

Hecuba: the queen of Troy and wife of Priamus. She had many children, including Paris, Hector and Cassandra.

Helen: the daughter of Zeus and Leda who was considered the most beautiful woman in the world. Paris from Troy carried off Helen from her husband, King Menelaus of Sparta. That act triggered the Trojan War.

Helios: the sun god and son of Hyperion and Thea.

Hephaestus (Vulcan): the god of fire and son of Zeus and Hera. Although he limped, he was a talented blacksmith who made magical weapons for the gods and heroes. He was married to beautiful Aphrodite.

Hera (Juno): the goddess of marriage and queen of Olympus. Despite Zeus' many love affairs, she remained his legitimate wife. She had three children with Zeus: Ares, Hephaestus and Hebe. During the Trojan War she favored the Greeks because Paris from Troy said her rival, Aphrodite, was the most beautiful goddess.

Heracles (Hercules): the son of Zeus and Alcmena. In a moment of temporary insanity brought on by Hera, Heracles killed his wife and children. To atone for his crime, he had to accomplish the twelve labors ordered by King Eurystheus of Mycenea: 1) he killed the Nemean lion; 2) he killed the Hydra with many heads; 3) he captured the wild boar of Mount Erymanthus; 4) he captured a sacrted deer; 5) he killed the birds of Lake Stymphalus; 6) he cleaned the Augean stables; 7) he captured the bull of King Minos of Crete; 8) he tamed the mares of King Diomedes; 9) he obtained the golden belt of Hippolyta, the Amazon queen; 10) he stole a herd of cows from the monster Geryon; 11) he saved the dog Cerberus; 12) he stole the golden apples of the Hesperides. Heracles successfully completed all twelve labors but died poisoned by the blood of Nessus, the centaur. After his death, Zeus brought him to Olympus to live with the gods.

Hercules: the Roman name for Heracles.

Hermes (Mercury): the son of Zeus and Maia and messenger of the gods. His winged sandals made him extremely fast. He accompanied the dead to Hades and was the god of wayfarers, merchants and thieves.

Hesperides: Hera's secret garden where she kept immortal golden apples. The nymphs of the Hesperides watered the tree.

Hestia (Vesta): the daughter of Cronus and Rhea and sister of Zeus. She was the goddess of the hearth.

Homer: the famous Greek poet and author of *The Iliad* and *The Odyssey*, epic poems that narrated the story of the

Aeolus *Heracles* *Erinyes* *Hermes* *Hector* *Europa*

Trojan War. He was born around 850 B.C. For a long time his poems were thought to be the works of different authors. Modern critics, however, believe the two works were written by a single author who adapted and rewrote earlier stories.

Hyperboreans: people that lived in the extreme northern regions where Apollo lived for half of the year. The Hyperboreans never grew ill or old.

Hyperion: the son of Uranus and Gaea who married his sister Thea.

Iapetus: the son of Uranus and Gaea and the father of Atlas and Prometheus.

Icarus: the son of Daedalus, the builder of the labyrinth where the Minotaur was held captive by King Minos of Crete. The king became furious with Daedalus and imprisoned him and his son in the labyrinth. Daedalus built wings made of feathers and wax so the two could escape. They took flight towards Sicily. Daedalus arrived safe and sound, but Icarus carelessly came too close to the sun. The wax in his wings melted and he fell into the sea and drowned.

Io: Princess of Argo, she was loved by Zeus, who turned her into a cow to protect her from his jealous wife Hera. Hera discovered the trick and had Argus, the monster with a hundred eyes, stand guard over Io. Io was freed by Hermes and escaped to Asia by way of a passage of water that became known as the Bosporus, or "passage of the cow."

Iphigenia: the daughter of Agamemnon and Clytemnestra. When it seemed the Greeks were going to lose the Trojan War, the seers asked that Iphigenia be sacrificed to the goddess Artemis so she would help the Greek army. Agamemnon was forced to consent, but Artemis showed pity on the girl and replaced her with a deer. Iphigenia was carried to Tauris, where she became a priestess of Artemis.

Iris: the goddess of the rainbow.

Janus: a Roman god with two faces whose image was placed on doors to indicate the entrance and exit. The temple of Janus was in the Roman Forum and its doors were closed during times of peace. The first month of the year—January—was named after him.

Jason: the Prince of Ioclus in Thessaly. He grew up far from the kingdom because his uncle Pelias had usurped his father's throne. Once he was an adult, he returned to lay claim to the throne, but Pelias sent him to find the Golden Fleece. The task was difficult but Jason brought it back with the help of his valiant companions (the Argonauts) and Medea. He returned to Ioclus and killed his uncle, the usurper.

Jocasta: the wife of King Laius of Thebes. She became a widow and married a stranger, Oedipus, after he freed Thebes from the bloodthirsty Sphinx. When she discovered Oedipus was her son, she committed suicide.

Juno: the Roman name for Hera.

Jupiter: the Roman name for Zeus.

Ladon: a dragon that guarded Hera's garden of the Hesperid.

Laertes: the father of Odysseus.

Laius: the King of Thebes unwittingly killed by his son Oedipus.

Lapiths: people of Thessaly whose King Pirithous was a friend of Theseus. During the wedding between Pirithous and Hippodamia, a memorable fight occurred between the Lapiths and the centaurs, whose terrible manners had offended the bride.

Lares: Roman spirits shown holding a cornucopia. They protected homes and descendants.

Latona: mother of Artemis and Apollo.

Leda: mother of Helen of Troy, Clytemnestra, Castor and Pollux. She was seduced by Zeus, who disguised himself as a swan.

Maia: the daughter of Atlas and the mother of Hermes.

Manes: the souls of dead Romans.

Mars: the Roman name for Ares.

Medea: an enchantress and daughter of the King of Colchis. She helped Jason obtain the Golden Fleece and regain the throne of Ioclus that was usurped by Pelias. When Jason fell in love with Creusa, Medea killed her and then murdered her own children.

Melampus: a mortal with the gift of prophecy. He understood the language of animals and cured the daughters of the King of Argo whom Dionysus had made insane. He married a daughter of the king as a reward.

Meleager: the son of the king of Calydonia, he and Atalanta killed a wild

Phaethon   *Galatea*   *Janus*   *Giants*   *Gorgon*   *Icarus*

boar. Meleager fell in love with Atalanta and gave her hunting trophies, a gesture that infuriated his uncles. After Meleager murdered his uncles, he was slain by his mother Althaea in revenge.

Menelaus: King of Sparta and husband of Helen of Troy. When Paris kidnapped Helen and brought her to Troy, Menelaus and other Greek princes declared war on Troy.

Mercury: the Roman name for Hermes.

Metis: goddess of prudence and a Titan's daughter.

Midas: the King of Phrygia who asked Dionysus to transform everything he touched into gold. He later realized his mistake: he could no longer eat because bread turned to gold and he could not caress his children without turning them into statues. He begged Dionysus to free him from this evil gift. When he submerged himself in a magical spring, these powers disappeared.

Minerva: the Roman name for the goddess Athena.

Minos: A king of Crete and son of Zeus and Europa, he was raised by King Asterion of Crete. Poseidon cast an evil spell on Minos' wife Pasyfae, who mated with a bull and gave birth to the Minotaur. Mortified, Minos kept the monstrous Minotaur in the labyrinth. After defeating the city of Athens, he ordered seven maidens and seven youths to be sacrificed to the Minotaur each year. Minos became one of the three judges of the dead in Hades.

Minotaur: a monster with a human's body and a bull's head, he ate human flesh. Theseus, with Ariadne's help, killed him.

Mnemosyne: the daughter of Uranus and Gaea. She is the goddess of memory and the mother of the Muses.

Moirae (the Fates): heavenly spinners named Clotho, Lachesis and Atropos. The first spun the thread of life, the second determined its length, and the third cut the thread, thus determining when life ended.

Morpheus: one of the thousand children of Sleep, whose job was to take on human form and appear to humans in their dreams.

Muses: daughters of Zeus and Mnemosyne (memory), they danced and sang. Clio was the goddess of history, Euterpe the goddess of music, Thalia the goddess of comedy, Mepomene the goddess of tragedy, Erao the goddess of lyric and love poetry, Terpsichore the goddess of dance, Urania the goddess of astronomy, Polyhymnia the goddess of sacred poetry, and Caliope the goddess of epic poetry.

Narcissus: a beautiful young man hopelessly loved by Echo, who faded away until just her voice remained. Narcissus fell in love with his own reflection in a pool; he pined way and fell into the water and drowned. A flower that grew on the spot was named after him.

Nausicaa: the daughter of King Alcinous of the Phaeaces. Athena used her so the Phaeaces would help Odysseus continue his journey after he shipwrecked on their coast.

Nemesis: a daughter of the night and the goddess of retribution.

Neptune: the Roman name for Poseidon, god of the sea.

Nereids: sea nymphs.

Nereus: an old marine god, the son of Pontus and father of the Nereids. He could turn into any type of animal.

Nestor: a Greek hero, he was the the grandson of Niobe, whose children were slain by Artemis and Apollo. To atone for this crime, Apollo let Nestor live the same number of years as were taken from his uncles. Thus, Nestor lived to a very old age.

Nike: the goddess of Victory, portrayed with open wings. She was one of the early gods of Olympus.

Niobe: the daughter of Tantalus who gave King Amphion of Thebes seven sons and seven daughters. She boasted of her superiority over Latona, Zeus' wife who had only two children, Artemis and Apollo. Artemis and Apollo took revenge by killing all but two of Niobe's children. Niobe turned into stone.

Nymphs: young women who lived in the woods, mountains, or sea and personified the forces of nature. The Oreads were mountain nymphs, the Nereids were sea nymphs, the Meliads were goddesses of the ash trees, and the Amadriads were goddesses of all trees.

Oceanus: the son of Uranus and Gaea. He was the god of waters.

Iris   *Ladon*   *Latona*   *Medea*   *Meleager*   *Midas*

Odysseus (Ulysses): the son of King Laertes of Ithaca, he was a brave Greek warrior who fought in the Trojan War. After Troy was destroyed, Odysseus wandered for years before returning to Ithaca. He was persecuted by Poseidon, the god of the sea, because he blinded his son Polyphemus. He arrived home in Ithaca after twenty years and was recognized by his dog, Argus. He was wearing beggar's rags to surprise the suitors trying to marry his wife, Penelope.

Oedipus: the son of King Laius of Thebes, he was sent far from the kingdom as soon as he was born because an oracle predicted he would kill his father. Oedipus grew up in Corinth and thought he was the son of the king of that city. When he became an adult, he learned of the prophecy and left Corinth so he would not kill the man he thought was his father. During the journey he met Laius near Delphi and killed him during an argument. He reached Thebes and freed the city from the Sphinx, a bloodthirsty monster. He married Jocasta, the widow of Laius, unaware that she was his mother. When he learned the truth, Oedipus blinded himself and Jocasta committed suicide.

Olympus: the highest mountain in Greece and home of the gods.

Orestes: the son of Agamemnon and Clytemnestra, he was a child when his father was murdered. When Orestes grew up, Apollo ordered him to avenge his father's death. He married Hermione and reigned in Argo and Sparta after Menelaus died.

Orion: a huge hunter who killed the wild beasts on the island of Chios. In exchange for his deeds, he asked the king for the hand in marriage of his daughter. The king, however, had him blinded. Orion regained his sight by wandering East where the sun's rays healed him. He angered Artemis, who made a scorpion sting him. The scorpion and Orion were turned into constellations. That is why the Orion constellation seems to escape from the Scorpion constellation behind it.

Orpheus: a talented poet and musician whose music tamed wild beasts. He descended into Hades to save Eurydice, his dead wife. Touched by the music of his lyre, the gods of the underworld let Orpheus take back his wife to Earth on one condition: he could not look at her. Orpheus turned back once before reaching the sunlight, however, and lost his beloved wife forever.

Pan: the god of the woods and fields and joyous companion of the nymphs. He was part goat and played the syrinx, or panpipe.

Pandora: created by Hephaestus on Zeus' orders, she was given a box that she was never to open. Pandora became curious, however, and opened it. Out came all the ills that plague humans: war, vice, illness, etc. Only hope, which remained at the bottom of the box, was left.

Paris: the handsome son of King Priamus of Troy. Paris gave Aphrodite the apple of discord in recognition for her beauty. In exchange, she offered him the love of Helen, the most beautiful woman on Earth. She was already married to Menelaus, but Paris carried Helen off, an act that triggered the Trojan War.

Patroclus: a Greek warrior and friend of Achilles, he was killed by Hector.

Pegasus: a winged horse born from the blood of the Medusa when Perseus cut off her head. Pegasus was tamed by Bellerophon.

Penelope: the wife of Odysseus and queen of Ithaca. She faithfully waited for her husband's return for many years and was forced to fend off the advances of numerous suitors. She told them she would decide who to marry as soon as she finished weaving a cloth. To delay her decision, during the night she would unravel the weaving she did during the day.

Persephone (Proserpine): the daughter of Demeter and Zeus, she married Hades, the lord of the underworld. She spent the winter in the underworld and returned to Earth in the spring, when plants and flowers were in bloom.

Perseus: the son of Zeus and Danaë, he was raised by a fisherman on an island. He set out on a voyage to kill the horrible Medusa and succeeded with the help of Hermes and Athena. During his voyage home, Perseus freed Andromeda, who was being sacrificed to a sea monster. He married Andromeda and returned home to the island, which was ruled by an evil king. He used the head of the Medusa to turn the king and his courtiers to stone. Then he gave the head to Athena, who placed it at the center of her shield.

Phaedra: the daughter of King Minos and the sister of Ariadne. She married Theseus and had two children.

Phaethon: the son of Helios, the sun, and the nymph Climene. He tried to

Minotaur

Morpheus

Narcissus

Nemesis

Odysseus

Orpheus

drive his father's chariot but took it too close to the Earth. To prevent him from burning Earth, Zeus struck him with a thunderbolt and made him fall into the Po River. His sisters, the Elyiads, wept so much that the gods took pity on them and turned them into poplar trees.

Phoebe: the daughter of Uranus and Gaea. Her daughter was Latona.

Pleiads: the seven nymph daughters of Atlas, they were loved by the hunter Orion. The gods turned Orion and the nymphs into constellations.

Pluto: the Roman name for the god Hades.

Pollux: the son of Zeus and Leda and the immortal twin brother of Castor.

Polyphemus: the most fearsome Cyclops, he was blinded by Odysseus.

Poseidon (Neptune): the god of the sea and brother of Zeus and Hades. He emerged from the oceans on a chariot surrounded by fish, dolphins, and sea creatures. He married Amphitrite but loved Demeter and Medusa. His scepter was a trident.

Priamus: King of Troy and husband of Hecuba, he had fifty children. Priamus was slain by Neoptolemus, the son of Achilles.

Prometheus: the son of the Titan Iapetus and Climene. He created man from clay. To help humanity he stole the divine fire and was condemned to a horrible fate. He was chained to a rock and vultures devoured his liver each day. Prometheus was freed by Heracles and later forgiven by the gods.

Proserpine: the Roman name for Persephone.

Psyche: the beloved of Eros, who visited her at night. Although Psyche was not allowed to look her lover in the face, she disobeyed and lit a candle one night. When a drop of hot oil fell on Eros' face, he fled. Aphrodite, jealous of Psyche's beauty, tormented her. In the end Zeus allowed her to become a goddess and marry Eros.

Rhea Silvia: the mother of Romulus and Remus.

Rhea: the daughter of Gaea and Uranus and the wife of Cronus, with whom she had six children. The last son, Zeus, forced his father Cronus to give back his brothers and sisters whom he had devoured: Hades, Poseidon, Hestia, Hera and Demeter.

Romulus and Remus: twin boys born of the god Ares and Rhea Silvia. The two were thrown into the Tiber River by their father's rival. They were suckled by a she wolf and raised by the shepherd Faustolus. When grown, they decided to found a city, but when trying to establish the boundaries, the brothers got into a heated argument and Romulus killed Remus. Romulus founded his city (Rome) on the Palatine Hills and became its first king.

Saturn: the Roman name for the god Cronus.

Satyrs: also called Sileni, they had a man's chest and a goat's legs. They were demigods of the woods and companions of Dionysus.

Semele: the daughter of Cadmus and Harmonia, and mother of Dionysus.

Sibyl: one of the priestesses who interpreted the oracles of the gods at Delphi. As the sibyl slept, she heard the voice of Mother Earth and repeated the magic words. Priests interpreted the meaning and explained the prophecies.

Sirens: sea nymphs that sang so sweetly that sailors were lured towards their island and shipwrecked. Odysseus had his men put wax in their ears so that they would not hear the Sirens' song.

Sphinx: a monster with the head of a woman, the body of a lion, and the wings of a bird. She killed wayfarers who could not answer her riddle: What animal walks on all fours at dawn, on two legs at noon and on three at dusk? Only Oedipus gave the right answer: the animal is man, who crawls on all fours when a child, walks on two legs as an adult, and uses a cane in old age.

Styx: a river of Hades, the underworld.

Tantalus: a powerful king of Lydia or Phrygia. He revealed the secrets of the gods and stole ambrosia and nectar from their table. He was condemned to suffer thirst and hunger for eternity, even though he had water and food all around him. As soon as he stretched out his hand for something to drink or eat, the water and food would move out of his reach.

Tartarus: the underworld below Hades that had walls and a bronze door. It was used as a prison for the enemies of the gods, such as the Titans and Giants.

Telemachus: the son of Odysseus and Penelope. During his father's long

Orion *Pan* *Persephone* *Perseus* *Poseidon* *Priamus*

absence, Telemachus tried to oppose the suitors who were pressuring Penelope into marrying one of them so they could take over the throne of Ithaca.

Tethys: a sea goddess.

Thanatos: the son of night and the god of death, he was portrayed as a winged genie.

Thea: the daughter of Uranus and Gaea. She had three children with Hyperion: Helios, Eos, and Selene.

Theseus: the son of Aegeus and Aethra. He spent his childhood in Troezene and only learned at 16 who his father was. He went to Athens and asked to be recognized by his father, who was overjoyed. Theseus became king after his father's death. He defeated the Amazons and married Antiope, their queen. He was slain by King Lycomedes of Scyros.

Thetis: a beautiful Nereid loved by Zeus and Poseidon. Neither god married her because a prophecy said her son would be more powerful than his father. She married a mortal and they had a son, Achilles, the strongest Greek warrior.

Tiresias: a blind soothsayer of Thebes. Hera, displeased with her behavior during an argument with Zeus, blinded her. Zeus consoled Tiresias by giving her the gift of prophecy and the privilege of living for seven generations.

Titans: the children of Gaea and Uranus, they were towering, cruel creatures. The Titans declared war on the gods of Olympus and lost.

Titans: the children of Uranus and Gaea who ruled the world before Zeus and the Olympians defeated them.

Tithonus: a Trojan prince and brother of Priamus, he was loved by the goddess Eos (Aurora). Eos made him immortal, but forgot to request eternal youth. As he aged, Tithonus became smaller and more wrinkly until he turned into a grasshopper.

Triton: the son of Poseidon and Amphitrite, he was half man and half fish. He calmed the waters by blowing into a sea shell.

Troy: a city in Asia Minor which was mentioned by Homer in *The Iliad*. The German archeologist Schliemann discovered the remains of the city in 1871.

Typhon: a fire-eating monster with wings, and dragon heads for fingers. Cronus sent him to dethrone Zeus. While the gods fled in terror at the sight of Typhon, Zeus and Athena faced and defeated him. He generated other monsters: the Hydra of Lerna and the Chimera.

Ulysses: the Roman name for Odysseus.

Uranus: the personification of Heaven and the husband of Gaea, the Earth. He was the father of the Titans. Uranus was dethroned by his son Cronus, who was in turn deposed by his youngest son Zeus.

Venus: the Roman name for the goddess Aphrodite.

Vesta: the Roman name for the goddess Hestia.

Virgil: the Latin poet who narrated the brave feats of Aeneas in the epic poem *Aeneid*.

Vulcan: the Roman name for the god Hephaestus.

Zeus (Jupiter): the supreme god of Olympus and lord of the thunderbolt, Zeus also created rain, snow and clouds. Like all the Olympians, he belonged to the second generation of gods. His mother Rhea saved him from his father Cronus, who wanted to devour him. The goat Amaltea suckled him in a grotto. When he grew up, he seized his father's throne and later married Hera. His many children include Athena, Artemis, Apollo, Hephaestus, the Muses, the Graces, Hermes, Ares, Tantalus, Perseus, Minos, Dionysus, Heracles, Persephone and the Hours.

Romulus and Remus

Sibyl

Sirens

Triton

Uranus

Zeus

Index

INDEX

This index is arranged in alphabetical order.
The words in **boldface** type show you the title
of a page where a subject is treated in depth.

Editor-in-chief: Elisabetta Dami
Editor: Adriana Sirena
Layout: Laura Zuccotti
Graphic design: Valentina Ziliani

Contributors
Luisa Cesana, Paul Cloche, Tuvia Fogel, Nuccia Fuga, Cristiana Giraudi,
Angelo Mantovani, Laura Ori, Francesca Pierangeli, Alessandra Pugassi,
Patrizia Puricelli, Giuseppe Recalcati, Alessandro Rusconi, Laura Sanchioni,
Remo Turati, Miriam Valdameri, Giovanna Zanotti, Giuseppe Zuccotti.

Consultants and Researchers
Franco Angelini, Luca Astori, Alessandra Bialetti, Luca Budicin,
Cosimo Finzi, Chaja Fogel, Cesare Gelli, Emilia Parisi, Gianni Zampieri.

Illustrators
Susanna Addario, Art Studium, Simonetta Baldini, Severino Baraldi, Gaia Bellettini,
G. B. Bertelli, Sandro Biffignandi, Cecilia Bozzoli, Giovanni Bruzzo, Piero Cattaneo,
Sergio Cavina, Alessandra Cimatoribus, Beatrice Corradi, Daniela Daledo, Arturo Del Castillo,
Chris Foss, Luana Freno, Flavio Ghiringhelli, Amedeo Gigli, Ezio Giglioli, Carlo Jacono,
Massimiliano Longo, Elena Mandich, Manuela Mascherini, Claudia Melotti,
Pier Angelo Montanini, Rosalba Moriggia, Maddalena Motteran, Nemo, Salvatore Palazzolo,
Umberta Pezzoli, Maria Piatto, Achille Picco, Mattia Pirro, Alberto Ponno, Laura Rigo,
Sergio Rizzato, G. B. Ronco, Rudolf Sablic, Alberto José Salinas, Paolo Salvaggio, Studio Rosso,
Rocco Tedesco, Marina Vecchi, Robert Weickmann, Matthew Wolf, Tony Wolf.

Page 1: field of poppies (M. Wolf). Pages 2-3: North American swamplands (G. B. Bertelli).
Page 4: Bees in the beehive (M. Wolf). Page 383: Hector and Achilles beneath the walls
of Troy (P. Cattaneo). Page 384: Christopher Columbus' ships (S. Biffignandi)

Pages 278, 279, 280 illustrations courtesy of The Walt Disney Company (Italy)
© Disney Enterprises, Inc.

Original Italian edition: © 1996 Dami Editore, Italy,
entitled *Enciclopedia Dami, prima enciclopedia illustrata per ragazzi.*

This edition published in 1997 by Tormont Publications Inc.
338 Saint Antoine St. East
Montreal, Canada H2Y 1A3
Tel: (514) 954-1441
Fax: (514) 954-5086

Translation: Daria Kissel for Language Consulting Congressi (Milan)

ISBN 2-7641-0362-X

Printed in U.S.A.